BARCELONA TO BEDLAM

BY GUY NATHAN

*T*HERE ARE NO WHOLE TRUTHS; ALL TRUTHS ARE HALF TRUTHS. IT IS TRYING TO TREAT THEM AS WHOLE TRUTHS THAT PLAYS THE DEVIL.

Alfred North Whitehead. *dialogues.*

D0493596

THE INFORMATION CONTAINED IN THIS BOOK IS AS A RESULT OF EXTENSIVE ENQUIRY, RESEARCH AND INVESTIGATION AS WELL AS INTERVIEWS AND COURT PAPERS SUPPLIED WITH THE AUTHORITY OF THE VICE-CHANCELLOR, THE RIGHT HONOURABLE SIR DONALD NICHOLLS.

CONTENTS

FOREWORD

By Reg Drury, 30 years ace News of the World sports reporter, and a Spurs supporter for all of those years.

Alan Sugar v Terry Venables must rate, without any shadow of doubt, as the saddest fixture in the history of Tottenham Hotspur since the club was formed in the gaslight era of the end of the 19th century. The financial clout of Sugar and the soccer know-how of Venables did, indeed, appear to be the "dream team". It was claimed to be on the back pages of the big selling tabloids.

It seemed, at least in theory, that Spurs had everything it takes to become a force in English football comparable with Liverpool of the Seventies and Eighties. But in less than two years the White Hart Lane allies became High Court enemies — and the dream had ended.

I unashamedly admit to being one of those who, mistakenly and briefly, believed that the combination of money and brains would at very least inspire Spurs to a third League championship to follow those won in such stylish fashion by Arthur Rowe's push-and-run side of 1950-51 and Bill Nicholson's double-winning team ten years later....

I must confess to a personal and sentimental stake in seeing Spurs back on top of the soccer world. I wrote my first-ever match report, just a few months past my 15th birthday, on a 1-0 Spurs victory over Portsmouth in a war-time competition in February, 1944. The game took place at White Hart Lane, then used on alternate Saturday afternoons by Arsenal as their "home" ground because Highbury was used as a civil defence post, and the report appeared in the "Enfield Gazette & Observer" — who paid me the kind of fee which wouldn't even buy a Sunday newspaper these days.

During the years that followed, as I graduated through "Sport" magazine and the now-defunct "Reynolds News" to the "News of the World", where I spent nearly thirty years as a chief football

7

writer, the soft spot for Spurs remained. I dealt with nine managers, kicking off with Joe Hulme and then Arthur Rowe, Jimmy Anderson, Bill Nicholson, Terry Neill, Keith Burkinshaw, Peter Shreeves, David Pleat and Terry Venables in turn. Most of them enjoyed their purple patches in spite of, rather than because of the club directors at the time.

None of the nine achieved lasting success, a la Liverpool, for various reasons. Maybe Rowe, who led Spurs to the Second and First Division titles in successive seasons, would have done but for ill health which led to his premature resignation. Perhaps Nicholson, the longest serving of the managers over nearly 16 years in command, would have kept Spurs on top if the side which reached the peak had been younger.

The one legacy of both Rowe and Nicholson was total commitment to a sophisticated way of playing the game. The teams they fielded provided genuine entertainment for the spectators more often than not, and undoubtedly far more than many sides who subsequently won the English championship. And even if not as successful, the men who followed Nicholson as manager stuck to the same principles of sending out teams to play attractive football.

Football is loaded with tradition, fashioned in a bygone age and maintained by those who took pride in keeping up standards. That is why the whole of the soccer-playing world still expects the present Real Madrid to display the quality of the days when Puskas and di Stefano ruled the roost. Why every country which comes up against the modern Hungarians are apprehensive, refusing to accept the reality of a very ordinary team because they still see the ghosts of the Magyar masters who dominated the game in the early fifties.

So Spurs fans, ever inclined to kid themselves at times and harbour ideas above their station, still have great expectations of the way in which their team should play. They not only want their favourites to win, which would satisfy the followers of most other clubs — they want them to win with a panache which will make them the envy of the rival supporters as were the teams fashioned by Rowe and Nicholson. I labour the point because this is the spotlight into which Venables stepped when he returned to White

Hart Lane as manager in November, 1987, some 18 years after leaving the club at the end of three seasons as a player.

The fact that Venables had not been one of the most popular of Spurs players didn't matter at all. His second coming was hailed as a sign that golden days were ahead at Tottenham — and understandably so. Terry had built a deserved reputation as one of the finest coaches, with one of the sharpest brains in the business. Not only in his native London where he worked wonders at both Crystal Palace and Queen's Park Rangers, but further afield in Spain.

He was unknown so far as most Continental observers of football were concerned when he arrived as manager of Barcelona. It wasn't the easiest of assignments — Barcelona had not won the Spanish championship for 10 seasons and were in the process of parting with the world's finest footballer, Diego Maradona.

That was, in many respects, Terry at his greatest, responding to a challenge and beating the odds. Barcelona won the Spanish title at the first attempt and were only beaten in the European Cup Final the following season in a penalty shoot-out. I observed him out there at first-hand, dealing easily with players and fans and speaking Catalan fluently enough to ensure that his messages got across both in the dressing room and at press conferences.

With hindsight, I firmly believe it was a pity that he ever came back to English soccer — where he couldn't get the same top-level response to his ideas as he did from Continental players — and to his native London, where he seemed convinced that being a manager of a football club simply wasn't enough.

Venables, even when I met him first as a Chelsea player just out of his teens, was always striving to be ahead of the game; going for his next target before sitting back to enjoy what he had just achieved. It is equally true that he could never be just a face in the crowd. His tendency was to be a leader of the pack, and in those early days at Chelsea it was the fact that a young team revolved around him, often off the field as well as on it, that led to an inevitable clash of personalities with manager Tommy Docherty and Terry's transfer to Spurs in May, 1966.

So everybody agreed, Venables was the ideal choice — almost the *only* choice — when Spurs suddenly needed replacement for David Pleat, who in his only full season as manager had taken the club to the FA Cup Final, the semi-finals of the Littlewoods Cup and third place in the First Division table.

Chairman Irving Scholar, who had wrested control from the old school of directors four years earlier, was getting impatient for success. He had hesitated to move for Venables when Keith Burkinshaw departed at the end of the 1983-84 season, but in 1987 he chased his man to a holiday hotel in Florida where Terry was taking a breather after leaving Barcelona.

Scholar was so committed to the Spurs cause that you hoped he would hit the jackpot. He and Terry were going to be "mates" in a modern set-up instead of the old relationship of chairman and manager. But it all ended up in tears with the football club burdened by debts piled up because well intentioned business ventures of the parent company, Tottenham Hotspur Plc, went sadly wrong.

Venables could have walked away, his reputation untarnished. But, instead, he felt it was his role to become saviour of the club by finding a person, or persons, then unknown, with the kind of cash to buy out Scholar and stage a total take-over. There were several false starts which commanded headlines on the sports pages of the mass circulation papers as well as the city pages of the self-styled quality press. But Venables bounced back from the disappointments, guided Spurs to an FA Cup Final triumph over Nottingham Forest and kept hoping someone would turn up.... Someone did.... Alan Sugar.

It is doubtful if either of them really knew what they were getting into when they joined forces in the summer of 1991 as the TV cameras zoomed in on a press conference at White Hart Lane one Saturday morning. Sugar had never in the past displayed any deep interest in football and it's hard to believe he would have invested in a commercial venture of which he possessed such scant knowledge. Venables had never previously been associated with a partner of such immense wealth.

It is hard to know what prompted Sugar to ride in on a lilywhite charger to rescue Spurs. Perhaps it was for the sheer satisfaction of outwitting Robert Maxwell, who was suddenly getting into the take-over act. Maybe it was the thought of a high profile like those enjoyed by the billionaires who own top Italian clubs such as AC Milan and Juventus.

Whatever the initial reason, it is clear that Sugar has enjoyed much of the publicity which goes with our national game. It puts the occasional mention in the financial columns in the shade, even for a Premier League player like Mr Amstrad. And Sugar clearly felt it was worth enduring loutish abuse outside the High Court and his Essex home at the time of his split with Venables.

Guy Nathan, I have known since his birth in 1939. We were brought up in the same block of flats, and he, like Venables and Sugar, is an East Londoner and matured in an area where you kicked a ball around until it got too dark and where you had to support either Spurs or Arsenal to be accepted as "one of the lads".

Like me, I suspect he would sooner have written about a third League Championship.

Reg Drury.

TERRY VENABLES — A CARING MAN

In 1989 I collapsed with what turned out to be a cancerous blockage in the lower intestines. The day before my fiftieth birthday I awaited my pre-med visualising the orange sized lump that might kill me. I had said goodbye to my wife and to my darling eight-month-old granddaughter, my first, and lonely was the feeling of the day. Not remorse, not even fear. To be frank I was pissed off that I might 'peg it' before I could see Gary Lineker kick his first ball for Spurs.

My son had been to the Ground to tell the ticket office that I might be late re-ordering my season ticket, but to hold it anyway. Questioned by the staff he explained why I would be late ordering.

It was 12 midday, one hour to go. A nurse brought me a letter. It had the THFC imprint on it…. It read….

'Dear Guy,

I have been informed that you are particularly unwell and at present are in hospital.

I would like to take this opportunity of wishing you a speedy recovery, on behalf of the Directors, Management and Players here at Tottenham Hotspur.

Signed…Terry Venables.'

Whatever business dealings may be questioned, whatever revelations may come to light in the future, whatever and wherever Terry Venables, the family man, the husband, the father, finds himself, I would like to record my eternal thanks and gratitude.

Given a short while to live after the op., I am certain in my mind that I owe much to the inspiration that letter has given me.

By the way, I am not a ghost, and, so far, by the grace of God I am in remission.

Guy Nathan.

PREFACE

When the Terry Venables dismissal from his post as Chief Executive of Tottenham was formally announced on the morning of the 14th May 1993, I, like many long-standing Spurs supporters' was quite naturally shocked. For many days thereafter argument, speculation and discussion raged among my family members who all follow the Lilywhites. My brother and I have been 'going' since 1946 and my two sons since they were around four years old, some 26 years ago. My wife has accompanied me to numerous matches, many away from home, over the last 33 years. You can imagine the main topic of conversation whenever we all got together.

I had just completed a biography on a long-term Auschwitz survivor and although I was preparing the final chapters of my third published novel, the idea of interviewing Terry in order to write about his period at White Hart Lane began to dominate my thinking.

One day in July, after Terry Venables had finally lost his claim to be reinstated as Chief Executive of Tottenham Hotspur Plc, I took the bull by the horns and telephoned Terry's Club, Scribes West International, and to my surprise he returned my call shortly afterwards. I explained my idea and he listened carefully and without interruption. Then he responded:

"It's funny that you should ring me just now because it is only a couple of days ago that I received a similar offer from Penguin Books. They want to do my complete life story and would look to bring the book out at the end of 1994. Your idea of a shorter consolidated version has great appeal. What would you call the book?"

"Barcelona to Bedlam," I replied.

He roared with laughter. There seemed to be an immediate rapport.

"You are a Spurs supporter, I take it?" (He obviously did not connect me with the dying man to whom he had written in 1989.)

I replied: "Since 1946. Strangely, the first game I saw was Arsenal versus Coventry. I was seven at the time and even then I was disillusioned with the Reds. It was only after I watched Spurs versus Blackburn that I knew I was going to be a supporter of their kind of football."

"Perhaps we had better meet, or maybe you would fax an offer through. My Literary Agent, Jonathan Harris is handling these matters; I'll ask him to contact you."

A few days later his Agent telephoned and a meeting was arranged.

Along with a director of the publishing company, Tony Marchant, we visited Scribes, had a couple of drinks while waiting, and then were joined by Terry and his charming and lovely second wife, Yvette. I explained the sort of book we intended to write.

I will admit to feeling desperately sorry for Terry at that time, as I had considered him to be very badly treated. Surely, if there were great differences at Board level, other means than a public 'flogging' could have been found. I warmed to Terry. Jonathan left to attend a football match, and Terry, Tony and I continued to discuss many aspects of the convoluted, recent events at Tottenham. Terry swore to us that he had never done anything wrong in his time at Spurs; he was confused and obviously annoyed, to say the least, by the way he had been treated by Alan Sugar.

(See chapter on meetings with Terry Venables.)

Yvette, who had left us to attend to the bar more than an hour previously, joined us when Terry was called away by the arrival of Teddy Sheringham. We were introduced, and I wished Teddy luck in the forthcoming season. We said little else as the centre-forward was clearly agitated and wanting to tell his former manager about his discussions with Ossie Ardiles who had just been appointed the new manager, and had the Ruddock situation to deal with. I was a little surprised that Terry Venables should be entertaining the player at such a time.

As the weeks went by, Jonathan Harris exchanged telephone conversations with me and my colleagues to which end a meeting was arranged for August the 3rd.

During those telephone calls, Harris explained that he was not going to conduct a Dutch auction, but others had entered into the fray to persuade Terry to write for them. Harris also requested that we reveal our source of backing finance.

The discussions of August the 3rd are detailed in a later chapter within this book.

A further meeting, following several telephone conversations and faxes with and from Jonathan Harris, was arranged for August the 26th at which Eddie Ashby, Terry's confidant and business associate, would be in attendance as we were bringing with us a gentleman by the name of Roger, who was representing our backers, as by this time we had learned that something in the order of a quarter of a million pounds would be needed to secure Terry's signature on a contract.

There was, however, a significant difference between what we were bidding for and what the other publishing houses required from him. They, without exception, were seeking to publish his full life story which they intended to produce at the end of 1994. We, on the other hand, required to produce a book about his time at Tottenham following his departure from Barcelona, to be issued in the early part of 1994. We had explained to Terry that we felt that he wasn't ready for a full autobiography as he surely wasn't finished as a football man, and that the interest of the public was very much centred upon his recent dismissal by Alan Sugar.

Our discussions were concerned with Terry contributing to this book possibly as a prelude to the full monte at some later date when his future was more clear.

In September, two television programmes, BBC 1's Panorama and Channel 4's Dispatches disclosed what they alleged to be inappropriate business dealings that involved two payments by Tottenham in cash; one of £58,750 paid to an agency called First Wave Sports Management, run by Frank McLintock and his partner Graham Smith and another of £200,000 paid to a Mr Santin for his assistance in the transfer of Paul Gascoigne to Lazio. There were further allegations which are detailed in later chapters.

It was then that we finally decided what form this book would take and we sought to set up a further meeting with Terry to discuss this.

Since then innumerable faxes and telephone calls have been exchanged with Jonathan Harris. Terry feared that a further contribution might prejudice the full autobiography that he clearly intends to write at some time in the future, or that our investigations might take a line unfavourable to him.

We expressed our continuing sympathy for his plight, never feeling that payments which were made by Tottenham Hotspur with Alan Sugar's consent should have led to the public display of ill feeling emanating from Sugar, and resulting in Terry's dismissal.

We offered to meet Terry again on or before the 27th of September, but each and every proposed meeting has been resisted by Jonathan Harris, presumably acting on behalf of his client. I even had a secret meeting with Harris which I reluctantly attended at Fat Sams restaurant in Gants Hill, with a view to resolving what was becoming a widening gap. Dealing with agents in the absence of the principal is invariably ineffective, unproductive and worst of all incomplete. The meeting struck me as useless and ludicrous without Terry's attendance, particularly as Harris suggested that it could be Alan Sugar who was financing this book.

By this time Roger and his backers had withdrawn when they learned of the television presentations, and we had made alternative financial proposals.

Quite properly Jonathan Harris was doing his best to protect his client, but he wanted assurances and information from me that I was either not able or unwilling to give in order to gain Terry's further support. I realised then that I would have to make do with only one serious interview with Terry Venables.

As for Alan Sugar, whom I knew during my formative years and later during my teens, far from financing this book he has not only refused all requests to talk to me, but has also sent a memo to every employee at Tottenham Hotspur to do likewise.

I remember him as a bit of a wimp, who definitely did not accompany the crowd of lads who each and every Saturday went to White Hart Lane during the 50's. Alan was not among the giggling lads who went to the game from rail stations such as Bethnal Green, Hackney Downs, Rectory Road and Stamford Hill eager for victory and the joy that a good result would bring to a Saturday evening's entertainment and pursuits. I doubt if he remembers me and certainly is not in contact with any of the 'gang' who still get together from time to time. Certainly not now that he has achieved such prominence and wealth.

I seem to have ruffled his feathers for some reason. I had a good laugh when friends of 20 years employed at Tottenham read out the memo that he had sent to, it seems, everyone from the gateman to the financial director.

It poses the question…. What does he think that people like Gary Mabbutt, Ossie Ardiles and Bill Nicholson might tell me that he didn't want supporters and public alike to know…?

The book you are about to read is a result of several interesting and informative meetings, interviews and very careful scrutiny of the court hearings and judgments that followed Terry's dismissal, as well as comments and views from the Vice-President of Barcelona Football Club and those of Terry's predecessor as manager of Tottenham Hotspur, David Pleat. Its production has involved months of investigation and research.

I have attempted to bring to supporters and the public details of one of the most controversial and fascinating periods in the history of Tottenham Hotspur and indeed of football itself.

To all who have helped me, in particular my editor Jeffrey, Reg Drury and Tony Marchant, Director of the publishing company; not least my wife and to my secretary Nicola Hope, I offer my sincere thanks, for without them I couldn't have written Barcelona to Bedlam.

Guy Nathan, *January 1994.*

Chapter 1
THE PROTAGONISTS

In the black corner, grim faced, determined, fifty-three-year old Alan Sugar, born Hackney, London, E.8, weighing in with an alleged personal cash fortune of £37,000,000, variously Chairman, Chief Executive, Director of several companies spread across the globe, including a vast publicly owned computer marketing, selling and distribution organisation from a base in Brentwood, Essex; married, two children, resident in a vast walled and iron-gated house in the 'upper echelons' of Chigwell, also in Essex. Mother, Fay, 85 years old on December 31st 1993, quite happy, but resident in an old aged home situated some three miles from his home. A good son, he pays the bills.

In the white corner, Terrence Frederick Venables, twinkly eyed, smiling man about town, born East Ham, mostly resident Dagenham, Essex, weighing in with nowt known in his bank, drinking and eating club owner on London's exclusive Kensington High Street. He has connections with many questionable companies, and with a bankrupt right-hand man, but is rated as one of the best football coaches in the world. Married for the second time, to Yvette, two daughters from first marriage.

Alan Sugar
Noted for spotting a hole in the market when he was a young man by realising the value of low-priced home computers. Quickly and successfully established himself in that field by visiting Japan, Hong Kong and Taiwan with borrowed money, and arranging for companies in those lands to manufacture the special style of equipment that he envisaged would make him a rich man. From a rather quiet, somewhat inoffensive teenager, he now enjoys a position of much respect and consideration from the international business world, and the 'City'.

In 1991 he noted that Terry Venables was seeking a partner in an attempt to buy out the existing Directors who controlled

Tottenham Hotspur Plc. At first Venables refused his ministrations, but came to terms with Sugar as others had dropped by the wayside, agreed to back him in his bid to oust Scholar and Bobroff, the major shareholders.

On March 15th 1991 he realised £33.8 million from the sale of 42.75 million ordinary shares in Amstrad Plc, reducing his holding to 36.4 per cent. The Company, Amstrad Plc, some three months later, was valued at £274 million. Mr Sugar's personal holding was then valued at £100 million. He remains as Chairman and Managing Director.

On taking over Tottenham he immediately affirmed that the pension rights of all members were fully safeguarded, a matter of great concern to the entire populace who had read of pension fund irregularities in the dealings of Mr Robert Maxwell, who had himself been involved at one time with a Tottenham takeover, and had reportedly loaned Tottenham £1,000,000.

On the 21st June 1991, jointly with Edennote Plc, he purchased 3,644,000 shares in Tottenham Plc, which enabled him and Venables to control the Company. He then wrote to all the other shareholders requesting that they did not sell their shares to him and Terry, because under a special rule he and Venables were obliged to make an offer for ALL the remaining shares. Naturally, he was able to pay outright for those shares without effectively causing a 'dent' in his personal wealth, whereas Venables' Company, Edennote, did not have the funds in place at the due date, and had to borrow the money from Alan Sugar for a few days.

This, the first instance in his dealings with Venables that 'raised his eyebrows'.

On December 6th 1991, having failed in attempts to mortgage the ground, he floated a four-for-seven 'rights issue', some 5,820,313 shares of 25p each at £1.25 per share, and underwrote those shares himself giving him a voting advantage over his 'partner', who was unable to take up his entire allocation. This time he was happy for investors to increase their holdings as the money would have flowed into the Club, but few were able to do so.

From that point on, Sugar became a virtual dictator at Tottenham, causing the computer arrangements to be altered so that results were recorded at his personal base in Brentwood, awarding himself a 'company to company' income of £50,000 per annum, and securing an ears-and-eyes protection with the appointment to Financial Director of a close associate, Colin Sandy, effectively decreasing Terry Venables' autonomy and authority. Sandy continued to undermine Terry, and in taking a credit rating on Eddie Ashby (which showed that Ashby was an undischarged bankrupt), Terry's right-hand-man who described himself as Tottenham's General Manager in correspondence, he eventually precipitated the eventual split when Sugar asked Terry to sack Ashby, which he failed to do.

By then Sandy was investigating documents and expenditure and questioning practically everything that Terry was doing off the football field.

On 14th May 1993, Sugar, with the backing of his Board of Directors, dismissed Terry Venables, having offered to purchase Edennote's shares in Tottenham, and to compensate that company for the loss of their service contract.

Distraught at the loss of his position at Tottenham, Venables then forced Sugar to defend legal actions against him, his private company and Tottenham Hotspur Plc.

Terry Venables
Following a successful time at Barcelona, Terry joined Tottenham Hotspur as Manager, after a holiday which may have been taken in order to create a time-gap following the departure of his predecessor, David Pleat, in 1987, if we are to believe that Irving Scholar wrapped up a deal with him long before Pleat's departure.

When he joined Spurs they were languishing near the bottom of the then Division 1. The teams were being 'managed' by an amalgam of senior players. In his first season, he lifted the team to a much higher place in the League and consolidated their playing staff and generally settled the Club after the furore of David Pleat's widely reported and alleged personal misbehaviour.

The team played a stilted style of football that was attributed to Terry's limited opportunities with the staff that remained under his control. Spurs went out of the FA Cup in disgrace, losing to Port Vale, and Terry disposed of Neil Ruddock to Millwall, and

Ossie Ardiles to Blackburn, and later made a major sale when he sold Chris Waddle to Marseilles for in excess of £4,000,000.

He signed, among others, Gary Lineker and Nayim from his old club, Barcelona, and Paul Gascoigne from Newcastle. Spurs continued to play in a rather controlled manner, with no wingers except for an occasional flurry from midfielder Paul Allen, and with backs restricted to play in their own half.

In 1991, his team reached the pinnacle of his success at Tottenham, when they beat Arsenal in the Semi-Final of the FA Cup and Nottingham Forest in the Final at Wembley. He had since signed Paul Stewart from Manchester City, Paul Walsh from Liverpool and Justin Edinburgh from Southend.

Clive Allen, formerly Tottenham's free goal scoring centre-forward was allowed to leave.

Long before the Cup Final, it was widely reported that Tottenham were in financial difficulties and arrangements were made to sell Paul Gascoigne to Lazio of Italy, but a serious injury received in that Cup Final affected the payment and release of the monies that Tottenham were due to receive for him, and delicate negotiations were conducted in an attempt to please the Midland Bank and a number of other creditors. In this matter Terry engaged the services of an Italian restaurateur, a Mr Santin, to assist in those negotiations, albeit that Lazio's Financial Director and their London solicitors spoke perfect English.

By this time Terry had launched a takeover campaign for Tottenham's shares and in that matter he needed a partner, because he alone could not raise sufficient to 'effectively take control'. Enter a number of interested entrepreneurs, but it was the erstwhile Alan Sugar who won the day and enabled Terry to elevate his own position to that of Chief Executive.

Meanwhile, there emerged a letter, which appears not to have been shown during previous Board meetings which questioned whether Mr Santin's involvement and interest for which he was paid £200,000 in cash had been necessary. A dispute arose as to whether the fee that was arranged for Gascoigne's transfer was £4.8 million before Santin's entry onto the scene, or whether it had already been agreed at £5.5 million. It was even alleged on a number of occasions that Terry had received a kick-back from that deal, particularly as Santin invoiced Tottenham for the amount on an invoice emanating from a Swiss company with only an accommodation address.

After Terry's rise to the Boardroom, he appointed a former manager of Tottenham, Peter Shreeves, to run the team affairs. Much as it had been during Mr Shreeves' previous stint as manager, in 1985, the performances of the First Team were poor. Spurs finished the League competition very near the bottom, losing more home games than at any time in their history. Shreeves' one year contract was not renewed.

Venables then, with the Board's approval, started to devote more time to the playing activities of the Club and less to the commercial enterprises which were being introduced and implemented by others.

To assist him, he appointed former Tottenham and England goalkeeper Ray Clemence and former Liverpool player, Doug Livermore. After some three weeks of the '92/'93 Season, he signed Teddy Sheringham from Nottingham Forest for £2.1 million in circumstances that are described elsewhere in this book. Teddy was at first a little slow for Tottenham's playing style, but soon improved and became the Club's leading goal scorer, later being included in the England squad. Spurs first team, although not winning any of the competitions, played well, particularly at the end of the season and the supporters began to feel that something big was about to happen. In the final games of the season, Spurs scored five against Norwich, four against Leeds and Southampton (the latter goals in just four minutes forty four seconds), three against QPR and Wimbledon, and beat the old enemy, Arsenal, both home and away, although they lost to them in the Semi-Final of the FA Cup by 1-0.

During the close season, Alan Sugar sacked Terry, and a great deal that had been confidential became public knowledge.

Terry was appointed Director on the 21st June 1991. His Agent has suggested that a personality clash coupled with a loss of respect began on the 22nd June 1991.

Terry indulged in many other interests along with a partner whom he appointed as a special assistant to him and the Board at Tottenham, and who had been, or was currently involved with 43 companies, many of which were facing liquidation, or were actually being wound up.

Terry had invented a game for sale to the public called 'The Manager' and much was learned about his activities in this matter. We know that both the printers and the assemblers lost enormous sums through not being paid. Suddenly, those who believed that Terry Venables might do for Spurs what two predecessors Messrs. Arthur Rowe and Bill Nicholson had done, lost faith in him as news of his 'other' interests became widely reported.

Following much litigation, which he himself instigated, Terry languishes in his Club, Scribes, also reported as being in enormous financial difficulties, with his reputation damaged, but not I hope, beyond all repair.

Newspapers such as the Sun have reported that Terry's convoluted background may be ignored by the FA as they seek a replacement for recent England Manager, Graham Taylor. This rumour has been denied by Graham Kelly, Chief Executive of the Football Association.

The Venables Record:
Played at every level of representation in the English football world, including the senior England Team. Won, as a player, an FA Cup Final medal when representing Tottenham, in 1967. Spurs beat his former major Club, Chelsea, by two goals to one. (For the nostalgic, Frank Saul and Jimmy Robertson scored for Spurs.) Also played for Chelsea and QPR.

During his management career, won the Third and Second Division Championships with Crystal Palace, reached the FA Cup Final (against Tottenham!), and won the Second Division Championship with Queens Park Rangers, won the Spanish League and the Spanish Cup and reached the European Cup Final with Barcelona; won the FA Cup with Tottenham in 1991.

SOME FACTS ABOUT TOTTENHAM AND AMSTRAD Plc
In the financial year ending 31st May 1993, during Terry's stewardship, Spurs turned over approximately £25 million as against £19 million the previous year. Players and match expenses were £13.8 million against £7.4 million the previous year.

Although turnover was increased by 31.5 per cent the profits dropped by approx. £700 thousand to £3.158 million. Current assets were worth only £2.1 million while they owe £12.6 million, but of course they are not insolvent due to the fact that not included in those figures are 'Fixed Assets', which include the Ground etc. £33.241 million.

It is also interesting to note that the staff had increased considerably: Players and associated staff from 81 to 90, increase of 11 per cent; Administration from 51 to 60, increase of 15 per cent; Selling and distribution staff from 11 to 20, practically double.

The 'emoluments' of the Directors totalled £442,258, up by 10 per cent, of which £11,700 related to Pension Fund contributions.

In 1992 the Chairman's emolument was nil, but Alan Sugar has received through his Jersey Company, some £20,835. The previous Chairman, Irving Scholar, received only £3,068. The highest paid Director, Terry Venables, received £357,198, as opposed to £267,500 paid in 1992.

At 1st June the players had cost Spurs £11.7 million and during the year Terry had purchased a further £6.578 million worth, but had sold some £4.668 million worth, leaving a current player valuation, less amortisation, of approx. £11 million worth. Interestingly the sales include that of Paul Gascoigne, who made a profit for Spurs of £2.8 million on his purchase price, and who by way of injury and delayed transfer earned Tottenham a further approx. £450,000 in interest which was held in escrow until he was finally passed fit for transfer to Lazio.

As a Company, Tottenham owed the bank almost £12 million at 1992 year-end accounts, which was down to £4.28 million by 31st May 1993.

Since that year end, Tottenham have signed Dozzell, Calderwood, Kerslake and Hazard for a total of £3.45 million, and sold Ruddock, Tuttle, Hendon and Paul Allen for a total of £3.425 million, a minor deficit of just £25,000.... Ossie is balancing the books!

Most recently, Gordon Durie has been sold to Rangers for a reputed £1.2 million and now Ossie is well in credit.

At the time of writing information has been publicised about a series of Company loans made to players which have not yet been repaid, including, allegedly £25,000 to Captain Gary Mabbutt, allegedly £75,000 to Paul Stewart and £126,000 to Ossie Ardiles, Terry's successor as Tottenham Manager, at a time when he was a Spurs player.

Alan Sugar has called for an armistice with the Football Association; in effect he is asking for all past misdemeanours to be wiped away against his undertaking that no such irregularities will occur again, while he is in control.

The alleged loans were almost entirely made during Venables' administration, with perhaps the exception of those made to Ardiles who received his 'loans' during the period of Irving Scholar's Chairmanship.

In addition, Tottenham and Ardiles are facing threatening litigation from the Chairman of West Bromwich Albion who alleges breach of contract when Ardiles left them to join Tottenham.

AMSTRAD Plc

Amstrad Plc is much bigger than Tottenham, and makes no profit at the moment, but Sugar has been praised by the 'City' for reducing losses from the previous horrendous trading year (during our infamous recession), to a lower figure than had been anticipated....

Turnover: £356.6 million; loss of £70.9 million.

The nearest shareholder to Alan Sugar is a Mr K. Ashcroft who owns just 870,000 shares.

Interestingly, although it is widely known that Rupert Murdoch, one of Margaret Thatcher's favourite sons, is a close associate of Sugar's, Amstrad makes no political donations.

The Group has offices in Germany, Australasia, France, Italy, the Benelux Countries and until recently, Spain, which was sold during 1993. Sugar's Company owed £8.476 million to its bankers, which is less than Tottenham owed when he came in as Chairman.

He is reported as earning some £219,000 in annual salary and I wonder whether Sugar may have given himself a rewarding contract with Tottenham Plc, because Venables/Edennote were paid £225,000 per annum, which was more than Sugar's wages from Amstrad.... It's a thought....

In the contents of this book I think it may be interesting to quote from a letter written by Alan Sugar on the 23rd July 1993 to Tottenham Independent Supporters Association (TISA), in reply to a letter from them. Since he clearly wanted his position to be understood, I do not suppose that he will object to my reproducing what he has said:

"Thank you for your recent letter regarding Tottenham Hotspur and Terry Venables. I am sorry that it has taken me a bit of time to respond, but that is because I wanted to wait until the Court had determined whether Mr Venables should be permitted to remain as Chief Executive and then to give the dust some time to settle.

"You have been very critical of me and the Board for the action we have taken against Terry Venables. I cannot agree with your sentiments, but I respect your right to make them and I have some understanding of the emotions and feelings that have led you to such a view. Although I cannot comment at this time on some matters, I feel it is appropriate that I should make a number of points.

"The first point I should make is that the Board's decision to terminate Mr Venables' contract was not related to his abilities as a football manager; he was sacked as Chief Executive of the company. I can assure you that the decision was not taken without a great deal of consideration, but the Board did have good reasons for taking the decision. I cannot detail the reasons at this time as the Court case is continuing and these matters are sub judice and I am therefore not permitted to discuss those matters in public.

"You will of course remember the financial difficulties Tottenham were suffering in 1991 prior to my acquiring my initial share holding in the company. I am determined that Tottenham will not suffer those sort of problems again.

"I know that there has been much comment in relation to that initial acquisition with regard to the amount of money that Terry Venables put into the company. I should set the record straight. The majority of the money Terry invested was not put into Tottenham; it was passed on to the third parties in order to acquire their shares in Tottenham. The only benefit that the club gained from Mr Venables' investment was the money he actually put into Tottenham which was £800,000. This was not sufficient to save the company and therefore the club. I had to inject £6 million into the company in order to secure its immediate financial future. That is a substantial sum of money and I would not have invested that sum if I was not committed to ensuring that Tottenham had a successful future.

"It is because I am determined to do the best for Tottenham and because I have its best interests at heart, that the Board have appointed Ossie Ardiles as manager. His footballing beliefs are totally in tune with Tottenham's great traditions, and already, even before the season has started, the players look to be thriving on Ossie's determination to play football the Tottenham way.

"He was a great player and I am sure that he will prove to be just as great a manager. He may not have the managerial experience of Terry Venables, but all the recent evidence is that great players can turn out to be very good managers. Look at Kenny Dalglish, first at Liverpool and now at Blackburn, Trevor Francis at Sheffield Wednesday, Johann Cruyff at Barcelona and of course Franz Beckenbauer. If you have been a long standing and devoted follower of Tottenham Hotspur, you would have had the pleasure of watching Ossie Ardiles in his prime at White Hart Lane and I am sure that you will want to give him your full support when the season starts. Ossie has already proved himself at Swindon and West Brom and has built a potentially successful team at Newcastle, although not given time to demonstrate what a good team he had built. Both I and the Board of Directors felt the time was right for Ossie to prove himself in the Premier League and I am sure he will be a great success.

"Comment has been made that I did not regularly visit White Hart Lane every other Saturday to watch Tottenham until I decided to rescue the club with Terry Venables two years ago. That is true.

However, that does not mean that I did not follow the fortunes of Spurs or was not interested in the club. I was born in Hackney, very much Tottenham's catchment area, and was taken regularly to see Spurs play by my father. I come from a family of devoted Spurs supporters; my brother is as much of a Spurs nut as anybody you could meet.

"Whilst I was busy trying to make my own way in the world since the age of 16 I did not often have the time to go to White Hart Lane, but always looked out for their results and continued my interest as best I could. I have enormous admiration and respect for people like you who support Tottenham week in and week out, season after season, in the foulest weather imaginable. Do not think that because I was not there on the terrace I loved Tottenham any less.

"It upsets me when remarks are made to the effect that I care less about Tottenham than Terry Venables does. As I say above, I have always been a Tottenham fan and want them to be as successful as possible, like any other fan. Terry Venables, of course, was a professional footballer and is now a professional football manager and therefore is paid to give his all for whatever team he is involved with. He, of course, initially started life with Chelsea before spending a few seasons with Tottenham before moving on and then going into management with Crystal Palace, QPR and Barcelona before returning to Tottenham.

"There have also been comments about my apparent desire to run the football team and/or interfere with the running of the football team. This is totally untrue. I am not and nor have I ever professed to be a football expert. I love watching the game, I love supporting Spurs and I want to make Spurs successful, but I do not have the knowledge or experience to even begin to suggest how the team should play or what players should be bought and what players should be sold. I never interfered with the running of the football team when Terry Venables was in charge of that and I can assure you that Ossie Ardiles need have no fears that I will interfere with the football side now. I will not do so.

"Contrary to rumour I do not want Tottenham Hotspur to be another 'Wimbledon'. I want them to be the best club in the land, the best in Europe. My dream, like that of any other Spurs supporter is for Tottenham to win the Premier League, the FA Cup, the League Cup and the European Cup and as many trophies as possible. Above all, I want them to play good and entertaining football in the great tradition of Spurs, so that Spurs fans not only enjoy success, but only watching that success.

"My time and expertise will be devoted to making sure that the club is run properly on the commercial side so that there is money available for Ossie Ardiles to buy players and provide the sort of support he needs to keep Spurs a great club. I need not remind you of the financial difficulties Tottenham faced in 1991, that despite winning the FA Cup the Club could have been wound up. Only this week the troubles at Barnet have again been in the news. I am determined that Tottenham will not suffer financial difficulties again, but am equally determined that Tottenham are successful and are competing in all competitions and are hopefully winning some silverware.

"I wish the business with Terry Venables had never taken place, but unfortunately it became unavoidable, as unpleasant as it was. Although the Court proceedings are still outstanding, at least everybody in the club now knows where they stand and with Ossie Ardiles as manager, I look forward to future success. I hope that you will continue to support the club in the way that you have always done and will together with me, get behind Ossie in the coming season. Having witnessed the success that Arsenal had last season, I am even more determined that Tottenham succeed this season and to help Tottenham to do so, I hope the club can count on your support to encourage the players and make sure there is a great atmosphere to encourage the good football and the success it should bring.

Dear Ms....The first home game is against Arsenal and I don't have to tell you that your support at White Hart Lane will matter when you visit our ground.

Yours sincerely

Alan Sugar."

Chapter 2
THE BARCELONA INTEREST

BARCELONA FOOTBALL CLUB. Snr. NICOLAU CASAUS de la FUENTE IENE, VICE-PRESIDENT BARCELONA FOOTBALL CLUB

When I finally agreed to accept the commission to write this book, I decided that it would be imperative to meet with someone who was at Barcelona Football Club, and of course, who knew Terry Venables well during his time there as what we might term 'the manager'.

To say that I was surprised to receive a return fax agreeing to my request, and that the second most important man in the organisation, for that is what Barca is, would see me, is an understatement.

Our interview was arranged for 5 pm on the evening of Tuesday 8th December, but as I was arriving on the previous Friday, I would be able to be a guest of the Club at the home game with Longrones on the Saturday evening.

I collected two tickets at around eleven thirty that morning, my wife accompanied me, at the reception hall, but only after passing several hundred people watching an under eleven game where one of the teams was wearing the traditional 'Barca' shirts: the famous wide-striped red and bluc. On leaving reception, I immediately noticed a gantry some twenty feet off the ground of about one hundred feet that extended to what I construed was the Stadium. Not thinking on that matter any further we returned to Barcelona city and spent the day wandering around the Olympic Village, waiting until it was time to go to the match, which kicked off at 8.45 pm that Saturday evening.

We arrived back at the complex two hours before the game, being naturally nervous about connections and times of entrance etc., to find thousands of people exiting from the stadium at the far end of the gantry.

What could be wrong? Had the match been played and we had missed it? Did the guy in the hotel tell us incorrectly (my Spanish is not so good) the time of the game ending, or what?

Confused, we climbed the gantry and peered into the ground itself as the remnants of the supporting public drifted out. We spotted two young men standing around apparently in no hurry to get away, and approached them seeking their knowledge of our language. One spoke English fairly fluently and he was able to explain that the ground at which we were looking was only the RESERVE team ground. The capacity was about sixteen thousand. The ground had been almost full, even though the game, the reserve team game, HAD BEEN LIVE ON TELEVISION THAT SAME AFTERNOON!

"You did not miss the main stadium, did you...? It is big enough!"

We felt such fools, but then you would, wouldn't you...?

At that point I began to examine seriously just what Barcelona Football Club was all about. It was not a football club as we know it here in England. Or indeed anywhere else. It was an enormous complex with several stadiums, a block of offices the size of the Mansion House, and a serious contributor to taxes, and the social welfare of the main city. Barcelona Football Club is truly an institution in the real sense of the word.... It took us three quarters of an hour to walk around the perimeter of the ground, find the entrance that in some way related to our tickets, then to climb the 172 steps that led to the highest seat in the ground, five levels above the pitch. The enormity of the task that Terry Venables had taken on came home to me. This was not football management as we know it. This was placing himself in front of the most critical and scrutinising eyes. This was standing up and being counted beyond anything that could be imagined in the life of a football manager. Every move, every statement, every conversation, every selection, and yes, every result would fill several pages of EL MUNDO DEPORTIVO, and every other newspaper that was published in the State of Catalonia. This was placing oneself 'on the line' and only a big man, a very big man, confident of his ability, confident of his attitude and style, could take on a task such as this....

At Barca there are football teams at every level imaginable. The complex encompasses four football pitches, two main stadiums, an indoor handball pitch, an ice hockey arena, a roller rink, parking above ground and under the main Stadium for 8000 vehicles, restaurants, bars, 1200 souvenir and food stalls, and even a residential 'farm house' for young players being brought on by the Club for future stardom. At entrance 7, there is a hall filled with toys and playthings to enable supporters with children to deposit them before the game and collect them afterwards assured of perfect safety and care.

I remember, presumably like most of you, when my children used to cry on seeing their dad leave on a Saturday afternoon for a match at Spurs. Not so the Barcelonians.... Their kiddies look forward to a home game. Saturday in Barcelona is not a day when you go to watch your favourite team play, it is a day of football festival. Under 19s at three thirty. Reserves at six, and then one of the finest teams in Europe at eight thirty or eight forty five. There are 110,000 members (owners) of the Club. They purchase a 'billet' at the commencement of each season, which entitles them to attend all of the sporting activities and all parts of the grounds. With 750 supporter chapters across the globe, Barcelona boasts the largest membership of any football club world-wide! The press room has in excess of 200 seats, 24 radio booths, a conference room with capacity for 250 guests, and is equipped with public address and simultaneous translation systems. There is even a television production set for interviews and documentary purposes.

I did not intend to write about the game that night, but something happened that was so ironic that I feel that I must make mention of it. Remember Holland versus England in the World Cup preliminaries...?

The score was nil nil when the centre-forward broke through for Longrones. Just he and the goalkeeper eye to eye, face to face. The edge of the penalty area, when the defender of Barcelona tripped the advancing forward. A free kick outside the box, the offending player SENT OFF. (As some believe that Koeman should have been when he did the same thing to David Platt.) Later on, one, and then two one to Longrones. A penalty to Barca. Who stepped up to equalise…? You've guessed it, the man himself, Ronald Koeman who had been brought on by Johann Cruyff as a second half substitute….

On the Tuesday, as arranged, I turned up in awe of the pending interview. Everything was so vast. Vice-President Casaus himself so important.

Would you believe that he couldn't speak a word of English? To the rescue his secretary Mercedes: fluent English.

For an hour she wrote down the questions in Spanish and I arranged to return the following evening to listen to and record the answers which I then had to get translated here in England.

Before commencing to relate the very interesting comments of Snr. Casaus, I must mention that the interview was conducted some two hours before Barcelona played their European Cup match with Monaco, which they won by two goals to nil.

The office of Senor Casaus was as one would assume, both opulent and palatial. Modern large furniture, thick pile carpet, and outer offices housing several personal staff, including the English-speaking aforementioned Mercedes who seemed to have more work to do than was humanly possible. This while the seventy odd year old Vice-President shuffled around his office at a steady pace, calm and dignified.

He began by telling me that the main Stadium was completed in 1957 to house 90,000 people and that further tiers were added to increase the capacity to 120,000. That the smaller stadium came first and was now used only for the second team and other full time professionals, which surprisingly only amounted to 22 players. I asked him how they managed on such a small playing staff, and he suggested that that is all that is needed if one has amateurs, juniors and part time professionals on the staff which actually complete a full playing staff of around seventy or so. Each group is kept separate and is under the control of a main 'technico' who each then come under the numero uno, which during the eighties was our Tel. I asked him how Terry had fared during his time at the Club.

"Terry Venables is a good 'technico' with strong views and firm discipline. I am the man who travels to each game away and am the man to whom the 'uno technico' is responsible. We had a good relationship. A very good relationship. I found him to be extremely amiable, good to get on with and most of all I regard him as a friend."

I then asked him about Maradona and Schuster.

"Terry Venables would have liked to keep them both. Maradona is his own man and even though Terry was coming to the Club at the time when he had decided to leave the Club, I think for Napoli, we were unable to retain his services. He is a fine player, but sometimes as in all great players, a little temperamental. Schuster was another problem that all blew up in the press. He was out of contract and Terry could not play him. The more he could not play the more he wanted to leave. Eventually as you know there was a court case, but we let him go a little reluctantly. I believe that Mr Venables would have liked to have kept him, that was my impression."

"I am interested to know what your reaction is to the problems Terry has had in England recently."

"We have heard some things but not a great deal, When your book gets published here in Spain we will know more. At the moment, we have great sympatico for Terry. He is popular with all here at Barca."

"Were you aware of the alleged meetings between Irving Scholar and Terry Venables even while he was still your technico?"

"We had a tournament way back in '85 or '86 and Mr Scholar came over with David Pleat for that match which was with Tottenham. Since that time I have never spoken to him, not even by telephone. We had no idea of any meetings. You seem to know more about that than us."

"Are you at present happy with your current technico, Johan Cruyff?"

"Without casting any aspersions on Terry Venables, or any other of our previous technicos, Mr Cruyff is absolutely wonderful. He has achieved so much and we have the finest team in Spain at the moment. We are in the European Cup, final stages, and are currently top of the Spanish League."

"It has been rumoured that Mr Cruyff may not return to Barca after the World Cup in America when he takes over the Dutch National Team."

"At the moment Mr Cruyff is on a contract and we are hopeful that he renews that contract for ten or twenty years."

"Should he not do so, would you consider a return to the Club of Terry Venables?"

"Mr Venables is my friend and will always be so. It would not be right to discuss that while Mr Cruyff is in charge still. What I can say is that Terry was a good man and will always be welcome back here...as a friend."

(I mention that I inquired of the translator whether there was any inflection in Senor Casaus's voice giving a real hint of what he was actually saying.... She replied that in her opinion he was trying to say that he liked Terry but he would not able to return as Coach.)

We were able to chat thereafter for a short while, somehow making each other understand, and I gauged that much of what he was saying was that Terry was really popular with all people during his time there, with the Directors and players and the supporters. He was, in fact, a gentleman, who would always be welcome in Spanish Society, but that his days of coaching that Club again were over. Finally he mentioned how wrong the newspapers had been to suggest that Terry parted in bad faith.

"That is so untrue," he stated....

THE OFFICIAL BARCELONA SUPPORTERS CLUB, LONDON

In the Don Pepe Restaurant, Frampton St, London, I interviewed the Presidente. This is a powerful body who were in constant touch with the Club and carried out the work needed to market tickets and clothing and souvenirs in this Country, as well as arranging for overseas trips.

There are seven hundred and fifty Chapters of the Barcelona Football Club across the World. Each has a committee and president. They meet, usually, once a month, and discuss recent events, instructions from home base in Spain, ticket enquiries, commercial sales and propositions, membership applications, and all matters concerning the massive enterprise that is the 'Barca' football club, so famous, World-wide.

The Presidente of the London Chapter is Senor Bonaventura Alsina i Soler. Unfortunately his English is limited to a formal greeting, and 'thank you'. As my Spanish extends to "Dos cafe con liche caliente" (two coffees with hot milk), you might expect that there was some difficulty in communication.

He couldn't keep saying 'good afternoon' and I couldn't continue drinking coffee all day...!

The Secretario is Senor Jose Font Planas, who, fortunately, had a great command of our National language. Additionally, there were five members of the Committee, including one, Ramon, who spoke the two languages fluently, and was in Barcelona at the time of Terry Venables' occupancy of the coach's post, and who has been a resident of London for the past three and a half years.

I established that they were all very much in touch with recent events at Tottenham. They probably had more information than I at the time. Through Ramon I asked El Presidente what were his thoughts on all of the matters.

"I know Terry Venables well. I have been to functions with him both here and in Barcelona. I know him to be a kind and pleasant man; a wonderful host and most of all a very good coach. To a Catalan, Terry is remembered with reverence. We had not won the Spanish League for ten years until he arrived. He introduced some fine players, like Archibald, Lineker, Schuster and Hughes. He came just before Maradona left us in dismay and confusion. I do not know Alan Sugar. It seems that there is a conflict of personality. I believe that Mr Sugar should have shown some dignity and resolved his differences with Mr Venables from inside the Club. Anything is better than what has happened."

Ramon took over the conversation for himself.

"When Terry first came to Barcelona we had been starved of success. He introduced a brand of football that was new to us. It was faster, and more aggressive. Coupled with the normal Spanish skill it was a delight to see and we had much success under him."

"Didn't he play the offside a lot?"

"Ah, that is where you English differ from us. We see the offside rule as one to take advantage of. We see the tactics and the cleverness of the coach as a wonderful thing. In England, even at Spurs where I have been many times, the cheers are for a high cross ball, and a leap in the air from big centre-forwards. The ball invariably is headed out and the defence rushes out to create an offside situation and the crowd boos. In Spain we heartily applaud that. It is all part of the intricacy of the game and all down to the cleverness of the coach.''

"I take it you have also met Terry?''

"We all have. He has been here to a meeting when he came over for a break.''

"Tell me about his time there, if you can, in chronological order.''

"Huh?''

"Order of events in date order.''

"Oh, I see. Well, when he first came we doubted whether he had the technical skill for a top Spanish club. Your football is so much rush and dash and fitness. Soon he had earned a reputation for skill coupled with the best of what is good in England. He came, not only to the Football Club, but also to Barcelona. To Spain. To the people. He speaks Spanish well. He mixes well, and always has time for anyone. He never turns his back on anyone, be they supporter, critic or player. So, we won the League and he was a hero. Then we entered the European Cup, and we were still a wonderful team. We finished second that season, but we had great sympathy for him when we lost to Staua in the European Cup Final at Seville. It was not his fault. What could he do, take the penalties himself? Then after that he had terrible trouble with Schuster. He didn't want to play for Terry and he wanted to leave. The Club officiados refused his request for transfer. The Club was in turmoil, but still we had faith in Terry. Schuster took the Club to court for unfair practices. Have you met with Terry yet?''

I told him that I had been down to Scribes and met and drank with Terry and talked to him, and met Terry's wife and agent and business partner.

"What do you think of team managers having outside business interests?''

"Look at Cruyff. He has more business across Europe than the Presidente of the Club! They get paid so much from their work

40

and from their advertising and television appearances that it is natural to invest and to make interest in those investments. With Terry Venables it makes no difference. Football is his first love…. Always!''

''What happened when it was announced that he was leaving Barcelona?''

''We were not very surprised. There had been newspaper reports that the Spurs Chairman, Scholar, had been seen in Barcelona and that, after the Schuster business, Terry was not so in love with the administration at Barcelona. We knew really what was on the cards…. On the cards, is that good English saying?''

''What was the football position then?''

''We had lost, I think, five of the first six games. We were very near the bottom, and this gave the Board excuse to release him. I think maybe he knew his days were numbered and that he had a job to go to.''

''What is the attitude now to Terry, regardless of all this business with Alan Sugar?''

''Soon, Johan Cruyff is to manage the Dutch national side if they beat you in Holland and get to the World Cup. If he stays on with Holland and there is a vacancy, the word in Barcelona is that Terry will return. We would welcome him with open arms''.

(Holland 2, England nil.)

It was clear that they were privy to something which had only been rumoured here in Great Britain. At Board level you have read that they do not see Terry returning….

I noted the whole Committee's concensus of agreement to everything that Ramon had told me. They were enthusiastic to validate his comments and all wished Terry the very best when I next see him and to tell him that they would welcome a visit to their monthly meeting at any time.

Downstairs in the restaurant lobby, I felt like a king. Every waiter and member of staff, including the owner, awaited my arrival and offered their comments. They were all, without reservation, in support of Terry.

The owner of the restaurant insisted pleasantly that he tells me of the many times he had met Terry in both countries. How he regarded him as a friend. How he wished him to return to the restaurant where he had eaten many times, whenever he was able. He told me that Ossie and many of the Spurs players ate there, and he enjoyed them all. If he wasn't a Barcelona supporter he certainly would be a Spurs man.

I'm not advertising the restaurant, but if you like Spanish food, then I have never had better...!

Outside I was surprised to see one of the people that I had been introduced to waiting for me, leaning against a wall, smoking in true 'Strand Cigarette' style. NOT A MUGGING...!

"Hey Senor, I tell you truth more than you know."

"Go on."

"I work in hotel in Barcelona, when season before Terry Venables leave us. I sometimes head restaurant waiter, sometime concierge. I see this man, Irving Scholar and Terry together many times. One time Scholar stay at hotel, Terry visit and speak much to him. They seem arranging business deal."

"What's your name?"

"I speak no name. I not want trouble. I know Terry Venables and I know he make arrangements to leave Barcelona before job is coming free. I know. I must go now. Goodbye.... Good luck."

(The David Pleat thoughts coincide with what this man told me. I cannot verify the truth of this without asking Terry and/or Irving Scholar. It does pose the question, however, as to whether David was indeed set up in some way. Did Scholar want him out as he had now 'fallen' for Terry as his manager? Was all that trouble that Pleat found himself in, just one long carefully planned excuse for Scholar to get rid of him and procure the services of the man he now wanted? He, Irving Scholar, has been accused of 'becoming tired' of people in his life rather quickly and changing allegiances as soon as a new 'love' comes into his life. Perhaps we ought to ask his second wife, who lasted just a few months...?)

Chapter 3
THE BEGINNING FOR TERRY VENABLES — THE END FOR DAVID PLEAT

The final whistle blew and Terry knew that his dream now depended entirely on his players' ability to score more penalties than the inferior opposition who had resisted all efforts by the Barcelona forwards to penetrate their goal. The Staua Bucharest defence had done everything that their coach had asked of them, when they came into the game, knowing that they were inferior in technical skill to the opposition, and at a great disadvantage with the European Champions Final being played in Seville. It was 1986.

Shades of England's efforts against the Poles way back in 1973 ran through Terry's mind, and it was then that he realised that this was not going to be the crowning glory of El Tel's career.

In his first season as coach Terry had taken his army of red and blue shirted athletes to the summit of their ambitions when, contrary to all claims to the title by Real Madrid, he had won the Spanish First Division crown amid wild acclaim and deserved flattery. Players such as Schuster from Germany, and Lineker and Archibald from the UK, had given the steel to the playing set up that was all that was needed to oust the prolific Real from their throne.

The Catalans praised Terry Venables and to them he was a God among men.

Then came the catastrophe; for Staua, the opponents in the final of that all important European football competition, the one that would indirectly provide the excuse for his transfer to Spurs, were not considered worthy opposition and the result should have been a foregone conclusion. But football possesses its own logic, an unseen power that so often defies reasoning, fitness, experience, history and reality.

Some might call it karma.

Sitting on that bench that evening in 1986, Terry Venables called it something else!

The loss of the European Final to the Bucharest side was how it all started to go wrong in Spain and equally, how it all seemed right at the time for the return for Terry to the UK....

For two years Spurs had been playing some of the best football since the glory days of the early sixties. Under thoughtful and tactically wise Manager David Pleat, they had adopted a five man mid-field that contained such wonderful exponents of pure class as Glen Hoddle, Ossie Ardiles and Chris Waddle. Not that Tony Galvin, Richard Gough, Gary Mabbutt, Chris Hughton and Ray Clemence were not playing their part, but they had lost the FA Cup Final on the 16th May 1987 to an inspired Coventry, the first time Spurs had ever gone down in that competition at Wembley, and then, during the middle of the '87/'88 Season, the Manager was publicly scandalised, when, David alleges, the Sun Newspaper rendered his position as Spurs Manager untenable.

The Spurs Board under Irving Scholar, utilised this apparent opportunity to make a change in management, which in any case had been widely forecast. Rumour of secret meetings between Terry Venables and Irving Scholar had already been noted in several journals. The Star had predicted this change in a major editorial.

David Pleat may one day take the opportunity to reveal certain facts about the events that led to his departure. There are relevations to be disclosed, but this book will not be the vehicle within which they will be recorded. Suffice to say that there seemed to be a great deal of 'skulduggery' involving a number of people whose interest in those matters can certainly be described as 'vested'. David, for the moment, refuses to disclose the roles played by either Terry Venables or Irving Scholar or a certain public relations company at that time.

The end came for Terry Venables as the football coach for Barcelona F.C. in the Autumn of 1987, by which time David Pleat in his capacity had already ceased to be Manager of Tottenham, after which the Spurs team was temporarily managed by an amalgam of Gary Mabbutt, Ossie Ardiles and Ray Clemence supervised by Trevor Hartley.

When Terry arrived the squad appeared to be in disarray and they were near the bottom of Division 1. Obviously, the idea of the squad being managed by their contemporaries was not working out too well. When Pleat left Spurs, they were in third position in the First Division… (now the Premier League)…but slipped to near the foot before Venables had arrived.

But the Messiah cometh!

One might think that David Pleat has less than fond memories of Spurs and his time there, but not so. He is philosophical and, I believe, regretful of the fact that it all went sour for him. This, despite losing Glenn Hoddle to Monaco at the end of the '86/'87 Season. David felt that prospects were good for the team and that one more season might have brought the ultimate prize, the First Division Championship. Certainly those who remember the team that played three League Cup Semi-Finals against Arsenal, and the FA Cup Final against Coventry and finished third in the League, will remember the football side with great affection. The balance of the mid-field five, Waddle, Allen, Hoddle, Ardiles and Hodge, was something for any opposition to contend with. Clive Allen at centre-forward scored 49 goals that season, and missed as many.

On the 27th September I rang David at Luton and he agreed to a meeting at Luton's ground, just before the reserves were about to play Portsmouth. By coincidence, Scott Houghton was playing for Luton, transferred by Ossie Ardiles at the beginning of the current season, and Guy Butters for Portsmouth, one of the players shifted out from Spurs by Terry Venables.

During the telephone conversation, which lasted for nearly half an hour, David clearly stated that he often spoke in warning to Irving Scholar about Terry Venables and indeed while Spurs were playing in the Juan Gamper tournament in Barcelona, only one month after David had taken over, they went out together for a meal.

Pleat felt even then, and indeed predicted as much, that Venables would be a Spurs Manager while Scholar held the reins.

Pleat also thought that Terry's outstanding knowledge of the game, from a schoolboy, through to his management of Barcelona, would be too great for the enthusiastic but technically ignorant Directors to cope with. He also knew that Terry was involved in many other business activities....

Irving, was very keen in his attempts to make Venables his next manager. He regarded Pleat's warnings as sour grapes, although David believes that he has been proven right.

Irving Scholar, like an errant husband, had initially fallen for the idea of David being Spurs Manager and welcomed him with open arms, allowing him almost complete authority, but gradually, as he learned and absorbed much of David's experience, he began to involve himself more in the day-to-day management of affairs (a manager's nightmare!), and effectively reduced David's authority.

When the crazy tabloids wrote unsubstantiated stories about Pleat, and continued to effectively crucify the man, Irving, David believes, was in regular touch with Terry, a man he greatly admired, and he took the opportunity to make a change. It was a case of off with the old and on with the new.

In fact David says that according to Scholar, Terry Venables was a hero when the Chairman stood and cheered from the terraces during Terry's stint as a player for Tottenham.

I would be less than honest if I did not print my own feelings on that matter. David did not wish to discuss those personal events in detail, naturally, but I still have to admit to being a Pleat man where football is concerned.

David had been a good man for Spurs and the right man at the time. He had become one of the leading authorities on the game during the World Cup in Mexico 1986, and clearly spotted the 4/5/1 system which he evolved at Spurs. His astute asides on television were a joy to listen to; he seemed to approach the viewer with a respectful, intimate, conversational style, rather than the elitist manner in which so many of the so-called pundits address the public.

We met at Luton on 6th October 1993, to discuss his time at Spurs. Referring to his appointment, he said...:

"Firstly, I don't want to get involved with the Sugar/Venables stuff in detail. We all know that there is so much to that. I expect you know more than any of us."

"There are so many aspects of running a club. There is so much."

"What about your days at Spurs? Can we start there?"

"Irving told me that it was a match made in Heaven, but when I arrived at Spurs I felt somewhat like a usurper of the glory and history that was in existence. There were so many that had been there for a long long time before me and I knew beyond doubt that I was on trial."

"Did you have an assistant?"

"Yes, Trevor Hartley. I also had coaches and a chief scout, and there was always Bill Nicholson, but I quickly realized that the more staff that you have, the more people you have around who are able to tittle-tattle and talk to the media and generally, sometimes inadvertently, undermine your authority. You see, at first, the Directors listened and learned but soon Irving would begin to offer his views and then suggest how one player or another might be selected, or how some players might be available for possible transfer."

"What about the fact that it was the biggest club you had been called on to manage?"

"It was so different. At Luton we have one laundry lady. At Tottenham there were four. At Luton there are what, 30 or so stewards. At Spurs more like 230. Facilities for the crowds were ten times bigger, although arguably not better than here at Luton. I always believed that…. I don't want to go into great detail about Irving. We had a decent relationship, but there is much to tell, and I am too close to many things that have happened."

"You told me that you were wary of the Board employing Terry. That was six years ago, long before all the recent stuff took place."

"No-one will deny that my successor was a man who was a fine coach, mainly with players he had already worked with, which I suppose is often the way. The newspapers and the media people haven't been coached by him and they haven't played for him…. Personally I'm not certain that he is as good as they make out. There are others who haven't had the backing. Pointing to his record there is a lot to examine. Crystal Palace, for example, had an intake of some outstanding youngsters in one season. Players like Hillaire, Nicholas, Swindlehurst and Samson, and Terry took them to the position where they were dubbed, and indeed called them, the 'team of the eighties'. Do you remember that...? Then Terry left them the following season. I think that the Board told him he was getting involved with too many other things. You should speak to Ron Noades. Some call Terry the 'Lifeboat Man'. He has been known to get out when he sees the down-swing coming.... After his exploits at Barcelona, Irving was very thrilled at his achievements. He won the Spanish League, but there are only two clubs that can do that, or certainly at the time there were."

"Barcelona and Real Madrid."

"Exactly. Not to take anything away from him. He got to the final of the European Cup, which was played in Seville, which was a very boring game which Staua got the blame for. I do believe that Terry is bright, and he has a reputation for being a talker and appearing to accept what you say and generally he is very pleasant. I remember once when Charlton were playing QPR and there were fourteen off-sides in the first half. The crowd were slow-handclapping. It was at the Valley, and QPR were away. Then in another game, when he was the manager of our opposition, here at Luton, he was quizzed in the press conference afterwards about his tactics....

He replied: 'I don't know what you are on about. The crowd enjoyed it. They were definitely clapping...!'

That's Terry; glib. Always with the quick answer. He doesn't court popularity but he runs it very well."

"Why did you feel the need to discuss Venables with Scholar? This point really intrigues me."

"Irving worshipped him, thought he was a very fine coach but I knew what he would be getting himself into. Irving was also a person that developed quick favourites. If, for example, Laudrup would be on the television, he'd come in on the following morning and ask me to consider him for Spurs. It was a way of imposing his opinions."

"Did he like Nico Claesen?"

"I think he thought that one of my good signings. Irving at

times had good opinions. I once observed that Mitchell Thomas would go forward like Amoros, and Irving totally agreed with that. There was a lot about that player, but in truth Terry failed to develop that when he played for him at Spurs.

"Sometimes Irving was very forgetful. I think that it may be the mark of a businessman. Terry also often forgets things."

"Like what?"

"We have had our differences on what was agreed about a loan player or things like that. I have no doubts though about Terry as a fine coach. I do believe that he is good, but perhaps not as good as he is made out to be by people like Jeff Powell of the 'Mail'. Terry enjoys trading too much. Look at the players who have come and gone at Spurs. My God, I'd pay four million for Gazza and Lineker right now. Who wouldn't, but where are they now? I sometimes think that he enjoys the trading as much as the development of the player. He's sharp but at the end of the day, salary alone, and I know what he was on when he arrived at Spurs, would make anyone successful; it also encourages independence. Venables was the Messiah, and didn't he impose his demand! He was the one who moaned about salaries a few years ago, but he had no problems at Tottenham about his own. The things that he demanded, and was given, reduced the Board to little more than observers. I guess that Terry would have gained particular pleasure out of seeing off Irving and Bobroff. It would be like an achievement for him."

"Regardless of cost?"

"Absolutely; and look what it has cost him now. In fairness he has treated me properly although he always asks: "David, why do you insist on having the last word?""

"And what do you reply David?"

"Because you do, Terry."

"I discussed with him once why Clive Allen could not play with Nico Claesen. In some ways managers help each other."

"Are you a particular friend of Terry's in the game?"

"No, not a close friend, although he is quite personable. I am an acquaintance. Most managers aren't really close friends, but we get on, all of us, reasonably. It's competitive."

"What about George Graham's purported friendship with Terry?"

"They have been around together for some time, but even with those two I think that their friendship is based very much on rivalry. Now, George, there you have a top man. A man I much admire. He has come up through the ranks. He has been a coach in the lower divisions with Palace, QPR and Millwall, and now all his experience is being turned towards a very successful Arsenal. I guess that Brian Clough is one I respect a great deal as a manager. He helped me get my first managerial job when I was coming to the end of my career at Peterborough. Put in a really good word for me and that is how I got started. I like Brian. 'If you are good enough you are young enough. Don't feel humble here, there are not that many good managers around.' I think that Peter Taylor, if he could rise in his grave, would say the same thing now. To summarise it, I have to say that I always felt that Terry would be a strong opponent to the Spurs Board and it turned out that way. I could have read and written the book before this all happened. Venables is a football man and football people do basically resent the scenario of Directors who come in for reasons of property and/or profit and start throwing in their ideas. They actually think that it is their prerogative and privilege. With Scholar I knew that Terry would tell him to stick his nose out of it."

"As with Alan Sugar."

"Exactly. That is clearly what happened. In the end Terry's career has turned a full cycle. That he has ousted Irving, is an amazing achievement. Irving was Tottenham through and through. Alan Sugar, I have no doubt, was armed with a lot of information by Irving Scholar. A lot of information, and he knew what had happened with the Venables takeover."

"What do you actually think about a manager of a top club having an entrepreneurial bent and a multitude of outside interests?"

"I don't think it can work. What I never understood at Tottenham was that Terry Venables came in as the Manager, and spent a lot of money on a lot of players in a very short time, most of whom are not there now. Nayim, Bergsenn, Lineker, Gascoigne, Walsh, Van den Hauwe, Fenwick and others and therefore became a trader."

"And Scott Houghton, who is in your reserve team now? You will of course remember when the lights went out at Spurs a couple of seasons ago, and Terry brought him on, or at least Peter Shreeves did, and he absolutely destroyed you in the last twenty minutes or so."

"Yes, we have him here but the lad needs to think a great deal harder about his game if he wants to compete at the top level. To go back to that time, Terry then changed the set up and appointed Peter Shreeves to look after the team. People in the game, cynical people, said that that wouldn't work. Terry was bound to override him, and he would not be as in charge as he thought. One year later out goes Peter and in comes Ray Clemence and Dougie Livermore. Another change. He was forever changing. Players, managers, they all come alike."

"A bit like a chameleon?"

"You said that! He has this very expensive looking grey coat, probably Harris tweed, and I used to watch him come out of the stand like a Messiah and onto the bench to give his views and make gestures which suggested that he was the main man, advising Clemence and Livermore what to do, and of course everyone thought the man a genius. The man in the grey coat. However, I must say in his favour he did make good substitutions putting on two at a time like he did. I remember the game against Manchester City; he got most of the credit for that victory when they got through the Cup. Poor old Clemence and Livermore never got a mention. Are you speaking to them?"

"Well, Clemence had declined my invitation. I think that he thought I wanted only the inside dirt from him, which was his mistake. Livermore is still in Sugar's employ and he has gagged them all at Spurs."

"I'm sure that sort of thing got up a lot of people's nose. I remember Jeff Powell of the Mail. A Venables man through and through. The man can do no wrong. The bias of many of the newspapers can really affect people in the game. Terry is a hero to Powell. Some people in the game are amused at his reverence. I believe that he has little appreciation of some of the better coaches in this country. People like Howard Wilkinson, Howard Kendall and Dario Gradi who are some of those who have really proved themselves without the resources that Terry has often had at his disposal. In Terry's favour, he is very bright and has always got an answer. He can be difficult to deal with at times .... The one thing that always happens with Terry is there is an argument about who said what and what was meant, particularly if you loan a player from him. He seems to change what was said in the beginning. When I bought Phil Gray, there were all sorts of wrangling caused by what Spurs would get if we sold him on. He's with Sunderland now. Then when I loaned Paul Moran, there was a disagreement on what the deal was. Terry even admitted that he was a hard man to deal with, but selling and trading players is Terry at his best.... I have to give him credit; excellent substitutions, but responsible in part for playing the off-side rule to excess, which tends to ruin the entertainment value of a game, closing down space and preventing play. I'm not suggesting Terry Venables' teams do not play football, and score from that football.... He's not bad at all at set-pieces. He certainly is a thinker.''

"When he first came to Spurs he played without wingers after Chris Waddle went. Spurs have had twenty seven wingers since the War, nearly all internationals, and I for one did not like that idea. I thought he brought that with him from Spain.''

"He saw what he'd got and that was the way he chose to play. Perhaps he didn't have any good wingers in the club,'' David replied.

"What about Moran for example?'', I asked.

"He, unfortunately is always just off the top. I think maybe he isn't strong enough. Galvin was at the end with a bad knee. Waddle liked the central position most of all, and of course Paul Allen liked the wide open spaces of the right side. With Waddle, I had to persuade him to stay wide, that it was the best for the team, but he did a good job. He was a reluctant winger. I looked to play him just off the front two, but Glenn was there. I finally got to know the answer to Glenn. Play a couple of good strong lads around him for support, put Ossie behind him to bring the ball out from the defence.''

"Similarly to the way Ossie as Spurs manager plays now with Samways and Dozzell?''

"Exactly. Yes, Waddle was the ideal man for that five man mid-field. Hoddle with plenty of bodies around him, Ossie linking them all together, and the underrated Hodge, the classic inside left. Allen was the thrust. It was really one of the most exciting formations ever. A superb combination."

"Can we get to the Cup Final?"

"I played a not entirely fit Chris Hughton who was not as good on the right side. I, perhaps, should have given the job to Gary Stevens. He was certainly fitter. There were so many who were playing with knocks after the three League Cup Semi-Finals, I knew that once extra time was on, we would have difficulty in playing the game out. Goffey was labouring. Mabbutt could not feel his toes at all; clearly when that final intended cross hit his legs and dropped over Clemence's head, he didn't even feel the ball make contact. What a brave man that guy is. I'll tell you, Gary Mabbutt is one of the best in football, the personification of every manager's dream. He plays with such a handicap, yet you never hear him moan or say anything out of place. He's an absolute delight. We deserved a trophy that season."

"I know some of the hardships, I am a diabetic myself. It's sometimes hard just to get up in the mornings let alone play for twelve years at the top level. I admire that man so much."

"I've got so much to tell, and I'm keeping most of it back because one day when I give it all up, I'll write my own story about it all. The joys and the anguish."

"I just want your thoughts as they are now, David."

"All I know is that I have not been at all surprised...."

"By the Venables-Sugar thing?"

"No! Not surprised about that. I predicted it. I also saw a Spurs Director long ago at a testimonial dinner for that Middlesex fast bowler in London, and he told me even then that he was acting as mediator. Their problems have been going on from almost the start of their partnership. I knew sooner or later there would be a split there. When I left, they had a good team. The only problem being that Glenn had done his extra year. Funny, we had already agreed with a club about his transfer and then he went to Monaco who were not the people we had reached agreement with."

"Which club?"

"I can't tell you that, it isn't fair to them. Enough to say that they weren't very happy with Tottenham. And then afterwards I was surprised to read in one of the tabloids, suggesting that I left Terry a shambles. He inherited a shambles. He had to say that. He had to. You have to try to pretend that when you come in it's a shambles, and that you are the one starting at the bottom and going to make it better. I left it after the most successful season since whenever. We were wavering only during the last three or four games. We played ten kids at Everton, for which we were fined £10,000, later reduced to £5,000 on appeal. I had to do that, the first team squad were nearly off of their feet after playing so many high-pressure games. I played John Polston, Moran, they are all the kids that were up to it. It was then all aggravation, what with Cup Final tickets, press and media, and interviews and oh so many things. Very difficult, with so many commercial things and so many games behind us. At the end of the day, there was no shambles and Terry Venables knew that. But that's football. I remember those Semi-Finals. Do you know, Guy, that we were only behind once in all three games, and that was right at the very end of the last game. We had so many injuries and players out there with knocks. Ray Clemence was at the very end of his career, and was just beginning to lose some of the mental agility and bravery that besets great keepers after many years in the game. In the League we had lost 4-3 at Coventry and Regis and Houchen were causing us terrible problems in the air. That is where a manager relies so much on his keeper."

"Is that about the time Ray Clemence said that he had always favoured being a line-keeper, whatever that may be?"

"I make no comment on what that is."

"Would you say that looking back on your days at Spurs, when it was clearly a great experience, and since when you have been with Leicester and Luton, that you really enjoyed managing a club of that size?"

"Yes, oh, yes. I'd do it again."

"Well you are not too old, and nobody in or out of the game doubts your ability."

"For sure. Spurs was the type of club you rarely appreciate 'til afterwards. So many people to contend with. Lots of people, all very nice polite people, but the traditions can work against a new boy. Bill Nicholson was always there. Others had been there for donkeys' years and I was the incoming boss. Very difficult atmosphere. Security, reception, outside shows, visiting dignitaries, hotels, travelling, accounts departments. So much to deal with, it's hardly any wonder when some players say that they rarely see the Manager. All the time a manager has to watch his back. There were the scouts, Ted Buxton, Len Cheesright, Bill Nick and John Moncur; they were all there, but a manager has the responsibility of the whole thing. For all they can do for him, the Manager has the overall control."

"The buck stops there!"

"Right. The more people you have there the more those little things get out, the more loyalty becomes a problem. It's a hard position to hold at a club the size of Spurs because you are in the spotlight all the time. Stupid things, like being rung on a Sunday at home because one of the players is up to no good. Once there was an incident where one of them was caught up by being in the wrong place at the wrong time regarding some stolen jewellery, and had to make a statement in the Police station. Down I had to go. Being a manager of a top First Division, or should I say Premier League team, is a seven-day non-stop job. Particularly in London. You have to be a London boy to know all about the London scene. The clubs and the watering holes. Players being thrown out, club managers getting in touch and all of that. I'm not a London boy. I'm not connected with that scene. In that respect, unless you are used to all that, it is very difficult to get to know every player's habits and get to know their favourite places. Whereas in a smaller club you can see everything on a one-to-one basis. You tend to know all the dives that the players visit and some of the landlords, and they know where to get hold of you and often what to do for the best. At a big club I also had the opportunity of seeing and getting the best youngsters and really it is a marvellous institution. I love Spurs and have done so since I was a 15 year old schoolboy international. I was courted by Bill, but I decided to stay in my home town and with the local club. Maybe it was not a good decision but I have always opted for some happiness and I was happy at a small club. In many many ways it was good at Spurs. Irving said it was a marriage made in

Heaven, until he married Terry Venables, so to speak. Talk is cheap but it is very hard when the Chairman is very much — sometimes in the nicest possible way, but not always — into things. The phone is ringing internally constantly. I remember one argument we had over my cancellation of the Christmas dinner. I thought that there wasn't much enthusiasm amongst the players for it. Some were going home to Ireland and other places and I cancelled it. Irving went mad. He loved to serve the players' meal with Douglas Alexiou. Said it was a tradition at Spurs. The lady who cooked the meal at Broxbourne, her husband was very ill. The groundsman who helped to get the supplies in was very busy that week. I just thought it was the right thing to do. I was fed up with thinking about Christmas dinners. Irving came on the phone and stormed: 'Who do you think you are?' It was such a big thing to him. I said, "O.K., we'll have another dinner at a more convenient time. Do whatever you want.' He screamed: 'You can't do that! You can't do that! Who the hell do you think you are?' All of a sudden you find you are there and your authority is being questioned, and the Chairman suddenly wants to be the Manager and you can feel the usurping of your position....

They'll have kicked off in the game. I'll have to go now."

"Can we meet again?"

"Definitely. It's nice being able to reminisce. I'll see you again, give me a ring."

I went back to Luton Town Football Club, feeling welcome and knowing that David would speak freely, and honestly.

It's what the man is all about....

"Last time we met, David, I spoke to you about Tottenham and football in general, but little about yourself. For those readers who remember you at Spurs and for all those who admire your efforts, can you tell me about David Pleat's career?"

"I was born in Nottingham in 1945."

"Did you come from a happy home?"

"Yes, I had a very normal boyhood, very happy, very family orientated."

"I went to grammar school, I played for the school, for my district, for Nottingham Boys and Nottingham Primary Schools, for the County and for England Boys. It was a Rugby school. I played that game as well, but football was my first love. In the County side were several other players who have since made it in professional football. There was Mick Jones, the old Leeds centre-forward, Alan Birchenhall who played for Chelsea, Morris Bembridge who turned to golf and became a very fine golfer, Richardson the left back of Derby County at one time. It was a very good County side. I played outside right. I decided to stay on at school to get my 'O' levels, which I did before joining Nottingham Forest where I played for seventeen years and thirty three days, which was a record for a long time. That record has gone now. When I was a Schoolboy International, I played my first game against Scotland and we won five three. I scored then and I scored in my first game in the First Division for Notts Forest against Cardiff. Rodrigues was at left back. I was then the youngest player to turn out for them. I could have gone to a number of clubs but I chose the home town team. When we beat that Scotland team at Wembley I remember Barry Fry (The ex-Southend United manager and former Barnet chief, now at Birmingham) at inside right. It was a great side and we were all regarded as outstanding. Bobby Moncur was at left back for Scotland, George Graham was in their side... That was some Young England team, I can tell you!

The manager that signed me for Notts Forest was the late great Billy Walker, and then I played for Andy Beattie, and finally for Johnny Carey. Carey bought a couple of other wingers and by then I became surplus to requirements. I signed for Luton Town, but then suffered a very bad injury, just before I received news of a big club's interest. Eventually, I was freed by Alan Brown. I had a real bad back problem. Reg Burr was the Chairman then, the man who is now at Millwall. I moved to Shrewsbury, to Arthur Rowley, and then to Exeter under Frank Broome. I respected him as a player, and I had a good few years there, and then I got married to Maureen, who was a Luton girl, at around that time. Later I moved to Jim Iley (ex-Spurs) at Peterborough, and then I got a call after eight months to go as manager of Nuneaton Borough. If you are good enough, you are young enough. Clough and Taylor said 'take the job. It's a young man's game'. Brian had just taken over at Hartlepool. I still played sometimes at

Nuneaton. My last game was at Yeovil, on the slope. My back was so bad that I had to go into traction. That was it, I couldn't play again. I then came back to Luton in a coaching capacity under Harry Haslam. I worked on the commercial side for a few months and then turned to full time coaching as assistant. The first team coach then moved to Detroit and I took over. Then Harry Haslam moved to Sheffield United and asked me to go with him, but I was offered the manager's job here and decided to take that. I got lucky and I worked very hard at it, and success followed all that hard work. I was one of the youngest qualified coaches at the time. I remember my sister sending me Eamonn Dunphy's book for a present. It's called 'It's Only a Game'... She was telling me something!

I based my game on counter-attacking. First year I saved us from relegation. Then we were thirteenth in the Second Division, and then we were eighth, then we were fifth, then third and just missed promotion. Tragic day. Won the last game of the season, 3-0, but Swansea won at Preston which buggered us up. Toshack went up. The following year was a delight for me. We had a record number of least losses. We lost only four times the whole season. We went up to the First Division, having won the Championship with games to spare. Graham Taylor's Watford followed us up in second place.

That year I met Brian Clough on holiday. I asked him what keeps him going. Typically, Brian answered:

'It's bloody upstarts like you and that Taylor fellow.'

"In my first season in the top flight, we nearly got relegated but we scored a winning goal in the last game with three minutes to go, and we celebrated as never before in the coach on the way home from Manchester. That day would make a book in itself."

"How long were you at Luton before coming to Tottenham?"

"About nine or ten years."

"While you were there, Aleksic, your goalkeeper, transferred to Spurs."

"Oh yes, I let him go for about £100,000. I was making good profits for Luton then, as I am now, by selling. Only trouble now, is I can't buy to replace."

"He'd gone by the time you came?"

"Yes, he's in South Africa now. I also sold Paul Price to them. I took Bill Nicholson to Wales, to Wrexham, to watch them play the Russians. The Russians were superb. Paul did alright but I think Wales lost. Spurs signed him and I made another sale. I seem to have been selling players all my life."

"Has that been a burden to you?"

"Definitely. It is something that Terry has not had to do to survive. Maybe with the exception of Gascoigne, who he had to sell to raise some important money. Selling, selling, selling. That's all I have seemed to have to do. There was a club like Tottenham who bought when I wanted to buy a player. Mostly, now, I have to sell and accept someone in part exchange who is not my ideal choice."

"Reflecting now back to the time when you left Tottenham, do you think that there was justification for Scholar to sack you, because one can remember the great success that you had?"

"I can't really answer that question, but what I can tell you is that you or no-one can understand the pressure that was brought to bear."

"Just something the public might like to know, David, on a personal basis.... Is everything O.K. with you and Maureen? Are you still married to the same gracious lady, and basically is everything O.K. in your personal life?"

"Wonderful. Me and Maureen are as strong as ever. We've been married for many years, we have a son who has gained a 'First' in medicine at Jesus College, Oxford and a daughter who is a qualified beautician, Joanne."

"Finally, David, your aspirations?"

"My present position is unsatisfactory. I'm working in an awful vacuum at this moment. I definitely would like to manage a top club again. The experience at Spurs has taught me a great deal, and I feel ready again to do justice to a top Premier League Team. The only satisfaction is grooming youngsters to better things, and watching them develop. Because the expediences of football most people want immediate results, but it all takes time with young players, and therefore the credibility of what one is doing doesn't stand out.... I remember one thing.... A certain journalist approached me to say that Irving Scholar wanted to see me. I thought..., Tottenham, aha."

"Shreeves was still there at the time?"

"Yes. Irving wanted Shreeves out. After I saw him I waited for a while, and then I think I telephoned and I was told…. 'Look, David, there's a bit of politics at the Club and they look as though they are going to keep Shreeves for another year.' I was terribly disappointed, and asked the reporter why my hopes had been set up. Why? What had changed? I told him not to contact me again. Then a year later, Irving came in for me again. So what happened to me was a repeat of what had happened to Peter Shreeves. Irving was adept at changing everything and setting the future while still involved with the present. I left Luton with a strong and able playing staff, and I left Terry Venables with the same at Tottenham. That year our record speaks for itself."

"David, I have thoroughly enjoyed our discussions. Can I just ask you whether you feel that when you have finished with team management you will want to go in as say, General Manager, or Chief Executive like Terry?"

"I'd like to stay in the game at that sort of level, but I don't feel that I would want to own a club like Terry. General Manager seems O.K."

"Can I warn you from my own experience? It is one terrible job to have. Not only do you have the team manager looking over his shoulder, but you have the board looking down on you."

"Yes, I expect you do. It's interesting that…. That assessment. People that have spent thirty or so years of their lives, playing, coaching, managing, must be better equipped to direct the fortunes of a football club. Particularly if they are intelligent, and have studied everything."

"The last question, I promise. Trouble is you are so interesting and open to talk to, I could go on all day. Tell me…. Analyse for me the current word on everyone's lips…. THE BUNG…!"

(David became a little annoyed at this, for the first time. He raised his voice and suddenly became rather formal.)

"Look, Mr Nathan…. Where do you think a manager of a football club is going to get fifty grand, or the like, to pay another manager for releasing his player? I can assure you most managers earn decent money but it is a short life, any indiscretions reach the grape-vine quickly; and there will be no future prospects for this type of manager. Ask any of them! It isn't managers that are in question. I know that the press go on about it, but if it is demanded, and I am not at all sure that it is, then the Chairman is the one who approves the payment and signs the bloody cheque. Everything is minuted. Everything is logged properly. Do you think that Boards of Directors sit down approving 'bungs' and how to put them through their books? It's a lot of old rubbish. If a payment is made, then it is the Chairmen who have that responsibility.''

His Chairman came in at that moment, wanting David to meet some other Chairmen who were visiting Kenilworth Road, and I left, thankful for the experience of talking to a straight and honest man whose knowledge of football is clearly extensive and beyond question.

I look forward to reading in the press that David has joined a top club and to the later success of that appointment....

Chapter 4
THE MEETINGS WITH TERRY VENABLES
3rd August and 26th August 1993

I have already explained that initially Tony Marchant and I had a meeting with Terry at his Club, Scribes West in Kensington. Because of the difficulties we are having with his Agent, Jonathan Harris, I specifically describe this as a meeting and not an interview, as for once, I left my little tape recorder behind me, but, on the way home sitting idly in a cold train carriage, we made many notes as to the conversation. Authors are blessed with almost photographic memories.

After some initial banter which is mentioned in the preface, I began to ask Terry several questions with regard to the events that led to his dismissal.

I asked him about the 'Question in Sport' programme on which he appeared one week after Alan Sugar. Sugar was reticent during his TV 'trial' and often referred to his answers being sub judice. Terry, however, was frank, and it was to is credit that he never slagged off Alan during the broadcast.

I asked Terry, almost immediately, why Jimmy Greaves appeared to have a go at him, and come out on Sugar's side.

"I have no idea," he said. "I have always got on well with him whenever our paths crossed, and although we aren't mates, we've never had a cross word. He certainly gave me a hard time, but I think I held my own."

I made no comment. There was little to add. Jimmy Greaves was entitled to his opinion, which, since that broadcast, has been somewhat borne out.

At this time, it must be said we only knew of the allegation by Alan Sugar, alleged in Court, that Terry had requested fifty thousand pounds from him for onward payment to Brian Clough in connection with the Teddy Sheringham Transfer.

The television exposés on Channel 4 and BBC 1 had not been broadcast, and the newspaper reporters had failed to attend the 14th of May hearing, and seemed not to be there when the Judge listened intently to arguments.

It was therefore early in the saga that later ensued when we met officially for the first time.

A time when Terry was feeling low, and was totally bemused by the rapid events that had resulted in his dismissal from his post at Spurs, and had destroyed his dreams, and effectively, his life....

At this time, TISA and, I believe most of the Country, were feeling sympathy for him and aggression toward Alan Sugar, who was seen as the ultimate tyrant in the events that had taken place.

Yvette, Terry's lovely second wife was taking it all in her stride, carrying out her duties as hostess at Scribes, serving what drinks were being ordered by the very few paying customers. Apart from ourselves there were less than six other people around. The staff outnumbered the customers! There was a receptionist, another man sitting idly behind the counter reading a newspaper, a chef, a couple of suited men, a soulful pianist and a lone elderly barman, who later came to our notice in another way. He was called Nick. Now I mention that because in a perfectly innocent way, his name was mentioned when Tony and I had a meeting with a renowned News International employee, who stated that he had been a friend of Nick's for many years, and that it was the barman that had informed him of three publishing companies who had visited Scribes in order to offer Terry over £200,000 for his life story: later confirmed by both Terry and his literary agent, Jonathan Harris.

Blithely and without concern, the newsman told us the names of the other three publishers trying to involve themselves in the hottest property around, notwithstanding the ever newsworthy Princess of Wales.

Openly I stated to Terry that my Publishing Company was there to do a similar thing, publish his story, but our idea was not for the full life history, just for the five and a half years he had been at White Hart Lane.

We never wanted the full 'monte' for several reasons. Firstly, we didn't and still don't believe that Terry's life has in any way finished. We believe that he will rise again, probably overseas at first, and the events of the past will fade like wisps of cloud on a windy day. Of course, people will always remember the accusations and there will always be some who say that there is no smoke without fire, unless someone somewhere has decided to tell the absolute truth.

(See my interviews with McLintock and Graham Smith, and you will draw your own conclusions on the £58,750 cash payment.)

The other 'questionable' payment of £200,000 was not envisaged as a course that would prove in any way successful as an investigation. The mere payment of such a large sum in cash, and in response to an invoice raised by a company with a post-box address in Switzerland, speaks for itself.

It has been alleged that Terry split that money with restaurateur and Italian linguist, Santin. Whoever alleges such a thing must prove it, but I defy him to do so. For Santin will not tell what happened to the money and I doubt that Terry will, assuming that he knows!

I asked Terry how he was feeling; this, after Jonathan Harris had gone to his football match, and after Yvette had left us alone to talk things over.

"How would you expect me to be feeling?"

"I'm sorry to be insensitive. What I meant is, well I don't really know.... Just that.... How are you feeling?

"Stunned is the answer. Shell-shocked."

"What happened? Why did he turn on you like that?"

"If I knew I would tell you. I promise you I don't honestly know."

"I think it was shitty, the way he has behaved and the way that he has dragged Tottenham down into the mire."

"And the way that he has treated me."

"Precisely, if you state that you have no idea why he has done that, and that he had no reason."

"I can honestly state that I have no idea why he has turned on me with such ferocity."

"Can it be this alleged payment to Brian Clough which has upset him? The one made in cash?"

"Look, you know a bit about the game if you have been going to football for all those years. Sometimes there are certain commissions that need to be paid to a number of people. It isn't as if it is the first time, and certainly won't be the last."

"Presumably, he organised the cheque anyway?"

"Exactly."

"But the money was paid in cash?"

"The Agents wanted it that way."

"It's unbelievable.... Not that you paid another manager some money, if that indeed was what happened, but the reaction of a top businessman like Sugar. I even use Amstrad myself. Why the hell didn't he just call you in and say that he didn't like the idea and request that you look for another centre-forward? There *are* others, even though Teddy has improved immeasurably since his arrival at Spurs."

"Alan Sugar knows nothing about the game. He came into the game for profit and sees Spurs as another company to control alongside his computer company. Football is special, and the people in it are professionals."

"Did he interfere in player selection and the running of the team?"

"No, not really. I had to talk with him for money needed to sign players, but to be frank, I hardly ever saw him. He spent nearly all of his time down at Brentwood."

"Didn't he attend games?"

"Sometimes he comes, but not if there is something to do connected with Amstrad. That takes priority."

"What about other people at Tottenham? Do they back you?"

"Some.... Most I think, but he has some of his own people there and they of course do his every instruction. Sometimes it was like working with your enemies."

"The old trick. Put your own people in and undermine the bloke that's trying to get on with the job?"

"As the months passed by, I began to feel less and less like the Chief Executive. Colin Sandy and a bloke called John Ireland were appointed by him, and they tried to take over the role of Chief Executive.''

"Surely not on the football side?''

"There are many aspects to running a Club like Spurs. It isn't just picking or coaching a team. It's tickets, and commercial enterprises and interviews, contracts; things like that.''

"They have their own commercial manager.''

"Yes, they have managers and professionals in every department, but they all answer to the Chief Executive.''

"Or are supposed to?''

"Exactly.... Sugar reckoned that there wasn't room for the two of us.''

"I remember being at school, and for five years I was at sea,'' I told him. "It was the same there. People running to the teacher, or the Chief Steward with stories, tittle-tattling like mad.''

"That is how it was. I never thought that it would come to this though. The man's a.... I don't know what.''

"Do you think that you might have been better staying at Barcelona?''

"There was a great feeling at Spurs in the beginning. I have never regretted being there, but it hasn't exactly ended happily.''

"Do you intend to fight on? I understand that the Courts have given you a couple of weeks or so to find three hundred thousand pounds to cover legal costs should you lose the fight.''

"I'm going to fight him all the way. I believe that I am in the right, and that the unanimous verdict of the supporters is behind me.''

"And the general public. What I have heard is that there is a vast majority of people who are shocked by what has happened and cannot believe that you are out, including me.''

"I believe that I can beat him and get back in again.''

"You still want to buy his shares?''

"I am trying to arrange that.''

"That'll cost you an awful lot of money. That's assuming he would sell in the first place.''

"The Courts can make him do that.''

"Isn't that what you have just been to court about? They want some money up front?"

"Yes, I'll get there."

"Terry, I know this is personal, but how did you manage the interest payments to the loan company who lent you the money to buy the shares in the first place? I calculated that it was more than you were earning from Spurs."

"I did and I am still managing to pay them. Don't ask me how. It's been a terrible burden."

"What about your current income?"

"I have business interests that pay me sufficient to live on."

"But not enough to continue with your former life style surely?"

"We're managing, Yvette and I?"

"I believe that your daughter got the sack too."

"Yes, silly sod kicked her out of the Club as well."

"Terry, how do you think you can fight a man with such wealth and power?"

"I have to trust the advice of my legal people who think that I have an absolute right to buy him out."

"Don't you think that you might have been wiser, and indeed still be wiser, to accept a settlement and call it a day?"

"I am determined not to let that happen."

"If I may say so, I think, pragmatism rules."

"If you had your heart in something, wouldn't you fight for it?" Tony Marchant now....

"If it were me, I'd knock the bastard's teeth out and then stand there getting everything that is due to me. I'm not a football fan myself, but I wouldn't let a bloke get away with it like this Sugar has."

"Look, Tel, I'm on you side," I intervened. "I openly admit that even though I knew Sugar when we were young. You have got to be the best man to run Spurs, but there has got to be more to it than what has already been published. You say that you have no idea why he sacked you."

"I'm telling you the truth. I have no idea except to say that he told me that there was no room for the two of us. Do you know, he is such a fool, that he once told me during a match that the crowd should be singing out 'Alan Sugar's Blue and White Army'.... I looked at him in amazement and he stormed out."

"You were watching a match?"

"Yes, it was during one of the games."

"Did he sign the cheques?"

"Yes, over a certain amount. He had to."

"So, if he now complains about 'bung' payments, why didn't he do so then when he signed the cheque?"

(We have since learned that Terry had autonomy up to £50,000.)

"You ask me...! We discussed it. I told him what it was for, and he signed without question."

"Every cheque?"

"Every one over a certain limit."

"What about this book, then? I hear that you have several offers from others to do your life story."

"Yes, but they can't bring the book out until the end of ninety four."

"And we see a book coming out now."

"That attracts me. I don't honestly think I could write a book about my life in the time scale, but I have to consider all offers."

"Look, Terry. Your life hasn't finished. You may yet return to favour somewhere, and quite soon. What happens if you do eventually get the England job? You'll have to write about that or the book won't be complete."

"Yes. I know, that's what I like about your idea.... And the title. It was that which made me ask Jonathan to talk to you."

"The other consideration, is where you will be in a year's time. I hate to use the phrase, yesterday's man, but it could be that you will be managing a team in Australia or Argentina or back in Spain and your life story will not have the impact a book offered to the public now would have."

"In the main I agree, but I am not sure that I could even help you with an abbreviated version the way things are. I am spending every day with lawyers and barristers. What can I tell you anyway? If I put the money into the Court most things would become sub judice anyway."

"O.K., that's true, but the book wouldn't be published until the end of this year or maybe early next year. That gives you time."

"Maybe…. I like the idea of your book better than the proposals of the other publishers, and I like you. You seem to know a great deal about Tottenham and are clearly a thoughtful football man. Have you ever been in the game?"

"Yes I have, but that is another story…. If you can't speak to us in depth about the current affairs, what can we put in the book anyway…? Most of the football supporters of Tottenham, QPR and Crystal Palace as well as the Barcelona people know of your background."

"There isn't much to put in about the current stuff. I got into bed with Alan Sugar and it didn't work out."

"There is surely more to it than that. You are Tottenham. You are synonymous with what has happened at Spurs since David Pleat left. The football that the team played at the end of last Season has got everyone thinking that Spurs can win it all under your management."

"They did play well during the closing spell, I admit. For your answer you will need to ask Mr Sugar."

"You're very well controlled about it all."

"I'm not the sort of man to lose his rag."

"I know…. I have a friend at Spurs. Known her twenty years or more. She tells me one or two things. I know that in the main the staff are behind you. They have their jobs to consider but they are all pretty distraught at what has happened."

"That's nice of her. Who is she?"

"I'd rather not say, for obvious reasons. Just to say that she thinks highly of you."

At that point Yvette came over to top up our drinks and we had another short while Terry refilled his glass with the bubbly. I had read stories of a supplier of Champagne to Scribes seeking a winding up order for non-payment of a £7,000 account. The thought crossed my mind that Terry was in no position to be drinking the stuff at the time. It wasn't as if there were any paying guests in the Club. I admit to feeling true pity. The man was obviously shattered. Any members that might have been there on a Tuesday night had gone elsewhere. The effect of his dismissal by Sugar was far reaching. We carried on....

"Getting back to the book, and everyone knowing your background: We all know that you were brought up in Dagenham. That you always wanted to be a footballer, and that you have played at every level conceivable. What of your personal life?"

"I married young. Later I met Yvette and I divorced my first wife and last year I married Yvette. I have two girls from my first marriage. The rest is an open book."

"What about your other businesses?"

"I have the Club here and several other interests."

"How's 'The Manager' game going?"

"It did well in its first year."

"The football at Spurs at the end of last Season was so cavalier. What do you attribute that to?'

"Clem and Dougy did a fantastic job. Clem was so enthusiastic and being his first full coaching job he brought some great ideas to the team. A lot was due to the development of Anderton, and the improved sharpness of Sheringham."

"Look, I know that it is cheeky of me to ask, but why oh why has Vinny Samways never developed as a player. I mean why can't he even touch the ball with his right foot."

"I arrived too late for Vinny. If you don't get in there by the time a player is what...? Sixteen, seventeen, it is too late."

"What about his habit of running towards a Spurs player and closing him down before releasing the ball.... To say nothing of him standing there waiting to see what happens next."

"I have told him a thousand times. Release and run. If you watch him he will do it once and then forget all about it. I have a maxim about that. The last thing you teach a player is the first thing he forgets."

"And David Howells? Why can't he play for anyone except you?"

"David is a serious lad. I think that he has done really well on the strength of us playing him in almost every position on the field. He might appear to have been playing for years but he is still only young and really has his best position to find yet."

"I remember his first game. He played at centre-forward up at Hillsborough and he scored the winning goal in a two-one win."

"You remember that? What were you doing up there?"

"My son was staying in Manchester. I went up to see him and we went across Snake Pass to see the game. Howells was good. A thinking player, but his whole style has changed."

Tony Marchant, bored with all the talk of football:

"What about the book then? Are we going to have a deal?"

"There are several hurdles to cross first. One is that I am not sure that I want to do it and in any case, whether I can."

"Two hundred grand wouldn't go amiss right now though, would it?"

"No, certainly not."

"If you agreed to our proposals we might be able to get our backers to write to the court and satisfy them that you are good for at least two hundred thousand out of the three you need to find."

"You would do that?"

"That's the whole idea. You could take on Sugar and justice might be seen to be done."

"Would your backers do that for me?"

"We would need to ask them, but they know that we are coming here and expect us to return with some sort of deal," Tony concluded.

"I think that you need to speak to Jonathan again. He is doing this for me. I will speak to him and you can get together. What I will say is if I decide on the full version with another publisher I would like to consider Guy to ghost-write it for me."

"I don't think that you will find anyone more qualified, Terry. Guy talks about Spurs and knows a great deal about football."

"I think that it does require someone with that sort of know-ledge," Terry agreed. "Sorry, I need to leave you now; I can see Teddy Sheringham has arrived."

"Just before you leave," I asked. "Did Neil Ruddock consult with you about his problems?"

"I spoke to him several times. He's a good lad and I am

shocked that he wanted to leave but they have treated him abominably?''

"In what way?"

"He has an agreement. He is very loyal to his manager and he played his heart out for me. I think Spurs should make it up to him and Sugar should pay him what he is due. He won't find a much better and more committed centre-half than Neil.''

"Can I ask you one more thing and that is about your decision to drop Ardiles for the Port Vale game after their manager had expressed such fear of his inclusion.''

"If you remember, the ground was a foot deep in mud. Ossie was past his best and I didn't feel that the ground lent itself to his style of play.''

"A mistake on recollection?"

Terry rose and Yvette joined us. She was born in East Ham in Essex, and has known Terry for eight years. She 'knew' him during his years in Barcelona. She, like Terry, was relaxed about it all and confirmed that they were managing with all the publicity and stress that the whole awful events had brought to their lives. One thing for sure. She has great faith in Terry and seemed to believe that he would win through in the end....

Then something remarkable. We were beckoned by Terry to go into the main bar to join Teddy Sheringham and his friend. Both Tony and I stood aside but within earshot, while Teddy excitedly related his most recent conversation with Ossie Ardiles....

Sheringham: "I went in there and I asked for it straight out."

Venables: "What did you ask for?"

Sheringham: "Twenty grand a week."

Venables: "What did he say?"

Sheringham: "No way...."

Venables: "Say hello to a Spurs fan, Teddy."

I shook his hand, a little uncomfortably, and wished him luck for next Season. There was an obvious plot for Teddy, with Venables' assistance and guidance, to put pressure on Spurs' new manager Ossie Ardiles.

On the 4th of August we received a fax from Jonathan Harris.

Dear Guy,

It was good to meet you and Tony last night and further to our telephone conversations and discussions, I look forward to receiving your offer in writing on Thursday at my office.

As we discussed, the offer should address the following:

a) How you see the proposed book in terms of its editorial extent (the number of words) and the editorial content; in other words, what book it is that you want to publish and who will be writing it (please supply copies of books they have written before).

(Not staying for the meeting the previous evening, Harris seems not to have realised that I would be the author.)

b) Your proposed publishing timescale together with the target date for publication.

c) The financial parameters of your offer which needs to detail the advance that you are prepared to pay, the timescale for payment of that advance, together with the proposed royalty splits for both hard and soft versions. In addition, how you would deal with the serialisation.

d) We also require some background to your company detailing the experience of the personnel involved, the team that you would propose assembling to handle the task, your Curriculum Vitae or at least details of relevant publishing experience and the past companies that you have worked at. We would also require you to provide evidence of your ability to meet the proposed advance that you are offering, and I know that you have indicated that you have silent partners which, because of the sensitivity of the issues at stake for my client, I would require you to disclose. I am more than happy to sign a strict confidentiality agreement which will ensure that this information goes no further than myself or my client.

e) In addition, please provide a list of the titles that you have published in the last nine months together with some sample copies of the same.

As you know, my client reserves the right not to proceed with the production of the book concerning himself at this stage and, as I have already indicated to you, you are not to approach news-papers or the media at any stage in these discussions.

On another note, I know that my client enjoyed meeting you, and we both look forward to sitting down and evaluating your formal offer.

With kind regards.

Yours sincerely,

Jonathan G. Harris, Managing Director, Associated Publicity Holdings.

We faxed an offer that meant Terry would receive £200,000 in three tranches, of £65,000, £65,000 and £70,000. The first would be paid on engrossment of contract, the second on publication and the third two months after that date. After that, he would re-ceive a royalty of 99.5p per book sold.

A meeting was arranged for Thursday the 26th August at which Roger, our financier, and Eddie Ashby, as well as Jonathan and Terry would attend.

In the taxi ride across from Euston to Scribes I learned of a re-markable event that had taken place some two years previously which to me had some serious connotations....

Roger had been approached by Ashby when he was charged by the Board at Tottenham with the task of finding a mortgage company willing to fund Tottenham's loss-making enterprises: Effectively to provide much needed cash to shore up the Company while Sugar and his team, including Venables, turned the Company around.

That in itself was a remarkable coincidence, but it was when I enquired of Roger as to from whence his actual finances emanated, that I was suddenly alarmed and troubled; for he told me that there was one particular financier in Kensington, London, to whom he turned for the sort of amount that we required to buy the rights to Terry's book, but in other circumstances involving greater amounts, he reverted to a consortium of associates, all in the Midlands, and some who resided close by to his home in Sutton Coldfield.

After three meetings with Ashby he had pulled out of the Tottenham mortgage discussions when he realized that the task was too great a risk, that the ground needed much refurbishment before it could comply with the Taylor Report, even after a grant from wherever, and that his backers had lost interest after evaluating Spurs' Balance Sheet.

ONE OF HIS BACKERS WAS DOUG ELLIS THE CHAIRMAN OF ASTON VILLA...!

ASHBY, WHAT HAVE YOU DONE...?

Had he laid bare the finances of the then struggling Tottenham to a Chairman of another First Division Football Club? Could it have resulted in an acceptance of finance that left Ellis surreptitiously pulling the strings at Tottenham?

Bloody careless Ashby....

I am of the opinion that Sugar does not even know about this, to this very day, nor Venables, nor the Board...!

26th August 1993

When we arrived Terry was engaged with two or three other men. (It was shortly after this that he went to Israel amid much speculation.)

The meeting commenced in the small bar room, and immediately Eddie Ashby spoke to Roger, suggesting that he seemed to know his face, but couldn't remember where from. I was amazed.... He had met Roger on at least THREE occasions, twice at White Hart Lane....

Any ability that I might have tried to muster in order not to be biased against this man was eradicated by his unbusinesslike approach.

Admittedly, at this time neither of the two television programmes exposing Ashby's questionable business deals, or my discovery of the unfortunate family, the Bailys (Chapter 9) had taken place, but his reputation had spread before our meeting.

Tony Marchant and I sat silently while Harris and Ashby probed for information about who was behind Roger and from where the up-front payment would emanate. They continued to banter and eventually after some three quarters of an hour agreed that they would exchange solicitors and Roger would then provide the 'comfort' that Ashby and Harris demanded by way of an undertaking by the secret financier's bankers that the money would be available upon request. This information would be exchanged by the ensuing Tuesday, the 31st.

At that point Ashby became dismissive and ventured to rise and virtually see us off. I protested that Tony and I had come quite a long way and Roger even further.

"I would like to see Terry again. There is something that I have to say to him face up."

"I'm sorry Mr Nathan, the meeting is over. Mr Venables is far too busy with some other guys at the moment."

"I too am sorry, Mr Ashby, but I am sure that Terry could afford just, say, three minutes of his time, and then in the absence of any offer of repast, we would like to eat and drink, before Roger returns to the Midlands."

Annoyed at the lack of respect for his eminence, Ashby then left and returned with Venables.

We all shook hands and Terry looked better than when we first met him earlier that month. He was dressed in a smart dark suit and the usual blue shirt and bright tie. Similar to the one on the cover of this book. I told him of a method of writing this book that would provide him with virtually all the time that he needed to continue his efforts with Solicitors etc., although by now he had failed to deposit the money into the Courts for security of costs. Perhaps it was with that pressure lifted which caused a more relaxed and smiling approach.

He left, agreeing that he was very interested in our revised proposals, particularly as the call on his time was going to be less than he had imagined. We shook hands again, and he nodded in agreement when I suggested that subject to finance we had pretty well reached agreement. He really seemed to want the deal that we were offering. He was also very keen on the idea of me writing an abbreviated version of his life, now, and the full ghost-written autobiography at the end of 1994, or early 1995. That way, I explained, he would have two bites at the financial cherry!

Finally we had a laugh as Terry described himself as 'one take Terry', having sat for fifteen seconds only when he made the advert shown on television for Virgin, where he was reading a book entitled 'How to succeed in business', while piling granulated sugar into a cup of tea. The ad. ended with him tasting the tea, and then saying: 'UGH...SUGAR'. He did that with one take only, such is the professionalism of the man, and I believe, he received close to £10,000.

All the meals at the Club are priced at five pounds, and I have to say that the fresh Scottish Salmon salad was one of the best I had ever been served, to say nothing of the price. The entire bill for the three of us with coffee and two rounds of spirits each was just £27-00.

Fourteen days later, Terry disposed of this shares in Tottenham, all bar 100, and resigned from the Board.

By the ensuing Friday, Harris had been ringing on an almost daily basis advising that he had heard nothing from Roger. Our own enquiries to our 'man' were also being met with unreturned telephone calls and unanswered faxes.

Eventually, Roger phoned my home:

"I can tell you frankly that we have not met Harris's parameters because our backers do not feel that there is any security for the first payment of £65,000. Terry could take the money and then not complete the task of extensive interviewing. The further payments are not of concern, because they are to be made after the book is written."

"That's a bit far fetched, Roger," I replied. "Why would he blow the balance of £135,000 by not complying with the contract requirements?"

"It is that he may not have a choice in the matter."

"What on earth do you mean by that?"

"I can't tell you. Only for me to say that unless you can guarantee to us that he will, beyond any doubt, complete his obligations, we can't go ahead with the initial payment."

"How about insurance?"

"We would require accident and life in any case. You would need performance of contract insurance and I doubt if you will get that."

I promised to ring him back. My son works at Lloyds and if anyone could find this sort of cover, he could.

For two days my lad tried the Americas, Hong Kong, Thailand,

Tokyo, and finally, Saudi Arabia. An Arab Sheik who owned a private insurance company finally showed interest but in the end he demanded a premium that was to say the least, prohibitive.

I telephoned Roger in defeat.

"It doesn't matter much any more, Guy. That matter I attempted to hint at the other day will soon be public knowledge, and I am afraid that we have no further interest."

"Roger, I don't believe this. After all you have done insofar as coming down to Scribes and talking to Terry etcetera...."

"Guy, believe me, we had every intention of backing you in this project, but certain matters have arisen, that I am unable to mention at this time. Suffice to say that in just a very few days now, you will have as much knowledge as I. Perhaps if you were able to insure against performance of contract we might still have been in the game."

That conversation took place on Monday the 13th September 1993.

On Thursday the 16th September 1993, the BBC1 9 o'clock Newscaster, Martin Lewis, announced that the 'Question Time' Programme scheduled for ten thirty that same evening would be delayed by half an hour to make way for a special Panorama presentation about a certain manager of a Premier League Football Club and his irregular business dealings.

The details of that programme, to which the viewing public were given just one and a half hours' notice, are described in our chapter entitled 'The Media'....

A fax from Harris:

Terry is still very preoccupied in directions other than literary ones at this stage, but it is certainly an option that he would like to keep open. With this in mind, he has asked me to assemble a list of potential writers to assist him in this possible enterprise and, as I have already mentioned, we would like to include you on this list. If you are interested in fulfilling this role, could you please forward to me as soon as possible the following:
1. A Curriculum Vitae which particularly lists all your writing experience and background to date.

2. We would like to see two sample chapters from you which should be about football and I can, of course, brief you on this....

(He has to be joking! Jonathan Harris is twenty nine years of age and has to my knowledge never written anything published in his entire life!)

As far as my client's possible contribution to your forthcoming book, he is prepared to consider contributing to it if we can be satisfied to the following:

a) Could you please forward a detailed synopsis of the book as soon as possible.

b) Can you please confirm in writing who else will be contributing to your publication.

c) Will you please confirm in writing the basis of any remuneration you may be prepared to offer my client for participating in such a way.

I very much look forward to receiving your written response as soon as you are able, and I fully appreciate that the sample chapters may take a little longer to provide. I look forward to hearing from you soon.

Yours sincerely

Jonathan G. Harris
Managing Director

Still prior to the TV programme.

13th October 1993

Dear Guy,

Further to our telephone conversation of 10th October and your subsequent fax of 12th October, I thought it would be helpful to confirm the following:-

1. Your facsimile message of 12th October has been passed to my Client for consideration.

2. As soon as it has been discussed we will not hesitate in contacting you. I also confirm that he is in receipt of your fax of 6th October.

3. I note that you wish to be considered as the "ghost writer" should my Client ever decide to write his memoirs. To this end I look forward to receiving the article on football that you wrote some time ago which you promised to send.

(He means the story related to me by Tommy Docherty in Chapter 12 on anecdotes and my own experiences.)

contin.

In addition my Client has specifically requested that you reveal which league team you were General Manager of in the past. The fact that you have been a Coach and General Manager certainly lends credence to your case to act as his writer, as you obviously possess an active working knowledge of the game.

Your refusal to reveal such information can only serve to cast doubts as to your credentials in our eyes.

As to my Client's possible contribution to "Barcelona to Bedlam", I further comment as follows:-

1. I have confirmed with Terry your comment that "the bias we are writing the story with is in favour of your client".

2. My clients attitude to contributing is still dependent on full and satisfactory answers to the four requests for further information contained in my letter to you of 4th October. I have explained to him that as yet you are not in a position to confirm the value of the serial sale, in which you have kindly suggested he may share, but as soon as it is settled you will fully confirm this position. In addition, you will be supplying him with a detailed synopsis and details of who you have interviewed as soon as these interviews are completed.

3. With regard to your comment that NAP Ltd has commissioned this book, both you and Tony on more than one occasion have told me that you have been "commissioned" to do this work by people whose identities you have refused to reveal.

Accordingly, I now invite you to reconsider your answer detailed in 'point d' of your facsimile dated 6th October.

Your fax is utterly inconsistent with what you have previously told me and as a result serves to cast doubt on your written response. At this stage we might only be satisfied with legal warranties and full disclosure as to the true position but I will have to discuss this with my Client.

Several faxes at a frequent rate were received by us, but it was clear that the Agent was now only interested in gaining information, and that Terry had no real intention of doing anything on the literary front.

Finally, I will write what we wrote to promulgate that final fax from Harris:

14th November

To Jonathan Harris…Associated Publicity Holdings.

We are in receipt of your two most recent faxes.

We regret that we are unable to provide you with the information requested, without the removal of the word 'consider'….

We will require an undertaking from Terry that after relating this info. to him, he WILL spend as long as is necessary for our requirements by way of formal contract.

My recent attempts to contact him direct are in an effort to speak with him on the matter of the Premier League's request to me for details of our investigations. We are conscious of your client's well-being and the enquiry…, (To Terry) …which has again been answered by yourself, has little to do with book production.

In effect we are genuinely wishing to help where possible but your reluctance to meet is preventing the real issues which are Terry's life, not just a book.

You will know that we have spoken to many people and I can tell you that there is a conflict of information which does not auger well in a number of areas.

Failing your undertaking as requested we appear to be at an impasse.

Sincerely,

Guy.

NOTE:

I have always felt that Terry is advised badly by the people around him who all have a vested interest. I actually once wrote to him and Yvette begging them to give up the fight against the almighty Alan Sugar, take the money and run....

Any doubt that I might have had in respect of the people that he gathers around him, have now been eradicated by the resistance to a further meeting, that can only perpetuate the printing of facts that in some ways remain unexplained.

I have written to Rick Parry, Steve Coppell and Robert Reid QC, The Premier League Enquiry Committee, offering what I have on the basis that I am allowed to relate the evidence to hand personally to them....

There is just one further matter that I would address; and that is on the subject of Terry's legal fees, which many supporters have mentioned in as much as they are concerned by the advice that Terry has been given and the cost to him of the advice and the actual legal fees, confirming my above statement that the people around Terry have a vested interest.

It can be widely assumed that Terry's own legal bills must have been enormous. His Solicitors, Messrs. Kanter Jules Grangewood and the barristers that represented him are no slouches, and their services do not come cheap.

In advising him to continue his quest when they did, is it questionable that little consideration for the fact that Sugar's team would demand a large payment to be placed into court to secure the costs, should Terry ultimately lose, or at least provide security in a tangible form, was given; although it would be fair to assume that the eminent solicitors did advise him of the possibility?

What has now transpired is that Terry has lost everything, almost, while Sugar is still intact, all because Terry ran out of money and not because the court effected an ultimate damning decision. He has been forced by circumstances to dispose of his shares in Tottenham Hotspur Plc, and therefore with it any rights that he might have had to force Sugar to impart his holdings to him, and any chance to return to the Board.

Maybe, and it really is a long shot, another benefactor might buy Sugar out and then do the perverse thing and return Terry to the Club he loves. Who knows…?

What we do know is that on the 25th August 1993, one day prior to my last meeting with Terry, and after the time had lapsed for him to place the security into the court, Messrs. Kanter Jules Grangewood, or more specifically their Partners, Messrs. Kanter, Pottesman, Kanter…(No. 2) Begner and Isaacs, took charge of 500,000 shares in Tottenham Hotspur Plc, belonging to Edennote Plc, for a sum of £450,000.

Chapter 5
THE MEDIA

The first of the media reports relates to the LBC broadcast of the interview of Alan Sugar conducted by the eminent Andrew Neil, Editor of the Sunday Times. The live interview took place only four days after Terry Venables had won the first round of the battles that were to ensue:

SUNDAY 16th MAY

Andrew Neil: "Between now and noon, the Chairman of Tottenham Hotspur, Alan Sugar, will give his side of the Boardroom battle that has split the North London Club and left Terry Venables fighting to retain his interest in Spurs.

"Terry Venables will be back behind his desk at White Hart Lane tomorrow now that a judge has suspended the Tottenham Board's decision to dismiss him as Chief Executive of the Club. We will have to wait until the court hearing on May the 25th to find out whether Mr Venables has the law on his side for more permanent employment.

"When Alan Sugar joined Terry Venables at the Spurs Club in 1991, it was said by Sugar 'This is the dream ticket'. Two East End boys both successful, one in business the other in football. They have come together to save the Club. Alan Sugar looking after the business, Terry Venables the football. Now they have fallen out and Mr Sugar wants Mr Venables to leave the Club, leaving Mr Sugar in sole control.

"Now Mr Sugar has offered to buy out Terry Venables' stake in the Club, but Venables has said that offer was derisory. There has been a certain sympathy for Venables particularly reported in the sports pages since Friday's dramatic events.

"But joining me now on the line to give his side of the story is Alan Sugar. Alan, good morning to you."

Alan Sugar: "Good morning, Andrew."

Andrew Neil: "Alan, let's just go back to basics. Why did you decide to sack Terry Venables?"

Alan Sugar: "Well, Andrew, when I agreed to give this interview I did tell your assistant that it would be limited because as you have already announced, the matter has regretfully been brought into the Courts and the proverbial lawyers have told me to keep my mouth shut. But as you know me a little bit I will say what I can. First of all, Andrew, it's not Alan Sugar asking Terry Venables to leave the Football Club, it's the Board of Directors and we are intelligent people who have spoken of Terry's departure, we knew it would have been received in the manner in which it has in the press. Especially the back pages of the press and that alone must indicate that this thing has been well thought through and that the decision of the Board of Directors was taken with that in mind and therefore it was a decision that we thought was necessary.

Andrew Neil: "At what stage did you decide or did you and the Board decide or realise that Venables would have to go?"

Alan Sugar: "I and the Board.... Well, I had in particular given the matter a lot of thought in the past few months and I had numerous meetings with Terry Venables to try to discuss the future of the Company, the business and the Club and this manifested itself into the fact that on May the 6th I gave him a letter in which I outlined an offer. The letter was strictly private and confidential and to my great surprise he immediately disclosed it and showed it to other people and I don't just mean lawyers, I mean other people. That letter contained an offer to buy his shares off of him at the price that he had paid for them, irrespective of what the market price was. In fact what he had shelled out in paying for them together with an offer for cancelling his various contracts with the Company, and it also stated in there that I felt that this matter should be kept strictly confidential, private and confidential from the media and that if and when we were able to come to an agreement, that we would find some way of, kind of in a dignified manner, for both of us to part company. In other words it was presented in a very business-like manner."

Andrew Neil: "Did you think that this offer would fall on receptive ears because it was your understanding that Terry Venables is in some financial difficulty?"

Alan Sugar: "This offer was made with the intention of making sure that Terry would be able to walk away and not be placed into any financial difficulty. I mean, the fact is I, as his Chairman, you know, have to take his side and not be guided by what one reads in the press. He clearly borrowed money to buy the shares in the Company and obviously in borrowing that money he has had to pay interest etc, and that the costs if he left the Company, because the market in Tottenham Hotspur shares is very thin, in fact if you tried to buy 20,000 Tottenham Hotspur shares, it has the effect of the price going up 10p and similarly if you tried to sell 20,000 Tottenham Hotspur shares it makes the price go down and the thought of trying to dispose of, you know, millions of shares was just inconceivable and he would not get his money, so I felt it fair and proper to make sure that if he left, that I would make him the offer of taking the shares off of him at what they cost him and that's that. It has not been made in any way or form knowing that he has financial problems.''

Andrew Neil: "We now know, I understand that part of the money that he borrowed to buy the Spurs shares, the Company that he borrowed that from has collapsed and is now in the hands of the receivers who want the loan back. So therefore he is in some financial difficulties. That must have been at the back of your mind with this offer?''

Alan Sugar: "Andrew, I have heard that rumour and I do not know the arrangements that Terry made with those people. I am not privy to any of those contracts that he made with these people and that is firmly his business.''

Andrew Neil: "I understand.''

Alan Sugar: "All I know is that he borrowed the money, and whether he borrowed it with a company that has gone bankrupt, or whether he borrowed it from Lloyds Bank or indeed borrowed it from you, it has to be paid back.''

Andrew Neil: "I wish I had enough money so that he could have borrowed it from me, Alan. Tell me this, were you surprised, therefore, if you thought that this was a good financial offer you were making, that he has since described it as derisory? I assume because he has been offered a price for the shares that is no more than the price he paid.''

Alan Sugar: "Well, I am very surprised at his comments. I mean, I think his comments of it being derisory are, with the greatest respect to him, a lack of understanding of commercial matters, I mean, what he feels in his mind is that if someone wanted to pay him back for the investment that he made in Tottenham is not just to pay the actual capital sum that he paid out for the shares, he also considers that he has been paying interest on the money he borrowed. He paid legal fees and advisers' fees to arrange loans and things like that, he paid legal fees and advisers' fees to help acquire the Company and in his mind he believes that he wants to recover all that also. Now, I mean, I think that every businessman in the world would like to be able to do things like that, recover interest on loans that they took to go into business ventures but regretfully in the cruel, harsh world, I mean, that is a dream.''

Andrew Neil: ''Can we just clarify one thing? The split between you, the decision, certainly on your side to part company. Has that or does it not have anything to do with Venables' abilities as the Manager as Spurs?''

Alan Sugar: ''Absolutely not. Nobody is questioning his ability as a football coach. Absolutely not and it is a very sad day, it was a very sad day on Friday and everybody, every Director, everybody involved regrets deeply that it has come to this.''

Andrew Neil: ''So, therefore the disagreement is wholly a business one and as I understand it, comes out in your view from Venables preferring you to keep to a division of labour, that he runs the football side, you run the business side. In what way, therefore, did Venables want to get involved on your terms from the business side?''

Alan Sugar: ''Andrew, I don't want to sound corny here, but this is one of the questions which I have got to say to you, I plead the fifth, if you know what I mean. This is one of them where the Lawyers said, you know, that I have got to, you know, keep quiet.''

Andrew Neil: ''Can I just ask you on that legal advice, that because you are not before a jury trial, or this case will not be taken by a jury, it is going to be heard by a Judge, so therefore I don't quite understand why you are not at liberty to speak more about this? Since although LBC has enormous influence, we don't expect it to influence a High Court Judge?''

Alan Sugar: "Andrew, you are as familiar with the legal system as I am."

Andrew Neil: "Well, that is why I ask you that question...." (Interrupted.)

Alan Sugar: "And I don't know either, so what I best do is listen to the people that I am paying."

Andrew Neil: "Has it anything to do with the kind of company Venables has been keeping, particularly the kind of business company? I understand that one of his close associates who has been involved in the Club is a Mr Eddie Ashby, who has been involved in forty-three companies, sixteen of them in receivership, fifteen struck off the registrar of companies and eight in liquidation."

Alan Sugar: "Andrew, really you have put me on the spot, my friend and, you know, I can't really comment. I will say one thing. That this.... When we went into this thing two years ago it was a dream made in heaven. Me a so-called, reasonably good business man with good marketing skills and experience, or whatever and Terry, somebody involved with football. O.K., two East End boys who should be able to get on with each other and all that I can say is that if he had different people around him, not particularly restricted to this Mr Ashby that you refer to, but to other people, we would not be having this argument today and I blame Jonathan Crystal for everything that has happened to this Company in the past two years. I firmly blame him for everything and Jonathan Crystal, who is a Director, Terry will reflect in years to come how his dream to run and own part of a football club, was destroyed basically by Jonathan Crystal and nobody else."

Andrew Neil: "Now Jonathan Crystal, as I understand it, is a Barrister and a Director of Spurs. He voted with Venables at the crucial Board meeting. He is very close to Venables. I understand that he is everything from principal adviser to chauffeur."

Alan Sugar: "Again I don't want to comment on that. I think you should get comments about the way Jonathan Crystal conducts himself in respect to Terry Venables and other people."

Andrew Neil: "Is there any way though you can tell us why Crystal has been, in your view, such a malign influence on Terry Venables?"

Alan Sugar: "Well, let me tell you this, Andrew, you know very well that I went through a rather rough period last year in the Amshold privatisation, or the attempt to privatise Amstrad."

Andrew Neil: "I remember that."

Alan Sugar: "And you know that on many occasions I was criticised for not having any Non-Executive Directors. I have since, Andrew, become the world's greatest expert on knowing what a Non-Executive Director is supposed to do."

Andrew Neil: "You never asked me." (They both laugh.)

Alan Sugar: "But we have appointed some people through the correct channels and the correct people."

Andrew Neil: "I understand."

Alan Sugar: "A Non-Executive Director is supposed to be independent."

Andrew Neil: "I understand."

Alan Sugar: "He is supposed to be there, giving advice on behalf...in...you know, looking after the shareholders' interests and being independent from the Executives."

Andrew Neil: "And checking on what the Management is doing on behalf of the shareholders."

Alan Sugar: "Absolutely, Jonathan Crystal is not independent. It is blatantly as simple as that and unfortunately has been the cause of loading up bullets in a gun which regrettably Terry has been constantly firing and I don't care whether he is a Barrister or what, there are hundreds of people around that will concur that."

Andrew Neil: "Alan, when you.... When the Board took the decision, did you expect a legal challenge from Venables as the result of it?"

Alan Sugar: "Er.... Yes, we did, we didn't expect it at the time that it came, we felt that it would come afterwards or indeed we felt that it would be before the Board meeting which was called, you know, earlier part of last week."

Andrew Neil: "And on the 25th May, when it's going to be heard in Court 'cause it is only a temporary decision he got in his favour until the full Court hearing, will the current decision, whatever it is on the 25th of May, will that resolve matters or is it now going to be a protracted legal battle?"

Alan Sugar: "Andrew, I don't know. I am going to speak to the lawyers again tomorrow morning for them to sit down and try to explain to me in simple terms what the hell has gone on, 'cause, you know, I don't understand, I don't understand anything about this whole thing and they promised to explain to me what the system is going to do."

Andrew Neil: "I get from everything you say this morning, Alan, that whatever the Court decision, this is a dream ticket that cannot be put together again, it is a split, it's under?"

Alan Sugar: "Well, regretfully, with great regret, a decision by myself and the Board, both Boards, the Plc Board and the Football Club Board and regretfully we believe that it is unrepairable and we cannot go forward in any other way than we indicated last Friday."

Andrew Neil: "Finally, Alan, some of the fans reacted badly to this and have been attacking you, but you said that you knew that sort of thing was going to happen. Once this is out of the way, in what way do you intend to repair the damage that has been done with the Club supporters? How are you going to regain their confidence and get their minds back onto what's happening on the pitch, rather than the Boardroom?"

Alan Sugar: "Well, you know, actions, as you know, Andrew, are much louder than words. No one man is bigger than Tottenham Hotspur Football Club. It was established in 1882, it will be there long after you and I and Terry have gone and we have to do things with the best interest of the Club at heart. Obviously the fans want the football team to be strong, they want to go out and try and win. They want good management on the football side. We have got good management at the moment who work under Terry Venables, Doug Livermore and Ray Clemence and that's all I can say. We will apply the funds, the cash, in an appropriate manner that one should apply cash in the Football Club. The .... will tell the story. You know as well as I do that fans are very fickle. There is a distinct possibility, and I am not throwing this down as a challenge or a gauntlet, but three or four games into the season, if we win three or four games and the Manager becomes a hero and the team, the cruel harsh reality is that maybe Terry is forgotten. Maybe, I don't know. I am not trying to undermine him as a famous football personality. He will never be forgotten, obviously, but that is what fans are like, unfortunately. You know, I was told by other Directors of the Company that whilst it was a big bad blow on Friday, that the so-called reported hundreds of fans outside the door, in fact amounted to twenty-five and there were thirty cameramen and press. They had said on occasions in the previous regime when there were problems with the Club in the early Scholar days and things like that, that the riots, or not the riots, the disorderly fans were tens of tens thick, going back to the road, if you know what I mean. Obviously there are some fans there that are angry and I am prepared to stand up and be counted, and we will have to wait and see."

Andrew Neil: "Is the Club now on a firm financial footing and do you have the resources to develop it?"

Alan Sugar: "I believe the Club is on a firm…. Well, I know the Club to be on a firm financial footing. We are constrained at the moment, unfortunately by the Taylor report, obviously like every other football club is. It has come at a time when, you know, we could have done without it. We have to follow the rules and take the long-term view. But most certainly I have pledged on Friday, and that was the only thing I could tell the fans, that if I am allowed to have control of the Club with the Board of Directors, whilst I am there the Club will not get into financial difficulties."

Andrew Neil: "Is it your intention to appoint again someone who combines the roles of Chief Executive and Manager?"

Alan Sugar: "It's far too early to say that now, Andrew, regretfully the matter has been brought to the Courts and for the next couple of weeks the staff, the people, are going to be in total disarray as to what direction they have to work in, it's going to be very, very difficult and I can't really say at the moment."

Andrew Neil: "And have you turned your mind yet to who the new Manager is going to be?"

Alan Sugar: "The Manager of the Club at the moment is Doug Livermore and it has been for the last year. Terry Venables has been the Chief Executive."

Andrew Neil: "But still involved in the football side of the Club."

Alan Sugar: "Absolutely, but Andrew, I am the Chairman and

Chief Executive of Amstrad, and I am involved in the design of the products and selling them.''

Andrew Neil: "I understand. You have not yet turned your mind, at least not publicly anyway, to who the new Chief Executive is going to be.''

Alan Sugar: "Chief Executive? I think your question earlier was who the Manager was going to be; the Manager is Doug Livermore.''

Andrew Neil: "I understand that. What I meant was who is going to fill Terry Venables' place.''

Alan Sugar: "I don't, as I said…. What we are concerned about now is keeping the thing together. You know, these next couple of weeks, for the morale of the staff, the players and everything. Something has got to be sorted out, we have got to keep the status quo, peace, and when all that has gone and we know who is in charge and who's in control, then we can make those decisions.''

Andrew Neil: "If you have got an Executive Chairman like yourself and a Manager already in position, why do you need a Chief Executive?''

Alan Sugar: "You're doing the talking, Andrew, not me, as I said, maybe we don't, maybe we do. All I know is that I have never interfered with football matters, never intend to interfere with football matters, and the allegations in Friday morning's press that I am going to actually pick the team on match day is an absolute joke, I mean a total joke. I think I have been down to the dressing room twice in the whole time, two years, that I have been in the Club.''

Andrew Neil: "I want you to know that I am available, but Glasgow Rangers has first call.''

Alan Sugar: "All right.''

Andrew Neil: "Alan, thanks for coming on this morning, I know you are under difficult constraints, but it has been good to talk to you.''

Alan Sugar: "Thanks a lot.''

Andrew Neil: "That's Alan Sugar, the Chairman of Spurs, giving us his side of the case on what has become the most controversy on the sports calendar this year, the battle between him and Terry Venables.''

Although there were numerous newspaper articles and news bulletins about the conflict that was turning the football world upside down, it wasn't until the Panorama programme appeared on BBC 1 in September 1993 that the full extent of some of the corruption at Tottenham, which had only been whispered previously, opened the eyes of the public in general and caused the first real wave of doubt concerning the "hero' of Spurs, Terry Venables, from his loyal supporters.

Here is that broadcast:

Panorama opened with an introduction regarding the background to the High Court hearings that involved specifically Terry Venables, 'one of football's best known personalities'.

"Venables claims that he was wrongfully dismissed as Chief Executive from Spurs by Chairman, Alan Sugar", the Narrator informed us. "To the fans there was only one villain. Tonight Panorama tells the inside story of the biggest bust-up in British soccer, and reveals why Sugar sacked the Manager."

"In the realm of football, Terry Venables enjoys the status of a king, and until recently the control of his own castle. As a player he won the FA Cup and remains the only Englishman to represent his Country at every level of the game. When Venables converted from player to coach the success continued. Under his guidance both Crystal Palace and Queens Park Rangers won promotion. He returned to Wembley with QPR for the 1982 FA Cup Final"...(against Spurs, then managed by Keith Burkenshaw)..."Having conquered Britain he faced his biggest challenge when he took over as Manager of Barcelona. He wasted little time; winning the European Cup during his first Season."

(Totally incorrect..! He won the Spanish League during his first Season and then was beaten in the European Cup a year later!)

"Flags were unfurled in his honour, and Terry Venables was crowned 'El Tel', the finest coach in Europe."..

Trevor Brooking, the former West Ham and England midfielder, offered his expert opinion:

"As a player he was always quite a thoughtful midfield player and a lot of questions used to be asked from coaches and managers he used to play under. So he was absorbing that information, then, and then of course when he went into the management/coaching side, he was always recognised as a very thoughtful tactician. As coach I think he has been one of the most successful ones that this country has produced."

The Narrator: "Venables had one great ambition. In 1991 he formed a partnership with Alan Sugar and took control of Tottenham Hotspur. He was already Manager of the Club, but to move from the bench to the boardroom he needed £3 million. Although not a rich man, Venables raised the money. But within two years the marriage had collapsed. Venables was sacked and the Court case with all its costs forced him to sell his shares. The announcement came at the beginning of this month."

Venables was then shown making the announcement on television:

"Hello everyone... Long time no see. O.K., except for a nominal holding which I intend to retain I have sold all my shares in Tottenham Hotspur Plc. I intend to resign as a Director of the Company also."

The Narrator: "Venables says that he has lost a million pounds in the process and claims that neither he nor the supporters have been told why he was removed from the Club. Tonight 'Panorama' reveals for the first time how Terry Venables' corrupt business activities led to the dismissal from Tottenham Hotspur."

Enter on screen, Martin Bashir, investigative reporter:

"We will show how his ambition to purchase Spurs led him to unlawfully obtain a million pounds. The programme also reveals how he abused his position as Tottenham's Chief Executive, and how his personal advisor tried to cheat a major financial institution."

Back to the Narrator:

"The only reason given for the sacking of Terry Venables involved his choice of advisors, some of whom were employed at Tottenham Hotspur. The individual that attracted the greatest attention was his financial advisor, Eddie Ashby. Venables was to hire Ashby as Spurs' General Manager at a salary of £90,000. It was Paul Reviere that first introduced Ashby to Venables. Reviere ran a highly successful financial services company, selling pensions and other policies. As a football fanatic, he became part of the London soccer scene. In 1989 he and Venables began working together on the development of a new board game. They called it 'The Manager' and it was an attempt to re-create the excitement of running a football club. Paul Reviere spent 15 months developing the game, and then formed a company to promote it. That company was called 'Glenhope Management'. It's two other Directors were Eddie Ashby and Terry Venables. Once on sale it scored an immediate hit."

Paul Reviere now:

"It was launched in Harrods, I think in August 1990, and it got off to a very good start. We sold virtually all at departmental stores and I think we sold 25,000 by the beginning of the next year; taking into account the Christmas sales. There ought to be..er..running a good profit."

The Narrator:

"After working without pay for 15 months from his first-floor offices in Princes Gate, Paul Reviere was short of money. He decided to make his first substantial withdrawal from the Glenhope bank account."

Reviere again:

"I remember that we thought that there was probably about £34,000 there. The guy that controlled the purse strings and dealt with all of the financial side was Eddie Ashby, and when I asked him to tell what exactly we will be taking out of the Company, because I was experiencing cash-flow problems, I found to my horror that there was no money there."

The Narrator:

"Edward Moses Ashby has been involved with a number of businesses: The vast majority have been failures. He's been a director of 43 companies. 16 are in receivership. 8 in liquidation and 15 are in the process of being struck-off. Of the remaining 4, there are no details. Eddie Ashby had taken thousands of pounds from Glenhope's offices and transferred it to another company without Paul Reviere's knowledge. Ashby was doing the same thing at another of Venables' businesses. In April 1991, Terry Venables bought into 'Scribes West'. Scribes is a high-class private club in Kensington which had run into financial difficulties. One of Venables' first moves was to bring in Eddie Ashby as the Club's Finance Director. Despite using Venables' name to attract soccer stars and other celebrities, the Club continued to lose money. Geoffrey Van Hay, Scribes Managing Director, saw Venables as the last chance to ensure the Club's survival. He also knew that Venables was keen to expand his own business empire."

Geoffrey Van Hay (Former Managing Director Scribes Club West):

"Mr Venables saw Scribes as a launching pad. I think he thought that having such an elegant... the right premises would attract the right people. He loved being 'Mr Venables...Scribes West International'."

The Narrator:

"Two senior members of Scribes, Gavin Hans Hamilton, (another former Managing Director of Scribes), and Noel Botham, soon found that Venables wanted to take control of the Club. He promised to invest £50,000 and once again he appointed Eddie Ashby as Finance Director. Key Scribes accounts were then moved to the offices of Glenhope."

Geoffrey Van Hay:

"We were told that he was putting in £50,000. Later, when I asked had the £50,000 been actually invested, I was told by Gavin 'Not actually in the Club bank account'. I said 'What does that mean?' 'Well', Gavin replied, 'another bank account has suddenly appeared and apparently the money has been paid into that.'

" 'What does that mean....apparently?' Gavin answered....'Well we don't have access to that bank account, or to any of the statements, or to the cheque book.' "

The Narrator:

"This was part of.....(indistinguishable)."

Gavin Hans Hamilton:

"Geoffrey Van Hays, and my role was only to run the Club, and that all our efforts were to be concentrated on that, and we were to have nothing to do with the running of the financial aspects of the Club, and that will be handled by Eddie Ashby and Terry Venables."

The Narrator:

"During the summer of 1991 Scribes received a document which was to shock the shareholders. It was the latest development in the business-life of their Finance Director, and led to his formal resignation." (The document refers to a bankruptcy order against Edward Moses Ashby of the 3rd of June 1991.)

Geoffrey Van Hay:

"Gavin read it and said...'Oh my God, look at this.'...It was a piece of paper...'What have we got here?' he said. 'Ashby is a bankrupt!'

"I certainly knew that it was illegal for a bankrupt to be on the board of a company."

The Narrator then asked whether this information had affected Eddie Ashby's relationship to Scribes.

Gavin Hans Hamilton replied...."Well, he continued to run the finances of the Company."

The Narrator pressed the point..."And he continued to control the finances of the Company? Was that with Terry Venables' consent?"

Gavin Hans Hamilton:

"Well it must have been."

The Narrator:

"Another Scribes Director was Paul Reviere. He'd learnt that despite the Club's financial condition Eddie Ashby had been taking money out of the Company. As before, it was called an inter- company loan intended to finance another company."

Paul Reviere commented...."The money had been taken to pay wages of the printing company."

The Narrator continued: "Panorama has discovered that the money taken from Scribes and Glenhope was destined for an Essex printing works. Print Double had been manufacturing the Manager board game, but it was to become part of Eddie Ashby's attempt to build an illusory business empire, cheat the banks and raise money. The Company (Print Double) had substantial assets and Ashby agreed to invest a six-figure-sum. The Company Secretary, Chris Bowhay, expected the money to arrive in Print Double's bank account. But only one payment of £20,000 was deposited. Subsequent payments were late; this meant that Print Double had no time to clear cheques."

Chris Bowhay stated:

"The rest of the money after the £20,000 was paid over in

about half a dozen drops of about £5,000: twenties and fifty pound notes."

"How did you come across the money?" continued the Narrator.

"They asked us to meet them at a lay-by just off the A10. We would wait in the lay-by until a member of Glenhope turned up. He wound down his window and handed the money over."

"Did you know where the money came from?"

"Er....It came from....A couple of occasions it came from Glenhope, and he said that they had to raid Scribes to get the money and that's where he said it actually came from."

"He said they had to raid Scribes?"

"Yes."

"What did he mean by that?"

"There was no money in Glenhope and he had to get the money out of Scribes."

The Narrator:

"Although the money came out from those Companies it was routed through a venture capital company called Elite Europe. Alan Roberts, Print Double's Managing Director, was told it was backed by Terry Venables, though quite what he knew was unclear."

Alan Roberts, Managing Director Thamespad, Trainwell, Print Double, all in some form of liquidation:

"He led me on a little bit. He was gonna have 30% in the Company. We needed £150,000 from day one, but it took us probably ten weeks and over that period they actually advanced about £50,000."

The Narrator:

"Eddie Ashby was not registered as a director of Elite Europe but he always behaved as one. He identified a number of companies in serious financial trouble and then added them to his paper empire. Print Double gave the empire credibility because it had a large number of assets.

"More typical was the Independent Balloon Company. It was on the verge of receivership.

"Sue Cooper was one of four partners in the company. She advertised in a Sunday newspaper and Eddie Ashby replied, again using Terry Venables' name.''

Sue Cooper:

"I was quite impressed with Mr Ashby. They seemed to be financially secure. We, at the end of the day, got balance sheets. They had their bank accounts at Coutts & Co. (Bankers to the Royal Family.).... Mr Venables was regularly mentioned as having an interest in the Company, although I am not sure what that interest was. So actually I was impressed.''

The Narrator:

"IBC, the Independent Balloon Company, was to receive £15,000 from Elite Europe. Elite was also going to take on IBC's outstanding liabilities. But the money never arrived. Any profits that IBC did make were kept by Elite Europe.''

Sue Cooper said...."We feel that they let us down very badly, and our creditors. They didn't behave ethically and I am not sure if they behaved legally. They took our money. They took our stock. They gave us nothing in return. They just left us with our debts at the end of the day.''

The Narrator:

"Another worthless company that Ashby claimed was part of Elite Europe was Wetherall Baccarra, who had previous connections with the Wetherall clothing company in Liverpool, but after a boardroom battle, he was forced out. David Hodgkinson was on the Board of Wetheralls when Eddie Ashby was also a Director. He recalls that the Company was in receivership. Ashby still claimed that it was part of the Elite Europe empire.''

David Hodgkinson:

"I was surprised to hear in some detail that the Company was part of Elite Europe, in the ownership of Eddie Ashby, that he had listed in January 1991 Wetheralls as one of his assets, and was reporting a turnover £150,000 per year, with a net profit of £27,000 per year. At that stage the Company was in receivership. To my knowledge there was no potential whatsoever for Eddie Ashby to trade under the Wetherall name.''

The Narrator:

"Ashby was to use Elite to persuade finance houses to make substantial loans. It was shown with six apparently profitable companies. It said Wetherall Baccarra was successfully trading, but the

Company had been dissolved. Ashby had also distributed a balance sheet showing it had net assets of £597,000. This too was untrue. The balance sheet included equipment belonging to Print Double, but not its liabilities."

Chris Bowhay:

"I know they were trying to raise money on our machinery and our assets. Supposedly, the money would have come into our Company. If that were successful, I can't say whether it would have done. That's the opinion I got, what they were trying to do."

"Was that fraud?"

Chris Bowhay replied...."Oh, it is fraud because the machines were covered by hire purchase agreements.'

The Narrator:

"The balance sheet fraud collapsed. Print Double realised they were being quoted by Ashby as a wholly owned subsidiary of Elite Europe. They severed all contact immediately. Terry Venables' problems were not restricted to his choice of advisors. The Spurs deal was now imminent and he urgently needed money. In a final attempt to raise cash, he decided to cheat one of his former companies, Transatlantic Inns, which ran a number of public houses. Maceys is a West-End wine bar. It was one of 3 pubs managed by Transatlantic Inns. The others were the Cock and Magpie in Essex, a traditional country pub, and the Gramby Tavern in Reading," (A Whitbread House)..."a well-known music venue. Transatlantic didn't actually own any of these pubs, but had leased them all from various breweries. Terry Venables resigned as a Director of Transatlantic Inns on June 28th 1991. Despite this he entered into a transaction with another company to sell most of Transatlantic's property. Their major assets were the fixtures and fittings. This included things like the tables and chairs and even the pub's carpeting. Panorama has discovered that in August 1991, two months after he had resigned as a Director, Terry Venables arranged to sell and lease back the F&F of Maceys, The Cock and Magpie and the Gramby Tavern to a Company called Landhurst Leasing. He also sold Landhurst the contents of a fourth pub, The Miners, in Claremont Road, Cardiff. According to Cardiff Council, this pub, and indeed this road, does not actually exist. Landhurst Leasing's £1 million payment was deposited into Edennote, Terry Venables' private Company, not Transatlantic Inns. The money came in 3 tranches. Two instalments of £250,000 and a final payment of £500,000. The other Transatlantic Directors knew nothing of the sale of their assets, and they would have been more astonished to hear that Venables got more than £1 million for them. The maximum value of these fixtures and fittings is just over £100,000. That's about only 10% of what Venables' Company actually received. According to internal Edennote documents, £800,000 of the Landhurst money was paid out six days later to Tottenham Hotspur Football Club. This money alone enabled Venables to keep his part of the bargain with Alan Sugar, to purchase Spurs shares. Venables failed to disclose where the money came from. In the original offer document for Tottenham Hotspur he claims simply that £750,000 would come from his own resources. Why Landhurst Leasing paid Edennote £1 million in exchange for assets worth about £100,000, is hard to explain. Landhurst were paid a £10,000 arrangement fee, but they also received one other perk from Terry Venables. He instructed Spurs marketing department to provide Landhurst with a £20,000 executive-box for the entire Season. Box no. 44 in the West Stand. More importantly, Venables had achieved his ambition to become a controlling partner in Spurs. Terry Venables' decision to sell properties he didn't own at a vastly inflated price, and then put the money into his own Company, is unlawful. It hurts both the shareholders of Transatlantic Inns and those of Landhurst Leasing. Both Companies are now in receivership. Many football supporters regard Terry Venables as potentially the next England Manager. Tonight's revelations about his unprincipled business practices raise serious questions about that, and now his role as Tottenham Hotspur's Chief Executive is also being called into question. Besides putting Eddie Ashby on the payroll of Spurs, Venables began to mix his private business interests with those of Tottenham's. The Insurance Company, Legal and General, were in final negotiations with Spurs to sell financial products to the Club's supporters. As the deal was about to be closed, another Company, General Portfolio, whose Chairman was a shareholder in Scribes, suddenly replaced Legal and General. Panorama has obtained correspondence between General Portfolio and Terry Venables. The letter begins by referring to 'the common aims of increasing Scribes clientele and generating business for General Portfolio and Tottenham Hotspur'. So Venables' Club, Scribes, was to benefit from the deal. During their High Court battle, Alan Sugar questioned Terry Venables about invoices that concerned him. They triggered anxieties about the behaviour of the Club's Chief Executive. The first invoice was for a cash sum of £58,750.''...(Details of that invoice is given in the chapter on First Wave Sport Services, Chapter 6)...''The rest of the Board knew nothing about this work. There are two other invoices which the Board also knew nothing about. One is for £11,750 and is....'In respect of commercial consultancy on behalf of Tottenham Hotspur, Season 1991 and to include all expenditure, ie., fax, telex, telephone, travel and accommodation. This consultancy refers to feasibility study on own brand merchandising and the exploitation of all commercial opportunities at the Club.'..''..(This invoice is mentioned in the interview with Graham Smith, partner to Frank McLintock in First Wave Sport Services, Chapter 6)...

''There is another invoice for £17,625 relating to...'Commercial and public relation activities.'...Venables has so far failed to give any further details about this work.

''Alan Sugar was also concerned about a change to the contract of Chief Scout, Ted Buxton. Just before Venables left, he amended Buxton's contract, giving him the right to unilaterally extend the agreement. It eventually read..' The Company or its Chief Scout may, at its option, extend the agreement for a further period of two years. This meant that if Buxton was dismissed, Spurs could be forced to pay compensation for an additional two years.

''Venables' largest payment to an agent involved the sale of Paul Gascoigne to Lazio. He recruited Gascoigne in the Summer of 1989, but two years later with the Club in serious debt, Venables was forced to sell him. Although the sale was agreed before the 1991 FA Cup Final, Gascoigne suffered a serious knee injury, and the price had to be re-negotiated. Panorama has obtained a letter dated 20th June 1991, sent by Lazio's London-based solicitors to Tottenham Hotspur. It confirms that the Italian Club would be prepared to pay a price £5.5 million for Paul Gascoigne. Lazio's Finance Director, Giancarlo Guerra, confirms the details of Gascoigne's transfer from Tottenham Hotspur to Italy."

Martin Bashir: "When did Tottenham reach agreement with Lazio about the fee for Paul Gascoigne?"

Giancarlo Guerra: "I remember it should be about June '91. Two months after Paul's accident at the Cup Final."

"How much did Lazio agree to pay?" Martin enquired.

"£5.5 million," Guerra replied.

"Was this figure ever increased?"

"Never. It was impossible to increase because it was a close agreement. All the money was already deposited in the bank. The bank received a trust deed from us and Tottenham, and so it was impossible to change the figure."

The Narrator intervened: "Despite this agreement, Venables asked his old friend, Pimlico Restaurateur Gino Santin, to assist in the negotiations. According to Lazio he played no part in the early discussions and only met them well after the deal had been struck. A month ago Venables told the Guardian newspaper that he was able to push up the price for 'Gazza' to £6.3 million. Did Lazio pay 6.3 million?"

"No...Lazio paid £5.5 million."

"Not a penny more?"

"Not a penny more."

The Narrator again:..."Despite Lazio's insistence that the price for Gascoigne was never increased, Venables arranged for Spurs to pay Santin. The money was paid direct to 'Anglo-European Market Research and Consulting', a Swiss Company. The figure was £200,000.

"Panorama invited Terry Venables to take part in this programme, but he refused to accept the BBC's normal terms and conditions of interviews. His financial advisor, Eddie Ashby, also did not comment.

"Tonight's revelations may come as a great surprise for Spurs fans, who loyally backed Venables. His abuse of position and his unscrupulous business practices may make even the most ardent supporters think again...."

The Reporter....Martin Bashir....The Producer....Mark Killick....The Editor....Glenwyn Benson.

Then on Sunday 19th September, Channel 4 presented a special Dispatches programme, entitled 'The Inside Story'. Producer, Ray Ackerman has granted us permission to utilise the excerpts that we have carefully selected, basically, those that are not a repeat of what has already been introduced by Panorama.

In this programme, both Terry Venables and Alan Sugar make contributions. The first speaker is Terry Venables...

"Why weren't they there at the beginning? They certainly weren't there when I was dismissed. Three months later, when they have got to find reasons, they are coming up with all these allegations, which infuriates me, and is very, very unfair.'

Alan Sugar: "Quite honestly, nine folders of affidavit evidence, a four-page letter to his own lawyers outlines all of our allegations. Now I am not saying that he has to agree with me, but how would you get there and say....'I don't know what it's all about..I don't know, it's absolute nonsense.' "

The Narrator: "This evening Dispatches tells the full story of the biggest bust-up in British soccer history and reveals why Alan Sugar sacked Terry Venables from Tottenham Hotspur. — A screen caption appeared: 'The Inside Story' — In 1992 Paul Gascoigne was finally sold to the Italian Football Club, Lazio for £5.5 million..............The deal went through finally, two months after the Sugar/Venables take-over....There was one demand for payment that caused a Boardroom row at Spurs. The demand came from Iginio Santin."

Alan Sugar:.."Now I said to Venables at that stage...'Who is this bloke?' He said... 'Well, he is an Italian and he has done a lot of transfers before, he knows Milan.. He knows this...He knows that..He's a very well-known restaurateur...and entrepreneur, and I admit he is...He is quite well-known. There's no question of it. Now I know that, he is.. Quite well-known. Basically, he speaks Italian and we don't understand them when they are talking in Italian..He knows what makes them tick...Let him get on with it.' I said, 'OK, let him get on with it.' "

Terry Venables: "He is well-known, in fact he has done deals for... like Mark Hately and several other players who have gone to

Italy before. In fact he has got a restaurant in Milan.. The best one in Milan. I said to him see if you can see what you can do."

The Narrator: "So Santin was employed to help in the sale of Gascoigne. Sugar was happy, because Venables told him that Santin's services would be for free."

Alan Sugar: ..."I said to Terry at the time, what is in it for this Santin bloke? That's when he first spoke to me about it... Venables said to me... 'Look, you've come out of the computer business....You don't know anything about football.. People who are associated with football do funny things..Believe me, they do things just to be associated. They like to be associated with the high-life, the Gascoignes and Tottenham and all this stuff. You won't believe it, I know you're cynical..I know you're cynical but people do do things for no money'. I said to him 'I don't know many of those people, but I'll take your word for it.' Football, obviously, is strange....I've been associated with it now for about a month. I mean this was a little bit strange, but I was still a little bit sceptical, and I swear to you that those were his words to me."

"Santin claims the credit for getting the deal through, after Gazza was injured in the Cup Final, and for the money that was deposited in the bank," said the Narrator.

Speaking to Santin now, the first time that the viewing public had seen the popular restaurateur.

"Can we talk about the negotiations? Were they difficult?"

"Very difficult, because Paul Gascoigne was broken and we were selling a player that we didn't know if he could play again. Lazio were buying a player," Santin replied with a strong accent.

The Managing Director of Lazio, Lionello Celon, then came on to say: "When Mr Santin got involved, many, many points were cleared up and this was an essential role played by Mr Santin during these negotiations. Without his involvement the whole thing could have fallen through: Jeopardised and the whole transfer falling through, because of these misunderstandings. I'd say that from the point on where Mr Santin got involved, many things were cleared up and solved."

The Narrator then said that Mr Sugar was still unhappy after the transfer, and produced the Santin invoice from a Swiss

Company.......The invoice was mis-spelt and described Gazza as Paul Cascoine, and Lazio as Latio....

Mr Sugar: "It came as a bolt out of the blue! He tells me that the man wants 5%, and he said to me 'Yeah, I know, I know, it's come to me as shock also..I know, I know I told you that, and he didn't tell me NOTHING!.. He didn't say anything...He just came along...I thought we'd just got to give him a drink.' This resulted in me having a telephone conversation with Gino Santin with Venables on the other end of the line also, as a conference call....I was speaking to Santin for the first time and his attitude was very abrupt. He was like...'I don't even want to discuss it..Don't even tell me I'm not getting a fee....Don't talk to me about all this bull-shit!' were his words..I mean people don't do anything for noth-ing, basically that is a realistic comment as far as I am concerned, but I said to Terry, 'You told me that you didn't discuss a fee'....Venables said..'I didn't'..Santin starts to get all aeriated on the phone and basically says 'Look, I can just as well walk away from this transaction and stuff this situation', and I could see that this guy had a pretty violent temper, a typical Latin, and I said, 'Terry, you'd better sort it out with him.' "

The Narrator: "Venables also states that Santin's demand for payment was as big a surprise to him as it was to Sugar."

Terry Venables: "He done an absolutely magnificent first-class job. The problem was Alan Sugar, like he always thinks someone is stealing his money, he's neurotic about his money, so I said I would trust Gino completely. Gino never asked for money, I must be fair, and Alan said when he did ask for it in the begin-ning....'You never said that at the beginning'. ....And he didn't!"

The Narrator: Santin does not agree. He says that what started as a favour soon developed into a different role. He says when he started 'his company has to be paid'. He was paid on September 9th 1991. When the interviewer asked him to explain this, and why the Company was not registered and used an accommoda-tion address overseas, Santin ended the interview."

The cheque was in fact cashed. An inquiry to the Trusting Hand Company who operated from the Swiss address was met with a refusal to discuss Mr Santin.

Terry Venables:... "As far as I am concerned Santin was responsible for getting us over £6 million and for arranging two games with Lazio which earned us a further £300,000. He could have quite easily gone and done it for Lazio and we would have got £2 million less. He knew the breaking point of us and the breaking point of Lazio. He was instrumental in getting that deal done, there is no shadow of a doubt."

When Sugar came to power he alleged that Venables told him that they were only going to get £4.8 million for Gascoigne.

Alan Sugar:..."It was the subject of one of our first Board meetings. He advised the Board the money on the table from Lazio at the moment was about £4.8 million and the difficulties were in getting them to pay it, as Gascoigne was injured and like anybody with half a brain, they are not going to pay money across unless the goods they are buying are first-class. That's our understanding."

Although Lazio say that Santin was crucial to the negotiations, he did not raise the price.

The Managing Director of Lazio:..."I would like to repeat that when Mr Santin got involved the price was already established. Mr Santin was mainly involved at a crucial point which had nothing to do with an increase of the price, but only with the two guarantees that had to be given i.e. Gascoigne's ability to play ball and making the money immediately available to Tottenham."

The £5.5 million was on the table on June 20th 1991 TWO WEEKS BEFORE SANTIN GOT INVOLVED, AND THERE IS A LETTER TO PROVE IT. Alan Sugar stated that he was shocked, absolutely shocked with himself for being such a mug. Venables claimed he knew nothing about any letter and that everybody was saying there was £5.5 million on the table from the beginning. Asked if there was any explanation he says....."I don't know."

Venables then made a remarkable statement. He offered to pay a quarter of a million pounds to charity if anyone could prove that the offer was not as he stated. Alternatively, if it could not be proved, then those people who were accusing him should do likewise.

Alan Sugar:....."I saw Terry Venables as a lot of people do, in fact a very wise football man, knows everything about football, a very good entrepreneur, owns clubs and pubs, Barcelona and everything, made games and written articles and written books, all this type of thing, and I steamed in, in the normal Alan Sugar way, head first without any checking and I have only got myself to blame."

With reference to the aforementioned Landhurst Leasing Company, Dispatches was able to report that they had gone bankrupt in 1992 with debts of over £60 million, and that the Company is being investigated by the Serious Fraud Office. They also discovered that after Venables borrowed £1 million, he was committed to monthly interest repayments of over £55,000!....Venables said that he could demonstrate quite clearly that he provided personal funds of £1.4 million to buy Tottenham, not actually saying from where those funds emanated.

Alan Sugar:....."Anyway, make a long story short, comes the time to part with the 'mazuma', part with the cheque, Eddie Ashby calls me to one side and tells me there is a hitch. Terry's money isn't in place and won't be until the next day.

"In fact, I laid out the whole of the purchase money and I got it back ten days later. There's me, banging my hands on the table with the lawyers in true Sugar style, insisting that the deal goes through that night, and Ashby tells me there's a problem. I know it sounds stupid but that was really the first time I realised that Terry was using borrowed money."

The programme continued its very worthwhile investigation into the many aspects of Terry's business dealings, discovering a little more than had been shown on the Panorama programme, but nothing which has not been written about in this book, either by way of interview or Court hearing.

There was another conflicting statement from Frank McLintock, and you surely would have discovered by the time that you have read this entire two volumed chronology that there are more conflicting statements from almost everyone involved, than can be calculated on an adding machine.

Shortly before this book was ready for printing there were several stories in the press about many aspects of life at Tottenham. A new saga involved loans to Spurs players, including the new Manager Ossie Ardiles, which were never repaid and had been written off. Apart from Ardiles, who joined in the 70's while

Spurs were being managed by Keith Burkenshaw, Mabbutt who has been there for twelve years and Chris Waddle who was signed by Peter Shreeves when he was first Manager in the early 80's, the players who had received these payments were all under Terry's management.

Alan Sugar has pleaded that these matters should not be allowed to harm Tottenham since the Club is now virtually under new management. Irregularities at Swindon Town caused that club to be relegated, but this will surely be inappropriate for Spurs now that the new regime is in place. He also promised that nothing like that will ever occur again while Tottenham is under his control....

I, for one, believe Sugar totally, and I will continue to support Spurs even if he fails in his bid for final peace and we find ourselves playing in the lower Divisions next year.... As for Terry.... There is nobody more disappointed than I, after the letter he sent me, to find that I have been idolising a fallen hero.

Let's hope that the media have reason to report Tottenham's successes in the near future.

Chapter 6
THE FIRST WAVE SPORT MANAGEMENT STORY

The £58,750 paid in cash

ON 21st SEPTEMBER 1993 FRANK McLINTOCK WROTE AN ARTICLE IN THE EVENING STANDARD.

A payment was made to his Company, First Wave Sport Management, of £58,750 in cash by Tottenham Hotspur.

It was stated that no fee was paid to him for that article.

Frank is a full partner in First Wave Sport Management Services.

Frank took the decision to write the full story (as he put it) to end all the innuendo and rumour, which was damaging his reputation. He denied that he was involved in any kind of 'bung' and said that in this matter he had acted in the best interests of Teddy Sheringham and Tottenham Hotspur, both of whom he represented at the same time.

Frank claims that his services were utilised so often that he became part of the Tottenham team and had his own parking place.

"My relationship," he wrote, "started when Terry asked me to represent Paul Stewart, with regard to a new contract. Terry was worried about the stories that suggested Paul was homesick for the North."

(Paul Stewart comes from Moss Side in Manchester and was transferred to Tottenham from Manchester City. It was rumoured that his wife could not settle in London.)

Frank claims to have sorted Stewart out but six months later the problem arose again. Terry was worried about the effect of Stewart's unhappiness on the fans so soon after Paul Gascoigne transferred to Lazio. Frank claims to have sorted matters out, but it was clear that Stewart wanted to leave, so Terry asked him to sound out clubs in the North. Manchester United, Aston Villa and Liverpool were all interested. Stewart eventually moved to Liver-

111

pool for two and a half million pounds. (He cost 1.75 million originally.) After that Frank worked on the Andy Gray transfer from Crystal Palace to Spurs.

(He does not explain what he actually did.)

Frank then claims to have worked on the transfer of Neil Ruddock from Southampton to Spurs. Again he does not describe what he actually did. Incidentally, Ruddock is the first and only player to be re-signed by Spurs after being sold off. It was Terry Venables who originally sold him back to Millwall, following the loss by Tottenham to Port Vale in an F.A. Cup round.

Frank claims in the article that he spent a lot of time persuading Terry that Ruddock was a good player and he was who Spurs needed.

(Seeing how Ruddock had been at Spurs previously, after signing from Millwall, this would appear to be a wasted effort...! Frank was Assistant Manager at Millwall when Ruddock left them to join Spurs for the first time.)

Frank claims that it took him three months to complete the deal, after a Tribunal hearing to confirm the fee.

He also stated that he and his Partner, Graham Smith (former Director, Chelsea Football Club), travelled to Australia, America, Germany, Holland, Spain and Borneo on behalf of Tottenham.... He also claims that First Wave spent £69,000 on all this.

Frank says that he also went to Australia to look at Mark Bosnich, the goalkeeper who is now with Aston Villa, and brought a Russian and a Jugoslavian footballer for Spurs to look at, personally paying their air fares and expenses.

(Looking at Bosnich so soon after Venables had signed Erik Thorstvedt from Norway...! Neither the Russian or the Jugo signed for Spurs!)

Frank says that Precki, the Jugoslavian, was based in the USA and now plays for Everton. Spurs only paid the player's hotel bill while in this country.

Frank went to Borneo to fix up a game for Spurs.

(What a wide brief he had. It seems that Terry was doing nothing while Frank was doing all the graft and paying for it himself, to boot!)

He further states that he met with Terry and some American businessmen who wanted some form of licence to manufacture and distribute sportswear in that Country.

"There were hundreds of telephone calls. We spent our own money on videos of foreign players. We also helped to fix up overseas trips for the Chief Scout at Tottenham, Ted Buxton. I was virtually a part-time employee at Tottenham....

It is important that we mention that Frank was originally involved with Teddy Sheringham's transfer to Notts. Forest from Millwall, when he was there as assistant manager. Important because he states that Millwall received two million pounds for the player at that time.

The article mentioned disbursements by First Wave of £69,000 without relating this figure in any direct way to the £58,750 originally paid by Tottenham, or revealing its ultimate destination.

It was interesting and informative, as far as it went, but it left a number of questions unanswered.

At 8.30 on the morning of Tuesday 5th of October I therefore contacted Frank McLintock at his home. I wanted to ask him why his Company's invoice to Spurs for services rendered was paid in cash, and whether he would show me documented proof that the money was wholly or partly paid in connection with his involvement with the Teddy Sheringham transfer from Notts Forest to Tottenham.

Initially, he refused to meet with me but then volunteered some interesting details and finally agreed to a meet when his Partner, Graham Smith, returned from holiday.

I suggested to him that it had been alleged that he was no more than a collector for a source, alleged by Alan Sugar to be Brian Clough, the Nottingham Forest Manager at the time of the Sheringham transfer, who might be the ultimate recipient of the money. I further suggested that it had been alleged in some quarters that the £8,750 included in the payment was not, (as had been indicated by him and the Channel Four programme, Dispatches), the VAT, but his Company's personal fee, leaving the balance of £50,000 for the alleged 'bung'....

The reason for the return to Spurs of £8,750, in cash, where it was left in the safe and later discovered by Colin Sandy, was that Terry Venables had insisted that Frank's fee should come out of the overall £50,000 — for whatever purpose that had been paid — coincidentally the exact equivalent of the VAT on the sum of £50,000.

To explain the incident that has been highlighted by the media, First Wave were purported to have acted on behalf of Terry Venables in his capacity as Chief Executive of Tottenham Hotspur in the delicate negotiations surrounding the capture of the Centre-Forward of Nottingham Forest, Teddy Sheringham. At the time Spurs were reported as trying to sign the player, the newspapers ended almost every story with the conclusion that Brian Clough would not release him, particularly as Notts. Forest had made such a miserable start to the season.

We then all woke up one morning, some three weeks into the '92/'93 Season, astonished to read that Teddy had signed for Spurs the previous night.

Subsequently, First Wave submitted an invoice to Tottenham for the amount of £58,750.

Peculiarly, and indeed what has caused the trauma, is that Frank claims that he received a telephone call from 'someone at Spurs' to come to White Hart Lane and collect his money; having rung Terry Venables on several occasions because his Company needed payment having expended a great deal of costs for which they had not been reimbursed.

(You will read later in the legal chapters, that Alan Sugar has a very different view on how that sum was demanded by Frank McLintock.)

When Frank arrived at Spurs he was handed a bag, and in it was the £58,750 IN CASH. Subsequent to that collection, Terry Venables, who was not at the Ground when the money was handed over, telephoned Frank, and in a heated discussion demanded that £8,750 be returned. Terry insisted that Frank's invoice should have read...£50,000 INCLUDING VAT and not net of VAT. Subsequently, Frank stated that he personally returned the £8,750 which he saw being placed in the safe.

I told Frank during our telephone conversation that I was not out to castigate anyone and that I was prepared to allow him as much space as he needed to satisfy the readers and the public at large that the deal was as he had explained it. One certain way was to show me, acting as a sort of auditor, what had happened to the £50,000.

It really is quite simple. You receive some money, and you bank it and a statement from the bank proves it. If the Partners took some of the money for themselves before banking the residue, they surely would have banked some or all of it in their own personal bank accounts. Supposing they had paid some pressing bills with part of the money, then they would be able to demonstrate the acceptance by the creditors of some cash in settlement of outstanding invoices.

One way or another an audit trail would prove beyond doubt that they did not merely act simply as couriers for somebody else....

Frank's answer found the only explainable alternative.

"I can't demonstrate that to you, as we each took half of that fee. I put my half into my other business and Graham paid for a house extension with his. The builder who did the job may be able to confirm that, but if he didn't declare the cash he was paid with on his VAT return, then he obviously won't say anything. I can tell you that we have received all sorts of hassle over this. Graham is fuming at the allegations that we collected the money for Brian Clough. It just isn't true."

"What other business do you have, Frank?"

"I have a sort of electrical franchise business in Edmonton. I'm actually on my way there now to meet with an Australian agent. I franchise computers, televisions, audio stuff, things like that. I'm shortly opening another shop."

"Frank, I would repeat, we are not out to discredit you, but if you can clear this matter up, your agency will appear from the cloud.... The side effect will be that allegations against Brian Clough will be withdrawn and Terry Venables will be exonerated from spending Spurs' money inappropriately. What this will do for all of you, is to wipe the slate clean. I am offering you this chance."

"There are so many agents in this game that don't know a f..... g thing about football, and we do. We are not one of those that go around making all sorts of demands that are outrageous. You have to know the people in the game first.''

I then asked: "Why did Terry need you to negotiate anything for him in the first place? He was on good terms with Brian Clough, since the Spurs-Notts. Forest Cup Final. Why didn't he deal with it himself?''

"You have to know about managers' egos. When an enquiry is made for a player, the first reaction is: 'I'm not selling him to that cheapskate. He only wants to buy players cheap, and then sell them on for big profits.' So, to avoid this, Terry appointed me to act as the intermediary.''

"For £50,000?''

"That bill was for more than just the Teddy Sheringham transfer. I was involved with the Paul Stewart transfer to Liverpool, and with the Neil Ruddock transfer from Southampton. Much appreciation I got from him, too! He just left without so much as a thank you Frank! At least when clubs deal with me, they know they are dealing with someone who knows about the game and knows how it carries on. I have spoken to the Customs people and the Tax men and they are satisfied with everything.''

"Frank, give me the opportunity to tell the world about it and you are all in the clear, including Terry!''

"O.K., ring me Thursday week when Graham is back off holiday and we'll meet.''

(At no time did Frank ask for a fee, although I explained that we were prepared to pay for time lost and personal expenses incurred during interview.)

It is important to say that several newspapers printed a statement from Alan Sugar that, during discussions with Terry Venables while he was in office, Terry was alleged to have told him that "We need the fifty grand for a sweetener. It's the sort of thing that is done in football. You know nothing about the game; leave it all to me....''

Was the payment to McLintock's Company the sweetener he was purported to have told Alan Sugar about...?

Frank then went on to tell me that there was another invoice that he had submitted to Spurs for £10,000 plus VAT which was for additional services involved with the assessment and possible signing of other players, some of which did not materialise.

I did not pursue this further because I was mainly concerned at the time with the investigation of that one particular payment of £50,000. It seemed an awful lot of money (whether or not it included VAT) especially when Terry Venables and Brian Clough could have negotiated in their capacities as Managers of their respective clubs. Why should Venables and Clough, who have continually complained about agents, need an intermediary? Do managers and football clubs now need agent representation. Additionally, while I am reliably informed that Teddy Sheringham likes to do his own 'trading' with the clubs, being a bright and intelligent man, it is widely known that it is Frank McLintock who represents the player.

The scenario, as I understand it, was that Teddy Sheringham's Agent, Frank McLintock, was talking to the agent who was acting for Spurs, who was Frank McLintock, the Club paying for those services, to the tune of some sixty thousand pounds, while the two managers and the player himself played little or no part. This, when the fee for Teddy's signature was in excess of two million pounds. If only on the basis of vested interest, Frank surely had no moral right to act for both parties.

Ten days later...
I telephoned Graham Smith at First Wave and he told me that Frank had not been in touch as he had only been back from holiday for one day, but if he could help in any way, he certainly would welcome the opportunity to clear up the matter.

We made an appointment for Monday 25th October at 1 pm.

We arrived at the appointed time, my business associate Mr Tony Marchant and I, in Biggleswade, to make our way up to the second floor into a suite of sparsely furnished and well worn carpeted offices. Graham's own office was small, above a dentist's suite, and it was clearly obvious that the enterprise was being run within a low overhead budget, or maybe it was having cash-flow problems!

There appeared to be only one employee, a secretary, Sue. Certainly with all the high-profile tasks undertaken by this firm, I would have expected somewhat more salubrious surroundings .

There wasn't even a lift to take us up to the second floor, suite

17c. The entrance was narrow and restricting, the stairs the same. The walls of Graham's office were adorned with memorabilia and the desk was covered with papers, giving the impression that the organisation was active and busy. During the two-hour interview, he said that he only had until two o'clock as another client was due. No-one, in fact, had arrived by the time we came to leave, which was two forty five. During this period, the phone rang twice.

"The first thing that I would ask you, Mr Smith, is when was First Wave Sport Services formed?"

"Nearly four years ago," Graham Smith told us, "and it was an offshoot of a company called CMR Productions Ltd. We bought the sports-marketing arm of that business out, after I had left Chelsea Football Club, where I had been a Director for fifteen years. Our main business is sports marketing. We do have some soccer players."

"When did you form a partnership with Frank McLintock?"

"Approximately three years ago. Obviously, it was because of Frank's name and who he is. Frank has a rapport with the soccer fraternity. We could capitalise in the market place. He has a lot of expertise and knowledge and credibility in the game. Some agents don't have this and know nothing about the game, but Frank has been a player and a manager and coach and is now a soccer pundit."

"Frank is still a partner?"

"Yes, he's still here."

"Among the players that you represent, is Teddy Sheringham one of them, specifically?"

"First of all, Teddy is his own man. Teddy was also represented by Frank, under the name of First Wave, when Teddy moved to Nottingham Forest from Millwall, and again when he moved to London, Tottenham Hotspur, from Nottingham Forest. If any commercial deals can be set up, we will offer them to Teddy; if we can do a deal then fine. Teddy is an articulate man and is quite capable of doing quite a bit for himself. Great. But if we can capitalise on certain opportunities, then we will. That is what our trade is all about."

"When you represented Teddy and also Tottenham, was there a conscious vested interest that you were aware of?"

"Well, the situation was quite simple. We were actually in the Teddy Sheringham business doing Tottenham a favour. The money that we were paid by them was not for Teddy Sheringham solely. We were used, if you like, as a conduit in the whole of the situation because we had the car of the player. We didn't negotiate with Nottingham Forest. We can't negotiate with Nottingham Forest. It isn't allowed."

"Why is that? You did, after all, negotiate with Terry Venables."

"For Teddy's contract, yes, absolutely. We didn't negotiate anything to do with the fee and we didn't speak to Notts. Forest. The negotiations were done on a club to club basis."

"Between Chairmen and Managers?"

"Between Terry Venables and an official of Nottingham Forest, which I am not party to"

The phone rang, but Sue, the Secretary took the call.

"The subject of the £58,750 is primarily the point of this interview. We are here to establish beyond irrevocable doubt its whereabouts and its destination. I fully understand that the balance over £50,000 is an amount equal to the VAT, and Terry asked you to accept that the amount of £50,000 should include this amount.... That seemed to be for a number of services, some of which weren't successfully concluded.... There is a very fine line between working for someone under instruction, and an agent getting paid for results. Endemic in the word 'Agent' is to be paid for achievement."

"No, not necessarily so. To clarify that, the situation with any client is that he takes you on, and refers to the original agreement regarding the modus operandi. How you are being paid and what you are being paid for."

"Do you have such an agreement with Tottenham?"

"We had expended a lot of monies, a lot of time. Most of the time when those things are unsuccessful, you don't bill the people for it, but when the occasion arises, and you do have something successful, you capitalise on it to cover the failures."

"In effect the customer gets charged for the failures, anyway?"

No answer to that specific point, but Graham then hastily continued....

"That's what happened with Terry. We said, 'Look Terry,

you have asked us to deal with certain things. You want Teddy
Sheringham. We have Teddy's ear. We knew he was Forest's
man. It's about time you paid us some money. We have been
overseas and to a lot of meetings etc., and we could do with the
money.''

"Why America? To sign players?''

"No, this was nothing to do with players. You yourself said that
we carried out a lot of functions for Terry. It encompassed a lot
of activities.''

"When the Russian came here and he wasn't selected, that
wasn't your fault?''

"No, that was nothing to do with us. We had the opportunity.
Part of my business is away from the commercial side. We have a lot
of opportunities with fast-moving sportswear, Terry Venables
came to us....''

"He definitely came to you?''

"Yes, emphatically. He came to us and said 'We are doing a lot
of things at Spurs. We are getting involved in merchandising, and
we are looking at the trade show in Atlanta.' We were in touch
with a major sportswear company that wanted Tottenham rights
to produce related merchandise in America. We did a market
study. We went over there and carried out a study.''

"Terry Venables asked you to go?''

"Yes, absolutely. It was one of the things we were doing for
Spurs. Now when the Sheringham thing came up, and Terry was
desperate for the deal to go through, Frank said to Terry: 'I want
the money. You know that you owe us this money.'

"Getting money off of a lot of football clubs is difficult, but
Terry has always been a very straight guy, and he has always been
fair. Frank has done other things for him as well, which if he wants
to tell you about them that's up to him. They were not illegal
things, other things which were for the benefit of Tottenham
Hotspur Football Club regarding players. We felt that the figure
was a fair one to put on it. If you look at it logically, it only involved
Teddy Sheringham slightly for those services. If you look at it logically, look how much they could make on him now.''

"Logically, Mr Smith, Teddy's contract with Nottingham
Forest wasn't up. They had had an awful start to the season, and

for weeks Brian Clough said, 'No, no, no', and suddenly the public woke up one morning to find Teddy had signed. What changed Brian's mind? What suddenly made him release his top goal-scorer?''

"Brian's mind never changed about Teddy Sheringham!''

"O.K. what you are saying is that if the money was right, Clough would have let him go at any time?''

"If the truth was only known, Brian was not overjoyed with Teddy. He had scored goals, but Brian said his pace was suspect, and something else, Nottingham Forest play a certain way and Teddy didn't fit that. If you look at the history of what Brian had done in the previous twelve months, you would know that a number of people were brought on board, a number of overseas players were tried as strikers, you will see that they were definitely looking for a replacement. There is no doubt about that.''

"So the absolute objection to his moving in that first part of the season was all newspaper gossip?''

"I can't say anything about that.''

"You never heard or read that?''

"No, not at all.''

"So you weren't surprised when Teddy approached you to handle it for him?''

"It was certainly no bother for Teddy, because Tottenham Hotspur was a club that he would have walked on glass to play for. He is a London boy. He was made a good offer by Terry, and as I say, how much money did Nottingham Forest make on him?''

(Very little is the answer. You will recall that Frank McLintock said that Millwall received two million for him.)

"That was September 1992. When did you get the call from Terry Venables asking you to collect the money. The fifty grand?''

"I didn't get the call. I wasn't here. You need to talk to Frank about that. All I did....''

"Look, Graham, you are part of this business, a partner and you had no interest in when £58,000 was being paid to you...? After eighteen months of spending and receiving nothing on account for it?''

"No! No! Fifty grand may seem a lot to you, but in this business that is the sort of money that changes hands frequently. You don't know how much money I made in the last twelve months. It's not something that I get terribly excited about. We have a very good business here. At the end of the day it was a straightforward invoicing situation. We had a call from the accounts department at Spurs...."

"From the accounts department?"

"Yes, exactly."

"Not from the Company Secretary or whoever was in charge of payments, like Colin Sandy or Terry himself?"

"On the invoice it was for the attention of Mr Ashby. Eddie Ashby."

"The General Manager of Tottenham...? The man who called himself General Manager?"

"To be perfectly honest with you, and I am not being facetious when I say that £50,000 is the type of transaction we invoice for: our turnover is nearly half a million pounds. This is a big business, this. You might look at the offices and think, they are not much, but we keep our exes. down as low as we can, and the profits up."

"O.K. I accept there was an invoice. Everyone has seen that, but was it Frank or yourself that got the call to say 'come along and collect, we've got it for you'?"

"It was Frank. I wasn't even in the Country."

"Did anyone tell him it would be in cash?"

"No, no-one told him that."

"So why didn't they send it through the post like any normal company? Why didn't Frank just say 'Send it'? It's very strange to get a call and rush along to the creditor, drop whatever you are doing, to collect a cheque, if you weren't advised that you were to collect cash."

"Look here Mr Nathan..." (Getting angry now!) "you are asking me questions here. If you have researched this subject you will know that Frank planted a wonderful story in the Evening Standard...so you are asking me questions...."

(Tony Marchant had a copy of the newspaper in his briefcase.)

"I think that story was incomplete."

"Well, I don't think that, fine. You have your opinions and I'll have mine...." (Getting ready to throw us out!) "You know what happened. When Frank McLintock turned up at Tottenham Hotspur, quite frankly, he was given cash. He was staggered by this...! Why he was given cash, you should ask the Spurs people. We didn't ask for cash. If you have spoken to Terry, you will know the answer. He should tell you the story."

"Was Terry the one to hand over the money?"

"Terry Venables wasn't even in his office at that time."

(Didn't really mean to trap him, but what's the use of me speaking to Terry when he wasn't even there when the money was handed over?)

"I'm not being funny about this, but I wasn't involved. Frank is the one to ask about this. I can certainly try and help you. That is the idea of speaking to you here this afternoon."

Tony Marchant interceded:

"Look here Mr Smith, we are here to get the truth. We all hope to earn a bit, but most of all Guy wants to relate the truth to the public. That is why we are here."

"I understand. You'll get the truth because this is going further. There is going to be a Commission at the Football Association, an enquiry. There is a High Court case going on, and if Alan Sugar makes allegations against Brian Clough, then there is a potential litigatory situation. The other thing is that you have got to understand, when any money is paid to a company, it is entered into the books and the relevant taxes are paid."

"Can I just pursue the point that you have just made...? I have spoken to Frank as you know. I was on the phone to him for about half an hour.... I want you to know, and I cannot impress you sufficiently on this point, that if I could be satisfied about the ultimate destination of that fifty thousand, the matter is then dead. You, Brian Clough, Frank and Terry are in the clear."

"I'm not being funny, but I've had the decency to let you come here and take my time, and I'm telling you what happened. It's our money and we have paid the tax on it. Here are the accounts...." (Shouting now!) "I'm not giving them to you, but look, there are the figures for the current year ending June '93. Anyone in authority who wants to check it out, be they Inland Revenue, Customs and Excise, or anyone who needs to know...."

"It is I who needs to know...."

"But I'm not showing them to you."

"Mr Smith, can I explain? You have been a Director of a football club, Chelsea, and you will know as I do, the normal procedure. If you showed me your VAT return for the relevant period NOW, I wouldn't be able to determine whether that fifty grand was included in it. I wouldn't be able to identify that single payment. We all know that what you send to the VAT is a consolidated turnover figure, and without the backing documents relating to that figure, the detailed analysis, and not the summary, they are meaningless for this enquiry. As are the accounts you have flashed in front of me, because they are your annual accounts and do not show individual receipts. In any case they are not yet approved by the Inland Revenue, they are only the audited set."

"Every entry was made in the books, when we received the money and when the money was paid into the bank."

"A) Sir, you are refusing to show me that, and B) Frank tells me that you never paid any of that money into your business account, yet you state that you have paid tax and VAT on it. You must admit that it does seem rather bizarre."

"I don't have to show you anything. Why should I?"

"With respect, that is what we are here for. To give you the opportunity to clear this up."

"I don't have to show you anything." (Shouting again wildly!)

"What about Terry? You profess that he has always been straight down the line, that he gave your company plenty of work, yet you refuse to help him. One sight of the proof that I am asking you for, and he is back in consideration for another job in this Country, and who knows, perhaps even the England job."

"This is all sub judice."

"No it isn't. That is a reason that Alan Sugar used on television and everyone jumps on the bandwagon."

"Oh yes it is. There is going to be an enquiry about all this."

"Going to be? Going to be...? Not yet and possibly not ever. I have the feeling that an enquiry into anything more than the transfer values of players at Tottenham will be a major embarrassment to the F.A. and it is not in their interests to appoint a QC or anyone else who might have judicial powers."

"Sorry Mr Nathan. You will have to take my word for it."

"I don't doubt you as a man, Graham, but what can I say to a hundred thousand readers that the Partner in First Wave was not prepared to disclose evidence of the destination of £50,000? All you do is leave the question mark over you, and Frank and Terry."

Tony Marchant, attempting to cool things down:

"Let me say something. Without you and Terry we can only put in the book what we learn. If we can say that Graham Smith let us see this or that it clears everything up. What goes in the book is the truth."

"Why don't you address the problem...? You see, I have got to be careful what I do.... I am going to be perfectly honest with you now.... But this is.... I can actually take certain people to task. There's a lot of things that the newspapers have said.... I am now prepared to contact my lawyer about this. If I can actually show you the entries in the books, then fine. Until I get the O.K. from him I can't do that."

"Mr Smith, Mr Smith.... You are a businessman. You don't need to ask a solicitor for permission to show us the receipt of one single cash transaction included in a whole host of others....

"What I am suggesting to you is to ask the Customs and Excise people."

(Did he think, I wondered at this point, that we were brought in on the back of a donkey? Surely he must have known as well as anyone that the Authorities will not show us other company's documents!)

"Mr Smith, all we would find is the summary of the whole quarter's return. Unless we or they demanded a break-down of the input figure, we could never detect the one receipt that we are discussing...."

"They've been along and they have seen it."

(At this point I remembered an audit that I had once done which showed tax and VAT being paid on an invoice, but the money iteslf wasn't banked or accounted for....)

"If we could write that Mr Graham Smith then pulled out a document and showed us what we needed to know, that, Sir, ends the acrimony that is creeping into this interview. We are not here to trap you. We only require a simple sight of the bank statement, the withdrawal, anything like that and you are all in the clear. If we could just say we saw that the money was banked the next day."

"It wasn't banked the next day. Frank kept the money. Then he had to go back to Spurs and he saw Peter Barnes."

"To put the £8,750 back in the safe. Yes we are aware of that."

"And Spurs received a credit note, saying that the bill had been changed and that was it. We are not going to send credit notes and invoices to a club like Tottenham Hotspur, where the money can be traced back if we were doing anything untoward. Why should we take £50,000 and give it to this, allegedly, to this Brian Clough, and then pay tax on it? Pay the VAT on it, and go through all this rigmarole? It's utter nonsense if you look at it logically."

"To look at it logically, and maybe it is illogical, why is it impossible for you to allow me to trace the £50,000? Whatever people do, cash, cheque, draft, whatever, it is easy to raise invoices and credit notes and to make entries into books. Why won't you show me the whereabouts of the physical cash...? There is always an audit trail. Signed receipts, bank statements, cash purchases, anything, but it can always be traced."

"It can be traced, Frank must have told you what we did with it."

"Yes he did."

"If you have nothing to hide tell me what he told you." he suggested.

"Certainly.... He told me that the money did not physically go into this Company's bank account."

"I know. It came out of drawings."

"Sure, you can do that. If this isn't a Limited Company you can just draw what you want.... I know that."

"If you speak to my accountant...hang on, maybe that is the best thing to do...George Hey and Company.

"They won't speak to us without your authority and not before you have primed them. Their loyalty is to their clients."

"To be perfectly honest with you, what I don't like is, and I have been fair with you..." (Ha Ha!) "and there is only so much

126

that I am prepared to give you...NOT THAT I AM TRYING TO BE EVASIVE...NOT THAT I AM TRYING TO BE IN ANY WAY INTRANSIGENT WITH YOU...I am just telling you that that is the way it has to be. Until I get clearance, I didn't know what you were coming here for today."

"Hang on: I advised you on the telephone what the purpose of this meeting would be, and you must have spoken to Frank."

"Frank hasn't even spoken to me about it." (Pull the other one, Graham.)

"Just to clarify everything. Frank said that you split the money and he paid for some computer equipment and you used yours to pay for your house extension."

"Well, I don't see that I have to give that information to you."

"You don't have to GIVE anything to me, but it is in everyone's interest that you do, and I can find no reason for not doing so, if everything is above board as you say."

"I've got nothing to hide."

"Did you pay for your extension with that money? It only needs a simple yes or no."

"I had money of my own, but yes I did use that money for carpets and curtains and the building costs, which were all paid by cash."

(Dear me, according to Graham Smith, everyone deals in cash these days! At least those mentioned to me, that Graham Smith deals with.)

"I don't want people to know my business...."

(Why then did Frank talk to the Evening Standard?)

"At the end of the day, whatever aspersions are cast, I know what happened to that money and everything will be proved at the right time."

"Mr Smith, the right time for Terry Venables is YESTERDAY!"

"I would prefer the case to come to its logical conclusion, and that is, I am before the Football Association on the 26th of November. I would prefer you to go through the public channels, and with respect to you, I know you are writing this book, and I have said that I will try to help you, but to be perfectly honest with you, nobody is party to our information at this time apart from the

Inland Revenue, Customs and Excise, my Accountant and what is in that sworn affidavit…,"

(What sworn affidavit?)

"…and I am not prepared to divulge anything unless my Accountant and my Lawyer says it is O.K. to show these people the entry in the books."

(I did not pursue the matter of the 'sworn affidavit' as I already had the information on that in the Court papers.)

"I'm sorry Mr Smith. That isn't what we are talking about. I have explained about entries and documents and invoices. What I require to clear up in this matter in favour of you and Terry is evidence of what happened to the £50,000. The physical whereabouts of FIFTY THOUSAND POUNDS. It is a lot of notes and a lot of ready cash. It is the physical application of cash that is in question here; NOT the entries, NOT the invoices and NOT summarised accounts."

"In other words, what happened to the fifty K?"

"Exactly. Where is it? What was done with it? Did Frank keep it for several days in his house and then bank it, split it and what happened to it then?"

"I think he put his into his account, but I didn't."

"You said that you paid the builder with it."

"O.K. I did."

"Then you must have receipts, his invoices etc."

"You must be joking! If this is what you are looking for."

"I'm only looking for the truth, if only for Terry's sake."

"Look, if this is what you want I can give you the builder's name, but you will get no joy there. I paid him in cash and he didn't put it through his books. Nor probably did the shops that I bought the carpets from and the curtains. I can give you their names if you want. What can happen is that these people might get into some sort of trouble if there is an investigation. The Inspector of Taxes can come to me and say 'right, this £25,000 and what Mr McLintock's got; what have you done with it?' I'd say 'go and see this one and that one and I paid cash for the extension and the other things'. Obviously they wouldn't be paying the VAT."

"There is no VAT on buildings, so why should the builder have to hide it?"

"So, O.K., but the curtain and carpet people would have to. I spent £11,000 on those things. With respect to you, I don't see why I should have to explain these things to you. I am not being funny, who the hell are you? Terry Venables hasn't called me to say that you are coming. I don't even know if he knows you."

"Look, I am writing a book on events that involve you. It wouldn't really matter if Terry advised you or not. You are giving me information for a book that I am writing so as to enable the public to read the truth on all the matters about which they are confused. It is simply that. Terry Venables has no meaning here."

"I can literally tell you now, if my Lawyer is happy about giving you the information then you can have it."

"All I am saying, to repeat myself, is that I want to be able to tell the F.A., Alan Sugar, the public at large and any QC or investigator that is interested, Tom, Dick and Harry, that this is what happened to £50,000, beyond irrevocable doubt. So far, it is a matter of not being convinced, it is a matter of not being shown that absolute proof. I would like above all else to bring Terry back to the people without a doubt in their minds, and that beyond doubt the money did not go to another manager of another football club. If that option was open to me and it was my credibility that was in doubt, Graham, I would be screaming it from the rooftops. If I was a former director of a football club, if I was a captain of a double-winning side, if I had taken Barcelona to a European Cup Final, like Terry, and won the Spanish League, I would WANT to tell you these things, assuming our positions were reversed."

"O.K. Alright, two things. You want to clear Terry Venables' name? If you wanted to do this and I was Terry, I would have rung me or Frank and said I want you to do this for me. I haven't heard a word from Terry. Not a word about you."

"I shouldn't think that Terry knows that we are here. I don't seek his permission. I would still like to go to him and say I've got it. The other thing that you don't know is that Terry is thinking of writing his life story. We won't be the Publishers, but he wishes for me to consider ghost-writing it. He therefore has a conflict of interests. If he tells me more than he already has, will it detract from his autobiography? I can tell you that he isn't ready to write it anyway. His life is far from finished. His career isn't finished, and won't be if you clear this matter up for me."

"I don't think that you know everything that there is to know."

"Mr Smith, nobody knows everything. My knowledge won't increase either if you continue to deny me the access I seek."

"I don't know what happened between Terry and Alan Sugar, but I do know a lot more."

"I am not here to exonerate Terry Venables if the facts show otherwise, but the way that things are currently stacking up, it seems that regardless of whether you or Frank was paid large sums of money, Alan Sugar or his man signed the cheques in the first place. So in the end it is Terry, by way of circumstance, that we will be helping. It surely is Terry that needs whatever help he can get. Sugar is O.K. He still has his job and Terry nothing. Nothing has yet been proved either. All that we know is that Terry has suffered because he couldn't match Sugar's ability to pay enormous court fees."

"What I am saying to you, Mr Nathan, is that he hasn't rung me up to advise that there are two guys going around to help him. You have asked me to elaborate on public knowledge, by asking what has happened to the money. That, basically, is what you want. I can stand up in a Court of Law and say, yes, we had the £50,000, yes, we took the money, no problem."

"Yes, problem. Because I told you that an accounting action is not a result. Effectively, the money should have been paid into your business account and transferred out to the two drawers. Instead, it went straight into your own accounts and that's it. Well, to be precise into Frank's account, you say, and into your pocket or under the bed or something."

"Look, I say we have paid our taxes. I don't understand why, I am not an accountant, but everything went through the books. As a partnership we are allowed to take what we want. It is not a Limited Company. You can go and see the builder, do what you like. I don't mind. Ask him and he will tell you to fuck-off. He won't disclose his books to you especially if he didn't put it through his own books. The man tends to speak with his fists before his mouth, so be careful. You'll get him into trouble with the Tax people. You understand what I am saying. I don't want to get people into trouble, but if you choose to see him, then be it on your own head…. Quite frankly I can say to you there is a shop in St Ives and a shop in Chateris, Cambridgeshire, who took cash for the goods that they supplied for the extension. I have got to say this to you, the Tax Man might get them into trouble. I am not wanting to hurt them, you understand these things? I would be doing them a disservice. So, honestly, how can I take you one step further?"

"Let's talk a bit about the extension. You had that commissioned on the strength of the twenty five 'k' you were expecting from Tottenham?"

"No, I had my own money for most of it before it would all fall due, but I did have to buy the extras. All in all the whole lot came to more than thirty thousand."

The phone rang for a second time. Sue took it again and Graham was not disturbed. There was no sign of the impending visitor, or of Frank McLintock….

"As far as I see it there is still a litigation situation involving Alan Sugar and Terry Venables."

"Are you being called as an official witness?"

No answer….

"Venables as far as I am aware is still fighting, and I am not prepared to tell you any more. In my book this particular situation is still sub judice."

"I am not aware of any court case in this session of the courts. As far as I know Terry may sue for loss of contract, but I believe that that will be resolved out of court. The F.A. enquiry is not on yet, and in any case we don't know and nor do they whether the QC, if appointed, will have judicial powers. There is absolutely nothing preventing you from clearing up your name and the names of the others that have been mentioned in this saga."

"Terry Venables has never let us down. His image across the globe is first class. I am pleased that as you find out more and more you are finding that he is the innocent party in all this. People in the game laugh at Alan Sugar. He knows nothing and suddenly he is this high profile guy, and he has done Terry wrong. You mark my words. Terry Venables has been so straight and so honest, of course I would do ANYTHING to help him. No problem whatsoever."

"WELL LET US DO IT!"

"Of course I will do ANYTHING to help him, that is what I am saying. Alright, I'll tell you what I'll do…. What do you want from me? WHAT DO YOU WANT FROM ME…? Tell me what you want, and if I can help I will. That's what I can't understand. If I have got it, I will let you have it."

"O.K. Tell me how long it took to build the extension on your house?"

"I think I started it in the…it finished in the <u>October.</u> The last payment…."

"Just after Teddy signed for Tottenham?"

"Yes, I think it was the October…."

"You never had this work done on the basis of the anticipated receipt of funds from Tottenham…? You had this money of your own?"

"Not at all…! I made three payments. Two prior to receiving the money from Spurs, and one afterwards. I spent, I think, about eleven thousand on curtains and carpets and fitting it out…."

"All in cash?"

"Yes…in cash. I have receipts. I'd show them to you, but they are at home…. Look I would want to clear anyone's name, but at the moment nobody has been accused. It is all allegations by Alan Sugar, and I would be more than happy, and I am sure that Terry would and Frank would and I am damned sure that Clough would, for someone to come outside of the courts and say, 'right, you've done that, or you haven't'. Look at this business with Ron Atkinson at the moment. Somebody is now accusing him. O.K. they have got to prove it. There will be allegation and counter-allegation, and people that know us, as we are the ones involved, know that it is a joke. Like I have said to you we want to prove to the relevant authorities that there was no underhand dealing, speak to them…."

"O.K. That is what I want to do in my book. Speak to the public. With respect to you, how many of the public, particularly those in Sweden, Denmark and Norway are being given the opportunity to read about a pending court case involving Aston Villa and Mark Bosnich…. We see our book going to South Africa, Europe, the Bahamas, and many other English speaking places in the World. We have been asked to produce it in Spanish.

It is being stocked by every major retailer in this Country. The cover has already been on display in the World Book Fair in Frankfurt.''

"Let me speak to Terry.... I'll ring him now.''

(Smith picked up the telephone and rang, but was greeted by an answerphone. He placed a message on the phone explaining that he was being confronted by two men, Guy Nathan and Tony Marchant, and he would like to speak with Terry on the matter. He asked Terry to ring him back.)

"Why isn't Frank here...? He promised a further interview.''

"He has another business.''

"With respect, Graham, we know that. You have to accept that before coming to see you we have already gathered a great deal of information.''

"You know about the builders, and the other business of Frank's....''

"Yes, and about his franchises and that he intends to open another shop and open a franchise in Australia. We know about Mr Fox, your architect, but you have not said one single word that casts doubts on what we know, so you see we are pursuing the same end to all this. How can I convince you that we are on side and only wish to get to the bottom of this with a view to helping the situation, and Terry in the process?''

"You are not out to get anybody in the shit? What about the builder? He has taken money off me.... Cash.''

"Don't know what we are going to do about him.''

"It's a fact of life that he gave me two receipts...and then another.... Look, from my own point of view I don't care. People in football will still keep me in business..., I hope Alan Sugar will trip up. He has already tripped up over the Santin affair.''

"I'm sorry, Mr Sugar hasn't slipped up. There is still a question as to why Terry didn't employ an Italian-speaking lawyer, or accountant.... Why a restaurateur...? Why an invoice from a Swiss Company? Why £200,000? Personally, I could have found an expert for a quarter of that money....''

"Look, I've got to go now. I'm expecting somebody. I'll ring you tomorrow night after I have spoken to Terry and perhaps we'll all get together and crack this....''

At this point Graham asked me to switch off the cassette recorder while he obviously wished to relate something to me 'off the record'. In the pursuit of the truth there is no such thing as 'off the record'....

Tony Marchant asked him whether he had given Mr Clough £50,000 as alleged. His reply, heard but not recorded by us was as follows verbatim:

"That thing is off isn't it...?" (I confirmed that) "...I can tell you that it was not £50,000, but if you want to help Terry, you will know what to write."

Tony then replied: "What, forty, or about thirty?"

"You are here to help Terry...? It was around thirty...ish."

"Actually three or four days after we took the money, Frank and I put a large sum into a cash conversion plan. We put equal amounts in, and I know that he drew his out of his bank account."

(What, to cover the payment to Clough? Evidence of some form of useage of large funds but not the money about which we have been questioning him?)

"Presumably you can produce those documents?"

"I'll talk to Terry and my lawyer and my accountants. See what I can show you."

"Graham, you don't need permission to show me an investment into your Partner's Australian franchise business, and the dates that you put that money in."

(To be frank we couldn't get out of there quick enough! We left so quickly that I left the tape recorder and my briefcase on his desk. Realising my mistake, I climbed the stairs as quickly as possible for me, and he was listening to it along with his Secretary, Sue.)

There was no call the following evening as promised. Nor the next night....

Then a call from Sue to say that Graham hadn't been able to speak with Terry Venables.

Finally, Tuesday the 2nd November, a call finally came from Graham Smith, explaining that he had at last heard from Terry, who had advised him not to get in touch with us and not to contribute to this book. (Too late!) Effectively, Terry Venables warned him off from providing us with the further information.

According to Smith, he had spoken to his lawyer who had said that the matters were still sub judice based on the probability that Terry would sue Alan Sugar for wrongful dismissal. Rubbish...! Sub judice is now becoming the term for 'I've got something to hide behind'.... As far as we are aware, Terry has threatened a legal action for wrongful dismissal; but according to some news reports, Sugar's Solicitors, Herbert Smith, are claiming legal costs to a similar amount that Terry deems is owed, £550,000 on the remaining two years of his contract.... The answer.... A lemon...!

Smith then apologised for not being able to tell us more (officially), but suggested that if Frank McLintock wanted to talk to us further, it was up to him. Frank was away with Arsenal in Belgium for the game against Standard Liege....

And on, and on, and on....

I have to report that while we were speaking to the ebullient Mr Smith, another member of our team was speaking to the builder.... Those enquiries continued, as it was quite clear that we could expect no further information from Smith. I was unable to pursue the off-the-record comments, for that very reason, but I would have liked to find out the details of the cash delivery.

Below is the result of our investigator's enquiries.

The planning application was put in to Huntingdonshire District Council for the extension to Graham Smith's home on the 9th December 1991, ref: H1606/91. The approval was given in February 1992.

Mr Colin Fox, the Architect, left his home without leaving a forwarding address. We found out, however, that he had moved to Wennington, Cambs. He gave us the address of the builders, and confirmed that all of his fees have been paid, and long before the day of Teddy Sheringham's signing for Tottenham, which was in August 1992.

We contacted the builder, Tim Roberts, who at first was reluctant to speak to us, not because he hadn't entered the money and receipts from Graham Smith in his books, but because he was living in fear having been threatened by Graham Smith, he told us. Smith telephoned him from Japan, and left a message on his answerphone threatening to 'break his legs'. The builder lives in fear of the consequences, and has discontinued his pursuit of approximately £3,000, that, according to him, is still outstanding. He was paid a total of £28,120 in three tranches: 6th May 1992, £10,625...18th May 1992, £7,140, and 24th June 1992, £10,355.... Mr Roberts stated that because he became somewhat alarmed at receiving such large sums paid in cash, he personally consulted his bank manager who advised him that it did not matter how the payments were made as long as he paid the full amounts into his business account, and declared those receipts in his VAT return and annual accounts. All monies were treated thus, and Mr Roberts at no time indicated a requirement for cash, or that the job would be carried out as one to defraud the Revenue or VAT people.

ALL OF THESE PAYMENTS WERE OF COURSE COMPLETED SOME TWO MONTHS BEFORE THE PAYMENT OF £58,750 BY TOTTENHAM HOTSPUR TO FIRST WAVE SPORT SERVICES, WITH THE EXCEPTION OF THE REMAINING THREE THOUSAND IN DISPUTE.

The relevant invoice from First Wave to Tottenham for the money which Alan Sugar had been told was in respect of a number of different services, reads as follows:

FOR THE ASSISTANCE IN ARRANGING THE
DISTRIBUTION AND MERCHANDISING
NETWORK ON BEHALF OF TOTTENHAM
HOTSPUR IN THE UNITED STATES, TO
INCLUDE TRAVEL AND ALL CONSULTANCY
WORK INVOLVED IN THE PROJECT £50,000
VAT   £8,750

Total   £58,750

Oddly, the invoice bears the signature of Terry Venables, and the words in his own handwriting: 'Paid in cash'....

(Note: Usually the invoice should be receipted by the recipient, in this case First Wave Sport Services.)

I have to make mention of the incredulous situation of any company supplying services for 18 months, never once offering an interim invoice or seeking a payment on account, and finally charging the receiving company an amount some nineteen thousand pounds LESS than they purported to have spent..)

On Friday the 12th November, I received a letter from Rick Parry, acting on behalf of the investigation team of Steve Coppell, Robert Reid, QC, and himself, seeking the information I have detailed above. Mr Reid does NOT have judicial powers and therefore there is no question of sub judice!

I then wrote to Jonathan Crystal explaining that I needed to see Terry Venables before submitting the above information to the Premier League HQ I wanted to tell Terry what I had discovered and seek his explanation before relating the evidence to Rick Parry.

I received a curt refusal from Crystal but a fax arrived once again from Harris demanding that his terms and conditions be met while Terry continues to 'consider' making further contribution to this book.

On Monday 15th November I wrote to Brian Clough to establish whether he wished to throw further light on the matter, or make some comment. He failed to answer although I am assured that the letter was indeed passed to him by the Nottingham Forest administration.

As a matter of interest, Teddy Sheringham signed for Tottenham on the 27th August 1992, at a time when Notts Forest had won one and lost two in the first three games of the season, and were very near the bottom of the League. At the end of that season, they were relegated! Brian Clough retired. Sheringham had been the Club's top goal scorer....

Chapter 7
THE PREMIER LEAGUE —
RICK PARRY

*An interesting and revealing interview with Rick Parry,
Chief Executive of the Premier League, FA Headquarters,
Lancaster Gate, London, 20th October 1993.*

I do not have great regard for Graham Kelly, Chief Executive of
the Football Association.

Before I commence on my apprehensive, and indeed comprehensive interview with Rick Parry, I really have to relate the details
of a wonderful telephone conversation....

Let me say that in my estimation many of the problems
associated with the Football Association and the public, and
indeed with people 'in the game' lies with Graham Kelly. I think
that he is a poor media interviewee. He is protective and
political to the extreme. I believe him to be concerned only for
his superiors which means his job, and that his reticence and
defensive attitudes and comments lie behind an almost reclusive
'toffology' that governs English Football. If that sounds harsh, as
a long-term football fan, and one who has been involved on the
'inside' I am surely entitled to my opinions. I doubt if he thinks
anything of me, for he was not exactly forthcoming when I tried
to discuss certain footballing matters with him.

Three days after a telephone message to his office, he returned
my call.

"Mr Kelly, thank you for ringing me back," I said. "I'm writing
a book about life at Tottenham Hotspur during the past six years.
I would like to interview you in order to discuss several issues. A
sort of view from the FA."

"I have nothing to say about Tottenham Hotspur," he replied
without knowing the details of the proposed interview.

"Look, I'm not doing a crucifixion job on Alan Sugar or Terry Venables. I am also very interested in your comments about football in general, and perhaps the England team situation. It really would be a chance for you to speak to the people through the book."

"I have nothing to say about Tottenham Hotspur."

"Can I quote you then on your attitude to the people and the supporters?"

"I have nothing to say about Tottenham Hotspur."

"Is that the official comment of the FA?"

"I have nothing to say about Tottenham Hotspur."

"Mr Kelly, football belongs to the people without whom you would have no job and no FA."

"I have nothing to say about Tottenham Hotspur."

"Then why did you bother to ring me? I'll quote you verbatim, and tell the readers what a splendid bloke you are."

I put the phone down without saying goodbye, which I really never do. Why does this North Countryman with the poker face and the insipid image wind me up so much, even when I see him on television?

Go back to the Football League, Graham, or better still, the Rugby League.... If they'll have you...!

Following this unhelpful attitude, I approached Rick Parry, the Chief Executive of the Premier League, with some trepidation. His response was all together warmer. He agreed to an interview without reservation.

The entrance and foyer of the Football Association is all that I ever imagined it, steeped in century-old history, it exudes wealth and comfort.

The reception hall, after walking through the double glass doors, along the thickly carpeted hall was panelled in Oak. There were several armchairs and blue and gold moquette settees in convenient places. Pinned high on the panelling were portraits of Her Majesty, The Duke of Kent and Prince Charles making a presentation to an Arab. On the windowsills were two large porcelain figurines, each of three Spanish dancers in various artistic poses.

I approached the long counter behind which stood a very beautiful young lady whose name tag declared her as Anna Hrysyszyn. (Pronounced Rosician.) Against the walls free-standing solid wood and glass showcases displayed the gifts of a hundred years in the shape of ornamental cut-glass and crystal ware, silver tureens and plates, and plaques. After asking my name, Ann requested that I sign the visitors' book. Incredibly the last names before mine were those on the 14th, of Spurs Assistant Manager Steve Perryman, and what looked like the scrawl of Vinny Samways.

While I waited I wondered what Vinny might have done. Had he been accused of winning more than three tackles in one season? Perhaps he was being charged with heading the ball forward. I know, he was there for bringing the game into disrepute by kicking the ball with his right foot on at least one occasion since the goal against Marlow, and was being warned that this really must stop. It is unknown in British football folklore for a left footed player to do this and it must to be stamped out at any cost. Fined ten thousand pounds!

Before I could complete my imaginative speculations, I was approached by a medium height, dark haired white shirted man, whom I immediately recognised as Rick Parry, the first ever Chief Executive of the Premier League. We shook hands and he led me though a maze of offices to one secluded and sectioned off at the back of a much larger room. He seemed reserved and I was being invaded with thoughts that this was not going to be an easy interview, for he surely was aware of the telephone confrontation I had had with his counterpart at the Football Association, Graham Kelly, the previous week.

"Can you tell me Mr Parry how you came to be associated with the idea of a Premier League in the first instance?"

"I was approached in the first instance by Graham Kelly, who I knew well, to get involved on a consultancy basis. I was working with Ernst and Robb at the time. Management consultancy."

"You are an accountant then?"

"Yes, Chartered. I had recently finished a stint on the Select Committee for the Manchester Olympic bid. I needed to return to the real world and Graham suggested that an idea was forming for the First Division to break away from the Football League."

"Was Mr Kelly with the FA or still with the League as Secretary at the time?"

"Oh, he had left the League some time by then. This was in the back end of 1990. He told me that if the idea was to go anywhere it really needed the investigation by an external consultancy, not least to provide a degree of independent view."

"Was that with the sole instigation by Graham Kelly or did he tell you that the whole FA Committee had authorised this approach?"

"I believe the Committee had to approve the fees, but basically it was his baby, and upon his instigation. Whatever committee it was would have known about the approach."

"That was your obligation for the whole of 1990?"

"Yes, at least until the October of that year."

"The entire objective was to supply details of the ramifications of a quite radical move against the traditions of the Football League?"

"Not exactly, but yes to a degree. Graham was interested in what would happen and what the financial benefits of such a move would be. I needed to see what the structure would be, how it would work. The trouble was an immediate investigation to examine the promotion and demotion situation.

"Sort of would the Football League put up with it, and allow their members to go into the Premier League and vice versa?"

"Exactly."

"Did you get much co-operation from the Football League?"

"Well, the whole thing ended up in litigation with the Football League losing their claim that we were acting in some unlawful manner. The whole thing had to be chewed around by the Chairmen of the teams in the First Division. By May 1991, I had achieved most of what I set out to do, and it was then for the teams to resign from the League to form their own situation. That meeting was held here at the FA. Basically the Chairmen had to sort it out amongst themselves."

"They had a choice then?"

"No, not really, but it was they who felt the decision ought to be made by them to organise their own destination."

"If one said no, then he would languish in what we now call

142

our First Division, the old Second Division, and presumably lose out on the financial benefits?''

"Quite."

"Join us or else?"

"Not exactly, but you might put it like that."

"Was there a committee or did all the Chairmen attend that decision making meeting?"

"That first meeting was in May '91 and that was a very successful meeting. Every Club was interested."

"Presumably they had seen your report and you had recommended that the scheme goes ahead?"

"After the Cup Final..." (In which Spurs beat Nottingham Forest by two goals to one!) "...effectively that was how it happened. I had submitted my report to the FA and they immediately recognised that the entire approval of the clubs was needed for the whole thing to be a success."

"What disadvantages were presented by the FA at that meeting?"

"There weren't any disadvantages. The advantages were on the blueprint which provided for increased quality, organisation and of course, media presentation. The FA was keen on the eighteen club league."

"The FA was keen...? That is of interest seeing how it has turned out."

"Yes, but there were difficulties in deciding who would stand down. It wasn't going to be easy to ask some teams to drop down a division. The England team would benefit too. Gate receipts would rise. There was talk and compromise, but basically everyone warmed to the idea."

"What did you see the public getting out of all this, other than increased entrance fees?"

"The Taylor report meant a whole new world of football supporter. We discussed improved conditions, better facilities and things like that. The supporter has not been forgotten: at least not by the Premier League and not by me. The commercial benefits would enable them to do these things, but I have to say that the Chairmen were mostly interested in a new type of constitution."

"They were at loggerheads with the League then?"

"No, not really, but they were beginning to think that they had become institutionalised and their progress as individual Limited Companies was being impaired by some antiquated impositions and rules. I don't want to talk about the tails wagging the dogs, but they were out of step many times. One problem was the voting system. One and a half votes by each First Division Club, then a single vote per Second Division club and then the Third and Fourth, I believe that they had eight between them. It was complicated and cumbersome, and obviously restrictive."

"You mean that without the vote of the lower divisions the First Division lot could grab all the television money?"

"That has turned out really well, with the lower Divisions having their own contract with ITV."

"This voting system was on any issue?"

"Yes, any issue."

"Was there then a second meeting?"

"Yes, one with me acting as Chairperson and without any FA representation. At that meeting which lasted only two hours they agreed the basis of a new constitution. They agreed how everything would be shared. One club/one vote and decisions by two thirds to a third majority. No management committee. Income sharing."

"The income.... You mean how you, as the organisational body would derive yours.... From the supporters at the gates?"

"Not just that. There was television to consider."

"Were you aware then that you would receive television monies before the formation of the new constitution?"

"We weren't aware of how much, but of course we knew that there would be some. I had learned that when I was preparing the blueprint."

"Was any particular contract with a specific company favoured at that time?"

"No, not at all. Quite a lot had been achieved in a very short space of time. We had not looked at any proposal then, but we knew there would be several."

"A Dutch auction?"

"Possibly. It was a fairly dramatic end to that short meeting.

The clubs signed an undertaking to resign from the Football League."

"There was no mandate at that time for two-thirds majority?"

"No, we needed them all and they all responded. I seem to remember that one or two weren't able to vote at that time but we got their vote easily later on."

"Is there still a power base among the bigger teams? I know it is unfair to call clubs like Norwich one of the lesser clubs, because they are really holding up against the might of the bigger boys. This deal would be particularly good for clubs like them."

"They all have an equal vote, Norwich, Southampton and Manchester United. Obviously they were keen to join the scheme."

"That was when in 1991?"

"The clubs gave twelve months notice to the League and then the '92/'93 Season would be under the new regime. During that period the League took us to court."

"You won that case because you had the right to form a league of football teams in their own right?"

"Exactly."

"You then came to the formation of the new organisation?"

"No, not quite. At that stage it was possible that the League was going to appeal the decision. The majority could see the writing on the wall and the appeal was blocked or thought to be a non-starter."

"You would call it reluctant acceptance by them?"

"Realism. We wanted to leave something behind to the League."

"What has been left behind?"

"The primary benefit was their ability to actually get into the Premier, by virtue of promotion from their Division One."

"Is there a monetary arrangement by way of damages for their loss?"

"Yes there is one. There is compensation."

"Does this last forever?"

"That's initially for five years, but they also have the advantage of their own TV deal. They are actually making more money now than ever before."

"By the time that the new season commenced, August '91, you were now ensconced as the first Chief Executive of the new Premier League?"

"October actually. It wasn't until then that the Football League had its EGM and formally allowed the resignation of the clubs."

"The season having started, you were then still playing for the F.L. and on notice to quit?"

"Yes."

"Can we move now to the period May '92 until August '92 when the Premier League kicked off, so to speak. What happened in the close season?"

"I moved into these premises, not at that time, but I officially took up my seat."

"Are you welcomed unequivocally here at these premises?"

"Well, as the whole thing emanated from them, I do not feel in any way uneasy here. We all get on quite well, and there have been many discussions that have taken place, and the whole relationship is benefitted by the proximity."

"Was there much resistance to your appointment? People were known to say that you did not have a football background while your President was a banker, Sir John Quentin, and that this was not the qualifications needed to be the administrator."

"If the majority had thought that, I wouldn't have been offered a job. That's just a simple statement of fact. I never canvassed for it. It was unanimous for me to take charge at least for the first season."

"Were you living in Liverpool at that time? Do you have a family?"

"I lived in Chester; in fact I still do. I don't have a family and I travel down from there."

"What, stay in London for five days and go back for weekends?"

"No, I spend about three days a week in the office and the rest of the time I am either at home or travelling around."

"Getting back to the period between May and October '92, presumably you were involved in a number of new contracts, including what is often described as the infamous one with

BSkyB? Recognising that television was going to provide the lion's share of your revenue, can you tell me of the circumstances that surrounded that deal? For example, did all the Chairmen of the clubs attend that specific meeting, or was there a committee?"

"All of them attended."

"Presumably all the companies interested in showing live football submitted tenders in the normal manner?"

"Not in a sealed-bid manner. Every proposal was openly discussed and one assumes that each knew of the other's tender. We knew it was useless to try that. Each would make up his own composition and at the end of the day it was unlikely that the final deal would resemble the initial proposal."

"Did you have a time limit on the submission of those tenders seeing as how you had turned it into almost a public auction?"

"We played it right to the wire. It generates further excitement and usually it generates higher bids."

"You were totally pragmatic about it then?"

"Not entirely. We didn't mind who got the deal, but money had to be considered alongside public service. It was cat-and-mouse stuff really. We were quite flexible. We also knew that one of the companies would not submit its best quote until the eleventh hour."

"Can I take you to the process of the actual meeting. You are definitely stating that every Chairman was present?"

"Absolutely."

"Did you chair that meeting?"

"No, it was taken by Sir John Quentin."

"Will you clarify the confused newspaper reports that Alan Sugar allegedly held up the meeting in order to telephone BSkyB to advise them of the ITV bid and so to enable them to increase theirs?"

"I welcome this opportunity. It is really the only time that the truth of this matter has been questioned with the view to presumably relate to the public the true events of that morning. The meeting was not held up. We were in the Royal Lancaster Hotel and all companies submitting for the contract were advised that they should not attend. The foyer was full of reporters and media men and ITV representatives had ignored our request and were handing out details of their tender to all and sundry. A reporter has stated that he overheard Mr Sugar relating details of the ITV tender to somebody, whom I am told was sitting by the phone at White Hart Lane. That was before the meeting started. Later, I can honestly tell you that Alan Sugar declared his interest in a successful bid by BSkyB and VOLUNTEERED UN-RESERVEDLY TO WITHDRAW FROM THE MEETING AND TO ABSTAIN FROM HIS RIGHT TO VOTE ON BEHALF OF TOTTENHAM HOTSPUR FOOTBALL CLUB. It was the vote of all the remaining participants to that meeting that he should be allowed to vote. As you know, we voted to accept the most recently received bid by BSkyB. That vote was carried by the actual mandatory requirement of two-thirds to one-third, i.e. 14 to 6. I can also tell you that the newspapers were entirely wrong when they suggested that the Sugar vote was the casting one. That definitely was not the case. There are of course a number of enquiries that will need to be made regarding the recent events at Tottenham. The question addressed to the television contract is not one of them. Whatever might be said about Mr Sugar, his behaviour on that morning was impeccable and beyond question. The BBC's tender was linked to a joint bid by BSkyB and was submitted to me the day before by John Gregson.''

"Reports suggested that the ITV bid was greater than that of the BSkyB bid until Mr Sugar intervened.''

"I'll kill that one right away. The ITV bid was never more than the ones submitted by BSkyB. Mr Sugar succeeded in raising that bid to even greater amounts, and has done us all a great service.''

"BSkyB did not stand in the foyer and do what ITV did?''

"No they did not. It is also a matter of public knowledge that I, too, telephoned them. We had indicated that we wanted final bids the night before. ITV tried something on by waiting until the morning of the meeting to increase their bid, and then to engage everyone's interest.''

"I guess that that action did them more harm than good.''

"That's your comment. It was I that advised BSkyB that ITV had this morning put in a higher bid.... 'Do you wish to up your bid?' I advised them that ITV had turned up with a higher bid, and I thought it totally correct to advise BSkyB of what had happened.

The result of my own and Mr Sugar's actions was that we actually received £10 million more because of our telephone calls.''

''What do you think of the moral issue that only two per cent of the Country had BSkyB at that time?''

''What do you think, Mr Nathan, of people who go to football matches subsidising the armchair supporter? What we have done is to gather a large sum of money and to use that to the benefit of everyone in football. I feel that there is no moral issue to answer. The result may have been enormous sales of wall saucers for Amstrad but that should not detract from the overall effect of more and more people enjoying football in better conditions with better facilities, and a very good TV coverage of live matches. Pubs now show matches on Monday evenings and Sunday afternoons, and thousands more are able to see it live, as it happens. Attendances are 16.5 per cent up, and football is buoyant again, even though our World Cup prospects are now less than we had hoped for. I have read that we have lost £10 million, £25 million, and even £40 million by not getting to the Finals. It is ludicrous. When did this Country make that sort of money out of a World Cup competition? Sure, we have lost, but we'll come again. I am totally confident for the future of football at large and for the Premier League to be a success.''

''Can I now ask you about recent reports — indeed a programme on which you appeared recently on BBC Channel 2 discussed it, although you were not quoted, regarding the future of football as a whole?''

''I'll clear up the point about me not quoting. I actually said quite a bit in an hour and three quarters of question-and-answer routines. When the programme was shown, only what one would call the high-profile characters were left in. People like Jimmy Hill, and Malcolm Allison were quoted as almost an argument between two people rather than a general discussion. Only Mr Taylor for the PFA and a little of what Graham Kelly said was used to any effect. The show failed to bring in any level of optimism that we had discussed.''

''What can you tell me that the broadcast didn't?''

''I can tell you of our intentions of allowing nine year olds to attend at professional clubs for proper coaching. Our possible enquiries into legislating for the quality and possible qualification of Directors of football clubs, so that we don't have the Spurs situation repeated. And the possibility of licensing professional and reputable agents."

"You mean that at last you are going to look at the Continental idea of running perhaps eleven or twelve teams from the age of nine year olds? That you intend to impose regulations alongside those in Company Law regarding the suitability of Directors of football clubs, and finally, authorising the dealing with legitimate agents to represent footballers and others who ask for that service?"

"That is all in our thinking at this time."

"What about the Tottenham thing? Are you investigating them?"

"We are considering at this time the appointment of a Q.C. to examine the events and documentation that has led up to that awful situation."

"Would he have judicial powers?"

"Hard to say at this time."

"Do you fear his appointment, in as much as he may be so thorough so as to open a can of worms?"

"This is dangerous ground, Mr Nathan. Of course we hope that such a thing doesn't happen."

"Rick Parry, where do you go from here?"

"I need five years in total. I would love to see radical changes in the way that I have told you. I would like to see that through and the Premier League flourish under my direction and for all the beneficiaries.... The clubs, the Managers, the Chairmen, the public. Everyone. I believe that our football is healthy. I believe that we will overcome all the difficulties that are being put to us at this time. I believe that our footballers are strong and fit and are superb athletes and are capable of anything."

"Finally, Mr Parry. May I ask you whether there is a specific investigation into Tottenham Hotspur at this time?"

"I have already mentioned the possibility of a thorough look into them and indeed into the whole of football by an appointed Q.C. At the moment I can tell you that we are looking at player valuations."

"You mean the one point one million paid for both Nayim and Lineker. The fact that Nayim is alleged to be in Spurs books at £300,000 and in your books at £50,000? This seems no more than an accounting function. The overall paid to the two of them is not in question. It is just what each player is registered as costing or what each is valued at? Seems that as they have both been sold, the profit made is still reflected accurately in Spurs books."

"Precisely."

I thanked him following some two hours of interview, and left wondering where this man had been all his life! What would have been and would have evolved under this accountant's thinking, enthusiasm and integrity had he come into our National game earlier?

He was as open as his counterpart was close-mouthed. Indeed, he positively welcomed the opportunity to explain certain matters to me, whereas Mr Kelly obviously preferred to keep everything close to his chest, with, I would suggest, an unacceptable disregard for the public.

I have openly questioned some of the things I have found out about Alan Sugar, and indeed Terry Venables, but I am really happy that the matter over the TV deal was cleared up and that Mr Sugar has been exonerated from all suggestions of irregularity.

Finally, a message to Graham Kelly: Graham…. When you resign from the FA or they throw you out, please recommend that Rick Parry takes over. With a man like him at the helm, our game of football would benefit quicker, more successfully, and more openly than ever before, to the benefit and well-being of everyone connected with the game.

(Since writing this, credit to Vinny Samways is offered, for scoring against Liverpool…with his right peg!)

Chapter 8

TISA

(The Tottenham Independent Supporters Association)

Not to be confused with the Spurs Supporters Association....

The Association was formed in 1990 primarily to organise supporters and small shareholders into a group that would have some influence with the Spurs Board in the many things that were going on within the Club. Things like changes to the stadium into an all-seater, catering and toilet facilities, and general policies which directly affected the supporters. The idea emanated from a stance of dissatisfaction by the founder members Steve Davies, a solicitor, and Bernie Kingsley, a personnel manager of a large industrial group. Steve and Bernie have been dedicated Spurs supporters since their formative years.

Their idea to establish a body of men (and women) strong in opinion and belief, dedicated to the improvement of all things good at Spurs soon became an appealing one when more than eleven hundred shareholders and supporters joined their ranks.

It is difficult to compare their activities to the more established Spurs Supporters Association, but research tells us that the latter body has different policies and ideals. It is seen by many as a 'social' arm of the supporters, and has, over the years, enjoyed a good working relationship with the Club, while TISA has been more vociferous and demonstrative in its desire to influence what goes on. Not that the SSA do not desire the same ends, but their relationship with the Tottenham management has never been controversial, while Steve and Bernie have always seen their organisation as one to challenge and seek out, and by way of reasonable and democratic process, to make things better for the poor old down trodden supporter.

It may well be that the FA stance on supporter influence and involvement as of course the biggest contributors to the Club's income, welcomes this type of body. It certainly would seem that a powerful representation of supporters would not go amiss at Spurs. Someone, somewhere, is needed to prevent a totalitarian decision-making board who rarely consider the effects of their policies on the supporter and have of late fleeced them by wildly increasing entrance fees, over-priced undercooked food, miserable, antiquated toilet facilities, especially for women and children, and an unprecedented desire to attract the wealthier supporter to purchase strange looking glass boxes from which to view the matches.

There is nothing inherently wrong in maximising business, and to attract the people with money to spare, into the arena, but it is the fear that this is being done at the average supporter's expense that necessitates the welcome existence of organisations like TISA.

I met with Steve and Bernie at a London restaurant whose name and food warrants no mention....

The Tottenham Hotspur Independent Supporters Association was formed in September 1990, and not, as many people believe, one day after Terry Venables got the sack. The formation was influenced by the news that Robert Maxwell might take over the Club. Not that the founders were aware of the appalling financial involvement of the man, made public after his death, but because he was already involved at Derby and his son at Oxford and his reputation as a football club director had not been reported as one of unmitigated success. Indeed, the newspapers continually printed articles deriding his decisions and the many disagreements that occurred too frequently at both of these clubs.

Steve added that it was the poor record of Maxwell as a director and the fact that Tottenham were in financial difficulties that promulgated their concern, coupled with the fact that they did not believe that Maxwell had long term plans for Spurs, but was there trying to gain control, or at least, to support his friend Irving Scholar, with doubtful ambition. As it turned out, it has been reported that Maxwell loaned Spurs a million pounds to ease their immediate problems, but nothing eventually came from his attempts to join the board.

"Why did you think that he made advances to Tottenham in the first instance?" I enquired.

"It seems that he was a man who acted on a whim, and he could fancy being involved with Spurs in the same way that other people fancied having steak for lunch or something. We thought that he would like being part of Spurs only because he could continue being in the limelight."

"So that and the well publicised financial losses were at the root of your formation?"

"We were troubled by the direction that Tottenham had taken. We didn't know whether we could do much about it but we feared that they might go under and we thought that at least we could try to do something constructive."

"How did you physically go about forming the organisation?"

"We had a public meeting to start off with, at the University of London Union. We were helped in the organisation of that by the SSA. We publicised it through the Evening Standard, and about one hundred people turned up."

"Were they shareholders?"

"Many were, but not all. We then publicised it through the Fanzines (supporters magazines).... We appeared at the next Tottenham Annual General Meeting."

"Why not the name TISSA to encompass the shareholders?"

"We thought about that but we didn't want to represent just those that owned shares in the Club."

"Was one of your concerns the news that Gascoigne would have to be sold to ease the financial burden?"

"Yes, one of them but not all. We tried not to get involved with individual measures like that which may have needed to be taken. We were mainly interested in a long term relationship; our major concern being the long term direction. The management being settled and future programmes being established. The dodgy finances only helped us to believe in our involvement."

"How did you think that you could help or influence that situation?"

"First of all through pressure on the media. Through the Annual General Meetings because both Bernie and I and many of our members are shareholders."

"Do you have any idea at that time of inception how many, no, what percentage of shareholding was represented by your members?"

"At that time approximately twenty per cent of the overall were small shareholders."

"You were trying to co-ordinate them into one body?"

"That, unfortunately, is something we have not succeeded in doing. Currently, we think that only about one third of our membership have shares in Tottenham. It's a pretty small shareholding, say maybe two, three per cent. We are still very effective with public campaigns even though we represent only a small vote."

"Did you consider that your campaigns might be harmful to say, Irving Scholar...? Although we might blame him for the difficult financial position at that time, by stirring it up, were you actually doing any good?"

"It hadn't reached crisis point, and it may be said that if we hadn't been there Irving may have tried to ride out the storm. Or, worse, sell out to Maxwell!"

"It is interesting that you decided that Irving was the one to go, particularly in the light of who we have got to replace him. The eventual sale of the shares to Terry and Alan meant that the money that they paid was going to Scholar and Bobroff. Spurs therefore didn't benefit at all."

"The six million that was paid did not go entirely to those two. That isn't correct. Only about half went to them, the premium, the excess over the amount that they demanded, went into the Club.

"That doesn't entirely stack up with the amounts that Venables and Sugar parted with, according to sources."

"They bought thirty six per cent of the shares amounting to three and a half million at seventy five 'p' each. Some two point six million pounds. That is a matter of public record. They ended up having to buy more shares than just those owned by Bobroff and Scholar. They wanted the complete management buy-out."

"Did other directors sell their holding to them as well?"

"Tony Berry gave an undertaking that he wouldn't sell his holdings, and effectively, he was part of or allied to, that takeover.

Barry Kennedy, who was the next biggest shareholder, did the same."

"Berry was reputed to have somewhere between four and eight per cent. That could make quite a significant difference."

"Berry actually owns or owned at the time of takeover in 1991, eight hundred thousand shares which was eight per cent. Now, after the Rights Issue, that eight hundred thousand represents just about five per cent. He never bought any from the Issue."

"Did TISA approve the partnership of Venables and Sugar?"

"We contacted Venables because he mentioned at the AGM that he was interested in putting a deal together. Bernie asked him what his proposals were. He told us what they were and we figured that his heart was in the right place. We felt that if he was there the Club had a good chance to recover. He seemed the best man for the job. He was having trouble with a guy called Larry Gillet (Investor), and we felt that if Sugar was the man with the money, and he was the man Terry felt comfortable with, then we retained an open mind. I can remember doing an interview on a London Broadcasting Company programme with Andrew Neil (Editor of the Sunday Times).... It was on the date that the story broke about Sugar being involved and the point I made there was that unlike previous backers Venables had mentioned, Sugar was known to genuinely have the money. We knew of his resources and there was a degree of confidence in that."

"Did you at that time have any contact with Sugar?"

"We came in very late in the day."

"Did he try to contact you?"

"I suppose that he knew that Venables had been talking to us."

"He made no attempt to court you or gain your approval?"

"None whatsoever. It is interesting that after that, recently, he has taken umbrage at the fact that we supported Venables in the row. We had one meeting with him about ground capacity. We were talking about fifty thousand or so, and he just turned around and blithely said 'what has it got to do with you?. We don't get that amount of people here at the moment.' He seemed uneasy and rather loathe to be wasting his time talking to us. He is just not somebody who has the inclination to try and appease others. He seems to think that it is all his domain and not anybody else's business. He has a confrontorial attitude and seems to destroy any sympathy one may have to his cause."

"Intransigent, you would say?"

"I think that he believes that he is always right, and that he'll tell you what he is doing, and if you don't wish to believe it or have any other idea, then that's your hard luck, and you are now the enemy. That's his general attitude. He's used to people doing his every command without question and if you don't do it, well he can just change the people. He's very rich and powerful and let's you know it."

"Getting on to more recent events, let's examine how your organisation viewed the football side of things with both the Venables management and the later appointment of Peter Shreeves who took over when Terry moved upstairs."

"We were not particularly excited about it seeing as how he failed when he had the job after Burkenshaw left, although he did sign some good players. It certainly wasn't a good Season under him (1991/92).... I think that the general support of the fans was unaffected by his appointment. As long as Terry Venables was still there we were all sympathetic towards whatever Terry saw fit to do. As it turned out Shreeves lost some of that sympathy with what he did with the team."

"I personally remember the Scott Houghton thing. That was a mystery. And then Mark Robson had a go at Shreeves for an uncaring attitude towards him when he was out injured for months. Then Shreeves sold him to West Ham."

"Well, you wouldn't need to be a mathematical genius to count Shreeve's successes."

"Did you get involved with the relationship between Shreeves and Venables. It has been said that Peter wasn't left to actually run the show."

"We were told by Venables that Shreeves was left to do the job himself, and indeed, demanded that. Venables wanted to influence team selection and as far as we know, style of play, but Peter wouldn't have that. Clearly, as Shreeves actually failed, that was why he didn't get his contract renewed. Perhaps if he had allowed Terry to have a say he might have been more successful and even have been there now."

"How did TISA view the subsequent appointment of joint management of Clemence and Livermore?"

"We heard that they might have been appointed before Shreeves; the previous Summer. We were more surprised with the Shreeves appointment. Livermore was obviously very close to Terry, in the sense that they had worked closely together the previous couple of Seasons. The Reserves already had Clemence as team manager. It seemed that Venables would become involved with the football side of things again, and therefore Tottenham were unlikely to appoint another big name or outsider. Terry could certainly work with Clemence and Livermore, who were basically his disciples."

"Were you aware that by this time there were problems between Sugar and Venables?"

"There was some vague mention of it in the newspapers, and at about that time we saw Venables up at the training ground, and it was clear from what he said that he was having problems."

"What did he actually say?"

"He said that Sugar was accusing him of wasting his money. I asked Terry if the problem was becoming unmanageable. He said that he was managing and didn't see it reaching crisis point. We were concerned about it and thought of approaching Sugar but in the end decided to stay out of it. We never expected it to reach the confrontation that it did."

"Have you at any time had dealings with Eddie Ashby?"

"We first met Ashby in the Summer of '92.... No that's wrong. We met him at Scribes just after Venables had been appointed Chief Exec. He introduced him as his P.A. In the summer of '92 we discussed with Ashby the development of the ground. He was the one talking to us because Venables had so much to attend to. There was no suggestion that Ashby was making any decisions. He was acting as a go-between. He was instrumental in the sighting of the Legends Club on the lower east side of the ground and indeed it was us that suggested that name. He showed us the plans and very reasonably, sought our opinion."

"Why were you consulted in the first instance?"

"That was our relationship with Venables. Terry asked Ashby to find out from us what our thoughts were."

"You are saying that Terry had the foresight to include supporter opinion in some of the things that he needed to deal with?"

"Absolutely. That is why we thought he was the best man to run the Club after he was dismissed."

"Sugar never did?"

"Not directly, but we assumed that what Terry did was in agreement with Sugar's ideas. We were even consulted on ticket office procedure, and even the prices of seats etc. Everyone in the Club was encouraged to accept us."

"Did this continue throughout?"

"Yes, pretty well. There was a board meeting in February '92 to discuss the seating on the 'Shelf' because they were worried that they might lose a grant. The 'Minutes' were shown to us and in those it was agreed by them all that we would be consulted. It is actually minuted. There was a lot of things happening at the Club. There was the introduction of a Chinese food counter, and in all these decisions Terry talked to us, presumably Sugar agreed with this.... I think that we had some concern in the area of what you would call 'agreement'. We felt that consultation didn't always mean that we totally agreed and there was a feeling that they might say 'TISA were consulted and matters discussed with them and everything is O.K....' It wasn't always like that. In fact at that stage we were not convinced about an all seater stadium. Nevertheless, they did genuinely talk to us and paid attention to our views."

"When were you first aware that the crisis had arrived?"

"Not long before it actually became public."

"We were told about the Board meeting on the 6th May where Sugar threw a letter at Venables offering to buy him out. During that meeting we also were informed that Sugar swore at Crystal."

"Can we go back to the Rights Issue and as shareholders, what took place with you then?"

"In the original takeover they had agreed between them they had asked shareholders not to sell any of their shares to either of them. This was because they had agreed to invest an equal amount of money and obviously wished to maintain the status quo. They had to buy 36 per cent from Scholar and Bobroff. The intention was to spend as little as possible on the takeover so that they would have more money to put into the Club. That wasn't in fact, successful. They ended up with a total of 63 per cent. When the Rights Issue was announced, the request then was for shareholders to TAKE UP their entitlement. Sugar agreed to underwrite those that weren't taken up. They wanted the shareholders to do that as with any rights issue."

"What could have happened, then, is if Venables and Sugar took up their allocation and the small shareholders did the same, they still would have been equal partners."

"Sugar knew at that time that Venables could not afford to take up his allocation, and also that others would not do so. By underwriting the entire issue he knew from the start that he would end up with a majority. Sugar absolutely knew that."

"What did you think at that time? Surely you would be aware, as two professional men, that the balance of power was shifting?"

"We were encouraged to believe that the status quo would not change. Venables was entirely involved and we never dreamed that things would end up as they have. They didn't actually say we intend to go on as equal partners for the next ten years, but that was assumed."

"You had or have never been told by either man that it was the intention to remain as equals? This is very important seeing as you seemed to have the ear of Terry at that time."

"Terry did not comment, although we were in agreement that the Rights Issue was something that the Company was putting forward to raise money. Of course we realised what in effect would happen, but the management and voting power seemed to be something aside from this."

"Just as an aside.... What did you think of Terry's advisers who allowed this before an actual agreement on power was signed?"

"We assumed that they knew what they were doing. There was, however, a very specific item raised in Court which we identified, which I think that I mentioned in my affidavit that said in the letter we received.... 'Sugar intends to enter into an agreement' regarding regulating the disposal of their shares. That was clearly stated in both the mandatory offer document in '91 and again in the offer of the Rights Issue of '92. That was absolutely clear. We took that to mean that they would continue to work together as equals. Many joint ventures start out in this way but do not necessarily carry on like that. We always knew that Sugar had more money than Venables. We believe that Venables expected the status quo to remain throughout the association with Sugar, and we believe that Sugar was aware of this.''

"Tell me, have you met Colin Sandy?''

"Yes, we have…. I haven't spoken to him since the 14th May and I don't expect that he will speak to us now.''

"The reasons for that?''

"His loyalty is to Sugar and he isn't exactly on our side at the moment. Sugar now sees us as the enemy because we declared our support for Venables, only with the support of our members, and honestly because we felt he was and is the best man to run the Club.''

"At the moment then, TISA are out of favour and you have no contact with the Club?''

"Sugar still writes to us quite regularly, mainly complaining about what we are doing and insisting that we do not act for our members and wishing us to resign. Not about our health…!''

"After the split, both of you became very high-profile, but with Terry's position dissipated by Colin Sandy at the Club, and effectively in law, you still supported him.''

"Everything that we believed in evolved around Terry Venables being a central figure at the Club. We believe that as football supporters, he had done a pretty worthwhile job.''

"Can you make it perfectly clear to our readers how and why you came to put the weight of your Organisation behind one and not the other.''

"Initially, we canvassed fifty members, of our thousand or so members at that time. Then we called an official public meeting which was held on the 23rd May (Nine days after Terry had been granted temporary 'relief')…about seven hundred attended. Ted Buxton and Bill Nicholson came along. We set out our feelings and then threw the meeting over to the floor. Our members, Ted Buxton and Bill Nicholson voted for our support of Terry Venables. In fact Bill was very upset about it. THE OVERALL FEELING OF THAT MEETING WAS IN SUPPORT OF TERRY

IN AS MUCH AS HE SHOULD NOT LEAVE THE CLUB. If they had voted differently we would have reflected their feelings. We did speak to Sugar on the day of the dismissal, the 14th May, before the board meeting, early in the morning. What he said was that he was disappointed in what I had said on GMTV earlier on. The night before, at a sportswriters' dinner, Terry had announced that he was going to be sacked. I was asleep and Sugar telephoned me at home, that morning. He asked me not to publicly support Terry until I had heard his side of the story. I asked him what that story was, and he said he wasn't able to tell me at that time. I told him that we have faith and confidence in Terry and until he discloses something that would change our minds, he must expect us to support Venables. From that point on he has been, what?, offended might be the right word."

"What happened as the conversation developed? Did he get annoyed or argue with you?"

"He became agitated and said that he would speak to us after the Board meeting, that afternoon; but you know what took place then."

"Did he indicate or seem to be aware that Terry had lined up his legal people for an injunction hearing?"

"None whatsoever."

"So even you didn't know about the hearing; and therefore didn't attend that.... In fact even the hordes of pressmen never knew about it?"

"Obviously, because none of them were at the High Court that afternoon. They were all around the Club and up at Enfield for the testimonial of Eddie Baily. That was not the game that was discussed in the Court. That game was on the ensuing Tuesday."

"What took place in the ensuing eleven days after the 14th May until the hearing on the 25th?"

"On the next day, Saturday the 15th, we had a meeting with several members, during the Cup Final (Arsenal vs. Sheffield Wednesday).... We made two decisions. The first, to write to all our members and to get a postcard campaign going. The second to call a public meeting for Friday 21st May. We continued our support of Venables, and we made our reasons clear, that he was still the best man to run the Club, and we purposefully refrained from using controversial language and from insulting Sugar."

"During that week you appeared on Television again and expressed your unreserved support."

"Yes, and then on the Friday about seven or eight hundred people attended the meeting. There was massive support for our policy. We wanted to make it clear that we were not anti-Sugar as much as we were pro-Venables."

"Invariably, that isn't possible."

"I remember Alan Sugar being asked by the media whether the two of them could work together. Maybe they could negotiate. He said very clearly, and on many occasions thereafter, that there was no room for both of them. By definition we then felt that Sugar should be the one to go."

"Tell me; what did you think of the decision to temporarily return Terry to Tottenham?"

"They had a meeting at Herbert Smith, the Solicitors (Sugar's) to decide on the way to work. Sugar couldn't be seen to be obstructing that because he would be in contempt. They mutually agreed to try and get on for that short time. The South African tour was cancelled."

"What about TISA after the hearings of the 25th May and the 10th to the 15th June when it was decided that the Board acted correctly?"

"Our view now is that Venables will never return and the best thing is to get behind Spurs and Ossie Ardiles. Except that Mr Sugar is still somewhat unrelenting, and is pursuing a path to try to get us removed as coordinators of TISA."

"How is he doing this?"

"He insisted on us holding a referendum to assure him of the support of the majority of our members, and when the results were announced showing 95 per cent behind us, he is now demanding that he is allowed to hold his own vote. He is attempting to gain access to our files of members so that he can circulate them himself. He has written to us."

"May I reproduce those letters in the book?"

"We think not, but we will give you certain details."

"Why not allow access to the public?"

"Because in our opinion they are libellous and insulting to our integrity, and we are going to sit on them before deciding whether to act upon them or not."

"You, in fact, are seeking peace with Spurs and Sugar but in effect you are being hounded still by the avenging Alan Sugar?"

"In effect, yes!"

"Do you believe that eventually, there will be peace?"

"Probably not with us at the helm, but hopefully, there can be some ground for us to meet on."

"If Mr Sugar invited you back you would accept such an invitation?"

"Yes, of course, but that seems most unlikely. There is some further correspondence, and it is difficult to know what will happen. We certainly have no persuasion on who can or cannot be Chairman of Tottenham Hotspur Plc, and we believe that he shouldn't attempt to alter our structure to his own satisfaction."

"What you are saying is that he now has everyone at Spurs doing his every bidding and he would like your Organisation to get in step?"

"It seems like that."

"Do you think that he intends to be at Tottenham for a long time, or that he will leave when Tottenham, as a commercial commodity, has no further money making potential for Amstrad?"

"He has said that he would like to leave his shareholding for his children, but basically, we are not sure that he will be there forever."

"Unlike the Andersons who were here for donkey's years, or the Hill-Woods at Arsenal...? Has he ever told you of his life-long support for Spurs?

"There is a letter that he sent to our members. In it he says that he went to Spurs as a young man with his brother and his Dad, but we are not sure. Certainly his brother is a keen fan, but there is no proof that Alan ever accompanied him."

(The letter is reproduced below.)

"When he came in in 1991, he never then mentioned that he had ever supported the Club. Certainly he has to be more interested now. He declared in his letter that he spent his teens making his way in the World. Presumably that means that he couldn't come to Tottenham.''

"What do you think is the overall effect of all this on Alan Sugar, and indeed Terry Venables, 'though he has told me that and I will be producing that in the chapter on him.''

"Well, you have seen Terry since we last met, so I will talk about Sugar. The effect on him, being a very determined character will be to prove us and all those that still think that Terry was best, to make Tottenham successful, which after all, is what we want.''

"Penultimately, I would like you to imagine that Terry raised enough cash to return and buy out Sugar. What then would be your personal view and that of TISA...? Bernie?''

"I think people would like him to be involved, but that would suggest more disruption and people would not be keen on that. Life moves on. We have a situation now where he has been re-placed and Ossie has started reasonably well. I think that it is all somewhat hypothetical and won't ever happen.''

"Steve...?

"There is always the scenario whereby another might buy Sugar out and the new chairman appoint Terry as whatever. I'd like to see Terry back, but I think that his time has gone.''

"Finally, what about Ossie Ardiles?''

"Well, he was not only the right appointment to appease Sugar's critics but also the right appointment in any case, but I would like to see his team play more of the football he creates in the other team's half. At the moment so much is played in our own half, and it is relatively ineffective.''

I thanked them both for their most informative interview, joined TISA myself, and arranged to reproduce several docu-ments that they mentioned during the interview for the readers' interest.

SINCE THE DISPUTE SEVEN HUNDRED MEMBERS HAVE BEEN ADDED WHILE THERE HAS BEEN ONLY ONE FORMAL RESIGNATION...!

TISA NEWS...NUMBER 8...SUMMER, 1993.

WHY HAS TISA SUPPORTED TERRY VENABLES' EFFORTS TO REMAIN AS CHIEF EXECUTIVE OF TOTTENHAM?

The short answer is because the overwhelming majority of members supported it.

It was a widely held view that with the addition of one or two new players, Tottenham would be a real force next season.

What of AMS's ambitions for the club? By contrast, he does not appear driven by an ambition to see Spurs, for example, win the League Championship.

He has talked of how he will not see Spurs in financial trouble whilst he is in charge, which is gratifying, but hardly the limit of supporters' ambitions for the club. He has spoken about qualifying for Europe. No doubt he would be delighted if Spurs wins a trophy but that does not seem to be his primary concern.

His lack of understanding of football is worrying.

Nothing that has happened since TV's sacking, including our detailed consideration of AMS's affidavit, has not led us to change our view that it is in the best interests of Tottenham for Venables to remain Chief Executive.

EGM...CANCELLED...2.00 PM...30TH JULY 1993

The board has intended to call an EGM for 2.00 pm on 30th July 1993 at White Hart Lane, for the purpose of sacking Jonathan Crystal as a Director of Tottenham Plc.

TV HAS ALSO PROPOSED RESOLUTIONS FOR SHAREHOLDERS TO CONSIDER:

1) That Steve Davies be appointed to the Board of Directors to safeguard the interests of supporters and ensure that decisions which affect supporters are taken after consultation with them.

We hope to have your support for this motion.

2) To dismiss Tony Berry and Douglas Alexiou as Directors.

Berry and Alexiou were directors during the Scholar/Bobroff era when the company got disastrously into debt. Why should we have confidence in them now? Therefore, we would intend to support this motion.

A LETTER SENT TO BERNIE KINGSLEY 2nd JULY BY ALAN SUGAR, ON TOTTENHAM HOTSPUR HEADED NOTEPAPER.

Dear Mr Kingsley,

Thank you for your letter dated 26th June.

As you quite rightly state, you are entitled to your opinion — I do not have to share it. It is my opinion that you are not a Tottenham Hotspur supporter, you are a Terry Venables supporter and I am afraid that the stance that you have taken publicly clearly indicates this. TISA, or any other supporters organisation, is very important and when the time is right you can be sure that an explanation of Mr Venables' dismissal will be given (the depth of detail of our explanation will depend on our legal status at the time). Most certainly a new going forward strategy will also be given.

I am not sure if there is such a thing as a database available for all TISA members. If there is, I would very much like to have this database as I propose to do the following:

a) Circularise to all TISA members a status report on the current litigation, as well as an update on current plans.

b) Suggest to all members that they have a democratic vote and appoint new leaders other than yourself and Mr Davies.

With respect to item b), the rationale behind this is that I feel that you and Mr Davies have clearly committed yourselves to a certain stance. No matter how convincing or factual the Club's arguments are, it would be rather embarrassing I should imagine for you to be able to make a 180 degree turn in your stance. Therefore, it would be most graceful for you both to step down in your capacity as leaders of TISA and support a democratic vote amongst all the members, to first of all appoint a short list of candidates and secondly, vote on those candidates. The outcome of such a vote will no doubt result in one or two new leading representatives of TISA, to which the Football Club Board will respectfully accept, and from time to time discuss whatever matters TISA wishes to discuss. Regretfully, too much water has gone under the bridge for me to consider discussing the affairs of the Club with you or Mr Davies in the future.

I will advise Mr Chris Belt of our Ticketing Department, of your decision not to renew your season ticket.

A.M. Sugar. Chairman.

Mr Sugar seems to think that the foregone conclusion is that there will be a new management of TISA once he can implement his referendum. That was in July 1993. TISA had an election. The results were as follows.
1) Was TISA right to support Terry Venables...?
RESULT: Yes...95% No...4% ABSTAINED...1%
2) Should TISA continue to support Terry Venables whilst there remains a possibility that he can regain his position at the Club...?
RESULT: Yes...90% No...8% ABSTAINED...2%
3) Should TISA continue to campaign on issues of concern to supporters, and pursue a dialogue with whoever is in control?
RESULT: Yes...99% No...1% (Everyone voted)
4) Should Steve Davies and Bernie Kingsley continue?
RESULT: Yes...95% No...2% ABSTAINED...3%.
    The result of the above was not believed by Alan Sugar. He wrote again to the joint Coordinators on the 1st September.

Dear Mr Davies and Mr Kingsley,
    I refer to your letter of the 25th August.
    Your letter of 25 August does not answer my question of why you state that Mr Venables is the best person to control Tottenham Hotspur; neither do your letters of 26 July and 5 August. Clearly you have no logical explanation.
    May I remind you that it was I that asked you to have a democratic vote of all TISA members. The statistics that you purport to have in my opinion are fabricated by you and do not represent any clear result of a democratic vote whatsoever. We do not know for example, how many people have replied to you. It may be that 10 people have replied out of a so-called 1000 members. We would like the opportunity to mailshot all of your members and to be responsible for counting the votes. It is unreasonable in any democratic vote that people being voted for are also responsible for collating and compiling the vote.

I have expressed to you in the past that it is virtually impossible for the Board of Directors at Tottenham to have any dialogue with you two gentlemen. This is not because we do not wish to listen to people that have another view: it is because of the vindictive attack that you have made on the Board in your one-sided presentation to the other TISA members. You have given no explanation whatsoever as to why we have gone forward with the current strategy.

I am also aware that you have written separately to Mr Ardiles requesting a meeting with him. At this moment in time the Board feel that no such meeting should take place with TISA until we have a clear understanding that the whole of TISA — or the majority of TISA — have voted for you two gentlemen to remain as their coordinators. Until such time as we are convinced of this (independently) we can not consider a dialogue with TISA.

Yours sincerely

A.M. Sugar

TISA replied thus:

Dear Mr Sugar,

We are in receipt of your letter of 1st September.

As you know, Mr Venables has given up his attempts to have himself reinstated as Chief Executive at Tottenham, and we have consequently brought our campaign in support of his reinstatement to an end. We consider that it is in the best interests of the Club to put its problems behind it, including our difference of opinion with you as to the merits of Mr Venables.

You indicated previously that you would like us replaced as TISA Coordinators. We have asked TISA members what they think and over 90% of respondents stated that they wish to see us continue, including most of the 8% who thought TISA should not continue to back Venables, and even the 4% who thought TISA was wrong to back him initially. You now accuse us of fabricating the results; that allegation is groundless and offensive.

We are an independent organisation, and have no intention of allowing you to write to our members and be responsible for counting the votes.

You have chosen not to accept that we have the support of TISA members and we note that you will not consider meeting with us, or a meeting between Mr Ardiles and TISA. In our view that is unfortunate, because we consider that, given the opportunity, TISA members can make a contribution to the development of Tottenham.

We have explained previously why we supported the reinstatement of Mr Venables and the fact that you do not accept that we were right to do so does not mean we have not given an explanation.

You said previously that we should accept Mr Venables is not returning to the club and look to the future. Now that we have done so we do not see how it will assist in relations between us to reiterate the reasons whey we supported his reinstatement.

We have not been vindictive. We have coordinated Tottenham supporters and articulated our members' views, as you would have seen had you been able to attend the Public Meeting held on 21st May 1993 (where approximately 700 Spurs' supporters were present). It seems that you blame the undersigned personally for the strong reaction of supporters to Mr Venables' sacking. TISA has acted responsibly at all times in exercising our democratic right to express our views.

We stressed the need for correspondence with the Board to be polite and for protests to be peaceful. The police praised the behaviour of supporters outside court and when we found that five or six people, who were not TISA members, had caused you problems, we endeavoured to persuade them not to do so.

It is disappointing that the letter from Mr Brazier was published in the match programme vs Chelsea. We note from the copy of his letter which you have now sent to us that it is addressed personally, signed 'John Brazier, Your pal on the Shelf', and that you replied thanking him for his 'kind words' and recording that you have endorsed his views '100%'. Mr Brazier's letter is insulting to TISA members in describing them as 'rent-a-mob' and to Steve Davies in particular. It suggests that Mr Davies has sought publicity for his own sake when in fact he has simply publicised the views of TISA. It accuses him of hypocrisy in attending a match after calling for a boycott of home matches.

The boycott policy was decided upon and adopted by those present at the Public Meeting of 21st May. At a TISA meeting on 24th June the policy was reviewed and a majority decided on reflection they intended to attend matches. The proposed boycott was therefore scrapped and this was publicised in TISA Newsletter #8, and in the press soon afterwards (i.e. before the start of the season). Some individual supporters have decided to either not renew their season tickets or not attend matches as a matter of principle: the undersigned decided not to renew our season tickets at least until the outcome of the section 459 proceedings was known, but have never said we would not attend any matches whatsoever.

Mr Brazier further says that the full facts of Mr Venables' dismissal are not known to the general public and by implication not known to us. Mr Brazier clearly does not know that, with the agreement of Mr Venables and yourself, we read your affidavit in which you set out your case including your reasons for losing confidence in Mr Venables.

From the start of the season the programme has generally (and conspicuously) avoided commenting on Mr Venables' departure and the circumstances surrounding it. As one could understand, it concentrated on information about the team and associated matters. It did not publish any of the letters which the club received complaining about Mr Venables, and nor would we expect it to. Indeed, it is generally the case that the programme does not criticise individuals, particularly in the way Mr Brazier's letter does.

In the interests of good relations between us we request that you print a statement on the letter page of the programme vs Oldham (18th September) making clear that the club disassociates itself from the insulting comments of Mr Brazier. If you are not prepared to do so then we propose that in the interests of fairness you give us the right to reply and publish a letter from ourselves, of equal length to that of Mr Brazier, and unedited.

The programme has a good reputation and, as you know, recently won a 'Programme of the Year' award. We consider that its credibility is at risk if it carries personal attacks on individuals or organisations but does not allow them to reply.

We will continue to look positively toward the future of Tottenham, to organise TISA and to support the Club we have both followed since the 1960's. If at some time in the future your attitude changes, we will be happy to discuss with you matters of interest to our members.

Yours sincerely

Steve Davies & Bernie Kingsley.

At the time of writing, there has been much correspondence through the auspices of a Mr John Fennelly who is the Press Officer of Tottenham and who also incidentally approves the Match Programme. Mr Sugar continues to press for a referendum and continues to request details of the data-based list of members of TISA. He has also suggested that this involuntary vote be contracted and controlled by Messrs. Touche Ross, the well-known Accountancy and Auditing Company, who, by chance, are also the Auditors of Amstrad.

Bernie and Steve are certainly not idiots and would not allow this to happen.

As a result, an agreement has been reached whereby the controllers of this referendum are to be The Electoral Reform Society, who of course are entirely independent.

The first signs are that Mr Sugar will not be successful in removing Bernie or Steve from their positions. The reason is simple.

THERE ARE FOUR COORDINATORS IN TOTAL. NOMINATIONS FOR THE REPLACEMENTS HAVE BEEN RECEIVED AND FIVE HAVE BEEN NOMINATED. OF THOSE FIVE, FOUR ARE THE SAME ONES THAT PRESENTLY HOLD THE POSITIONS INCLUDING, OF COURSE, BERNIE KINGSLEY AND STEVE DAVIES....

Hard Luck Alan.

The vote will be conducted during late November and all members listed on the database as at the 7th September will be included. Unfortunately my own membership was after that date, but I would like to use this book to record my vote.

IN FAVOUR OF BERNIE KINGSLEY...AYE.

IN FAVOUR OF STEVE DAVIES...AYE.

Chapter 9
THE BAILYS

Many a Spurs supporter will remember the side that played in 1949/50 who won the Second Division Championship and in the following Season, after promotion, the First Division title. Who can possibly forget the many Internationals who played then, from goalie Ditchburn right through to the accomplished Canadian who represented this Country on the left wing, Les Medley.

Of course we have to mention that Spurs present Life President and former double winning side manager, Bill Nicholson, was in that team, as well as the best England Manager of all time, the man who won the World Cup at Wembley in 1966, Alf Ramsey, at right back for the Lilywhites.

Distinguished as they were, and indeed are, it is to the partner to Les Medley, at inside left, Eddie Baily, the Cheekie Chappie to whom I refer in this chapter.

More to the point it is, coincidentally, his nephew Terry and niece by marriage, Valerie Baily, that warrants the mention.

For it was those two, as Directors of 'Dellprint' who were the main losers, when Terry Venables along with a guy called Paul Reviere and the aforementioned Eddie Ashby (later to describe himself as General Manager of T.H.F.C.), through their Company, Glenhope Products Ltd, decided to invent and market a game called 'The Manager'.

On a Channel 4 programme, the Company that was called into question was not only Glenhope, but another based on Canvey Island in Essex currently called 'Games and Print Services Ltd, but formerly known as Thamespad Ltd, and Trainwell Ltd

It all becomes somewhat complicated when it appears that Ashby persuaded Alan Roberts to allow the involvement of himself and his partners, by introducing £50,000 into Thamespad through a new company which they called Print Double Ltd

Without attempting to further complicate matters by describing the links between these companies, it would be adequate to say that Roberts received some of that £50,000 in cash by way of surreptitious meetings at various roadsides, but nothing like the full amount promised. According to Roberts, his company secretary would meet Ashby or his representatives by pre-arrangement and the car windows would drop, and a bundle of notes, usually amounts from two to five thousand would pass between them without hardly a word being said. Once Ashby apparently mentioned that the money had been sent by Glenhope, but in the main, Roberts accepted the payments without question.

Our investigations proved that Thamespad Ltd were more or less only the assemblers of that game, and that most of the actual work was carried out by the sub-contractor, Messrs. Dellprint. It was they who prepared all the printing of the hundreds of cards and the game board as well as the cover which distinctly showed the portrait of Terry Venables.

The tangled web of associated companies engaged and liqui-dated during Dellprint's association with Alan Roberts' group of companies and indirectly Glenhope, needs a qualified account-ant to translate the many events that resulted in a loss to the Bailys of something like eighty thousand pounds.

Dellprint is a family run business, Mum, Dad and two sons, with some ten additional employees. The loss of that vast sum, including an amount not yet invoiced, prevaricated the dismissal of some twenty five per cent of the staff. It has changed the lives of the Bailys for an unforeseeable future while they work diligently, night and day, to repay the debts that they themselves incurred as a result of this association with the Roberts/Ashby/Venables tie-up.

Simplistically it went like this.

Thamespad Ltd had been trading for many years with Dellprint, successfully, and there was no concern to Terry and Valerie Baily regarding payment for work carried out. Then, quite inconspicuously, they were asked in the normal way of events to quote and prepare the artwork for the game called 'The Manager'.

They were given the contract to print and supply.

At that time they had no idea that Venables, Ashby or Reviere had any connection with Alan Roberts the owner of Thamespad. Unbeknown to them was the fact that Eddie Ashby had promised

Roberts an injection of capital into his business, for which Glenhope took security by way of a large chunk of the shares in Thamespad.

Impressed by the fact that Terry Venables was connected to Glenhope Ltd, and needing a capital injection into the Company during a time of recession, Roberts gleefully accepted Eddie Ashby's offer.

The game produced, amid fanfares and special exhibitions, and display at Harrods, Mr Roberts, naturally, expected to receive the promised total investment and to be paid some one hundred and fifty thousand pounds for the completed work, out of which he would have reimbursed the Bailys for their part of the operation.

Terry Baily and Valerie visited the toy fair at Earls Court and there, they saw the results of their efforts proudly on display, and to be told by the girls on the stand that six thousand of the games had been sent to the British Army based overseas in Kuwait fighting against the Tyrant, Saddam Hussein. They of course had no idea that a planned subterfuge, to liquidate Thamespad was in mind.

Mr Roberts recalls that the investment was never realised in its entirety. Suddenly, from being a decent hard working toy and games manufacturer, Alan Roberts found himself caught up in intrigue, for after the announcement of the intent to liquidate, without Double Print settling the outstanding account, and, conversely, without onward payment to the sub-contractor, Dellprint, Mr Roberts could then be found at a factory in Corby called Trainwell Ltd, where they continued to produce 'The Manager' and also the best selling 'Trivial Pursuit'.

Only a short time after this first liquidation, Mr Baily travelled to Corby where he espied some of the machinery which Thamespad had operated at the Canvey factory.

The Bailys then received a letter from a firm of liquidators announcing Trainwell Ltd was in receivership. This came on the 13th March 1991 and had been sent by Messrs. Levy Gee & Partners of Chalk Farm, London, N.W.1, described as 'Corporate Support Services'.

We have discovered that Levy Gee also acted for the Company in presenting their original documents to the Company Registrar, and that the registered address of Thamespad Ltd, was changed to that of Levy Gee's on the twelfth of November, 1990.

In the letter which was referenced DJW, the initials of one of the Directors being Derrick J Wolf, but signed by another name indistinguishable to the eye, but nevertheless described as a Director, Mr Wolf openly discloses the debtors of Trainwell Ltd, and the amounts owed to them from various companies. As a result of these disclosures, the Bailys were to receive some fifty nine thousand pounds being various percentages of the total the Liquidator obviously expected to collect during his capacity as Receiver, and included some offers to Dellprint to release art work and film for other sums.

Among those debtors being called in by Levy Gee was a debt of £150,000 owed to Trainwell Ltd, by Glenhope Products Ltd. Of this sum the Bailys were being offered some ten per cent, i.e. £15,000.

Of the total offered by Levy Gee on all the money owed to Trainwell, which amounted to several hundred thousand pounds, the Bailys actually received seven thousand six hundred and eighty four pounds and fifty p…!

Clearly the question of what happened to the money paid to Glenhope for sales that they had made, which were reported as being quite substantial, is one issue.

During a television interview with Paul Reviere, a Director of Glenhope Products Ltd, he stated that he wished to draw some money out of what he knew to be a very successful enterprise, that of marketing and producing 'The Manager', but found the bank account to contain practically nothing.

Mr Roberts had another company described as a holding company, Thamespad (Holdings) Ltd. It was this company that owned the building in Canvey at which he first traded. Back he went from Corby to start trading once again this time as 'Print and Games Ltd'.

Once again Mr Baily has visited these premises and once again the machinery has been identified as part of the original collection.

I asked Valerie whether they were still trading with Alan Roberts.

She replied that business had to go on and before his involvement, specifically with Eddie Ashby, Print Double and Glenhope, he was a 'good customer'.

For two years Terry and Valerie Baily have struggled to 'stay alive'.

Their bankers, as is their wont, are allowing them to work on a five thousand pounds overdraft only. Every penny of their tiny profit is being paid to their creditors, following a moratorium that they voluntarily called. Their life quality has deteriorated and plummeted. They have had no holiday since 1991. They have not changed their car. Almost half of the staff have now gone and not been replaced. Their hours are long and arduous. They consider that at the present rate of turnover, limited by the reduced labour capacity and the low bank facility, it will take them all of a further six to seven years to pay the debt that they incurred.

I could not allow the matter to end there.

I contacted Harrods who confirmed that 'The Manager' was no longer being stocked and was no longer available, supplies having been discontinued.

I wanted to meet with Alan Roberts to find out the strength of the involvement of Glenhope Products Ltd, Mr Venables and Messrs. Levy Gee, the Receivers. It would be true to say that it is highly unusual for the Chartered Accountants who formed a Limited Company for a client, to also act as their liquidators. Perhaps that is a matter for the Institute of Chartered Acountants.

Below are details of my conversation with Alan Roberts, his Company Secretary, who was the one to collect the roadside handouts, and with Messrs. Levy Gee & Partners.

The Company Secretary: I have nothing to say. Speak to Mr Roberts.

I spoke to Mr Roberts.

"Terry Venables is suing the Daily Mirror for something that they wrote about him based on something I was supposed to have said. I rang the Daily Mirror and they asked me whether I could confirm or deny some allegations made on television to help their defence. In that light I am not going to talk to you."

I rang Mr Maurice Moses of Levy Gee and he stated that he would talk to me after I spoke to Roberts.

I rang Levy Gee again. This time they suggested that I put my intentions and points of enquiry into writing after which they would almost certainly agree to speak to me at a formal interview.

On Monday 26th October 1993, I wrote to Mr Moses explaining that I needed to know where the money that they were appointed to collect from Alan Roberts' companies debtors list, ended up. What happened to the money due from Glenhope Ltd? Indeed, had they been paid at all by Glenhope Ltd...? What was the nature of Glenhope's dealings and investment in Thamespad/Trainwell and Games and Print Services. Were Terry and his confidants on the Board of Directors, or shareholders of those Companies?

On the telephone Mr Moses was able to tell me that he recalls great difficulty in gaining information and payment. He had spoken to Terry Venables on only a couple of occasions, with the thrust of his enquiry being directed at Eddie Ashby and Paul Reviere. He remembers being 'constantly mucked about' by them.

Subsequently I received a letter answering to some extent the questions that I put to the Liquidators, Messrs. Levy Gee.

"Print Double attempted to acquire certain items of plant and machinery which were offered for sale as part of the receivership of Trainwell Ltd"

(O.K., but how did Trainwell get the machinery in the first instance when it originally belonged to Thamespad, Canvey...?)

"Correspondence has been exchanged between Levy Gee and Glenhope Ltd, the responses being signed by Eddie Ashby as Director of that company."

(In volume 2 of this book you will discover that Glenhope is now in liquidation!)

"Of the £150,000 owed by Glenhope Ltd, we have received a total of £18,000 paid in two tranches, the first one of ten thousand pounds, and a full and final settlement amount of £8,000. This latter amount was paid by 'EDENNOTE LTD'."

(Edennote is wholly owned by Terry Venables and was set up only for the purposes of arranging a management contract with Tottenham Hotspur Plc, and for a vehicle to purchase the shares in the Tottenham Company. The liquidators state that categorically, which shows beyond doubt Venables' involvement, and also that he has used one Company to pay the debts of another Company.... Naughty!)

"Thamespad Ltd is now in final liquidation; a final statement has been issued to creditors, and no more money is forthcoming."

(The Bailys have never received a final statement!)

"As regards to Trainwell Ltd, a meeting has been convened and a report required by creditors has been issued to all creditors."

(No report has ever been received by Dellprint Ltd!)

"Thamespad Ltd was not owed any money by Glenhope Ltd"

(So, no mention of the promised £50,000 and no mention of the capital that was actually injected!)

"According to Trainwell's books, there was a sum of £151,660 outstanding from Glenhope Ltd, but Glenhope have disputed this amount to the total of £105,109. Assuming acceptance of the dispute (the Receivers do not say why there should be such a dispute)...that left a balance of £46,551 which Ashby agreed would be paid in regular instalments over a period of five months. These arrangements were not adhered to, and accordingly a statutory demand was issued in September 1991.

"A winding-up petition was sworn on the 9th December 1991, but we accepted a completion of the said £8,000."

(The rights and activities of receivers and liquidators must surely be questioned. In settling with Glenhope for that puny amount, which no doubt was used in part to satisfy the fees of Levy Gee, absolutely no consideration was given to Dellprint and others that have suffered enormous losses.)

Certainly it seems that Ashby opens and closes companies at will, without consideration for the people that he is destroying, the job losses and the companies that suddenly find themselves in financial difficulty because of his antics....

What happened to the £151,000 plus the profit element which we know to be around 100 per cent, therefore a total of circa £302,000 and which must have been paid to Glenhope for sales by esteemed retailers such as Harrods and Hamleys etc?

Where is it? Who has had it? Certainly Paul Reviere hasn't, for he wasn't able to withdraw a relatively small amount when he needed it most. Eddie Ashby...Terry Venables.... Where is that money?)

The Receivers have now offered a further 10 per cent to Dellprint, some £800, as a final settlement against that which they lost in their dealings with the tangled web of companies in which Ashby and Venables were involved.

Just as a matter of interest the Receivers go on to advise us that of a debt owed to Trainwell by a company called 'Brandmakers' (they currently manufacture 'Question of Sport'), which amounts to over a quarter of a million pounds, of which the Bailys were to receive some £37,500, they have again been involved in a dispute and have accepted £11,500 in full and final settlement. The Bailys received some £1,725 against the initial expectancy of £37,500. Another puny settlement and another instance of the ultimate creditor being the sufferer.

We are advised that as a result of another winding-up petition a firm of accountants called Pannell Kerr Forster were appointed joint administrative receivers on the 30th July 1992. This of course means that Brandmakers are still trading, but being controlled by a receiver who effectively runs the Company.

Meanwhile Dellprint carry the financial burden of all these people's agreements, no doubt with their own fees in mind.

Yes, a receiver must be paid, we can none of us work for nothing (perhaps with the exception of First Wave Sport Services Ltd), but surely a consideration for the plight of the true losers must be paramount to negotiated settlements.

At some time after May 1993, Glenhope Ltd was dissolved, adding another branch to the fallen tree of failures directed by Mr Venables and or his aide-de-camp, Eddie Ashby.

To summarise specifically the payment by Edennote of £8,000 in full and final settlement to the Receivers of the Glenhope debt. To Make such payment while Edennote was itself insolvent is illegal, and I quote below the Company act under which the Bailys may well pursue through the courts, there interest.

In later evidence mentioned in Court during the hearings of the 10th. to 14th. June, Terry submits that he and other companies that he controls is owed over £1 million in respect of the monies raised to purchase the shares in Tottenham. Money loaned to Edennote. This, in addition to the money he borrowed from the Bank.

Now if we assume that Glenhope was one of those companies, it would account for why Paul Reviere was unable to withdraw any money out of the bank account of Glenhope, and more importantly, why the Bailys and presumably Thamespad and Trainwell and any amount of other suppliers remain unpaid as to their invoices.

Was the money received from the sales of 'The Manager' board game used to assist in the purchase of those shares? Or did Terry commit another 'dodgy' act when he used Edennote's money to settle the Glenhope debt with the Receiver?

Clearly, only an investigation will discover these irregular, if not unlawful payments.

Perhaps, those enthusiastic to respond to the 'Sun' newspapers' campaign to have Terry elected as England Manager will now know why the FA should not appoint him. How they, or indeed the whole Country would appear in the eyes of others, if shortly after the appointment, Terry was being investigated by an Inspector of the Secretary of State, for that is what it will amount to if the Bailys obtain their court Order to perpetuate such an action.

Company Act 432..Section XIV.. Paragraph a)....

'The Secretary of state may appoint an inspector to investigate the affairs of the company and report on them, if the court, by order declares that its affairs ought to be so investigated. The Secretary of State may make such an apointment if it appears to him that there are circumstances suggesting:

a) That the company's affairs are being or have been conducted with intent to defraud its creditors or the creditors of any other person or otherwise for a fraudulent or unlawful purpose or in any manner which is unfairly prejudicial to some part of its members.

Overleaf, you can read the letter that the Bailys have written to the Prime Minister and the Secretary of State.

Dellprint Limited

Registered in England No. 1528372

Lithographic-Printers – Platemakers – Designers

Attn. The Right Honourable Prime Minister,
Mr John Major,
10 Downing Street,
London.

Copy to the Secretary of State.   10/1/93.

Dear Mr Major,

My wife and I are writing to you on a very serious matter concerning Mr Terry Venables.

Attached to this letter is a copy of Chapter 9 of Author Guy Nathan's book, Barcelona to Bedlam. It explains our plight.

Through the good offices of the Publishers of that book, Messrs New Author Publications Ltd., their accountants and their solicitors, we write in an effort to get the Secretary of State to appoint an investigator to look into the affairs of Mr Venables and his partner Mr Edward Ashby, so that we might have a chance of recouping some or all of the money out of which we have been cheated.

Our hope is that the Secretary of State will voluntarily appoint such a man and not force us to resort to the Court to obtain an order instructing him to do so, which would cost us a great deal of money which we do not have at this time. We seek your assistance under Clause 432, Chapter XIV, item a) of the Companies Act.

We ask why should we have suffered for so long and why we look as if we are going to continue to suffer in the future, because of the unscrupulous activities of Mr Venables and his cohauts.

We have had no holiday for two years, and are unlikely to get one for many years to come. We have been forced to call a moritorium of our creditors. The bank have all but foreclosed on us. We have had to dismiss several staff. Our sons and us are working until midnight each day in order to pay back our creditors, while the perpetrator of these events is being hailed as our next manager of the England team. We have losr both customers and' suppliers. The FA, not satisfied with the ultimate humiliation of being left out of the World Cup, now seem to wish to compound their extraordinary decisions by electing a man whom we intend by one means or other to suffer

"Since I was a little kid."

"And you are what, twenty five or so?"

"Say, a supporter for about eighteen years or so?"

"I think the same as Kevin, really. When it first happened, we ought it was diabolical, but now I think it is a good thing. At the e everyone thought that Venables saved the Club, but Sugar is man that put the money in."

"Do you think that Venables was good for the Club when he s here?"

"The footballing side of it…. Yeah."

"Do you think we played well under him."

"Yeah, but we didn't win enough, did we?"

KEVIN THEN INTERRUPTED….

"Except that to win one FA Cup wasn't enough for the money spent."

"What about the time Terry appointed Peter Shreeves to run team?"

"That wasn't a clever decision."

"What about the Livermore/Clemence management?"

"They were much better. Definitely."

"Now they are gone, we start all over again? What about Ossie liles? Do you think he will have more success?"

"I think he will."

"What about the way Spurs are playing right now?"

"Best start to the Season for ages. I think they are playing really l."

"Summing up, are you saying that at first you thought that it s diabolical treatment of Terry Venables, but now as the facts beginning to come out, you have doubts?"

"If they are true. We don't know much yet."

"Are you warming towards Alan Sugar and away from Terry nables?"

"Well, we don't really know the facts, but I would say yeah."

"What's your name?"

"Purcell, Epping."

"What about your opinion?"

"Well, it's all been said really. I agree with them."

"How long have you been a Spurs supporter."

investigation for what we believe is fraudulent activity. We do not see that we, at our time of life, should carry the financial can for Venables' misdemeanours while he gets the top sporting job in the Country at no doubt, a massive salary.

Is it the desire of the relevant authorities to make England the laughing stock of the World?

Please help us, as without your assistance, it seems that the little people like us, and no doubt many others caught up in this web, will suffer while this man gets away with everything.

In your Citizens Charter our case is a serious test to examine whether we can expect the protection that you wish to offer in a classless society.

We want to know what happened to the money the Home Office paid to Glenhope for the 6000 'Manager' games that we printed, and which were sent to our forces in Kuwait during the Iraqi war. We want to know what happened to the money paid to Glenhope from Harrods, Selfridges and Hamleys and others. We know that the cost element of producing 25000 games was over £150,000. Add on Venables' profit element and the figure is around £300,000. What has happened to all that money and why haven't we been paid? What Venables has done to us is disgraceful.

You will see from the copies of letters received by Guy Nathan from the Receivers that Venables settled a £140,000 balance owed to creditors with an £8,000 cheque from Edennote. This is not fair to us. Why did the receivers settle for such a small amount? How come Glenhope had so little money that the insolvent Edennote, an associated company of Tottenham Hotspur PLc paid their debt?..

We seek your help as requested.

Yours Sincerely,

Terry and Valerie Baily. Directors.

Chapter 10
VIEWS OF SPURS SUPPO
AND THE CHIEF OF PO

I started interviewing some Spurs supporters outsi
before the Everton game on Sunday the 3rd Octob
my portable close to their faces, trying desperate
noisy traffic. I decided to make recordings at ever
Ground, so as to gain the views of the public wh
varying locations. A broad view.

I started at the North-East corner at the bot
Road.

Before writing their individual comments, I f
to point out that all of those interviewed had a
knowledge as those who had watched the two T
and read the papers.

My first supporter was a Mr Kevin Sisson of E
him:

"You are aware of the recent events at White H
do you view them as you know them at the mome

"When it first happened I thought that it was c
utterly wrong for Alan Sugar to get rid of Venable
thought that it was the worst thing that could be c
allegations are true then I think it was the right th

"What do you see as the allegations?"

"About the Santin business where he was supp
hundred grand, and eight grand turned up in th
like that. The whole thing was a complete farce, re

"And your name is?"

"Price, Epping."

"Are you a Spurs supporter?"

"Yes."

"How long have you been supporting them?"

investigation for what we believe is fraudulent activity. We do not see that we, at our time of life, should carry the financial can for Venables' misdemeanours while he gets the top sporting job in the Country at no doubt, a massive salary.

Is it the desire of the relevant authorities to make England the laughing stock of the World?

Please help us, as without your assistance, it seems that the little people like us, and no doubt many others caught up in this web, will suffer while this man gets away with everything.

In your Citizens Charter our case is a serious test to examine whether we can expect the protection that you wish to offer in a classless society.

We want to know what happened to the money the Home Office paid to Glenhope for the 6000 'Manager' games that we printed, and which were sent to our forces in Kuwait during the Iraqi war. We want to know what happened to the money paid to Glenhope from Harrods, Selfridges and Hamleys and others. We know that the cost element of producing 25000 games was over £150,000. Add on Venables' profit element and the figure is around £300,000. What has happened to all that money and why haven't we been paid? What Venables has done to us is disgraceful.

You will see from the copies of letters received by Guy Nathan from the Receivers that Venables settled a £140,000 balance owed to creditors with an £8,000 cheque from Edennote. This is not fair to us. Why did the receivers settle for such a small amount? How come Glenhope had so little money that the insolvent Edennote, an associated company of Tottenham Hotspur PLc paid their debt?..

We seek your help as requested.

Yours Sincerely,

Terry and Valerie Baily. Directors.

Chapter 10
VIEWS OF SPURS SUPPORTERS
AND THE CHIEF OF POLICE

I started interviewing some Spurs supporters outside the Ground before the Everton game on Sunday the 3rd October 1993. I held my portable close to their faces, trying desperately to avoid the noisy traffic. I decided to make recordings at every corner of the Ground, so as to gain the views of the public who arrived from varying locations. A broad view.

I started at the North-East corner at the bottom of Paxton Road.

Before writing their individual comments, I feel that I have to point out that all of those interviewed had about as much knowledge as those who had watched the two TV programmes and read the papers.

My first supporter was a Mr Kevin Sisson of Epping. I asked him:

"You are aware of the recent events at White Hart Lane. How do you view them as you know them at the moment?"

"When it first happened I thought that it was completely and utterly wrong for Alan Sugar to get rid of Venables. At the time I thought that it was the worst thing that could be done. But if the allegations are true then I think it was the right thing."

"What do you see as the allegations?"

"About the Santin business where he was supposed to pay two hundred grand, and eight grand turned up in the safe. Things like that. The whole thing was a complete farce, really."

"And your name is?"

"Price, Epping."

"Are you a Spurs supporter?"

"Yes."

"How long have you been supporting them?"

"Since I was a little kid."

"And you are what, twenty five or so?"

"Say, a supporter for about eighteen years or so?"

"I think the same as Kevin, really. When it first happened, we thought it was diabolical, but now I think it is a good thing. At the time everyone thought that Venables saved the Club, but Sugar is the man that put the money in."

"Do you think that Venables was good for the Club when he was here?"

"The footballing side of it.... Yeah."

"Do you think we played well under him."

"Yeah, but we didn't win enough, did we?"

KEVIN THEN INTERRUPTED....

"Except that to win one FA Cup wasn't enough for the money he spent."

"What about the time Terry appointed Peter Shreeves to run the team?"

"That wasn't a clever decision."

"What about the Livermore/Clemence management?"

"They were much better. Definitely."

"Now they are gone, we start all over again? What about Ossie Ardiles? Do you think he will have more success?"

"I think he will."

"What about the way Spurs are playing right now?"

"Best start to the Season for ages. I think they are playing really well."

"Summing up, are you saying that at first you thought that it was diabolical treatment of Terry Venables, but now as the facts are beginning to come out, you have doubts?"

"If they are true. We don't know much yet."

"Are you warming towards Alan Sugar and away from Terry Venables?"

"Well, we don't really know the facts, but I would say yeah."

"What's your name?"

"Purcell, Epping."

"What about your opinion?"

"Well, it's all been said really. I agree with them."

"How long have you been a Spurs supporter."

"Donkey's years. My whole life...." (He was about forty five) "Why has it all come out in football. The little man can't get away with anything, but these big blokes.... I think that the man Venables done brilliant while he was at Tottenham. Everything comes out now."

"Do you think he should have concentrated on football only and left the business side alone?"

"His football ability was never in doubt. Definitely he should have left the business side alone."

"O.K. Thanks. You'll see your name in the book.... Bye."

"When's it coming out?"

"January."

Kevin Preston from Heybridge in Essex.

"How old are you, Kevin?"

"Forty one."

"And how long have you been supporting Tottenham?"

"Thirty odd years."

"You've seen the changes then. Presumably you have seen the television about recent events at Spurs. What do you think about it all?"

"I would still like to see Venables here."

"Do you think that what has been alleged warranted his dismissal?"

"Not really, no. He may not be a good businessman but he is a really good football man, and that's what we really care about."

"Do you think that Alan Sugar should have moved him away from the business side and left him in charge of the football?"

"I think that would have been a good idea, yeah."

"So you are really a Venables man and would have liked to see us stay with him?"

"Yeah, I do."

Arnold Raven, also of Heybridge:

"How long have you been a Spurs supporter Arnold?"

"All my life. I'm forty nine."

"You first came when you were what, six, or seven?"

"Yes about nineteen fifty or so."

"You remember the old great team we had with Ditchburn, Ramsey, Nicholson and Eddie Baily?"

"Yes I remember them well."

"What do you think of the current situation?"

"I would like to see Venables back. Mainly because of the footballing aspect. The business side of things I feel that whatever has gone on has gone on. Whether that is right or wrong I don't know, but what I do know is that Terry Venables is the best man to have in charge."

"You don't have faith in Ossie Ardiles?"

"Yes I do have faith in Ossie, but I think Terry put Spurs on the right path and he should have been allowed to stay there."

"You are saying that Alan Sugar should have given him another chance and left him in charge of the football?"

"Yes, most definitely. It should have been done in a more dignified way. There's lots of things that people can rake up about anybody in business transactions, but everybody regrets making some decisions and does some things wrong, but the man was very good at football, certainly."

"Do you think that maybe the heavy interest payments that Terry had to contend with might have affected his judgement?"

"Yes, really that may be the case, but that is a business problem and not a football problem. It is where the two things are always opposite. If you go down the path that Terry is alleged to have done then you burn your bridges."

"Thank you both very much. Hope you enjoy the game."

(Even as we spoke none of us knew that possibly one of the best performances seen at Spurs for many a year was about to be witnessed. Spurs won the game by three two, scoring the equalising and winning goals in the final two minutes of the game. But it wasn't so much the result as the fluency of their play, and the magnificent effort that went into the victory. Alan Sugar, Steve Perryman and Ossie Ardiles must have been crowing after this incredibly exciting and professional performance.)

Tuesday 6th October 1993. The evening Spurs played Burnley in the second leg of the second round of the 1993 Coca-Cola League Cup Competition. The weather was at its British best with the rain teeming down in buckets. I decided on Tony's, the cafe whose walls had been adorned with photographs of Spurs teams since the fifties: Ditchburn, Ramsey, Withers (Willis), Old Bill Nicholson, Clarke, Burgess, Walters, Bennet, Duquemin, Baily and Medley. Ah, those.... I nearly said they were the days, but not so, for on the wall next to that one was the double team of the sixties. Who could forget Blanchflower, and Mackay and John White, Cliffy Jones, and later Jimmy Greaves. The restaurant was full of nostalgia and I remembered that it was the one where many of the players would grab a bit of lunch when they were in for treatment instead of being down at the training ground in Cheshunt. I remembered seeing Tony Galvin and Mickey Hazard there. I approached it and...it was closed. Tony had gone bust a few weeks previously and I was stunned. Tony's restaurant was not just your everyday greasy spoon cafe, but an institution in the lives of the early arriving supporter.

The only alternative was the Hotspur Cafe across the road. There were two lovely middle-aged ladies sitting at a table, and in a moment they were snared.

"Are you going to the match?" I asked.

"Yes," they replied in unison. I'm no sexist. Why not? The woman's angle.

"How long have you been going to Spurs?"

"Ten years a season ticket holder." Mary Nash of Hatfield replied.

"You've seen the changes at Spurs in management then since Keith Burkenshaw? What do you think of the football that we are playing?"

"It's very good."

"Do you notice any difference between the days of say, David Pleat and now?"

"Only when Peter Shreeves came in and once before after he left and just before Venables arrived, when Mabbutt, Clemence and Ossie were in temporary charge."

"Did you enjoy the football that Spurs played when Terry took over?"

"Well, he came into a very demoralised club. I think the footballers were the same but he lifted them. It seemed to take him a long time to sort them out but when he did they have played very well."

"You mentioned Peter Shreeves. What about him?"

"His team played badly, but I suspect that he is a very nice person and probably too nice to be number one at Spurs. I really see him as a number two under a better manager."

"As he is now under Glenn Hoddle at Chelsea?"

"Exactly."

"What about the present situation, or should I say the on-going situation. What do you think should happen now?"

"I think Terry should be allowed back to take charge of football matters."

"And what about Ossie Ardiles? Do you think he should then go?

"No, I think it would be good if they worked together."

"Interesting. Do you really think that that would work?"

"No, not really. It was Terry Venables that got rid of Ardiles in the first place. I would still like to see him back though."

"What do you see for the future? Do you see us going forward now under Alan Sugar and Ossie?"

"I think Ossie could be there for some time yet, but I am not so sure about Mr Sugar. I am not convinced that he doesn't see Spurs as a commodity, and if they let him down commercially, I think he'll sell out."

"What do you think of the recent dispute?"

"I think that we know only a little that has gone on. Perhaps your book will tell us the truth. There certainly was a clash of personalities. Both men are Generals in their respective fields, and an army does not need two commanders at the helm. Then her friend commented:

"I have to add that I don't ever think that Terry should come back to replace either Mr Sugar or Ossie Ardiles. The way Ossie plays football, and his ideas are how I like football to be played."

This highly intelligent lady then questioned me about the book and its title etc. I turned to her colleague and then wished them both an enjoyable game after her friend suggested that her views were exactly the same, except that she thought that Terry Venables should never return to Spurs in any capacity.

I wondered what a policeman might think or have to say about it all and about Spurs in general. I asked twelve constables if they were supporters but none were. There was an offer from one to be interviewed but he laughed when he told me that he supported West Ham. He then directed me to Inspector Colin Parsons of Tottenham Police Station, who, not only was in charge, but was also a supporter.

I asked him whether he had much crowd problem particularly after the announcement of the dismissal of Terry.

"No, surprisingly not. Through liaison with the Tottenham Supporters Association and the like, we have actually avoided any crowd trouble. There were several incidents outside the main gates shortly after the dismissal, but they were in the main quite humorous and nobody warranted either warning or arrest."

"In one of the court cases the Judge made reference to activities by some supporters that actually warranted his sympathy: In fact he allowed those matters to influence his adjudication. Were you involved at any time with the incidents referred to?"

"No, that was all handled by The City Divisions. I think that it was well documented on the television. The trouble was all around the High Court at the time of the first and second hearings. From a local point of view that never fed its way back to the ground."

"Have you been at Tottenham Station for a long time?"

"For the last eighteen months, but a Spurs supporter for considerably longer."

"So you have seen the changes in direction, and management?"

"Yes and they are definitely a change for the better. The co-operation of the present administration is so good that, although the police are not becoming complacent, our task has become significantly easier."

"In what way?"

"Well the whole situation has improved. The days are gone when we actually expect trouble. Now it is the exception rather than the norm."

"Do you think that the present Directors are responsible for that, and do you deal directly with Mr Sugar?"

"Certainly the present co-operation and liaison is very good, and the staff, the Company Secretary, Mr John Ireland, clearly acting under the Chairman's direction, are very good in helping us with our problems.''

"Do you deal with the Managers?"

"Only when an incident occurs inside the ground either during and after the game, or possibly before it sometimes. There have been very few incidents lately, and both Mr Venables and Mr Ardiles are unquestionably co-operative.''

"Taking your official cap off, and as a Spurs supporter, what do you think of recent events?''

"The recent events have settled down remarkably well. I took my lad to the Everton match and there was a good family attitude and friendly feeling about the whole ground. I had no qualms about attending the match.''

"As a civilian do you have anything to say about the departure from the Club of Mr Venables?''

"It isn't for me to comment on internal wranglings, but only to say that after an initial feeling of impending trouble the whole thing has settled and there has been less enthusiastic demonstrations and boycotting than we at first feared. I believe that emotions were flying high, but Mr Venables actually said himself that at the end of the day, the supporters support the Club and not just one individual. That seems to be the view that they have sensibly taken. This is demonstrated by the fact that there has been no trouble for the Police to deal with.''

I thanked him for his particularly sensible and informative comments, and hope that he enjoyed the game.

Finally, I have decided to print in summary the views of one, Lee Brier of Walthamstow. Lee is forty and comes to Spurs whenever possible, as mostly, he mans his market stall on a Saturday. Sometimes he finishes at about two, and if he can pack up in time, he makes it, just, in time to see the match. He has been a supporter for thirty two years.

I asked him the same questions as I had put to many, many others. In the main he agreed that the supporters had plenty of time for Terry Venables, who had probably been a little foolhardy. But what he said next captured my thoughts.

"But he isn't dangerous like the other one, is he?"

Lee, you have probably rendered this book as somewhat innocuous as you have summed it all up with just one succinct statement. Thank you.

Chapter 11
TRYING TO MAKE SENSE
OF IT ALL

At the time of writing, the dispute between Terry Venables and Alan Sugar has not been resolved, and may rumble on for a long time, but the fact is that Terry is now on the outside looking in whereas Alan is very much in control.

It is ironic that Sugar's position has been strengthened by the transcript of the Court proceedings which he was anxious that I should not see, and which are summarised in the second part of this book. Why I kept asking myself, did he refuse to talk to me or allow any of his employees to do so?

It seems that every employee, from the gateman to the Financial Director, received a memorandum from the Chairman which read: "If you are approached by a Mr Guy Nathan to contribute to his book about Spurs, you are instructed not to give him any information."

Fortunately, not everyone obeyed this puzzling instruction, although I have been told repeatedly that Sugar is not a man who puts up with opposition from his staff. I suppose he thought that I was on Terry's side, which is very interesting since at one time Jonathan Harris was worried that Sugar was financing my book!

As for the Court transcripts, Sugar had paid for these himself and he was unwilling to release them to me, although of course I offered to pay for copies. I had to go to almost the very highest judicial authority to obtain them as a matter of public interest.

What did the rich and powerful Chairman of two public companies think that an investigative writer like me might discover by sticking my nose into his affairs? In fact I might have done him a service, because at the end of the day the facts that I have discovered are not seriously to his discredit.

As for Terry Venables, who was quite forthcoming initially but who clammed up when my own and other peoples' inquiries began to raise certain questions, what were he and his advisers worried about?

So what have I learnt? Rather than sum up myself, I prefer to let readers form their own judgements.

They will want to look at Terry Venables as Barcelona Manager and Coach. He had some difficulty with the ego of one or more of his distinguished footballers, but whatever his problems with the players, he achieved a level of success that enriched the lives of the Spanish people, and particularly the Catalonians, to whom he was affectionately known as El Tel. He settled in well, learned the language and developed a love of the warm Mediterranean sunshine and life which those conditions and a considerable pay packet afforded him.

One of those questions I should like to have asked him, but was not of course given the opportunity to do so, was whether, and if so why, he became dissatisfied with life in Spain. Was he really so much in love with Spurs that he could not resist the blandishments of Irving Scholar, or did he perhaps see the move back to England as a further step to achieve his ambitions which later at least were seen to be greater than simply soccer management?

As a Chairman of Tottenham, Scholar was very much a Venables fan. He was not always wise in his judgements however, and his ill-advised speculation when he tried to market the Danish sportswear called Hummell was one of the reasons that Spurs' finances suffered so badly. He wrongly assumed that he could produce the kits under licence in this country and sell them to other clubs. In fact there is such competition between football managers and chairmen, to say nothing of the players, that the very fact that wearing Hummell kit would benefit Tottenham financially was enough to discourage other clubs from following suit.

In any case, a lot of managers are used to receiving some sort of 'bonus' from suppliers when they choose kit for their club teams and for sale through club shops. At the time, the standard First Division 'bung' was in the region of £4,000-£5,000, according to the importance of the club.

Scholar's judgement of Venables may have been wiser however. Terry was his new idol whom he wanted to replace David

Pleat. I should have liked to ask Terry whether part of his deal with Scholar was that he would eventually replace Pleat, and if so when, but in any event he did so when Pleat was struck by scandal. Had Scholar stuck up for Pleat, surely the whole business would have blown over. David was not a Government minister involved in some Profumo affair. He was surely a football club manager whose ability was beyond question. But Irving took the opportunity to replace him with Terry, enterprising, ambitious and with his eye on the main chance.

So October 1987 saw the arrival of El Tel at White Hart Lane. Opinions will differ about the quality of the football immediately after his appointment, but it was certainly not vintage stuff and Terry made a number of noticeable mistakes. For example, when after a week during which the Port Vale Manager declared his fear of his team playing against Ossie Ardiles, Terry left the Argentinian out of the side. Spurs lost and were out of the FA Cup! On the other hand, there was no-one who could have handled the winsome star from Geordie land, Paul Gascoigne, better than Terry. At first the lad played like a schoolboy, running into rucks of players who ganged up on him and, as a result, losing the ball regularly. Under Terry's sympathetic handling, he matured into someone who was adulated by the public, who recognised the true genius behind the often cheeky and cavalier style and the occasional loutish behaviour.

But Scholar's dream of revival under Venables soon became a nightmare when the Club ran into Financial chaos. Tottenham's bankers were becoming anxious about the extent of the Club's borrowings, which were calculated at over £11,000,000. One result was the enforced sale of Gascoigne to Lazio, delayed when the player seriously injured himself in the 1991 Cup Final. It was then that Terry revealed a rare business skill in helping together a deal that retained the Italian club's interest while still enabling Spurs to reduce their borrowing. An injured footballer, unable to play perhaps for a year, was virtually sold for a future transfer. Exactly how he managed this feat has been a subject of controversy, and it is another matter that I should have liked to put to him.

After four years at Spurs, Terry was happy to allow Shreeves to run the side while he himself borrowed to the hilt to elevate his personal standing. He had obviously foreseen the opportunity for a possible takeover. He had lost interest in being just another football manager. Ownership and general management excited him more. He had by this time met Eddie Ashby, who helped to convince that the glory which he felt destined for was to be found not on the football field but in the Boardroom.

Terry was sufficiently astute to realise that Robert Maxwell was an unsuitable rescuer to help him buy out Scholar. Ideally he wanted a sleeping partner with unlimited funds. Alan Sugar had the funds but was essentially a 'hands on' man. When it came to the crunch, however, Sugar was the only saviour around.

Terry never thought that a man like Sugar would remain discreetly in the background and leave everything to him, and in fact at first refused to speak to him until forced by circumstances to do so when other potential backers had fallen by the wayside. Sugar was as hard as a nut ever there was to crack and would hardly invest £9 million in an enterprise and retire like a lame duck.

Jonathan Harris once told me that things began to go wrong from the second day of their relationship. Terry doubtless over-estimated his importance in the set-up. One of his first actions was to dismiss Ian Gray as Managing Director and bring in the secretive Eddie Ashby as his right-hand man. I should have liked to ask Alan Sugar what he thought of this move, but in any case Sugar did not sit back and leave everything to the man who knew about football, which was probably just as well. Among his many actions, he brought in his own right-hand man, Colin Sandy, to act as his eyes and ears.

From Terry's viewpoint, Sugar took far too active a role. He saw fit to send faxes to the Venables home, demanding explanations for the most simple actions that had taken place earlier in the day, and on one occasion is alleged to have asked: "Have you any brains, Venables?"

Despite their East End backgrounds, Sugar and Venables are essentially unalike, certainly in their conduct of business. Alan may have battled and ducked and dived his way to the top. His flourishing enterprise, Amstrad, was testimony to his success, and he was perceived as a straightforward, honest man, albeit a little unforthcoming and inscrutable, to whom everything in business had to be above board and 'kosher'. Not for him the underhand dealings that are unfortunately the mark of the football world.

Terry a far less private individual, had made his life in football. It is curious that, despite the media attention given to the game, so little of the financial shenanigans that are a daily factor of the game of soccer, are public knowledge. Terry cannot be blamed for being part of the system, but I am convinced that Alan was surprised at what he found under the carpet.

Football is of course business, but I believe that it is a business that has a culture of its own, and I believe also that the intricate behind-doors dealings within the football world came as a shock to Sugar.

He may well have wondered why he should have been asked to sign a cheque for £200,000 to Mr Santin, for example, but the reason he did so was surely because he was told that Terry had promised this amount and that four per cent was normal since Santin was supposed to have increased Lazio's offer for Gazza and been responsible for Lazio placing the money in Spurs' bank. Why an invoice for Santin was apparently issued by an untraceable Swiss Company with a box number for an address may be irrelevant if the money was genuinely owed.

I wanted to ask Alan Sugar about the circumstances in which payment was made to First Wave, or more specifically to Frank McLintock personally, in cash, but of course I was not afforded the opportunity to do so. If money is due, it may not matter how it is paid, provided proper records are kept, but I suspect that the conversion of cheques into cash is a more frequent occurrence in the world of football than in the world of computers.

A number of matters have come to light recently, including the writing off of substantial loans to Spurs players, Ossie Ardiles among them. These of course were made before Sugar and Venables were in control, but Terry lived and breathed in a world where such things habitually happened, whereas they were probably alien to an outsider like Sugar. He had put a huge amount of money into Tottenham's coffers and saw the urgent necessity to protect his investment.

He has every reason to hope and expect that the various investigations being conducted in aspects of Tottenham's affairs will result in no more than a fine and warning, since he can hardly be held responsible for what went on before he took over. In this connection, a committee was set up in October 1993 to look into matters that bring the name of football into disrepute, and specifically those matters that have transpired at Tottenham Hotspur. Rick Parry, the Chief Executive of the Premier League told me that a concentrated effort would be made to gather evidence of irregularities, highlighted by Sugar's allegations against Venables, but that rapping people on the knuckles would achieve less than making stringent rules for the future. Steve Coppell, the former Manchester United and England winger and Crystal Palace Manager, made a similar point on BBC Television when he told Bob Wilson: "It won't be a whitewash or a witch-hunt".

Terry's downfall may have had something to do with the company he kept and the advice he was given. He was perhaps stupidly loyal to Eddie Ashby, with whom he was involved in a number of not always successful business affairs, and he was loath to detach himself from the man when Colin Sandy ran a check that revealed allegedly that of 43 businesses in which Ashby had been involved in, all but four had been the subject of winding up or receivership orders.

How did Venables finance his stake in Tottenham? Channel Four television disclosed borrowings of £1 million from Landlease Ltd, supposedly based on the security of £100,000 worth of furniture, fixtures and fittings, situated in three pubs owned by a company of which Terry was no longer a Director at the time of the loan. This company, now in liquidation, was allocated a 'free' box at White Hart Lane worth £20,000 per season.

Small wonder if Alan Sugar began to ask himself questions! Nevertheless Terry Venables had occasion to object to Sugar's conduct. These objections were fully aired in the Court proceedings. Among Venables' objections were the secondment of Tottenham's computer system to Amstrad headquarters; the manner in which Jonathan Crystal was sidelined; the introduction by Sugar of a contract to provide his Jersey Company with an annual income; the holding of an impromptu meeting at Arsenal Football Club, to attempt to dismiss Terry;

and unauthorised amendments to the minutes of Board meetings.

Readers of this book, who, like me enjoy the repartee of Court dialogue and battles will be able to read summarised versions of the eight days of legal argument, which contain fascinating affidavits, letters and statements in Volume 2.

The cynical among us may wonder whether Alan Sugar intended to boot out Venables from day one, particularly if we rely on what his Agent, Jonathan Harris told me. The questions that we could pose are: Did Sugar decide in those very early days to see off Venables as soon as the time was right...? Did Venables allow Sugar to join him, thinking that, 'This guy knows sod-all about football and will be an easy touch?' Or was there a slow build-up to eventual turmoil and disaster? These are the matters that I should dearly have loved to put to them both had they been willing, if only in the interests of truth.

My own version is that I believe Alan went into it all too soon and with his eyes closed, while Terry was desperate to find someone, anyone, to back his scheme after he had created such public furore in his efforts to oust Scholar and Bobroff. What Sugar found was a loosely run organisation, with Venables calling all the shots, protective of insiders, with its own way of doing things, and in a manner that was totally alien to the efficiency that had been introduced at Amstrad. When some of that easy-come easy-go treatment of many thousands of pounds bordered on the irregular and indeed, illegal, Sugar put his foot down. One must recall that he offered to buy Terry out with what would now certainly be termed as an acceptable offer, given what has gone on since May 14th.

Whatever the truth, Terry Venables gave Alan Sugar grounds for divorce, and Sugar jumped in.

CHAPTER 12
ANECDOTES AND SOME
INTERESTING EXPERIENCES

Although I am currently devoted to my trade as an author having written three novels and one biography of an Auschwitz survivor, I have previously had a number of experiences connected with professional football.

At one time I was voted the best junior coach in New South Wales during a four year stint in Australia, to return to the UK to join Arthur Rowley who was then a Manager of a Fourth Division club, that in the year of my joining him gained promotion to the Third Division. Later I looked after the new signings. This was a great time and I got to know all their problems, both serious and trivial that beset only the football player.

After the last player left our home, I was invited to help out with an ailing Fourth Division club in the North and for six months I acted as General Manager, meeting most of the press, a whole host of players, several managers, and numerous club directors.

I have been a football follower and Spurs fan all my life. It is with anguish that I observe the current football scene. Among more than 100 interviews which I have carried out recently, with the footballing public, I have encountered an increasing awareness that they feel they are 'being done' by the clubs, and the old camaraderie seems to be slipping away. As football becomes big business and slowly divorces itself from the 'man on the terraces', punters seem to be feeling that the game is no longer for them.

Glass boxes, pin-striped suited businessmen looking out of ivory towers where the bars distribute their G & T's and champagne are giving the average supporter an inferiority complex. Also, revelations of corruption, internal wranglings, and ticket frauds are among the many items that have encouraged disillusionment.

Recent events at our own club have not helped.

To be frank, there seems to be a difference between our image of the characters we idolise when they become public property and the men themselves. We find it difficult to separate their public and their private performances. The stars of football are like the film stars whom we praise for their performances, while failing to understand that they are also human beings with much the same problems as ourselves. Alan Sugar is not just Chairmanof Amstrad and Tottenham. Terry Venables is not just the public figure that we see on television and in the dug-outs.

Footballers in the main are not well educated. People like Tony Galvin and Ossie Ardiles, who have both had excellent educations, are the exceptions. Many youngsters with special footballing ability, prefer to kick a ball around, when they should be studying or doing their homework. Often, by the time they are fourteen, they are snapped up on schoolboy forms by a professional club and the thought of becoming one of the well paid stars that they invariably idolise becomes the object of their whole life. And why not? Education is good, but physical education is good, too. Any young man wanting to be a pro. footballer is bound to ignore the higher level of academic achievement. Achievement in sport is as worthwhile as any of the professions, and often more highly paid.

Now, the football manager is yet again a different personality than the player.

The manager who takes over a professional team is very conscious of his 'aura'. Invariably, no matter how good the team is that he takes over, he will begin to buy and sell. His greatest fear is that success will be attributed to his predecessor. Terry Venables, for an example, left Ossie a first class group of men, inspired by the 'Boss' (not forgetting the marvellous work of Doug Livermore and Ray Clemence), but Ossie has, somewhat because of injuries and disconsolate centre halves, made several changes. I think that he would be the last one to deny that among Spurs pros. are some exceptional youngsters. If, for example, Danny Hill and young Darren Caskie don't make the England team in due course we will all be disappointed. Andrew Turner is another who shows remarkable pace and maturity. Nevertheless, Ossie has signed, Calderwood, Dozzell, Kerslake and Hazard, while getting rid of Van den Hauwe, Fenwick and Tuttle in the first eight weeks of the current season.... He is reported to be hunting for further replacements. It seems not to matter that Terry Venables' squad looked like Champions at the end of last Season.

For what it is worth, I believe that Darren Anderton could be the spark that our National Team needs at this precise moment.

The managers often display peculiar characteristics in their search to achieve success. Strong elements of egotism and megalomania become part of and affect their personalities.

But their jobs are only as secure as their success, and they have much to put up with.

HAVING READ THE REVEALING INTERVIEWS SO FAR IN VOLUME 1, AND HOPEFULLY YOU ARE ABOUT TO EMBARK ON THE SERIOUS ISSUES DISCUSSED IN VOLUME 2, I OFFER A LITTLE LIGHT RELIEF WITH SOME OF MY EXPERIENCES WITHIN THE GAME.

The First Team had a game at three o'clock, one Saturday way back in 1972, but I was asked to go with the junior team to play Ipswich on that lovely pitch situated behind the main stadium. Arthur Rowley gave myself and the physio. our instructions and told us not to stop on the way back because the physio., especially, was needed to run the sponge at the main game in the afternoon. Fortunately, kick off at Portman Road was on time and we began with the well versed four-four-two formation that Arthur insisted upon. Within twenty minutes we were two down, and I was cheesed off at our total lack of attacking ideas. Turning to the physio., I asked him whether he didn't think that as they had no right winger in their four-three-three formation, wouldn't it be a wise move to free our left sided half back who was in any case a better winger.

"You gotta' be kidding. Arthur would slaughter us if we changed formation."

At half time I told the young lad, Ling his name was, to move forward and told the defence and mid-fielders to try and get the ball to him whenever possible. By mid way through the second half we had pulled the two goals back, and although the physio. reverted to the original formation with a quarter of an hour to go, we hung on for a draw.

When we returned to the ground, Arthur was busy with the

first team, but was pleased that we had drawn the game with Ipswich. I worked usually, on Tuesday, Thursday and Friday, but on the Sunday Arthur rang from his office and asked me to go down to the club. Expecting praise and possibly the offer of a full time position, I instead received one unholy bollocking.

I had changed his orders.

No matter that we were the better team after Ling moved up; no matter that we had drawn when a loss was going to be the undoubted result. I had done something which he had not ordained. Later we became somewhat closer. A bit like fighting the bigger kid at school who later found himself respecting the whippersnapper who gave him a tough time.

When Arthur was sacked after the team came straight down again from the Third to the Fourth, Dave Smith took over. I lost the assistant coaching job and he asked whether my wife and I could look after the new signings he planned. We were happy to do that: we received free tickets to all matches and two for the Cup Final if we chose to go. The extra income was not sufficient to feed and house the two lads who immediately came to us, but it didn't matter because I was working with my Father's business and the nepotism helped me to have as much time off as I needed as well as receiving a comfortable salary. Steve Goodwin was a fine player who deserved better than Fourth Division football. He had an almost Hoddle like ability to thread balls through the defence and create great openings for dashing wingers, one of whom was the other youngster who was staying with us, Andy Polycarpou (a close relative of the guy who plays Sharon's imprisoned husband, Peter Polycarpou, in Birds of a Feather). Andy was, academically speaking, not one of the brightest lads that I have ever met. But, put him into football kit and he was ingenious in what he did. Neither Steve or Andy seemed to particularly impress Dave Smith, who preferred hard working mid-fielders and battlers to the more delicate touches of our two house guests. But they were in the first team reasonably regularly, although neither saw eye to eye with the slightly eccentric manager.

One time, Steve had been growing a beard when, about to board the coach leaving for a game at Colchester, the manager spotted his dark growth.

"What's that fuzz around your face, Goodwin?"

"I'm growing a beard, Boss."

"Not in my team, you're not! Shave the bloody thing off, now!"

"I'm sorry, Boss, I like a beard. Having a beard doesn't make me any less of a footballer."

"It does in my team, get off the coach, you're dropped. Little Ronnie can take your place."

The Football Union Official had to intervene.

Managers can also be dictators: ....No, are dictators...!

On another occasion, it was 'Polly's' birthday. Now the Polycarpous are a well known dress and garment company with showrooms and offices in the West End of London and with major accounts on their books: People like Marks and Spensers and B.H.S. Although the family live in a modest terrace in Harringey, they are known to have a bob or two. Andy returned from training to find a beautiful BMW parked outside the house. He glanced at it nonchalantly, never thinking that his two brothers were waiting inside to present the keys to him. They were so proud of their nineteen year old brother who was receiving rave reports in the local and National media for his footballing prowess. Andy couldn't believe his luck and the love of his family expressed in the fabulous car he was being given.

The next day he proudly drove himself to the ground which normally was a walk for him. Now luck, and fate, play a big part in all our lives, and it was this inexplicable of all deatinies that ordained that Smithy should drive up in his company Rover at the same time.

"What's this? Won the pools?"

"No, Boss, it is a birthday present from my family."

"That's a better car than the one I've got."

Snorting and grumbling under his breath, Dave Smith muttered something like "I ain't fucking having that...."

When the team sheet was put up on the wall the next day, Andy was sub. For six games thereafter he never played, until finally with results not going his way, and a lot of criticism appearing in the locals, Dave picked Andy somewhat reluctantly. Twenty minutes into the game, Andy was carried off and never played again in the team, later moving to Norwich where he was finally rejected and is now working in the family firm.

I was sitting in my office, a leaky roofed board room at the Fourth Division Club's ground when the groundsman came in to tell me that Desmond Lynam was outside. I went out to meet him and greeted him with my name and title. "Great," he said, "I actually have come to see the team coach, Dave. Is he around?"

"He's not in his office, can I help?"

"Well probably. I'm doing a piece on the difference a few miles makes between various football clubs, and I am highlighting life at a struggling Fourth Division outfit to Manchester United."

"I think I better try to find Dave."

I knew where the team manager would be. It was one thirty and racing at Lingfield was about to start and the local bookie's would be the first place to try. When he heard that Desmond Lynam had arrived, he had forgotten about the appointment in his haste to make the first race, he began shouting and instructing me not to talk to him until he got there. His manner was incredibly rude and later I found out that it was all due to the fact that Desmond had the agreed fee of fifty pounds in his pocket and the coach was frightened I would pick it up instead of him. Perhaps it isn't known that many managers and coaches and people in the game will not be interviewed unless there is a bit of dropsy.

I was in Australia and Bobby Charlton came out there as a guest. Surrounded by about a hundred coaches and managers and adoring fans he was to demonstrate how to kick a ball properly and particularly how to take a penalty. Well, the vastly thoughtful Australian Administrator plunged a microphone into his hand, and Bobby, dressed in full kit, began to shoot at the goal while trying to talk us through what he was doing at the same time. Being a prolific smoker at the time he was soon out of breath and by the time he came to take his third penalty, all you could hear was a lot of heavy breathing, and laughing from the crowd as, what he was attempting, was just impossible. In halted spasms he apologised and glared at the admin. people, unable to continue. The whole bloody show was a farce. Later we were chatting over a drink, and I asked him what he thought distinguished one footballer from another.

"Take two men of roughly equal height and weight. Both as fit as they could be. What makes one a Division One man and the other unable to get out of the lower leagues?"

He thought hard and long over the answer.

"Do you know, Guy, I have often thought of that. I believe that it is intelligence."

Some ten years later when he was a Director with Wigan, and we were playing them at home, during the half time break in the board room I reminded him of our meeting in Australia and he laughed, recalling his embarrassment. When I suggested that the goal we had scored a minute before half time was a beauty and that our centre-forward was 'on his way to greater things' he became quite angry. Such is the competitiveness of great men.

Now the Charltons, especially Jack, are not exactly known for their merry attitudes.

I owned a hotel in the Midlands, fairly recently, and one day while I was resting at home getting ready for the evening session, my receptionist rang and told me that Big Jack had booked in, and wasn't very happy with his room.

Apparently, he was in town for an after dinner speech for the Round Table people who hadn't realized that he would need to stay the night. Both luxury suites were occupied, and there was just one room vacant in the whole hotel when Jack arrived unannounced. I decided to take him a bottle of champers and offer my apologies.

Thank God the room at least had its own en-suite facilities.

I knocked on the door. When he opened it he was dressed casually and had the television on.

"Good afternoon Mr Charlton, I have brought you a bottle of Champagne, compliments of the house."

"Who the bloody hell are you then?" he grunted.

"I'm the proprietor."

"So you're the one responsible for this bloody room. You can't swing a cat in here."

"If we had been informed of your arrival, I assure you we would have allocated a suite."

"I bet that is no better."

"Well, it is the one that has been occupied by Freddie Starr, Tony Knowles, and regularly by Ray Reardon. I am so sorry that the Round Table didn't book you in. We had no idea that you were coming to stay, although of course we did know that you were in town."

"You can take that bloody bottle away and bring me a pint preferably" he snorted, and closed the door in my face.

Now in fairness to Jack, he is a manager of an International Team and a World Cup winner and one of the most well known men around the sporting world. While I don't mean to be unfair, I feel that Jack, as soon as he heard that I was the owner of the hotel, assumed me to be one of the gentry, well heeled and Tory voting. Maybe I am wrong, but I think that Jack is happier with what he believes are the real men of this world. The working class as they used to be described. Later, after he delivered his speech, he came back to the hotel around twelve, well fed and 'watered' and asked very kindly whether he could have a pint. The bar was still open to residents who were having a late night pool competition. I smiled, gave him his pint. He thanked me coolly and wandered over to the table.

"Room for one more, is there?"

The lads were more than delighted to let him in. He played pool with them until four that morning, and it was as if he were one of them. He might have been a labourer or an office worker for all the 'side' there is to him. You really can't help but like the man, and it is no wonder that the Irish team are probably the best International outfit in Great Britain.

It is often read that a certain team is trying to sign one star or another, but that the negotiations are protracted and it could be a couple of weeks before the club get their man. Have you ever considered what it is all about?

Years ago a player couldn't wait to sign for Spurs and once there he never thought of leaving for another team until he had at least reached thirty.

Imagine.... Even though this is not an entirely imaginary conversation of the sort that takes place nowadays between a footballer's agent and a top manager, anxious to sign a real talent in the game.

"Hello, I'm 'Barry Smith's' Agent, Cyril. He wishes for me to negotiate his transfer and the details of his contract."

"He says he wants to play for us, and we want him to. Hopefully just a couple of things to iron out and we can secure his signature," replied the unsuspecting manager.

"Yes, just a couple of things. Now, about his fee. I know that he is due fifteen per cent because he didn't ask for a transfer in the first instant."

"Yes, that is right. Fifteen per cent."

"Now, what he says is that as he is not a company, can you pay the VAT if there is any, and certainly the PAYE tax...? Mind if I light a cigar?" (Taking out a Churchillian monster Havana!)

"I can ask the Chairman if he will do that. Is that all?"

"Just a couple of things more. As he is moving into a much larger income bracket I have advised him to set up as a limited company. Will you be able to pay his salary into the company?"

"I don't see why not."

"It's in Jersey."

"Oh. O.K. Don't see any problem there."

"Trouble is that he needs to be resident in the Channel Islands for a month before we can register the company. Are you prepared to sign him and then say that he has had a slight knock, and will be available at the end of the month?"

"That's a tough one. I can ask the Chairman, but we did want him for the Liverpool game which is on the 25th. Is that all?"

"Well, pass the ash tray will you? His main base will be here in London, and he is moving from the Outer Hebrides. What about the differential in house prices?"

"How do you mean?"

"Well, he will have a much heftier mortgage. We want the club to pay half the interest on his mortgage, or better still the difference between what he pays now and what he will have to pay."

"Well, I will have to ask the Chairman about that. Anything else?"

"Removal expenses?"

"Goes without saying."

"Carpets and curtains?"

"To £1,000."

"We want about five for that one."

"Where's his wife shopping for those, Harrods?"

"He intends to buy a big house."

"Perhaps we'll wait and see. Maybe the owners of the house he buys will leave the carpets and things."

"Shall we say then, up to five grand?"

"Up to five grand then."

"Now that my client is, how shall we say, coming among the big boys, he will need a good car."

"The standard car provided by the club, is a Sierra, a Rover or a Carlton. He can have a choice."

"We thought maybe a BMW or perhaps a Mercedes."

"That's what I drive, a Merc. When you see players driving one of those two cars it is usually because they are advertising for a dealer and he lets them drive one around for a couple of years and then changes it before selling it off."

"Perhaps my boy could advertise one, or better still, the club provide it. Also, we will need an undertaking that it gets changed every season."

"I will certainly have to consult with the Chairman on that one. Anything else?"

"Schooling. A man of my client's fame and value must surely send his daughter to a good school. London is not Scotland you know. Would the club be interested in supporting that idea?"

"Possibly."

"School uniform?"

"Possibly."

"School books?"

"Possibly."

"PE kit?"

"I would think our kit supplier could oblige with that one."

"You realize that when my boy is training, his wife will have to pick up the kiddie? She could do with a car as well."

"Might be O.K. Not the first one to ask that."

"Now I think that is all.... Oh, no. What about holidays?"

"Well, he gets the usual month in June and reports back for pre-season with the others."

"Oh, it isn't the time off he wants. If he goes say, to the Bahamas for three weeks, can he have a club Visa-card and charge it?"

"I'll have to ask the Chairman about that one."

"Now just one further item. Loyalty bonus."

"What's that?"

"Well, after he has played for say, six months, he should get a loyalty bonus."

"Hmm, six months you say. Maybe after a year or so."

"O.K. After a year, but a bonus paid after each year of the contract. Say forty grand after year one, going up by ten grand each year thereafter. We'll want a three year contract, with a twenty per cent share of the transfer fee when he leaves."

"I'll have to ask the Chairman about that one."

"Well, that's all, I think."

"Right, will your boy sign now?"

"Well, he is considering other offers. I'll be in touch. Thanks for the cigar...."

Many football managers are generous to players because they themselves receive many perks. They often have lucrative arrangements with kit suppliers. That could be one reason for the continual changes in the club's outfit. The other is of course to boost sales from the club shops. No sooner has a parent saved up enough to buy the little one the full kit he/she so desires for Christmas, when the bloody outfit becomes obsolete. And what about some of those designs? I watched the Ipswich goalkeeper in one of the most bizarre shirts I've ever seen. Arsenal's away kit last year looked like my kitchen curtains.

There is heavy competition to supply the kits to the Premier League clubs. This, like all the stories above is true.

A rep. for one of the major manufacturers called in on one manager who showed a great deal of interest in the design.

"Yes, I like that. We may be able to do a deal...."

"The governor sent down this little envelope for your expenses. I'll have the contracts ready in a couple of days. Just let me confirm the terms. Thirty-eight full kits free, plus two for the ladies team. We pay you £3 for every item of authentic kit you sell for us in your shops. They sell at £35-00 per shirt. £14 per shorts and £8-00 per pair of socks. Smaller sizes less five per cent."

"How much do they cost you?"

"Well, that isn't for me to say, but currently I'll tell you confidentially, it costs about three quid to produce a shirt and about a nicker for a pair of shorts. Socks come out at around seventy pence a pair."

"O.K. Just asking."

"Thank you, sir.... I'll be in touch."

In the envelope was four thousand pounds. Two days later the manager received the contract and tore it up.

The day after that meeting he had signed with another company. They had also left the same four thousand pounds in an envelope.

There was nothing the first company could do about their loss. The undercover payment could not be disclosed and they were left, biting the bullet the manager made.

For some time in the early eighties, I was a friend to Tommy Docherty. I visited, and indeed, slept in his converted barn in the Derbyshire Dales and met his lovely de facto wife at the time, Mary Brown, who many will remember was the wife of the Manchester United Physio., Laurie Brown, who now 'does for' the England Cricket Team. Tommy had lost his position as Manager of Man 'U' and he was scratching around for a living, acting as pundit to the commentator who broadcast for the BBC Saturday afternoon radio programme from various football grounds. I went with him to many games and one can't but enjoy the man and his anecdotes and stories. Tommy is a clown; the personification of the lovable rogue. He is surely responsible for that now famous saying, 'When one door closes in your face, there is surely another to come up and smash you in the head'. Well, at least his mother is. For it was she that told him that when he set off for his playing career with Preston North End.

Tommy also told me a story which is being published mid-1994 in a book of short tall stories....

There was this centre-forward who was a pain in the backside, but who had a good scoring record except for the previous five or six games. The manager of this club, who were in the Second Division at the time, was a canny Scot. Fed up with the player's continuous whining and whingeing and frequent demands for the team to pass to him more (Gordon Durie clone?), he decided to rest the player and bring in a young reserve who was knocking in goals from all angles. On the Tuesday when the players reported back from the week-end break, he called in the wimpish centre-forward and told him in no uncertain terms that he was out. Not even on the bench. In the reserves for at least the next half dozen games. The player went mad, and stormed out of the office, refusing to train that day, and arriving home in a ferocious mood. He spent the afternoon drinking cans of lager, and by evening was almost paralytic, swearing at his lovely young wife and ignoring his new born baby. His wife had been a model before the pregnancy and had earned almost as much as her husband, but recently, since she had to give it all up, the money had flowed out of the door and now he was to lose all his bonuses and disappear into oblivion. The next day he trained with the reserves, while the first team members eyed him warily. That evening his wife wanted to go out on the town to lose the 'blues' but our morose centre-forward declined.

She turned on the television and lo and behold there was a European match on and one of the protagonists was a highly rated English League team. After a few moments, the English team's striker went down in a heap and was carried off. Our man was duly disinterested except to comment that he had played with the injured player during their England Youth trials period.

The next day, Thursday, he finished reluctant and ilsolated training and was approaching his car when the manager's secretary ran out to ask him to attend a meeting in the boardroom.

Inside the office was the manager and a well built, beautifully attired man in camel haired coat with black velvet lapels, smooth white flowing hair at the temples. All that epitomises the Directors and administrators of wealthy football clubs....

"I was just telling Sam here, you know Sam?, how much we value you here at this club. How I have spoken to you and promised to build the team around you. How much the Directors of this club and of course myself rate you. I've told him that you are certain to be called into the England squad even though we are in the Second Div. But, I am afraid he has made me an offer for you that we can't resist and most of all we wouldn't wish to stand in your way of joining a top First Division club who are competing in Europe. Didn't I tell you that you were one of the best forwards in the Country? Didn't I? I'll leave you two together to discuss terms, son. It's a golden opportunity for you and I can only wish you well.''

The player signed.

So much for the integrity of managers!

I feel, finally, that I should reveal an experience, albeit reluctantly, of which I became aware, although it has nothing to do with Venables or Sugar. Unfortunately, it really is true, the names of the guilty are not quoted for obvious reasons.

I do not believe that many football matches in this Country are in any way rigged. Being a cynic, however, I am a firm believer that where there is money involved, there is bound on occasion, to be an element of 'graft'. On this occasion money was not the motive. It was just a case of how one man felt about another.

For purposes of legal protection, I will call the teams I am writing about, Team A, Team B and Team C. Let's have the manager of teams A and C entitled Mr X and Mr Z. Strangely, manager of Team B was not in any way involved. Maybe he didn't even know about it....

Team B were for the most part of the season top of the Second Division. Towards the end of the Season they began to falter and Team A moved to the top of the League. With one game to go, Team A were top, Team B second and Team C third. Only two were going to be promoted. As the fixtures worked out Team A were playing Team B at home for that last game.

The situation was that if Team A beat Team B and Team C won or drew it would be Team C that went up instead of the previous long time leaders.

On the Tuesday before the match, I met one of the players of Team B whom I had known for several years. I said to him:

"You've a hard game on Saturday. You must be losing sleep with so much depending on it.''

"No worry,'' he replied. "Mr X can't stand Mr Z. He told me that he doesn't want that bastard in the First Division with him.''

"So what happens?'' I enquired.

"Nought nought, that's what happens.''

"How do you know that?''

"Because Mr X has already told me. It's the best result for all concerned. We draw and they keep their home record and save face."

"I assume Mr Z doesn't know this?"

"Don't you fucking tell him either. Not if you want to see me in the First Division as well."

On the ensuing Saturday I watched for the result and the report. With just a few minutes to go, a forward of Team A's found himself with the whole goal in front of him from six yards out with Team B's goalie nowhere around. He hit the side of the post and the ball scrambled over the line, the wrong side of the goal-post.... The result...? Yes you've guessed it.... Nought nought.

Makes you think, doesn't it...?

VOLUME 2

Read now of the absorbing legal wrangles that took the two protagonists to seven long days of court hearings. Of how Alan Sugar came to allege that Terry Venables asked him for a 'bung' for Brian Clough. What Terry wrote to Alan and vice-versa. How the arguments and differences arose, and of how allegations and submissions were made exposing the two 'enemies' and their eventual disrespect and apparent hatred of each other. How the Gary Lineker and Teddy Sheringham transfers evolved, and how Tottenham had an interest in another manager before the appointment of Osvaldo Ardiles.

This sensational information is provided by way of personal permission of the Vice-Chancellor of Great Britain, Sir Donald Nicholls, whom we thank most sincerely, and with the co-operation of Messrs. Harry Counsell and Co, of London, without whom these papers, embargoed in the first instance by Alan Sugar from public release, could not have been reproduced for the reader's information.

This most alarming and sensational information was almost as fascinating to write, as I hope it is absorbing, to read....

BEDLAM 1993

On the morning of 14th of May 1993 at a special Board meeting convened by the Chairman, the Chief Executive of Tottenham Hotspur Plc was dismissed from his duties, with immediate effect.

Attending the meeting were Mr Alan Sugar, Chairman, Mr Colin Sandy, Financial Director, Mr Tony Berry, Director, Mr Jonathan Crystal, Non-Executive Director responsible for legal matters, and Mr Terry Venables, Director and Chief Executive.

Also with immediate effect, Mr Venables' employment contract was summarily cancelled, leaving him without any formal occupation within Tottenham Hotspur Plc, or within Tottenham Hotspur Football Club Ltd, which is a wholly owned subsidiary of the PLC, notwithstanding that he still remained as a Director of both and a major shareholder in the PLC.

Such a position was clearly untenable to both the remaining Board and Venables himself.

It would seem that Terry was not entitled to on the item on the agenda which concerned his dismissal. Only Mr Crystal voted in favour of retaining his services. By a two to one vote, Mr Tony Berry abstaining, and even though Colin Sandy held just one share in Tottenham Hotspur Football Club Ltd, Terry Venables had been destroyed.

His dreams and aspirations, perhaps his credibility, even, had been destroyed in one unemotional action by the Board of Directors headed by his one time partner, Alan Sugar, and he had no power to resist the resolution that effectively ended his career as a Spurs man.

But Terry surely knew that this was coming, for his Solicitors were already prepared to serve Tottenham and Sugar with an immediate petition to restrain the Board from acting on the resolution to dismiss him.

Under Rule 459 of the Companies Act, which allows such an application where it can be alleged that Directors are not behaving in a manner beneficial to the Company, he brought a rushed application to the Royal Courts of London that same afternoon applying for 'relief'.

This must have come as quite a surprise to those representing Mr Sugar, for they seemed neither prepared with documentation nor background when, before Her Ladyship, Mrs Justice Arden, the legal representatives of both parties lined up to argue their case.

Edennote Plc were represented by Mr Martin Mann QC, assisted by his junior, Mr Michael Gadd. These particular court proceedings alone run into an enormous number of pages and I have summarised them, concentrating not on the legalistic aspects but on the relevant issues of interest to the general public. The hearing was to be 'ex-parte', meaning that neither Mr Sugar or representatives of Amshold Ltd, the holding Company for Amstrad, or Tottenham Hotspur Plc would be allowed to speak on their behalf. Similarly, Edennote and Venables could only sit and listen.

Mr Mann, for Terry, opened by expressing his gratitude to Her Ladyship for accepting the case so late in the day. He advised the Court that Edennote was a Company wholly owned by one person, Mr Terry Venables who is the Manager and Chief Executive (Or at least he was until this morning) of Tottenham Hotspur Plc which is one of the respondents to this petition.

"I do not have to tell your Ladyship who Alan Sugar is," he said, "or that he is the majority shareholder in Amstrad Plc, the computer company."

"The PLC (Tottenham Hotspur) are represented by Mr Christopher Carr and Mr David Mabb, who act for Tottenham Hotspur Football Club Ltd, Alan Sugar and Amshold Ltd.

"These matters arise very simply. Terry Venables is a manager and organiser of National reputation — much loved by players, much admired by other managers and of enormous reputation in the football world both Nationally and Internationally. He was highly successful before he went to Barcelona and in Barcelona up until 1987 he was especially successful, taking that club to the European Cup Final whereupon he came back and joined Tottenham Plc's wholly owned subsidiary (the football club). He was equally successful here with that club, bringing it to FA Cup success in 1990.

"He is a man of unblemished character....

"Unfortunately troubles developed in 1991. It was then a company making substantial losses and its shares had been suspended on the stock market. As a result of some persuasion, Mr Venables was persuaded to participate in attempts to acquire the majority shares in the PLC. Initially he was unsuccessful in obtaining the funding, and ultimately, around mid-end of May 1991, or even early June after one or two approaches from Mr Sugar who had become involved along with a string of other entrepreneurs including Mr Robert Maxwell, Mr Venables agreed with him that they would together jointly bid for the shares....

"And that is where our story begins....

"They agreed that they would buy fifty per cent of the available shares each, and upon that acquisition Mr Sugar would become the Chairman and Mr Venables the Chief Executive. In essence there was a joint venture in those shares. That is not put in any legalistic way. They agreed that they would together bring success to the company, turn it around and they would together hold the positions that I have indicated. In due course the shares were acquired, as anticipated equally and they obtained their position."

(He makes no mention of Mr Alan Gray who was Managing Director, and subsequently dismissed after Terry took over as Chief Executive.)

"But it was not as easy as that because the Company had debts and they had incurred them and so in due course a 'rights issue' was evolved: Primarily by Mr Sugar, even though Mr Venables preferred to raise cash by way of mortgage. In that argument Mr Sugar prevailed with, no doubt, superior financial expertise.

"The shares were underwritten by the companies owned by Mr Sugar and Mr Venables...."

(It was at this time that the previously mentioned 'Roger', the financier, met with Eddie Ashby on three occasions and with Terry, just once, at Scribes Club. A rights issue for those that do not trade on the stock market, means that the company will issue more shares and when they are purchased by whoever wants them, can therefore increase the money flow into the company.

'Rights' means that for every share held by an existing shareholder a certain amount of the new shares will be offered in a pro rata, quantity. Underwriting means that if the shares are not purchased, the underwriters will pay for them themselves.)

"The terms of the underwriting arrangements were unequal as between them. So, the rights issue, if successful, meant that Sugar would end up with about twice as many shares as Mr Venables."

(The writer asks why Terry agreed to unequal underwriting in any circumstances? Was he so naive as to believe that all would remain equal? Perhaps he never knew Alan Sugar as the ruthless businessman that he has since proved to be. Assuming Terry could not afford as much as Alan, he was surely aware of the inequality that would result!)

"Seeing the result, Mr Venables expressed his unhappiness about it but was assured by Mr Sugar that whatever the result, if they had to take up the full amount of underwritten shares, they had a shareholders agreement.... AND HE WOULD ABIDE BY IT!

" 'Trust me' he had said at a meeting prior to the issue, at the Grosvenor Hotel in or about December 1991.... As luck turned out the two of them had to underwrite their respective interests and Edennote took up some more shares, and Sugar did likewise, with a resultant holding of approx. 46 per cent Mr Sugar and 23 per cent Mr Venables.... Mr Venables had financed his acquisition by borrowing and from other resources. He certainly borrowed two million of his investment from a series of transactions with a couple of finance houses, and we will see reference to those later. It was the way that he financed both the initial shares and the further issue amounts. In due course Mr Venables was awarded with a service agreement, which was entered into on July 22nd, 1991. This was signed and agreed before the Rights Issue in December of that same year.

"During the ensuing nine months differences had begun to arise between them. Mr Sugar had appointed Mr Colin Sandy, an employee of his company to that of Finance Director. The Board was split by this appointment as Mr Sandy was an employee of Amstrad/Amshold; against this were a Mr Tony Berry, a shareholder with around 4 to 8 per cent of the shareholding, and

Mr Venables and Mr Jonathan Crystal who is known to you as a Barrister, acting as an independent Non-Executive Director. Mr Venables would describe a progressive invasion of his duties by Colin Sandy who wanted to take over more and more duties, specifically with the computerisation of the merchandising of the company. This was a duty allocated to Mr Sugar."

(The author asks.... If the job of computerisation was normally that of Alan Sugar's, how could Venables complain that Sandy's activities encroached upon him? Sandy was clearly just helping Alan Sugar as his eyes and ears during his frequent absences.)

"Sandy's computerisation responsibilities would enable the ticketing and marketing operations to be linked to the Amstrad Headquarters at Brentwood. There were a number of difficulties. There was also a number of negotiations with Sky Television which ought to have been the province of Mr Venables."

(NOT SO...! You have read of what transpired in those negotiations in the interview with Rick Parry.)

"He felt that he was being left out of things. There were other difficulties. Matters came to a head at the beginning of this month when Mr Sugar served notice of a Directors meeting to be held this morning to remove Mr Venables as Chief Executive this morning. The position with Edennote was also severed. Votes were cast, and as a result Mr Venables's contract was terminated. The vote was equally divided, but the Chairman used his casting vote to pass the resolution.... I am corrected.... Quite rightly the vote could not have been equally divided. Mr Venables, because of his interest in the resolution was not able to vote, and therefore the Chairman was not called upon.

The point is that the Directors in what I call the 'Sugar interest' voted in favour of the resolution and so it was carried....

"We say very straightforwardly that the circumstances in which Mr Sugar and Mr Venables got together, and including the oral conversations indicate that Mr Venables has a legitimate interest in the management of the Company, and ought not to be deprived of exercising that right. The result is that he will be kept out of the Company to its serious prejudice and we say that it is conduct unfair to Mr Venables and to other shareholders who have proceeded on the basis that he and Mr Sugar will be jointly involved.

"Many shareholders have received such documents that indicate the agreement that Sugar and Venables will share the majority, and that the public sector are aware and are in express agreement with that.

"In those circumstances it is right for Mr Venables to bring a petition for the 'relief' which he will seek, and that in the circumstances, for him TO BUY THE SHARES THAT MR SUGAR HAD.

"I SAY 'HAD' BECAUSE ON A DATE UNKNOWN, BUT RELATIVELY RECENTLY, SUGAR SOLD THOSE SHARES TO A JERSEY BASED REGISTERED COMPANY CALLED AMSHOLD LTD!

"In those circumstances we ask that he is granted the relief to remain as Chief Executive, as was agreed between him and Mr Sugar, pending a full hearing, and for the benefit of the PLC, the Football Club, the team and the other shareholders who own 31 per cent of the Company and of course the supporters who number many thousands. That is that Mr Venables remains in charge of the marketing and football side.

"As you will see it is the considered opinion of Mr Venables, Mr Jonathan Crystal and of the Supporters Club, that the Club and everything to do with it will suffer enormously, should he be removed. Mr Venables is not just a football manager, but in his own way, an institution, without whom Tottenham Hotspur would not have done what it has on the field of play, and not achieved what it has in turning around a £2.8 million loss in 1991 into what looks like being a profit of £5.3 million at the end of this month.

"That, broadly, is it. We have to show you that there is a case to be tried. We submit that it is right for Mr Venables not to be displaced and left with just an action for damages, not from just a service contract. In no way can he ever be compensated with damages for what is essentially, his life. He would never have committed himself to the millions of pounds investment if he had known this was going to happen, and moreover Mr Sugar only did so knowing that his partner was Mr Venables. There it is, very briefly.

"May I take you to the petition?"

(Summary)

"The petitioner (Edennote Plc) is and was at all times owned and controlled by Terrence Venables. Up until this morning the manager of Tottenham Hotspur under a service contract issued in 1987. Tottenham Hotspur has been extremely successful under his management. In March 1991 he entered into negotiations with Irving Scholar and Paul Bobroff to purchase 3.6 million shares representing 35.8 per cent of the whole amount issued at that time. At the time he was the team manager and the Company was losing around 11 to 12 million pounds." (Accrued...Not annually). "In or about the middle of May 1991, Mr Venables entered into a verbal agreement with Mr Sugar that:

1) The said shares would be divided equally between the two of them.

2) Mr Venables would be appointed to the Board and made Chief Executive. Mr Sugar would be a Director and Chairman.

3) Because of that verbal agreement the two then purchased the shares in equal amounts, which resulted in each owning 17.8 per cent of the PLC.

In consequence of that offer they were required by Rule 9 of the 'City Code' to make an offer for the remaining shares held in the main by the public. I quote from the second paragraph of the letter of offer...."

'We have available approximately £7.5 million to invest.... We are pleased to say that we have undertakings from a number of shareholders NOT to accept our offer. If there are enough shareholders agreeing with us we intend to invest our money by way of proposing a Rights Issue which will allow us to make the capital injection needed. We agree that this will be the appropriate time to apply to the Stock Exchange for the lifting of the suspension of our shares....' Our short-term objective is, of course, to resolve the financial difficulties of Tottenham. Going forward, we believe that with the combination of Terry Venables' expertise in football and Alan Sugar's experience in financial matters we can put in place a plan for the company to be profitable on a long-term basis by focusing on football-related activities. This will hopefully open opportunities for the share price to improve. Alan Sugar has already been appointed as Chairman and Terry Venables as Chief Executive. NOW THAT WE ARE FIRMLY ON BOARD WE ARE BOTH CONFIDENT THAT WE CAN FULFIL OUR OBJECTIONS....'

The letter ends with a thanks to the supporters etc...."

(At this point the Barrister presented the court with details of Alan Sugar's personal holdings and of his wealth. From information gleaned by us on this matter, and also as to the state of Edennote at the time are simplified and listed in other chapters within this book.)

The Barrister continued in his efforts to present Terry's attributes and impress and influence the Lady Judge....

"Mr Venables has been the team manager of T.H.F.C. since 1987 and is a former Spurs player. He has had a successful career in football management, winning Third and Second Division Championships with Crystal Palace, reaching the FA Cup Final and winning the Second Division Championship with Queens Park Rangers. Winning the Spanish League and the Spanish Cup with Barcelona and also reaching the Final of the European Cup with them. Recently he won the FA Cup with Tottenham Hotspur...."

(What...? No mention that he also won a FA Cup winners' medal with Spurs as a player in 1967...?)

"Edennote was incorporated on the 5th March 1991.... No other business except the 'shares' in Tottenham Hotspur Plc.

"Mr Venables entered into a new term of employment contract for an initial term of five years. Mr Sugar refers to a loan note to Edennote Plc, under which borrowing was offered in the sum of 2 million pounds to enable Edennote to acquire the original shares from Bobroff and Scholar. Further you will see a security document offered by Pan Financial which states that should Mr Venables cease to be Chief Executive, that means default which constitutes termination of the arrangements with Pan."

(In other words Terry was borrowing the money from Pan Financial to purchase his shares, but the money did not arrive in time to complete the deal. Alan loaned him the money on the strength of it arriving, and the loan agreement with Pan said 'if Venables gets the sack, we are able to call in the loan immediately'.)

"So, there is potential serious damage to him by reason of the resolution. Over the page you will see that Mr Sugar and Edennote intended to enter into an agreement regulating the disposal of shares held by them. Not a surprising paragraph...!

"In fact, no agreement was actually entered into by them although as you will see, at the time of the Rights Issue an attempt was made, by Mr Venables, to get Mr Sugar to agree to allocating half of Mr Sugar's excess holding to the voting power of Mr Venables and for Mr Sugar to off-load those excesses within five years. Mr Sugar's rejection was expressed in language that I prefer not to mention in court...."

(Why not...?)

"At that time after the rights were taken up, Mr Sugar was left with approximately 46 per cent and Mr Venables 23 per cent.

"At a meeting at the Grosvenor Hotel on or about December 1991 Mr Venables spoke with Mr Sugar and advised him that as a result of the differential in shareholding, Mr Sugar had substantially greater voting power at any general meeting.

"Mr Sugar replied that:

" 'There can't be any problem because we have a shareholders agreement.'

"At the time there was a written agreement but this remained unsigned, on the reasoning by Alan Sugar, that he could not sign same until the Rights Issue had actually been completed. Consequently, in referring to there being a shareholders agreement, Mr Sugar was inferring that Mr Venables understood him to be referring to an oral agreement, mentioned previously."

(The Barrister then referred to the draft agreement that Terry tried to get Sugar to sign, testing whether Alan really intended to uphold what he alleged had been verbally agreed.)

"In the last financial year, ending 31st May 1991, the Company traded with a resultant loss of £2.8 million. Not withstanding Mr Venables' achievements, the relationship between him and Mr Sugar has deteriorated since about September 1992, and that that deterioration has been caused by Mr Sugar's determination to arrogate..." (to take over in a high handed manner) "...control of the Company to a progressively increasing extent and by other actions. Mr Sugar's determination to deprive Mr Venables of his ability to participate in the management of the Company culminated in a Board meeting, convened on the 14th May 1993..." (That morning) "...at which it was resolved that Mr Venables' service contract be terminated, and also that he consequently ceased to be Chief Executive of the Company.

"In acting as complained of, Mr Sugar acted in breach of the agreement and contrary to the legitimate expectations that the Petitioner has as a result of the said agreement, and of the reasonable expectations of the remaining shareholders. Mr Venables is fundamental to the operation of the Company and his exclusion would cause substantial damage.... Mr Sugar is accused of making management decisions of the Company without reference to Mr Venables as Chief Executive...."

(The Barrister continued with impressive repartee accounting for the faults that the Board were deemed to have in sacking Terry. The problem was much simpler than he had portrayed but he later offered exclusive evidence from an affidavit (statement) of Spurs Non-Executive Director Jonathan Crystal which was incredibly revealing. You will recall that Crystal was the only supportive vote for Terry when the decision to sack him was taken earlier that morning. Why I stated that the problem was much simpler than had been expounded by Barrister Mann was that the issue at hand was whether there was justification in the reinstatement of Terry contrary to the Board's wishes. That was all that was needed at this hearing. Documents, affidavits and evidence in support of his character and ability were not the issue and amounted to evidence that would be needed at a later hearing. Nevertheless, Mr Mann pursued the court in his efforts to blacken the Chairman and his fellow supporters on the Board by producing the Crystal statement....

BELOW, IS JONATHAN CRYSTAL'S TESTIMONY

"I have known Terry Venables fifteen years and retained that friendship even during the period when he was coaching Barcelona. I was involved in the attempt by Terry Venables to

230

obtain control of the shares in Tottenham at a time when the majority shareholders were Scholar and Bobroff. I am informed by Terry Venables, and believe that in or about May 1991 he was telephoned by Alan Sugar. Sugar requested a meeting which Venables then refused...."

(Terry was in negotiation with others, including Robert Maxwell, at that time.)

"Sugar telephoned Venables again and there was an agreement that Sugar would join Venables. The first occasion I really met Alan Sugar was in the Grosvenor House Hotel which would have been subsequent to the completion of the acquisition by Venables and Sugar of the shares from Scholar and Bobroff. I was present at the completion meeting held at the offices of Henry Ansbacher and I recollect that Mr Sugar appeared at that meeting late in the evening with his bank manager. I was led to understand by Venables in the period leading up to the completion of the share purchase and also on the evening of the purchase, that he and Sugar would be entering into the acquisition of the shares, on the basis that the shares would be split between them and he and Sugar would thereafter jointly own, control and operate the affairs of Tottenham Hotspur. It was my understanding that Sugar saw the acquisition as a commercial venture in which Venables would be an equal investor, whom would have control of the day to day running of the Company and the affairs of the football club. I cannot believe that Venables would have entered into any venture with Sugar on any other basis because Venables has spent many years in football and saw Tottenham Hotspur as an opportunity to be an owner of a football club.

"During all of the discussions relating to Venables' acquisition and control of Hotspur he always made it clear that he was not interested in being anything other than an owner and with a role as a Chief Executive of the Club. At no time, in my view, would Venables ever have contemplated a situation where he merely continued to have day to day control of the football team as manager. That would have been absolutely inconsistent with his substantial investment of money and his attempt to restore what by then was the tarnished reputation of Tottenham Hotspur.

"The purchase of the shares was completed. I did not become a Director until the 8th of August 1991. I was invited to a Board meeting at their Ground when I was proposed as a director, which appointment I accepted. I have, since that time, been a Director of the PLC in a non-executive capacity and on a date which I cannot now clearly recollect I became a director of the Football Club. The initial set up of the Board were that there were six Directors: Venables, Sugar, Crystal, Berry, Solomon and Colin Sandy. Solomon had become a Director in early 1991 when the Company was experiencing serious financial difficulties and Colin Sandy was, as I understood it, controlling an Amstrad company known as Amsop, but he was introduced by Alan Sugar as the senior Finance Director.

"In the succeeding months in my capacity as a Non-Executive Director, I attended the monthly Board meetings and contributed where I could to the well-being of the Company, by, for example, managing legal matters and handling Company affairs such as representation before the Football Association Committee and the like. My position as Non-Executive Director was not remunerated.

"In the initial few months, the Board was harmonious and Sugar was prepared to allow Venables to fulfil his role, as Chief Executive and as overseer of the football team. The Club had appointed an experienced manager (Peter Shreeves) who had the day to day responsibility for the team and, as it might be expected, the Board was faced with an avalanche of problems..."

(I have to put this in.... So was the team!)....

"...arising from the previous management of the Company, by in particular Scholar and Bobroff. The Company's executive leadership was faced with a loss for the twelve month period ending May 1991 in the order of £3 million, and the position subsequently has been in the first years of trading of the new Board, a profit of £2.8 million has been made and it is fully anticipated that in the second year a profit of £5 million will be made."

(Did this have as much to do with the beneficial receipts to Premier League Teams from the Sky Television deal, as with Venables' efforts? Certainly the home crowds were down under

Shreeves whose claim to fame was that the team lost more home games than at any other time during their existence and hardly the same team was played in successive weeks.)

"The first major issue of concern was the requirement for the Company to raise additional funding. The Board considered initially that the way forward was to seek to procure a mortgage over the Ground. Eddie Ashby, who had been acting as Terry Venables' assistant was <u>authorised by the Board</u> to seek to raise the funds by way of mortgage."

(Clearly at this time Alan Sugar was not aware of Eddie's involvement with several companies who had gone bust, and the man's personal bankruptcy problems.... This is when Roger, the financier, came onto the scene.)

"By late October early November Alan Sugar came up with the proposal that the Company should embark on a Rights Issue which he would be prepared to underwrite. That suggestion came about because, as I understand it, Henry Ansbacher had indicated that they would not be able to underwrite such a Rights Issue themselves. The question of a mortgage against the Rights Issue was a matter of considerable discussion."

(Borrow the money against an issue of further shares in the Company instead of against the Ground...?)

"And it appeared to me that Sugar was very anxious to rush matters along in relation to the Rights Issue. Venables during this period continually expressed his concern at the respective imbalance of the shareholdings and I clearly recollect being present being in discussion with Sugar and Venables when Sugar re-iterated that.... 'ANY RIGHTS ISSUE WOULD NOT ALTER THE ORIGINAL BASIS UPON WHICH HE AND VENABLES HAD ENTERED INTO THE ORIGINAL PURCHASE OF THE SHARES OF TOTTENHAM HOTSPUR Plc'."

(Then Barrister Mann)....

"And we are strongly reliant upon that observation."

The affidavit continued....

"Such assurance in my view went a long way to allaying Venables' concerns because it was inevitable that he would be unable to purchase his rights under this issue, and that fact was well known to Sugar and the Board. Certainly, I recollect that at the Board meetings which I attended when it was resolved to proceed with the Rights Issue, the question of the future operation of the Company was discussed quite openly and Sugar ASSURED THOSE PRESENT THAT THE RIGHTS ISSUE WOULD NOT ALTER THE STATUS QUO....

"The Rights Issue proceeded and the Company continued to operate as before. Venables was Chief Executive in fact and remained with that title.... I suppose from my point of view the first point at which I became uneasy about Sugar's attitude to the Company was at an Extraordinary General Meeting. I was present for this EGM which was also attended by a number of shareholders. Sugar took the meeting and when questions were asked from the floor, in particular in relation to the Company's policy relating to the payment of dividends, Sugar dismissed the questions as derisory in an offensive manner. It was clear to the other directors present that the shareholders were far from satisfied with Sugar's conduct and it was necessary for Venables and myself and the other directors to appease them afterwards. It was clear after this meeting that Sugar was disinterested in the views of any other shareholders other than himself and would certainly dismiss any discussions about the Company's financial strategy.

"The 1991/1992 season came to an end in May. The Manager (Shreeves) was on a one year contract which was not continued and it was agreed with the Board's approval that Venables would take a greater interest in the affairs of the Team in addition to all his other duties. Venables was very happy to assume these extra responsibilities, even if it meant, as became the case, that he was frequently working seven days a week. The football team required some new players and during the close-season, most at August 1992, the Club completed the acquisition of certain players, thus at the same time completing the sale of Paul Gascoigne to Lazio, which transfer had dragged on since May 1991. Sugar it will be appreciated had control of the finances of the Company and Sandy was appointed Finance Director. Sandy began to busy himself in areas in the Club in which he had no role to fulfil...."

(Had Mr Sugar become curious as to some of the extraordinary invoices a this time which he needed to question?)

"I cannot believe that he would have done so without the tacit approval and understanding of Sugar. By September or October of 1992 there began to emerge a fresh issue which subsequently led to enormous strife and contention.

"It needs to be appreciated that my understanding of computers is limited but what I did know was that a computer had a capacity to store information relating to, say, accountancy. Sugar wanted to locate the Company's computer information at Amstrad's premises at Brentwood. This whole issue is clouded in some confusion and also a great deal of contention. But certainly three of the Directors (Venables, Berry and myself) were concerned about this and, as appears from the minutes of the Board meeting, on more than one occasion Sugar directed that Berry and myself should investigate costings for placing the information on another computer bureaux. At the time this seemed a not unreasonable direction, but what was unknown to me was that Sandy, no doubt with Sugar's approval and understanding, purchased computer hard and software from the equipment which Amstrad held at Brentwood. Looking back, it is clear to me that Sandy and Sugar embarked on a scheme to create a situation where the Company had no real alternative either in terms of commerciality or mechanics but to place the information at Brentwood. Incidentally, I take the view that this was the second stage of Sugar's attempt to gain absolute control of the Company and renege on his agreement and promises to Venables.

"The issue of the computerisation created a great deal of friction and there was an uneasy peace and matters so far as I am concerned came to a head on the 3rd of December 1992. I informed Alan Sugar that I would be going to Mauritius the following week. I remember telling him that in terms, at the game against Arsenal on the 10th of December, because it had been the first time I had been away since I had been appointed as a Director...."

(Spurs won by one goal to nil...Paul Allen, now playing for Southampton, scored the winner....)

"He gave me no indication that he proposed any decisive steps during that period. The policy of the Company being that all contracts entered into should be sent to me for review and preferably for preparation. The purpose behind this was that the Company had previously entered into a number of agreements which were latterly disadvantageous for them. I had in mind in particular a catering contract which had been entered into in 1981 for a period of 20 years with virtually no provision for the Company to extract any sensible income out of that contract. During the period I was a Director I was involved in looking at a number of contracts and consulted on their preparation and it was a policy that was noted in the reports which I submitted at every board meeting.

"On the 17th of September I was informed by my Clerk and verily believe that a fax arrived in my chambers. The fax purported to be a copy of an agreement entered into between Amshold Ltd, and Tottenham Hotspur Plc, employing Sugar at a salary of £50,000...(FIFTY THOUSAND POUNDS) per annum to provide services for the PLC.

(It should be noted that under Football League Rules there was allowance for only one Director to be paid directly by a club. Under the Rules of the Football Association, under whose direction the Premier League falls, there is a different provision.... I quote....

'No club shall make any contract or arrangement pursuant to which a Director shall be remunerated save as permitted by the Football Association. Directors shall not receive a remuneration save for the fact that they are employed on a full time basis at the Club.'

For Tottenham Hotspur PLC to pay Amshold Ltd was an indirect way of Sugar obtaining a form of salary. He certainly did not qualify on the basis of full time employment at Tottenham, as it has been well publicised that he spent much of his time prior to Terry Venables' dismissal at the Headquarters of Amstrad....)

"I did not see the fax at that time because I was in Mauritius and there had been no prior indication that Sugar had it in mind to seem to extract an income for his position within the Company. When I returned to England at the beginning of January 1993, a board meeting took place at which I expressed my dismay of Sugar's behaviour at having procured the execution of such a contract. It seemed to me that Sugar had no regard to the interests of the Company, much less the views of the other directors and of the Board meeting. There was an extremely heated discussion in which Sugar took a personally, very offensive position towards me. It was certainly becoming evident at that stage that Sugar would get his own way come what may, and that position had been fortified by the events which I subsequently dealt with."

(Barrister discontinued his reading of the statement while he addressed the Judge.)

"I have seen correspondence to this effect: That Mr Sandy presented Mr Sugar with some drafts which Mr Sugar signed negligently, not realising that they were intended to be simply drafts rather than effectively executed documents. I think that is the gist of the correspondence that I have seen. So there is an explanation that has been put forward, but not one that I have accepted."

(He then referred to Crystal's statement again.)

"In the months subsequent to the discussions of the board meeting, the issue of the computerisation remained a continuing sore and I particularly remember one board meeting in which there was an exchange between Sandy and Sugar of a friendly nature when Sandy indicated that he had acquired some hardware for Tottenham, but on a subsequent occasion revealed that it was, in fact, OBSOLETE STOCK HELD BY AMSTRAD! Such an arrangement had never been disclosed by Sandy or Sugar to the Board and it was clear that Sugar was prepared to put the onus of Amstrad an himself in absolute priority to any interests of the Company (Tottenham!).

"Matters had subsequently come to a head at the board meeting held on Thursday the 6th of May 1993. The meeting was attended by all the Directors and it was evident that Sugar was in a particularly volcanic mood.

"At the commencement of the meeting there was a discussion about the 'Cadbury Report' (See below), and I proposed that the Company should, so far as it could, adopt the provisions contained therein. This was met with a very aggressive position by Sugar, who considered such to be impracticable. The matter had been discussed previously when the issue of the Cadbury Report had been discussed and it had been a matter which the Company considered should be adopted. The Board Minutes had been originally prepared by Colin Sandy in his capacity as Secretary, but from a certain date John Ireland was appointed as Company Secretary.

"SUGAR HAD DEMANDED THAT THE MINUTES BE FIRST SUBMITTED TO HIM AND HE WOULD THEN REVISE THEM AND THEN THEY WOULD BE CIRCULATED AMONG THE DIRECTORS FOR THEIR APPROVAL!"

(MY WORD…WHATEVER NEXT!)

"The Board Minutes for their approval on the 6th May referred to the previous discussion about Cadbury but contained the additional words…'IN RELATION TO ACCOUNTING'. That was not what had been previously agreed and it was not the first occasion that Sugar had sought TO ALTER THE MINUTES OF BOARD MEETINGS TO SUIT HIS POSITION AND INTERESTS. The meeting proceeded and at about four thirty there was a discussion about the computer arrangements. Venables went downstairs to, as I subsequently found out, obtain a report which he had commissioned relating to the advisability of maintaining Tottenham's computer information at Amstrad. When presented with this report by Venables, Sugar became very angry!"

(The Barrister then asked the Judge to read the next paragraph, to which she replied that she had done so.)

"I have never in my life seen such behaviour and it demonstrated in my view an absolute unfitness of Alan Sugar to be associated with the affairs of Tottenham Hotspur.

"Venables read a letter which had been posted to him and showed the letter to those present….

"THE LETTER CONSTITUTED A DEMAND BY SUGAR THAT VENABLES SHOULD LEAVE THE COMPANY AND IT CONTAINED CERTAIN FINANCIAL PROPOSALS TO REFLECT SUCH.

"Before leaving the Boardroom, Sugar telephoned someone and I understand at that stage…(inaudible) who was there in his capacity as Director of the Football Club and an architect in the development of the North Stand, to apologise for his behaviour. He did not at that stage apologise to either Venables or myself and I believe that he has never apologised to Venables.

"The following day when in my chambers, I received a telephone call from Alan Sugar when he indicated that he stood by every word that he had said but that he had been informed by Sandy that Venables considered...'He ought to apologise to me'...and he then offered some insincere apology." (Conjecture!)

"That disgraceful behaviour was followed by a further matter which occurred on Tuesday the 11th May 1993.

"On that evening Tottenham were playing at Arsenal and all the directors were understandably at the game. Venables and I arrived together at about six thirty five. Venables went to the dressing room and I went upstairs to the Arsenal Boardroom. Present there were Berry, Sugar and Sandy. At about six fifty Berry and I left the Boardroom to go to his car to get a telephone number and we returned shortly after at seven p.m. There was no indication during the whole of that evening that any board meeting of Tottenham Hotspur Plc had taken place in that Boardroom that night and indeed subsequently at the match, at all. The Directors were present in discussion with various people who were there.

The following day the 12th of May 1993, I received a fax from the Company Secretary enclosing a copy of a board meeting which had purportedly taken place of 7 p.m. of Tottenham Hotspur Plc at Arsenal Stadium."

(CAN'T YOU JUST IMAGINE IT...? "O.K. COLIN, THEY'VE GONE TO THE CAR. I VOTE VENABLES GOES. ALL IN FAVOUR SAY AYE.... AYE...AYE. MOTION CARRIED. GET US A CUP OF COFFEE WILL YOU...? BY THE WAY, WHAT TIME'S KICK OFF?")

AND THAT WAS THE END OF TERRY VENABLES!

"Such Minute is signed by Alan Sugar and purports to deal with the shares in Tottenham Hotspur Football and Athletic Co. Ltd I can state unequivocally that at 7 p.m. no such meeting took place. In any event, no notice of a meeting had been given to Venables and myself and, with great reluctance, I can only conclude is the fabrication of Sugar and Sandy with the connivance of Berry to which he sided with their stated aims in procuring the removal of Venables."

(Crystal, through Barrister Mann, then referred to a statement made at the meeting that morning.)

"I had subsequently spoken to Tony Berry at 12.50 p.m. yesterday when he acknowledged that no meeting had taken place at 7 p.m. on the night of the 11th. The meetings did not reflect what had taken place and the best thing was that it should be forgotten about. I did not and I do not think that the matter should be forgotten about because I consider that it is the clearest unequivocal example of Sugar's dictatorial and domineering behaviour, with an absolute disregard for the views and participation of any other director and shareholder. I consider the behaviour of those participating (in that meeting) to be outrageous.

"I have subsequently seen the letter of the Company Secretary date the 13th of May in which IT IS IMPLICITLY ACCEPTED BY TONY BERRY THAT THIS BOARD MEETING IS A SHAM...! I should state that at the board meeting last week there was a discussion about the manner in which the Company should proceed in the future. Venables had informed me that subsequent to a meeting that he had had with Sugar, Sugar had indicated that he was happy with the Team that finished mid-table and go two rounds in the Cup and not to venture too high.

"That, on any view would be a limited vision for a prestigious football club.

"When the discussion turned from the affairs of the Team to last Thursday's board meeting, Sugar unequivocally restated his position and indicated that HE WOULD BE HAPPY IF THE CLUB FINISHED FOURTH, FIFTH OR SIXTH OR SEVENTH AND WENT TWO ROUNDS IN THE CUP...! Tottenham Hotspur is one of the oldest and most prestigious football clubs in England. It attracts substantial support and in my view the supporters, who pay reasonably substantial sums of money both in relation to attending matches and purchasing merchandise, expect that the Club will at the very least attempt to compete at the very highest level and succeed. Tottenham has a history of success both in the League and in the Cup and in my view it would be totally unacceptable to supporters were the Club's stated position to be the limited ambitions expressed by Mr

Sugar. The point is of particular concern to me in that I have always regarded my directorship as being a stewardship or trusteeship of the Club for the shareholders, but particularly for the supporters.

"I would consider it as being a deception upon the supporters to expect them to pay money with the Company having as a hidden agenda, such limited ambitions.

"I agreed with Venables subsequent to the board meeting, TO STOP THE SALE OF SEASON TICKETS TO SPECTATORS WHILE THE PRESENT DISAGREEMENTS ARE RESOLVED and I entirely endorse that decision because the public should not be required to pay over money whilst....
1) There is uncertainty as to the future composition of the Board...and,
2) There is uncertainty as to the policy of the Company."

(See copy of letter appealing to fans to buy their season tickets anyway, signed by both Venables and Sugar and printed below along with a summary of the conclusions of the Cadbury Report.)

"Venables is fundamental to the operation of the Company. He has knowledge of all the activities of the Company and decisions are routed through him so that the Club has an overall strategy and direction. He is also fundamentally involved in the composition and performance of the Team and it is fair to say that, save in relation to merchandising, Venables is fundamental to the operation of the Company. It is beyond argument that if Venables is removed from the affairs of the Company it will have a massive impact upon the finances, morale and support."

(Mr Mann then addressed the Judge.)

"One of those factors, My Lady, which is not in evidence is that Mr Venables has told us that — It is better to put it this way: We have been informed by him that one of the most encouraging signs of recent years has been the way in which the parents of young men have been prepared to place their trust in him and assign their children to him for training to be brought up in the sport he so loves, and that is of course one of the reasons why his team, which is a young team has been so successful and why it is

241

fundamental that he should not be lost to the Club. Just one reason. Just an example."

(Back to Crystal's statement.)

"If the Company resolves to terminate Venables' position as Chief Executive, it would clearly be manifestly wrong, and there could be no basis for such action on behalf of the Board. I would therefore not consider it in the Company's best interest for such a resolution to be adopted and indeed I consider that there is no bona-fide basis upon which such resolution can be proposed other than to further Sugar's aim to obtain absolute control over the Company. I also consider that the removal of Venables will cause massive damage to the Company and the enormous significance is the fact that it will be absolutely contrary to the whole basis upon which the ORIGINAL VENTURE BETWEEN SUGAR AND VENABLES WAS CONSTITUTED — a basis it should be understood upon which I originally agreed to become a director of the Company. From my own point of view, I would never have become involved as a Director of a Public Company with all the responsibilities that that entails unless I had absolute certainty in my mind that, this principally being a football company, the day to day running of the Company and the affairs of the Team would rest with Venables who is massively experienced in that area, with of course Sugar's involvement with financial matters. I would never have agreed to serve in which Alan Sugar was the absolute controller."

"THAT IS THE STATEMENT WHICH MR CRYSTAL HAS APPROVED — INDEED, DICTATED HIMSELF — AND WHICH WE WILL USE AS THE BASIS OF AN AFFIDAVIT IN DUE COURSE.

(The essence of the Cadbury Report is that it is advisable, but not compulsory, that every PLC has a non-executive independent director on their board. Presumably, this is to protect shareholders not actually on the Board of Directors, and probably to care for their interests, as well as overseeing the formal requirements laid down by general company law. This, in addition to the responsibilities of the Company Secretary.)

Tottenham Hotspur

748 High Road, Tottenham, London N17 0AP
Telephone 081-808 6666   Fax 081-885 1951

Date as Postmark

Dear Season Ticket Holder

Both Terry Venables and Alan Sugar would like to state that whatever the outcome of the current litigation, Season Ticket Holders should not hold back in renewing season tickets for 1993/94 as this can harm the Club.

The Club, regardless of the outcome, must always come first as it will be here forever and both Mr. Venables and Mr. Sugar ask you to pledge your continued support by renewing your season ticket/s once again next season.

Your seats/standing places will be reserved for you up until 16th June 1993.

Yours sincerely,

T.F. Venables   A.M. Sugar

FOOTBALL & ATHLETIC CO. LTD.
MEMBERS OF FOOTBALL ASSOCIATION AND THE PREMIER LEAGUE

League Champions
1951 1961
League Cup Winners
1971 1973

Winners of the "Double" F.A. Cup and League Championship 1960-61
The European Cup Winners Cup 1962-63 & the U.E.F.A. Cup 1971-72 & 1983-84
Registered Office: 748 High Road, Tottenham, London N17 0AP
Registered Number: 57186 England

Winners of F.A. Cup
1901, 1921, 1961,
1962, 1967, 1981,
1982, 1991

The Barrister then addressed the Judge with a statement by Terry Venables....

"In so far as statements have been made regarding legal matters, I believe them to be correct. There was an agreement between Mr Sugar and me as related, upon which I relied. But if for any reason that agreement is not binding, putting it at its lowest, the matters referred to in my petition, represent a clear understanding as to what was reached between Mr Sugar and me upon which I relied. The whole basis upon which I, through the Petitioner (Edennote Plc), acquired a substantial shareholding in the Company and secured my appointment to the Board as Chief Executive Officer was so that I was in a position to control the management and lead it and the Tottenham Hotspur Football Team to a successful future. The whole basis upon which it was agreed between me and Mr Sugar was that we would both participate in the acquisition of shares, was so that he could invest further capital into the Company and use his financial skill to the benefit of the Company. In short, we were to complement each other in reversing the Company's fortunes. That is the basis upon which we discussed the matter and that is what I understood as being and relied on as being the position. Had I suspected otherwise I would on no account have participated with Mr Sugar; I would have proceeded alone or not at all."

(Then the Barrister explained the deal in the share agreements, and Mr Mann (acting for Mr Sugar), pointed out that although the Petitioner was Edennote Plc, the actual shareholder was Terry, but that he had charged the shares to Edennote and they were only the beneficiary.

Mr Mann then discussed the Tottenham's Company Articles and confirmed that the Articles for the PLC were those of 1983, while the Articles of the Football Company Ltd, were those of 1929. The PLC owns the Football Club entirely.

It seems that Mr Mann was clarifying the situation. Edennote purchased the shares in T.H. Plc on behalf of Terry who was the sole owner of Edennote Plc!)

There is an agreement in writing put forward by a Company called Linklater and Paines who appeared to have drafted the original share deal and made reference to any proposed Rights Issue. It said....

'Alan Sugar and Edennote each today purchased shares in Tottenham Hotspur Plc and Terry Venables is beneficially interested in the entire issued share capital of Edennote Plc. ALAN SUGAR AND TERRY VENABLES PERFORCE HAVE TODAY ALSO MADE ARRANGEMENTS FOR THE OFFER FOR THE REMAINING ISSUE OF ORDINARY SHARE CAPITAL. ANY SHARES WHICH ARE REQUIRED BY ALAN SUGAR AND TERRY VENABLES PURSUANT TO THE OFFER WILL BE SUBJECT TO THE TERMS OF THIS AGREEMENT. WRITTEN AGREEMENT FOR ONE OR THE OTHER TO BUY THOSE SHARES WILL NOT BE REQUIRED.

Then a clause discussing the purchase of further shares which seems to be the most relevant to the whole issue....

'NONE OF THE PARTIES TO THIS AGREEMENT OR ANY OF THEIR ASSOCIATES WILL AS FROM THE DATE OF THIS AGREEMENT BUY OR SELL SHARES IN TOTTENHAM OR ANY INTEREST IN SHARES IN TOTTENHAM WITHOUT FIRST OBTAINING THE WRITTEN CONSENT OF THE OTHER PARTY TO THIS AGREEMENT. THE CONSENT OF THE OTHER PARTIES TO THIS AGREEMENT MAY BE WITHHELD IF SUCH A PARTY IN HIS ABSOLUTE DISCRETION SO DETERMINES.

After five years the agreement for one or the other to sell or buy may not unreasonably be withheld.

Alan Sugar refused to sign this document!

"Mr Venables states that such an agreement was reached verbally, and produces this document (above) to show what was intended. Before the Rights Issue he prepared a similar document and you know what Alan Sugar said about that. Therefore Mr Venables has a legitimate interest which he is entitled to protect and safeguard. In the middle of May 1991 Mr Venables ORALLY agreed with Mr Sugar that shares would be purchased as to 50 per cent by Mr Venables or a company controlled by him.

"I think the background — I'm doing this on my own instructions — of Edennote was that it was to be a vehicle under which a number of prospective investors were to be joint bidders. When they were unable to provide their portion of the funding that was required, only Mr Venables was interested in pursuing it, at which point Mr Sugar appeared."

(This seems to reflect on the fact that the unmitigated praise heaped on Terry for saving Spurs is somewhat misdirected. The true saviour was, of course, Alan Sugar who stepped in when all else, meaning Terry's purported backers, had failed.)

"There is also the Service Agreement. There is nothing pertaining to the share issues in that; it is a standard contract which was for five years. It contains the usual termination conditions and was issued on July 2nd 1991."

(Later Barrister Mann advises the court that between Edennote and Tottenham there was an agreement for Tottenham to pay over £225,000 per annum of which the Company, Edennote would receive £125,000 from Tottenham Plc, and Mr Venables via Edennote £75,000 from the Football Club. He then says that in essence the aggregate amount was the same.

Not by my calculations! 75 plus 125 does not equal 225!

He then qualifies that, I think, by saying that there must have been some other benefits as well. This statement is particularly interesting.

That the amount paid, certainly even in gross terms before deductions for PAYE and NHI was not enough in its entirety to satisfy the interest payments on what Terry had borrowed. That is assuming that every penny was taken out of the Company, Edennote, when it was received!)

Then after reference to his 'junior', Barrister Mann referred to the 'additional' duties that Terry took on when he did not renew the contract of Peter Shreeves. I hope I have this right, but it seems to indicate that Edennote then began to receive the salary that was previously paid to Peter in addition to the £225,000....

Mann states:

"When he (Peter Shreeves) left the Club Mr Venables took over his managerial and coaching duties, and the Club took on the payment responsibility of remuneration, through Edennote, which had hitherto been the responsibility of it to Mr Shreeves."

(I wonder whether Terry acquiesced to the additional salary withdrawal, when Ray Clemence and Doug Livermore took over for the season 1992/3? Or were Tottenham now paying three coaches?)

Then Barrister Mann made what can only be described as a partly false statement to the Judge.

"But for the resolution, he is Manager and in charge of all football-related activities."

Now, maybe he did not intend to mislead the Court. I am sure that he knowingly did not do so, but he left out reference to Clemence and Livermore who were not sacked at that time, nor had either man made any public statement of intention to leave. To this day, Doug Livermore is still there in a coaching or scouting capacity. Throughout the season 1992/93 the supporters would clearly see those two sitting on the bench, particularly Clemence who was more demonstrative than Livermore, and who often stood to shout or gesticulate to the players on the field. Yes, often Terry would be seen down at the dug-out when some change in personnel or direction was needed, but it was clear to all, as to who was conducting the coaching. As a point of issue it might be argued that Mr Venables was in overall charge, but the implication was that if Terry was not reinstated, the football side of things would collapse.

The Barrister then admitted being 'foolish' to leave the flow charts of the management set-up at Spurs behind in his office. Did this show Clemence and Livermore? Would it, had the Judge been shown this flow chart, denigrated his statement regarding the current footballing importance of Terry…?

Barrister Mann then explained that Mr Sugar currently owns about 48 per cent of the shares, Edennote 23 per cent. Tony Berry commands the vote of, but may not own all of around 8 per cent and the remainder are with those supporters who took up small quantities in the beginning when the Club became a PLC in the early eighties, and some Institutions. He assured the Court that those people who are members of TISA (Tottenham Independent Supporters Association), among whom were many small shareholders, would use their voting power in favour of Terry Venables.

Such assurance given with absolute consultation? Or conjecture on his behalf...? (See chapter by TISA Coordinators.)

Finally, he makes his conclusive submission. He had been addressing the Court for two solid hours....

"We submit that there is sufficient evidence of actual and potential damage to the shareholder including and other than Mr Venables by reason of his denial, the denial to him, of participation and rights in management consistent with that legitimate expectation, and we submit that under section 37 and the principles in *The American Cyanamid* this is sufficiently clearly arguable case for appropriate relief, at least to hold the status quo until the matter can be properly argued with the relevant parties present (inter partes)...."

(Don't you just love the next bit...?)

"In the meantime the Club is without the authority of Mr Venables. There is work to be done. There are PLAYERS TO BE COSSETED. There are arrangements to be made for overseas tours. AND NONE OF IT CAN BE DONE WITHOUT HIM. No-one can be brought in at short notice to replace him.

"WE SUBMIT OF COURSE THAT THERE ISN'T ANYBODY IN ANY EVENT TO REPLACE HIM....

(We must realize that the Barrister was doing his very best to influence the judge. That is his objective; but does he really believe, or would the Judge, come to that, that there is anybody in this entire World who is that indispensable?)

(The American Cyanamid referred to is reference to a case admitted into English Law in 1975 the judgment being all about a similar situation that the Court was dealing with here. The case was between American Cyanamid and Ethicon Ltd. The approval of the application was made by the Appeal Court. See Vol. 1, Page 504, All England Law Book.)

After some quick fire questions on clarity by the Judge Barrister Mann made reference to the type of case the Court was dealing with and I quote:

"This is, of course, a very unusual case in that I do not think it has ever before happened that a manager of a football club has had such a direct and substantial interest in his own club and has been an owner in it. Football managers come and go like goodness knows what. They are perhaps the most ready targets of any of the entertainment industry.''

(Perhaps he had never seen some of the football that was played by certain teams in the Premier League. He might have been loathe to describe them as part of the 'entertainment industry'.)

Finally, pretty exhausted, Barrister Mann answered a few more of the Judge's questions such as one about the shortness of time between the possible granting of the 'relief' that was being applied for and the full hearing. She also sought confirmation of the wealth of Edennote, which was described as £1.2 million based on the 1.5 million shares that the Company purchased with its own funds and which were not encumbered by a finance agreement, that being at the then value of each share at 89p. This becomes an important issue later down the road.

In answer to the question about the shortness of time Barrister Mann confirmed that there cannot be any damage done in the next few days.

(Previously, you will recall, he indicated that everything might collapse if Terry wasn't instantly reinstated.)

Finished now with his submissions, his task virtually complete, Barrister Mann sat down to allow Barrister Mr Christopher Carr QC to offer his opposition to the application; making it very clear that he had no time whatsoever to prepare anything in advance, which confirms the opinion that Terry got it all set up in advance after the word spread of his pending dismissal, and Alan had no idea that Terry would immediately be seeking the Court's involvement.

Being caught with your pants down, you might call it!

Barrister Carr's first submission was that nothing had been presented which even begins to justify the grant of 'relief' over that period.

"What is it that the shareholders believe that we might do in the short period between now and the full hearing that may damage or irreparably harm their interests? The substance of this application is that this is an application whose effect will be to obtain specific performance of a contract of employment pending hearing of a full petition. No evidence of irreparable

249

immediate harm has been placed before your Ladyship. The question for today is simply, what ought to be done in the — whatever it may be — two or three week period pending an effective hearing of the motion? What is the harm to which the Petitioners can point, which they will suffer in that period, and which necessitates the grant by your Ladyship of a form of relief which requires mandatory performance of a contract of employment for that two or three week period? My respectful submission is that, despite all the matters which my learned friend has read, and which no doubt will be relevant on the hearing of the petition, he has not put forward one single sentence of evidence or argument which addresses the question — and the only question — which is for consideration this afternoon. I think that my Learned Friend has not completed his own evidence at this stage and has told your Ladyship on instructions only. He therefore still has to put his evidence into proper form in advance of the interlocutory hearing. We for our part will have to reply to the allegation. But the position as it stands at this moment, is that there is nothing before your Ladyship which even begins to justify relief. What is it that is feared or alleged that the Respondents to this Petition are about to do which will in some way cause prejudice to shareholders or would in some way produce irreparable harm over this period. What is it that is alleged or feared or about to happen or said which will be productive of irreparable harm?"

The Judge then commented:

"I had not understood the case to be put that way. As I understand it, the case is being put on the basis that this is an on-going entity with substantial football related activities. I cannot be specific, but as I understand it they involve not simply running a team but many other things as well, including supporters, functions, tours abroad, and examples have been given. In the light of the on-going nature of these activities, I think that it is being said the Company will suffer damage through the loss of the person who has hitherto been successfully running those activities. That is the allegation as I understand it."

(Clearly, at this point, had nothing but reasonable argument at his elbow. This was not impressing the Judge.)

Barrister Carr replied:

"Yes, I first of all pointed out that in order to protect that interest, what is at issue and what is sought, is a mandatory order in respect of a contract of employment, but if one then asks, what is the evidence that over these three weeks — or whatever period it may be — that those wide interests, those interests previously mentioned, what is the basis for the suggestion that those interests are in some way going to be damaged? All the material that you have heard has been directed towards the proposition that there is some form of arrangement or understanding or agreement entered into between Mr Sugar and Mr Venables to the effect that Mr Sugar would in some way preserve equality or would not in some way secure additional control, and this represents some equity between the parties. That is one of the bases that it is put, as I understand it. Over and above that, it is said that Mr Venables had his own independent position as a shareholder pure and simple.

"In addition to that we have quite a long statement from Mr Crystal in which he describes a number of episodes which he found offensive and which obviously will have to be dealt with. But in respectful submission none of that material suggests, or is evidence of, any risk of harm to the interests of the Club. As to the evidence, the mechanism designed to protect these wider interests is wholly inappropriate....

"IT IS ALMOST THE FIRST RULE OF THE LAW OF SPECIFIC PERFORMANCE THAT YOU DO <u>NOT GRANT THAT SPECIFIC PERFORMANCE OF A CONTRACT OF EMPLOYMENT</u>.

"It is also the first rule that in these type of injunctions, you only grant them in cases of extreme urgency. There are two formidable obstacles against this application.

"In support, what is suggested is that relief of this kind is necessary in order to protect the interests that the Club is concerned with, but in my submission is no answer at all to the objections to which I have referred because there is no evidence that these interests of the Club face any risk of any harm during the next two or three weeks, much less irreparable harm.

"As I understand what my Learned Friend said, he says that Mr

Venables has special skills and expertise in connection with football. He does not claim that Mr Venables has these special skills and expertise with regard to interests wider than just football; he directs them at football for reasons which are understandable. Mr Venables has a distinguished record in this field.

"It is not said that Venables' continuing presence at the helm of management is required in order to safeguard the PLC interests. If one examines football itself, the thing at which Mr Venables is particularly skilled, the Season has come to an end. No football is being played. There is no occasion in these next two or three weeks, insofar as one can see, for any particular football experience or skill to be used so far as the Football Club is concerned.

"So My Lady, my submission really is this: There are formidable obstacles in the way of this application. They relate to the nature of the relief sought and the circumstances in which it is sought. There is no answer to those objections in the form of risk or imminent harm occurring, and the like because there is no evidence to support that.

"My Lady, I refer to Mr Venables' draft affidavit. He says:

'If the court is minded to grant my application for injunctive relief, to prevent any purported termination of my employment taking place, it is of great importance that such relief be granted without delay. I work a seven day week and at weekends I carry out a substantial amount of work including staff interviews, discussions of contracts and player training. This weekend would be no exception. In addition work needs to be carried out this weekend in relation to a match against ENFIELD this Tuesday and considerable preparation needs to be made this weekend for a planned tour by the Team to South Africa commencing next Wednesday, on which I had intended to travel.' "

(A game at Enfield on Tuesday, and a tour of South Africa on Wednesday.. Barrister Carr then continued having completed the item from Terry's statement that he needed to refer to.)

"That indicated two things. First of all, it shows that there are footballing activities, beyond the Season — trips to South Africa and the like, and your Ladyship should have those in mind. But, in addition to that, what it shows is that the case for urgency is a case which involves football activity. He refers to staff interviews, discussions of contracts, player training. He does not suggest that there are any wider interests which would be jeopardised or threatened over the next short period. So the wider interests really do not enter into this application."

(If Terry was going to South Africa who was going to look after the shop in his absence? Referring to wider interests, Barrister Carr meant that there was no necessity for his reinstatement to Chief Executive, but only as a football manager. We all know that with Clemence and Livermore there, Terry's involvement was not paramount to the continued well-being of Team and surely Sugar would be able to run the Company.)

The Judge then made a comment: "The affairs of the PLC include the management of the Football Club."

Barrister Carr again: "Yes, that I follow. What one then has is this. Mr Venables suggests that he needs to be there to carry out this work which he describes in his affidavit. The question is simply this…. Is there on the evidence, any indication satisfactory to you that some irreparable harm is likely to arise in these next two or three weeks of a character which justifies a virtually unprecedented form of relief — mandatory order — as to the contract of employment? Your Ladyship can only form a view as a matter of impression today. On the one hand you have to balance the application, bearing in mind that we have had no opportunity to deal with any of the matters that have been put forward. Your Ladyship knows that Mr Venables has had notice since Monday of this week of the fact that this meeting was going to take place today, and we appear in court on ten minutes notice. Bearing in mind that the application is not particularised or described. There are many wider matters referred to, but what is the particular harm, the particular risk to the Club, to the PLC, that results from Mr Venables not being present in his management capacity over the next three weeks? There is virtually no evidence of any relevant irreparable harm.

"I submit that when one does the exercise of examination, there is no contest. There is no evidence of extreme urgency shown in this case.

"The order that is sought restrains Tottenham, its directors, servants and agents from acting on the purported resolution that the directors made this morning insofar as it terminates the service contract of Mr Venables. It is not said that this morning's meeting was improperly convened. It is not said that the resolution that was passed was an improper or invalid resolution."

The Judge interrupted: "I think that it is being said, is it not, that the resolution was unfairly prejudicial and therefore should be set aside and is of no effect? It is rather different from the usual case where the employer gives notice under contract to an employee. There is no doubt about his capacity to do that."

The Barrister replied succinctly.

"The issue is indeed whether there has been unfair prejudicial conduct. That is an issue to be resolved at the full hearing. The present issue is what protection should be given to Terry Venables. I am saying that there is no serious issue to be tried so far as this application is concerned. In a sense when one has got the difficulties that stand in the way — procedurally, mandatory, and contract of employment, and the urgency of the matter, when one has got those, it is not so easy to disentangle balance of convenience for that of serious issue. I would submit that the Petitioner puts in evidence exactly what his concern is to explain why it is relevant to the interests which he seeks to protect.

"With great respect the Court has not got the chance to examine such evidence this afternoon. My Learned Friend took two hours to go through a vast amount of material which goes to the question of whether he has an arguable case. In my respectful submission, it is simply quite inappropriate to come before the Court seeking the form of relief without any material substance to support it.

"In his draft petition in the first prayer the Petitioner seeks an order requiring Amshold Ltd (Jersey) to sell its shares to the Petitioner. In the second part he then seeks an injunction restraining the termination of the employment contract. As my Learned Friend said, he will not need part two if he gets part one. The only relevance of this injunction in connection with the contract of employment is somehow to preserve the position if preservation be needed on a temporary basis, pending the full hearing of the petition. In my submission the interim period does not require Mr Venables' position to be preserved. If there has been a termination of the employment contract, it is difficult to see on what basis it could now be said that there should be an order requiring that contract to be performed.

"IF THERE HAD BEEN A TERMINATION, THEY ARE GONE. THEY ARE AT AN END. THEY ARE FINISHED.

"If a contract has actually been terminated, as opposed to one that is in breach, it is difficult to see how the Court, taking it sequentially, could ever grant a prohibitory injunction restraining a party from acting in breach. I cannot throw any light on what my Learned Friend has said, only to say that the contract has been terminated.

The Judge made, then, an accurate observation....

"I had not read it that way. I thought that the allegation was that the resolutions" (Passed by the Board that morning) "PURPORTED to terminate the contract."

In answer, Barrister Carr....

"It is not the READING of the order that is in question, it is what my Learned Friend told you in argument. I think I heard him correctly. He first pointed out the terms of the resolution that was passed."

The Judge: "I think that we have the notice to convene a board meeting, but not the resolutions."

Barrister Carr: "I have only got the notices calling the meeting as well. I do not think that I have got copies of the resolutions either. I think my Learned Friend then said.... 'That the resolutions' — he will correct me if I am wrong — 'gave an authority to terminate' and then, after taking instructions he said.... 'The contract of employment has been terminated.' "

Terry's Barrister Mann: "A letter has been received, as I understand it, purporting to terminate the contract. That is as far as we can go. Accept that a letter has been sent. My Friend can make what he likes of it...!"

Barrister Carr then read the originals of the minute that resulted in the resolution to end Terry's career at Spurs....

'I am writing to give notice that your employment with Tottenham Hotspur Plc and another letter being about the management agreement with Edennote Plc has terminated with immediate effect, and your P45 will follow shortly in the case of the employment contract.'

"I do not know whether your Ladyship wishes to see those but both contracts are terminated with immediate effect.

"There was application by the Petitioner to prevent the termination of those contracts and to prevent the meeting at which those decisions were taken."

"That may be an issue in the full petition," said Justice Arden.

Barrister Carr: "It is said that the meeting was not called properly or did not take place properly, because it was unfairly prejudicial. I SUPPOSE THAT IT WOULD HAVE TO BE SAID THAT ANY RESOLUTION PASSED AT THE MEETING CORRESPONDINGLY LACKED LEGAL VALIDITY. So far as the respondents here today are concerned, they have sent letters to finally terminate those contracts.

"There are one or two more matters, although I am so lacking in instructions at this stage. I would draw attention to the two agreements.

"One, in or about the middle of May 1991 Mr Venables orally agreed with Mr Sugar to purchase shares in equality, that is to say 50 per cent each. Two, that Mr Sugar would be appointed Chairman and Mr Venables Chief Executive of the PLC. Both of these agreements have been performed. Then there is reference in documents issued to shareholders re — Rights Issue — to a POSSIBLE AGREEMENT OR INTENDED AGREEMENT TO BE MADE BETWEEN MR SUGAR AND MR VENABLES. BUT THOSE AGREEMENTS REMAIN TO BE NEGOTIATED.

"Not merely to be executed, but to be negotiated.

"Therefore the basis for an argument that some legitimate interest or expectation by Mr Venables is extremely thin. It is not suggested that the agreement that Mr Venables would be appointed to Chief Executive was intended to guarantee a job for life. That could not seriously be put forward.

"My Lady in my present state of instruction I cannot take this any further."

Justice Arden: "I have a recollection that under English Law 459 one of the specific forms of relief the Court can give at the end of the day is a making of regulations for the conduct for the management of the Company."

There followed great reference to other decisions of various courts, including one that was taken in a case involving the 'Blue Arrow' Company, with Tony Berry as their Director at the time, but basically Barrister Carr was trying to point out the difficulties that would arise if Terry was reappointed as Chief Exec. while the present Board remained, as he, by now, was in direct opposition to the Chairman and others.

"It amounts to a shareholder coming along to the Court and wanting to take over the management of the Company in order to protect his interest as a shareholder."

(This working on the fact that the contracts had already been terminated and therefore at this point Terry was nothing more than any other shareholder albeit with a large holding in the Company. Makes sense, but surely Terry had a little more 'entitlement' than that?)

In response Justice Arden suggested that Terry, if re-appointed would not be there to control the Board but would be subject to the directions of the Board.

(In that case the Board could tell him to have a holiday for two or three weeks until the full hearing and he would gain little, except salary.)

"If one examines what we have got," Barrister Carr, who had very recently pronounced that he had done all he could in the light of insufficient instruction, carried on…"where this leads to is for Mr Venables to re-assert his management in circumstances where the Board have in the exercise of their powers said…. 'We don't want you to carry on.' It is very difficult in the reality of life to suppose that it can be in anybody's best interest to have a senior manager in the saddle carrying out management activity where he is in flagrant disagreement with the Board. It is quite plain that relations have completely broken down. The only question can be, is it appropriate to force Mr Venables onto the Board when they have decided that they do not want him? Is it appropriate to force Mr Venables onto the Board, because that is the only way — the only possible way of protecting his interests as a shareholder? Once one poses that question, it is obvious that that cannot be right. The issue is unsustainable as a matter of principle. Life would be unworkable in any practical or realistic sense, if the Board and the Chief Executive were thrown together as continuing bedfellows, given the state of their relationship. How can it operate if Mr Venables remains in office? It is not viable.... That is my submission."

The Judge then asked whether he would like to comment on the terms of the Pan Financial agreement which clearly stated that should Terry lose his job, the whole of the two million that he had borrowed would become immediately repayable if they were to exercise their rights under the loan agreement.

Barrister Carr then stated that apart from Terry he did not know whether the remaining board members knew of the existence of this clause in the agreement with Pan Financial.

"That cannot be relevant. Their powers (The Board) cannot be curtailed or affected by what Mr Venables has agreed with a financier. Bankers and financiers often demand extraordinary powers but we all know that they do not necessarily exercise those powers. There is no evidence before the Court as to whether this organisation proposes to exercise its power to declare a default. This point therefore is simply in limbo. Further damages would likely to be an adequate remedy in respect of the losses that would occur if the finance company did exercise their right to repayment of the capital and interest due.

The Judge then asked if Mr Mann would care to respond.

He rose and said: "Outside investors in this case were entitled to assume that Mr Venables and Mr Sugar would together turn the Company around, as they had stated in the Rights Issue offer documents, which they read and which formed the basis upon which those shares were retained and have subsequently traded.

"This is not an employment case. It is almost perhaps, a bit of fun to say that it is because it is easy to say when it is a contract of employment that the contract should not be performed by the Court. Here we are there is no harm at all in allowing Mr Venables to remain in this position as it was before the resolution taken this morning. I note that no criticism has been made of his conduct whatsoever. The idea that he, by carrying on in his managerial position for the limited time suggested, which may be necessary, will cause difficulties in that management or the management of the Company is frankly absurd.

The Judge then enquired as to which Directors, other than Terry were Executive. (Meaning which ones received pay.)

"Is the Finance Director also an Executive Director?"

"No, he is not. There are no others. Mr Sandy is employed by one of the Amstrad companies, Amstrop, as I understand it. Mr Sugar is not one either."

(Note: The arrangement between Amshold Ltd and Tottenham Hotspur Plc to pay him £50,000 per annum; but he is still not regarded as a paid director! Nor does he have any rights under that contract formed and signed while Crystal was in Mauritius.)

"There is no-one other than Mr Venables. Involved in his leaving is that someone would step in to his shoes to run the Company in its 'Vanguard' at the helm of the ship, and goodness knows what consequences that would have on the shareholders. It would undeniably cause massive damage to the Club and the Company."

Lady Justice Arden: "I propose to rise for half to three quarters of an hour to reflect on the submissions which have been made."

(That was it! Terry dismissed in the morning, and as the dark evening clouds of conflict and confusion gathered around the Royal Courts of Justice, so his fate was being determined. How he longed to speak up and tell her Ladyship that he was being unfairly and prejudiciously treated.

The acrimony that had been gathering between the two protagonists was finally being sorted out in a court of law, by a lady Judge whose need it was to determine the result by way of legal consideration. In these austere halls of ruthless justice, no consideration for his family, their aspirations, his reputation or the Spurs supporters would be made.

For almost six years Terry had taken the Club from a lowly position, arriving when morale was at its lowest to a position which confirmed Spurs considered right to be up there with the best. Then came the news that the financial position of the Company was such that the Midland Bank were considering enforcing their right to demand return of the £11 million that

Tottenham owed them. With that in mind, Terry borrowed, pledged and strove to help save the Club and to realize his ambitions to take the helm to guide it to safety.

At a time when both the financial position and the team were at the point of imminent success, his world had collapsed around him. Matters which were confidential by nature, and which were previously agreed by the Chairman, initially, were now being used against him. What was behind Alan Sugar's determination to get rid of the man with whom he had committed a future to, and who had not, in the public's eyes, warranted this astonishing ill treatment. It quickly became obvious that there was more to this than had been discussed on this day.

Even a victory, temporary as it might be, would stave off the inevitable, for Alan Sugar is a mighty adversary. A man, humourless, inconsiderate and ruthless in fulfilling his aims.

Ultimately he would be the victor, of that there would be no doubt.

The Judgment followed later that evening....

THE JUDGMENT GAVE TERRY HOPE...FALSELY

At the time when the media ought to have been gathered in their numbers awaiting with bated breath the result of the afternoon's dramatic arguments, most were outside the main gates at White Hart Lane, anticipating the emergence of the protagonists from their place of employ. Few, it would seem, knew or anticipated the swift action of the Edennote team. Many of the eager newspaper reporters detailed to follow every event were actually in the 'Arms' having a pint, unaware that the real dramas were being played out some seven miles away in the Royal Courts. But soon after learning that they were waiting in vain, many made their way to the City to line up alongside hysterical fans and excited cameramen and broadcasters.

But they had missed the real events. The disclosures of Jonathan Crystal.

All that was available now, was the judgment.

Would Terry be returned to former glory? The ramifications of a favourable decision would be widespread as the reinstatement of the Chief Executive would, under the rules of

459, allow or permit the courts to order Mr Sugar to sell to Terry or Edennote his shareholding in Tottenham Hotspur Plc. That would be the side effect, although judgment in his favour would of course satisfy the immediate requirement which would be to turn around the resolution to cancel his contract of employment. If, however, the Judge in her wisdom, decided that no harm would beset the Company should the board resolution stand, at least until a later hearing which would have the full evidence before it, then the signs were on the wall that Terry was not going to succeed.

An hour passed and the hearing was re-convened.

I summarise the judgment because most of the argument was about the date of the next hearing. Both parties wished for a final resolution and sought an early date, with the Sugar team pushing for a date slightly earlier than the Venables team. As Terry's side were obviously more prepared, that seemed a little strange, but time scales were laid down so that the Judge could have time to read the evidence and affidavits of the various participants.

The Judge:

"The application for relief is made by the Petitioners, Edennote Plc, who are twenty three per cent shareholders in Tottenham Hotspur Plc who are one of the respondents. I should point out that the respondents have had little notice of this application and have therefore had to make their submissions on little preparation.

"The relief sought is for an injunction, pending an effective hearing at a fixed date.

In summary, the Company, the PLC, should be restrained from acting on a termination of contract for the employment of its Chief Executive. Further injunction is sought to prevent the PLC from permitting its wholly owned subsidiary, Tottenham Hotspur Football Club Ltd, from terminating a management contract with Edennote Plc. Within that contract Edennote provides the services of Mr Terry Venables.

"I am told that today the Board of the PLC have PURPORTED to terminate the contracts to which I have referred.

I have been given a great deal of information orally because of the urgency of this matter. The information that I have been given includes many significant matters, including the allegation that there is no-one else on the Board to run the Companies.

"Reference has been made to a match on Tuesday next at Enfield and to a tour of the players to play matches in South Africa. I do not accept therefore that the Season has effectively ended.

"The proceedings are a proposed petition under 459 of the Companies Act, but that petition has not been presented at this Court.

"I make reference to an oral agreement made in May 1991 and subsequently to a conversation in December 1991, prior to Rights Issue during a meeting at the Grosvenor House Hotel in London. During that meeting it is alleged that Mr Venables made reference to the inequality that would result if Mr Sugar were able to purchase shares in the Rights Issue. It is then stated that Mr Sugar replied.... 'Trust me — even if I pick up all the shares, we have a shareholders agreement'. Mr Venables then offered an agreement which Mr Sugar declined to accept until after the Rights Issue had been made. This agreement referred to the oral agreement allegedly made in May 1991. There is the question of the appointments of Mr Sugar as Chairman and Mr Venables as Chief Executive. It is not clear, after those appointments were made as to how long those appointments should remain.

"It is further said that the removal of Mr Venables and the termination of the management contract will cause damage to Edennote's substantial shareholding interests in T.H. Plc. I shall deal with that allegation before reference to the earlier ones of contract cancellation.

"It has been said that Mr Venables is a very distinguished football manager and an institution in this field of life.

"I am satisfied there is a serious issue to be tried as to the damage that would ensue if Mr Venables no longer performs his role as Chief Executive. I am told that T.H. Plc, has made a major financial recovery under Mr Venables' management.

"IN THE LIGHT OF ALL T HAT I HAVE HEARD, I AM NOT PREPARED TO ACCEPT THAT THERE IS NO CREDIBLE EVIDENCE OF IRREPARABLE HARM TO THE PLC AND CONSEQUENTLY TO THE SHAREHOLDERS WHICH WOULD RESULT FROM THE REMOVAL OF MR VENABLES."

(Terry had effectively won the first round which gave him and his advisors both the right and the encouragement to continue down the sticky path of litigation in the future. He emerged from the court victorious and waving gleefully to the crowd outside, and to the joyous relief of the supporters and many of the reporters who at this time believed that an injustice had been done. Terry stated to the media: "It's going to be alright.")

The Judge:

"Now as I have mentioned the primary relief sought by the Petitioner is an order that they buy out the shares held by Amshold Ltd (of Jersey). Of course, at the trial the Court could reflect any fall in value of the shares in the buy-out price. But if there is no relief and the shares fall in value, as a practical matter this form of relief would in my judgment be illusory. Edennote would not want their shares in the PLC which has been adversely affected by the removal of Mr Venables. If that occurs and if it no longer has Mr Venables as its Manager or Chief Executive. Further I am told that some players will leave and that supporters will go elsewhere or not renew their Season Tickets. At the time of trial the respondent Company's business would, if these allegations are true and proved, be that of a substantially different company from that which it is today.

"Reference has been made to a financial agreement between Edennote and Pan Financial which could result in the finance company's ability to call in their loan if Mr Venables has left his post. I have not considered that in depth at this stage.

"In all the circumstances I am satisfied that I ought to grant some form of relief. I do so partly influenced by what I have been told. NAMELY THAT MR VENABLES IS THE PERSON WHO IS PRINCIPALLY RESPONSIBLE FOR THE FOOTBALL RELATED ACTIVITIES.

"I thus envisage that it would be possible to ensure the smooth running of the Company if relief is granted."

The Judgment virtually concluded at that point.

Mr Carr for Mr Sugar tried to gain some advantage by asking the Judge to limit Terry's activities by restricting the 'relief' to only his management of the football team and its activities. There continued an argument as to what 'football related activities' meant. Football TEAM activities were not the same as football RELATED activities.

Mr Carr: "We are seeking to confine the relief which will preserve the football activities, and which will therefore enable us to stop him (TERRY) doing things which he has done previously on the commercial side, which the Respondents believe is not in the interests of the PLC, or the Limited Company. You will appreciate that the Board and Mr Sugar have not acted frivolously or lightly. There are SERIOUS REASONS why they have done what they have done."

Mr Mann: "The purposes of the order which your Ladyship envisages is to preserve the status quo. That is to preserve the functions which Mr Venables was carrying out before this morning's resolutions."

Mrs Justice Arden: "I am not proposing to impose restrictions today of Mr Venables' activities, in order to enable the Companies to run smoothly. However, I leave it open to the respondents to apply for restrictions on proper evidence. I would hope that if evidence is put forward which justifies restrictions, that those can be agreed and that the parties will attempt to discuss the matter rather than referring it straight back to the Court, since I am concerned that the parties efforts should be focused on the effective hearings due, and in due course, if the matter proceeds to trial."

Barrister Mann then suggested the form of order that Mrs Arden makes and that a good day for the next hearing would be on the 25th May 1993.

The judge intimated that should matter proceed to trial then it would need to be at the next 'session' of the Court which starts in October. These type of courts sit in a session until July 31st each year and then break off until October.

We now know that October 11th 1993 was the appointed date.

During the ensuing period of twelve days it was widely thought and expected, that Terry would only need to attend the further hearing and all would be well. Who can blame him? The entire Country, supporters of Spurs and others not even associated by any stretch of the imagination, believed that an injustice had occurred.

TISA, the body representing an active group of supporters and shareholders declared their unmitigated support of Terry's reinstatement.

The team under him, and coached by Doug Livermore and Ray Clemence had ended the Season with a flourish. Young footballers were coming through in the guise of Darren Anderton, Andy Turner and Nicky Barmby, each of whom had contributed to an exciting end to the Season with amazing things happening on the field of play.

Under the administration that existed at the end of the '92/'93 season, the supporters were considering the quality of the squad of players sufficient to win the Championship, League Cup, and FA Cup all in the ensuing Season.

Such were the achievements during the period January 1993 until the last game in May.

The pinnacle, the summit of Terry's efforts of over five years at White Hart Lane was in sight. Terry had stated that he wouldn't accept 'ten million' for the youngsters at the Club or the potential that was just coming to fruition.

It was therefore, no wonder that his publicly unanticipated dismissal was to cause the furore that ensued over the following twelve days.

The media reported Terry's every move and those of Alan Sugar. Each made guarded statements, aware of the sub judice situation. Sugar intimated that there was much for the public to know before they made up their minds. His house and car were damaged and he was hustled out of court through the rear exit to avoid the hostility of the supporters who continued to invade the Royal Courts' enclaves. At that point in time there is little doubt that Alan Sugar was the 'bad one'. Players, such as Teddy Sheringham, Neil Ruddock and Jason Cundy made it absolutely clear that they would only stay at Tottenham if Mr Venables remained in office. Such was the kudos and popularity of the man.

It was, however, surprising that others on the playing staff did not join that throng, but common sense applied; the calming influence of the experienced Gary Mabbutt, the long serving Club Captain, prevailed.

Many thought that if the unbelievable should happen, and Terry lose in the next round, then further players would follow the leads of the three openly vociferous players before them. Vinny Samways, somewhat less openly than the others, seemed to join their thinking. David Howells who had emerged as a talented 'defence screen' under Terry, and indeed who never performed for anyone else in a like manner either before the conflict or since, was another believed to be angry at Terry's dismissal.

As the protagonists returned to their respective lives to plan their attacks for the game that would be played in the court of law instead of on the football field, the media and newspapers began to ask 'How could Terry afford the legal fees? What income did he have, should the eventual decision go against him?'

Suddenly there were leaks as to the contents of affidavits. Sugar was suggesting that there was corruption involved and that Terry's associates were undesirable. The word 'bung' became common among the tabloids. Other football managers and their agents and associates were mentioned with restraint, but the seeds of doubt began their slow embrace and intrusion into the Nation's previously biased thinking....

And then, to May 25th 1993.

THE HEARING ON
25th MAY 1993

Terry Venables must have hoped that this day would result in a conclusive judgment in his favour, following the temporary relief he had been granted on 14th May.

Similarly, Alan Sugar, who had been taken by surprise by the force and speed with which Terry had attacked him in Mrs Justice Arden's Court, must have hoped that these new proceedings, before the Vice-Chancellor, Sir Donald Nicholls, would finally resolve matters in his favour.

Neither man can have welcomed the chaotic and farcical situation that had prevailed during the previous eleven days.

During most of that time, instead of being at his desk at Brentwood or in his opulent offices at White Hart Lane, Sugar was ensconced with his legal advisers, preparing a vigorous conter-attack in an endeavour to show that the reinstatement of Venables to the position that he had enjoyed prior to the 14th was neither practicable, reasonable nor acceptable to himself, other members of the Board and indeed staff and managers of all departments.

The fact that Terry pursued a weakish case indicated that he had been buoyed up by the first judgment, and perhaps he was confident of final victory. He reckoned perhaps without Sugar's powerful ammunition, so ably employed by his new counsel, Mr Philip Heslop, who sought to interpret events in his client's favour and in a very different light from the way they had been put to the previous judge.

Immediately after the ruling on 14th May, a meeting had been held at the offices of Herbert Smith to work out an interim arrangement whereby Venables could continue to act in his capacity as Chief Executive, but in practice the outcome was wholly unsatisfactory.

Sandy and others communicated with Venables by way of memorandum. There was no contact at Board level except in the

267

presence of highly paid solicitors. The planned trip to South Africa was cancelled. Most importantly, from Terry's viewpoint, a Board meeting on 17th May further undermined his position. It was called for the purpose of dismissing his right hand man, Eddie Ashby.

Venables found himself isolated by a hostile board where even Crystal was made to feel like an outsider, his own position having become tenuous following his affidavit at the initial hearing and his falling out with Sugar.

The situation was intolerable to all concerned. The Club Secretary, Peter Barnes, presented an affidavit to the Court, pointing out the problems that were being created in negotiations with the box and season ticket holders, who were telephoning constantly with enquiries for clarification of what was happening at the Club, and of course many supporters were not renewing their seats for the forthcoming season while matters were in limbo.

One of the very few actions that Sugar and Venables jointly undertook at this time was the signing by them both of a letter to all members, urging them not to withold their money for renewals since this would seriously damage Spurs' finances.

The Commercial Manager, Mr Rollo, swore an affidavit that sales were being affected by the uncertainty. Mr Alexiou, who had been re appointed to the Board having previously served under the Scholar administration, confirmed in an affidavit that all was not well and healthy at Board level. Players contracts, of which there were eleven to be renewed, could not be agreed because the Board was unwilling to allow Terry to deal with these matters, which of course he regarded as his responsibility.

Worse still, some of the players were taking a partisan position, making statements to the media, almost universally in support of Terry.

As Philip Heslop told the Judge:

"Could I have a word about the interim regime? It arose from the discussions that took place with Herbert Smith after the hearing of 14th May. It was at the suggestion of the Board that Mr Venables attended with his advisers to see whether any sort of regime could be agreed, could be worked out in the intervening period.

"The vital point about all of that is that the regime was set up firstly as a regime entirely designed to work out in the short term. I think you asked about the question whether all the various matters which would have to be dealt with by a Chief Executive had occurred in the intervening period, or whether one was simply postponing them. The answer is that many of the hard decisions that the board need to take in conjunction with their management have simply been postponed in the interregnum. They have not been taken. The reason they have been postponed, or the time has not arisen when they need to be taken, is that the Board do not believe that in the current conditions they can have confidence in Mr Venables to take the sort of decisions that are being postponed. Therefore you should not be seduced into thinking that the interregnum regime is a recipe for a longer period.

"The other point is in Mr Sugar's affidavit. There is evidence that in any event the regime has already caused a lot of difficulty.... That difficulty is likely to be compounded were these matters left to run.

Mr Heslop also referred to the matter of Eddie Ashby:

"As far as Mr Ashby is concerned, complaint is made that in some way this is all part of a plot to undermine Mr Venables' position. The reality is that Mr Ashby was not really acting purely as a personal assistant to Mr Venables. He was acting as a de facto general manager and furthermore he regarded himself as being separate to and above the authority of Mr Sandy. This issue has been rumbling on for some time. Learning that Mr Ashby was a bankrupt was bad enough, but we now have the affidavit of Mr Sandy relating to the number of companies with which Mr Ashby has been involved and which had gone into insolvent liquidation.

"It is really very odd that the Board should be expected to leave in place a General Manager, not merely a PA, a man with that sort of history. Far more important than the bankruptcy is the fact that the record seems to indicate that he has an extremely unsuccessful commercial past."

In Mr Heslop's submission, having considered the various options, there was no realistic alternative to, and the balance of convenience came down firmly in favour of, Tottenham being allowed through its Board to decide what was in its own best interests.

"They have resolved," Heslop said, "that Mr Venables should go. Right or wrong, that is their duty. There is no reason for the Court to intervene and I would ask your Lordship not to grant a continuance of the relief to Mr Venables in what has now become very bitter circumstances."

Following an adjournment, the Judge decided that he had heard insufficient evidence, and there was a lack of time that day, for him to overturn the earlier decision. The case would have to be continued at a later date.

Alan Sugar wanted a date later that same week but Terry Venables' counsel said that such an early continuance was impractical because of a looming Jewish holiday. Bearing in mind that Sugar is Jewish and Venables is not, there is something quite amusing about that. In the final result, a new date was agreed: 10th June!

So the parties had to put up with each other at least for a further sixteen days, time for more disruption at Tottenham, more evidence, more affidavits, more protests, more public statements; but time also for Terry Venables to take what was on offer and run.

Why did he refuse the full amount he had paid for his shares, £450,000 for the service agreement with Edennote and damages for the loss of his personal work contract?

Did he still really think he could win? Was he in no way worried about the allegations in Sugar's affidavit concerning invoices and payments? Did he think that he could match Sugar financially? Did he think that he could actually get rid of Sugar and run Tottenham himself?

What advice was he being given?

Was it a question of his pride ruling his common sense?

Whatever the answers — and of course I was not allowed to put these questions to him — Terry rejected compensation and resolved to fight on.

FOUR DAYS OF HEARINGS OF JUNE 1993, COMMENCING THE 10th

THE BATTLE OF TWO GIANTS.
As early as the 21st January 1993, according to documents in our possession, Alan Sugar wrote as follows to Terry Venables.
"Dear Terry

I feel that it is better for me to put my concerns in writing so that you can understand my current position.

On reflection, going back nearly 18 months when we made the joint take-over of Tottenham. I did not for one moment imagine that you would need to go to the length that you have to fund the transaction. That, however, is a past matter and not worth discussing", then referring to Eddie Ashby, "Nothing that he has done since he has been with the Company has been done in any professional manner. Many of the arrangements that he has made have been done on the basis of his commercial judgement which, in my opinion, is bad. If I speak very frankly, I observe that there is somewhat of a comfort factor of you having Eddie around in your life. Whilst this is none of my business, I appreciate that he handles many of your other financial matters and has been instrumental in rearranging your financing, etc, and obviously advises you on Scribes and your other businesses. I believe I have diplomatically allowed you to take the helm of the Company and be seen publicly as the Chief Executive running the organisation. I have always, when speaking to outsiders or members of the press, spoken about you with the utmost respect and have never implied in any way or form other than you are the person running the organisation, and that is how it should be if the organisation is running properly. BUT I AM AFRAID TO SAY THAT I DO NOT BELIEVE THAT THE ORGANISATION IS RUNNING PROPERLY AND I THINK WE HAVE A LONG WAY TO GO TO PROFESSIONALISE IT.

In hindsight, I was too hasty in the acquisition of Tottenham in not checking how the Company would be run on an ongoing basis.

The reality is that 20% of the Club belongs to you and 50% belongs to me and the reality is that when you go out and spend money on players, you are spending 50% of my money and in most cases, I know nothing about it. I think, up until now, I have been pretty dam reasonable in allowing you a completely free hand..... We have lots of empty boxes and we have a problem coming up at the start of next season with lots of renewals coming up. we have no contract for ground signage. I have personally asked you a few times to make sure that BSkyB/BBC are happy with the televising and I personally feel that a one day a week discussion with Rollo is not good enough.

I do not know whether we are going to resolve these differences between us as I get the distinct feeling that anything that happens publicly that implies that I am more senior than you in the Company seems to annoy you and seems to be taken very personally. I repeat that I say nothing to imply this to anybody.

If we are unable to work things out sensibly, then I believe that the only other approach is to discuss alternative plans for each other and those alternative plans of course, if implemented, should be done in the most businesslike and professional manner without unsavoury, unnecessary friction. But one thing is for sure. I am not going to carry on in the way that we are at the moment. Either you recognise my position in the Company (between ourselves, there is no need for public recognition) or I believe we should seriously sit down and resolve alternative ways which could only result in one or other of us departing from ownership of Tottenham, who I for one do not wish to do.

I would respectfully ask you not discuss this matter with Jonathan Crystal and take your time to reflect on these words and call me when you are ready to discuss the matter in detail.''

VENABLES' REPLY:

"In view of the contents of your memorandum it is better that I respond in writing so that you have time to reflect before we talk. The one thing I do agree is that we cannot continue as present.

Our original deal was joint ownership with equal shareholding and a shareholders agreement to protect the other. You pushed through the Rights Issue rather than raising finance on the properties. You knew I did not have the extra money. The reality is that our contribution, and ownership of, the Company cannot simply be measured in the money we have put in.

You talk about your money being spent. It is mine as well. You were to be Non-Executive Chairman of the PLC with an FD-Finance Director — I was to be Chief Executive with a General Manager. You have also become Chairman of the Football Club. You dealt with Gray. You were happy to deal with Eddie — What do you mean you do not know what he does? I RUN THE COMPANY WITH HIS BACK-UP..... Your view of Tottenham shows you misunderstand the business. The teams and there performance are paramount. I need to be at the training ground."

(Mr Mann then interrupts this letter by commenting that some of the misunderstandings may have arisen from the fact that the training ground is located away from the main Stadium implying presumably that Mr Sugar misunderstands Mr Venables' absences from his office.)

Continuing Terry's reply:

"That is where the football product is, just as you are at Brentwood for Amstrad. In a perfect world, and if we want to catch up with the likes of Milan, the Stadium is for match days and the heads of department (other than finance and commerce) should be at the training ground where the main activity goes on. I wonder if you know what I do all week, or what has been achieved in the last 18 months.

Supporting the team are the commercial/admin. departments who also report to me. To say that there is no direction means you are either ignoring what I do or relying Colin sandy for your information. It seems that you are concerned about the amount of time I put into the job. Most normal business people work five days, Monday to Friday. My week inevitably seven days. This week, for example, on Saturday morning I was at the training ground working with the youth squad all morning and the first team all afternoon. Sunday I was at Norwich. Monday business was as usual.

Eddie has worked hard for the Club's benefit."

(To say nothing of the £90,000 per annum salary he received!)

"You told me he was involved with fifteen companies with Mr Pay. That was enough for to act, but it turned out not to be the case. Colin Sandy then said that Eddie had set up a business with Mr Pay and again this was false. He had failures, but is not alone. I understand that you now want him to leave but I disagree. There are also failures on the part of Colin Sandy.

1) The computer system for stock control is still not up after 14 months despite three full-time assistants.

2) Management accounts are never on time.

3) Board minutes are at last moment.

4) No reconciled merchandising accounts since May.

5) He altered staff without reference to the Board or Jonathan Crystal.

6) He cut across my actions and caused unnecessary problems. A good example is his involvement with Paul Allen where he was asked merely to deal with tax implications of his testimonial.

Moreover, his actions over your contract are at best disgraceful. I asked him specifically if anything had been done and he said 'No'.

I would hope we share common goals — a successful team in business. To suggest I am annoyed at your profile of the club is absurd. It seems to me that the reverse is true. Also it is disturbing that YOU FEEL YOU WERE THROWN OUT OF MY OFFICE LAST SATURDAY. I have no wish to be rude, indeed I pride myself on not being so, but to take further you point about being asked to leave while I saw Doug Livermore and Ray Clemence, I find your position incredible.

We are in contact most days and you are well aware when I am serious about player purchases. You seem to deal with newspaper speculation when you could ask me. You read in the newspaper that I am interested in Wilkinson of Middlesborough. You get wound up or someone winds you up when I have not about him. If you asked me I could confirm that it is mostly newspaper speculation.

I should hardly need to tell you the hours I have worked on matters I resolve. Also my activities require me to spend a great deal of time off site because the business is not confined to the activities of the ground. It is just not like Amstrad.

I do not understand your reference to my dreams. I have never mentioned it. You must have read it in the Daily Mirror.

Once again you refer to my financing arrangements. Let me make one thing clear; I believe Jonathan Crystal and the other senior members of staff respect your position as Chairman and joint owner of the Club. It needs mutual recognition, understanding and respect. If you are not happy with that I will sit down with you to look at alternative ways forward. THE SOONER THE BETTER.''

Small wonder than that Mr Mann again representing the Venables' interest told the Judge, in fact, the Vice-Chancellor, on the 10th June 1993, the first day of the new hearing:

"The position is that Mr Sugar and Mr Venables have fallen out with each other. They do not get on, and one of them has to go. Matters have deteriorated to such an extent that it is unlikely that they would be able to ever get on with other in the long term.''

In other words whatever the legal basis of the Court proceedings the substantial issue was.... which of the two men would run Tottenham Hotspur. In boxing parlance, there was no room for a 'points decision'. One of them had to knock the other out!

Representing the 'Sugar team' the formidable Philip Heslop assisted by Mr Mabb, who you will recall acted in the senior capacity when Terry applied for the injunction on the 14th May. Now, he is there as support. In the other corner the old guard of Barrister Mann, and Mr Michael Gadd, knowledgeable, armed with good if inconsequential evidence, and surely at a disadvantage!..

David, without the 'sling'...... against Goliath.

The Object.. To once and for all decide whether Terry Venables had a legitimate claim to be reinstated. Whether indeed the Board of Tottenham Plc behaved correctly when they ended his career. Now, the evidence of people like Neil Ruddock, Frank McLintock, and many others who all aired their views!...

The Ramifications. Should they uphold the ruling of Mrs Justice Arden of the 14th May, chaos would surely rein in the high towers of White Hart Lane. It would undoubtedly mean that the Board would need to resign and alan Sugar would need to make arrangements to sell his shares, even though this trial, whatever the result, would not adjudicate on that subject, or indeed, preclude Edennote from pursuing that course.

If, on the other hand, the Judge overruled that original adjudication, then Terry would have to leave his job, and be left with a claim for wrongful dismissal and damages, but his integrity was already being called into doubt.

Billed as the penultimate of the trials, it was obvious that failure for either team would result in careful consideration as to the worth of progressing further spurious claim.

Commencing the proceedings was a special Barrister appointed by Alan Sugar who was there to discuss the timing of a hearing that was all about an illegal approach that Alan had made to Jonathan Crystal on June 1st.. As that hearing, after much argument, was put down to be heard at the end of these proceedings, and is written about later, we shall continue with the main issues.

The Lord Irvine of Lairge, the especially appointed Barrister left the Court on another mission. Philip Heslop took over...

Mr Heslop addressed the Court: "It is not accepted that the current regime is workable, or that it should be extended for a moment longer than necessary. The matter of an injunction remains a matter of the utmost importance and urgency. The problems facing the company remain. They have not been diminished, even if a temporary regime has been hobbled-up.

The forefront of my submission is that so far as the Company is concerned, it is right to bear in mind the prejudice it alleges if the injunction situation is not resolved as soon as possible. It has always been recognised as urgent."

Mr Mann: "The course I propose to take I hope will shorten these proceedings realistically. I wish to deal with it in three sections. The first being a short introduction. The second, how that fits into conditions that we have to satisfy. There is a draft amended petition."

Mr Heslop: "I am not against evidence being introduced late providing I am able to do the same for the Respondents. There is an affidavit from a Mr Staunton which I have not had an opportunity to consider. Regarding the amended petition, I only received those amendments yesterday I have strong objection to certain of the amendments, and as long as that is understood, then my Learned Friend and I can each take our own course. the amendments will strongly contested and my Learned Friend should not think that they are agreed. Some of them are vital!''

Mr Mann: "I have no anticipation of agreement or otherwise. We put them before your Lord as an appropriate way of dealing with them."

(At this point, I should perhaps say that the contents of this chapter have been condensed from over 200 pages of transcript, much of it repetitive, and parts of it easily comprehensible only to lawyers. I have done my best, briefly, to refer to all the important issues and arguments in a way that should interest the 'lay' readers, and particulary football followers, without raising any legal eyebrows. It is a bit like putting the pieces together in a gigantic jigsaw puzzle, but I hope that, at the end of the day, the reader will have managed to complete it for it is fascinating to write of the ingenious approaches of both sides, particularly Mr Heslop, and the way that they work everything around to their clients' advantage.)

Mr Mann continued:

"This is a battle of two giants. The first is Mr Sugar and his Company, Amshold Ltd, a giant of the industry. the second is Mr Venables, a giant of the football field, who has made his mark in an outstanding career, both nationally and internationally, and whose reputation is one of the highest and undisputed.

"At first sight an objective observer, may say that Mr Sugar should have control. He owns 46% of the shares. That, in a publicly quoted company, is the controlling interest. It has been said that his interest is 48%, but either way it makes no difference. Mr Venables has 23%, a round figure.

"When they originally purchased their share on the 21st June 1991, they did so under the publicly accepted plaudit of 'SAVIOURS OF THE PLC'. It was described at the time as a joint Venables/Sugar ticket. We say that they had an agreement to share control; they would not out-vote each other. Mr Sugar would take a back-seat as Non-Executive Chairman, although he would have responsibility for the financial affairs. In a press release it was de-

scribed as Mr Sugar having responsibility for the 11 off the field"...
(the £11 million owed to Midland Bank) "and Mr Venables the 11
on the field. If there were no companies involved that would be described as a partnership; a joint venture. In such circumstances if
they fell out the Court would grant injunctive relief to prevent the
exclusion of one or the other or a dissolution. As there are various
companies involved, we say that the partnership arrangement
should ride above the Articles of the companies.

As the main Companies involved are PLCs the question arises
as to whether Mr Sugar should go back on the partnership agreement. There is nothing the articles which prevents Mr Sugar from
outvoting Mr Venables and using a casting vote in relation particular matters in the Boardroom."

(In a Limited Company, each Director has one vote regardless of the number of shares that he may hold in that Company.
Should a tie on votes occur on an issue, the Chairman can use a
second, casting vote. Should an issue become, say, intolerable or
totally unacceptable to a Director, he may, if he owns or can rely
on 75% of the shares, ask the other shareholders for their support. Realistically, if he can find that degree of support he
doesn't need other directors support anyway. Where there is no
Director owning more than 49%, and he does not have the support of other shareholders, an aggregated vote of the other
shareholders could oust him from his position. It is usually recognised however, that major shareholders have a seat on the
board.)..

"This is precisely a case where those who are not party to the
arrangements, the small shareholders owning approximately
30% of the shares, between Mr Sugar and Mr Venables, have nevertheless accepted the existence of that arrangement."

The Vice-Chancellor: "If you are right, what you are suggesting should be the long term regime operating within this Company."

Mr Mann: "That simply affects the long term arrangements
between Mr Venables and Mr Sugar. It should not affect the way
the Company runs in any way at all."

The Vice-Chancellor: "How much would that cost Mr
Venables?"

Mr Mann: "It will cost whatever the valuation would be put upon it."

The Vice-Chancellor: "Let us be specific."

Mr Mann: "Shares are trading at about a £1 each, so we thank that it would cost about £6 million."

The Vice-Chancellor: "And is you Client able to raise that?"

Mr Mann: "The answer to that is YES, I am so instructed."

The Vice-Chancellor: "Do you have evidence?"

Mr Mann: "That is not the case at the moment, no, because we have not gone that far."

The Vice-Chancellor: "This is only a temporary application, I must have some regard to the likely outcome. Must I not?"

Mr Mann: "The position is this. If we are successful, we will be given an opportunity to buy out Mr Sugar."

The Vice-Chancellor: "Very well!.. I do not think that you should be given an opportunity simply on the basis of: 'Now I will go away and see if I can find some money'..... You have to have some reasonable ground for believing that this is a serious possibility. That is why I asked is there any evidence. I am asking whether this is an achievable course."

(Surely it was evident at this early stage that the Judge who had seen hundreds of pages of evidence in advance of the hearing, was correctly leaning towards the Sugar claim. Time, Terry to call it a day!)

Mr Mann: "My instructions — there is no evidence — that this a course that is achievable. For the purposes of the petition, evidence will have to be filed to that effect. That is something that we fully accept. We have no evidence at the moment. We are not aware as to how the mechanism of such a purchase would be put together."

(It's a strange world. If Terry needed to sell just his shares in tottenham it would be difficult to find a buyer because he would have a minority interest in Tottenham, and there would be no guarantee from Mr Sugar that purchaser would be given a seat on the Board. That would cost about £3 million. If, however he should win the right to buy out Sugar, and including his investment into Tottenham that would cost probably £10 million, with a further amount needed to perform to the 'City Code' and offer to buy out all the shareholders, maybe, then he would need, say £15 million, that would be easier to raise because he would have absolute control.)

"Our instructions are that it would be possible for Mr Venables to adduce evidence that funds would be made available. The real point is that we are asking to purchase Mr Sugar's shares in the interests of the Company as well as Mr Venables. The important thing is that Mr Venables is left in control so as to direct the Company."

The Vice-Chancellor: "I accept that Mr Sugar and Mr Venables can't now get on, but what is the basis upon which the Court should decide as to who shall buy out whom?"

Mr Mann: "I shall come to that later. The basis shall have regard as to who is at fault. If Mr Sugar is found to have been at fault, it would be wrong for him to continue to run the Company. If Mr Venables has tendered evidence of his ability to purchase Sugar's shares, then that should be sufficient to exercise discretion in his favour. As to who should be in control, we will show the Court circumstances that will include the fact that without Mr Venables, Mr Sugar would not have been in a position to make his purchase in the first instance. Mr Venables would not have risked his capital and his financial security, except on the basis of an agreement or understanding which he thought would protect his position. This is a bonafide application to put Mr Venables in control in the Company which he fought save. We submit the existence and breach of a legitimate interest, such as to amount to unfair prejudice. We further submit that there has been bad faith on behalf of Mr Sugar and Mr Sandy.

"I propose to run through the heads of complaint to particular aspects of the evidence which are relevant.

"There is the appointment of Mr Berry who was involved and sincerely criticised in the 'Blue Arrow' affair, and the appointment of Mr Alexiou, on the 14th May, who was a Director of Tottenham when the take-over was sought and when tottenham were in deep financial difficulties. We also say that Mr Sugar and Mr Sandy cannot be relied upon to look after the interests of the minority shareholders."

(Reference there to the cancellation by Sugar of acceptance of the Cadbury report!)..

"Further, it is suggested that there can be no continuance of the injunction because 'no new Manager can be appointed', which is a point for reinstating Mr Venables. May I quote from Mr Sugar's affdavit?... 'Neither I nor the majority of the Board with whom I have discussed this matter, i.e., Berry, Sandy and Alexiou, consider that Mr Venables is essential for any of the activities. What is clear to myself and the majority of the Board is that until the injunction granted to Edennote is lifted, the Board cannot effectively bring in a successor for Mr Venables who can carry out these functions.'

"The prospect of somebody of Mr Venables' calibre or sufficiently close to it, accepting the appointment, when there are many other opportunities, must be very remote indeed."

(Personally, as a supporter, I find this insulting to Tottenham. the opportunity to arise for a manager to come to the likes of Tottenham are rare, and cannot be compared to managing West Brom or any other team excepting say, Arsenal, Manchester United or Liverpool. Most managers would give their right arm to manage Spurs, even with the Boardroom wranglings!)..

Further with Sugar's affidavit..

"It is the opinion of the majority of the Board with whom I have consulted, that Tottenham will not suffer the massive damage to which Mr Crystal alludes, should Mr Venables' removal be confirmed. Once his removal has been confirmed we would then move to ensure that a proper management structure be put in place for the football team, which would be able to deal with any concerns the team may have and reassure them as to the Club's future. while the injunction remains in place, then I believe that the Club will suffer damage if the Board is unable to appoint a new team Manager from within the Club or recruit a new man from elsewhere.. FOR EXAMPLE, GLENN HODDLE, A FORMER TOTTENHAM PLAYER, WAS MANAGER OF SWINDON TOWN AND WOULD HAVE BEEN UNDER CONSIDERATION AS A POSSIBLY NEW MANAGER OF TOTTENHAM, BUT BECAUSE OF THE INJUNCTION THE BOARD HAS BEEN UNABLE TO APPROACH MR HODDLE AND HE HAS NOW SIGNED FOR CHELSEA.!.. The injunction needs to be lifted as a matter of urgency so this situation can be dealt with Tottenham is also being prevented from playing a proper part in the close-season transfer market. If a new manager is to be appointed, then he will, no doubt, have his own ideas as to which players Tottenham may wish to purchase. Until this matter is cleared up it is very difficult for any decision to be made."....

(So, Tottenham wanted Hoddle in the first instance)..

Mr Mann: "That begs the same question. Whether if the injunction is discharged, any new Manager capable of performing the role, which Mr Sugar envisages, would be prepared to accept an offer of a contract. We would submit that the likelihood of that is very little. All this results from the breach of an agreement."

The Vice-Chancellor: "That is the issue. You are now addressing what sensibly can be done. Saying that it all flows from the breach of an agreement is begging the question, and that is the issue."

Mr Mann: "There is an inconsistency of approach. Mr Sugar has not appreciated, it seems that there would be any difficulty in the Club carrying on without a replacement for Mr Venables at all. the two submanagers, Mr Clemence and Mr Livermore, are regarded as sufficient to to satisfy that role. I mention an interview of Mr Sugar by Mr Andrew Neil on London Broadcasting Company News Talk Programme on 16th May."

(The reader has already seen the full interview in the 'Media' chapter.)

Mann then refers to two items in affidavits presented by both Venables and Sugar, which comment on how the interim regime is working...

Venables: "Since the hearing of the 25th May, I have been continuing to carry out my duties under a regime that has been agreed between solicitors. I have encountered no insuperable problems in following the regime and all staff have been very helpful to me..... But then I have always enjoyed a good relationship with staff."

Mr Sugar: "In relation to the need for the injunction granted by Mrs Justice Arden to be lifted, I repeat what I said on the 25th May. An emergency interim regime was agreed following the Court hearing, and a true copy of that regime"....

Sugar's affidavit continues... "It is the opinion of myself and the other members of the Board, with whom I discussed this matter, that it would be impractical to continue this regime until judgement on the petition or any appeal therefrom."..

(Until a full trial in October/November 1993, which is expected to last for a month. That would mean Terry being at the Club until well into the new football season.

Sugar's affidavit referred inter alia to an alleged refusal by Venables to carry out what he called 'a reasonable request' from him, conveyed on his behalf in a letter dated 2nd June from John Ireland, Company Secretary of the PLC.)

"I submit that it is inappropriate for Tottenham to be forced to remain any longer in a situation where a reasonable request by the Chairman and subsequently confirmed by the Board, is met with such a response." Sugar stated.

Sugar contins.. "In connection with Mr Venables' adherence to the terms of the regime, I refer to Mr Barnes' affidavit which to my mind amounts to a breach of the agreement."

Mr Mann: "We will have look at that in due course. In addition Mr Sugar exhibits copies of a memorandum from Mr Ireland", and a letter from Mr Gray" (former Managing Financial Director).. "and an exchange of correspondence. I will take you to those.."

Sugar refers to some of the invoices paid by the Club with presumably Terry's permission and upon his instigation: "I have no knowledge of the services which have been provided and to which invoices relate, nor have Mr Berry, Mr Alexiou and Mr Sandy.."..

THE EXHIBIT DATED THE 2nd JUNE.

IRELAND TO VENABLES:

"Alan Sugar has asked me to request from you a written explanation as to the reasons for t he foliowing payments:

1) A payment of £20,000 to Eric Hall, which you have asked to be paid to him only in the last couple of days, without further delay.

(Eric Hall, is a players' agent whose reputation has been questioned and discussed frequently by the media.)

2) The sum of £10,000 plus VAT to Eric Hall in August/September 1991.

3) The sum of £50,000 plus VAT to Frank McLintock in August/September 1991.

(We know the answer to that one.... Don't we?)

'Alan has spoken to Mr Bobroff and Mr Scholar, Ian Gray, Tony Berry and Douglas Alexiou, and none of them know the reasons for payments numbered two and three. accordingly, please ensure that your written explanations are placed before the Board meeting on Thursday.''

Mr Mann: "This note was given on the Thursday while Mr Venables was in the course of preparing the final details of his evidence. His response, through his solicitors, follows.''....

Letter in response from Kanter Jules and Grangewood...

'Mr Ireland has forwarded to our Client a list of details for tomorrow's Board meeting. We attach a copy of it for your assistance in case you do not have it. As you know our Client has to serve his evidence today, you will understand therefore that his priorities will be dealing with this evidence and other pressing Club matters. We understand that Messr. Sugar and Sandy are privy already to the reasons for the itemised payments, presumably therefore, the Board does not need any further information, urgently.

'You may think that it is naive but why does Mr Sugar want written reasons now? Presumably he has a reason? Is it for litigation?

'Of course, it it is for the purpose of the litigation concerning our respective Clients, you ought to first make an allegation. Does Mr Sugar wish to make an allegation with regard to these payments?

'The content is a number of allegations which were made in Mr Sugar's affidavits. We think that in order to try and justify ex post facto, (after the event)... the termination, and we believe this is simply part of the same process of trying to dredge-up criticisms which could be laid at Mr Venables' door, for a reason which is not associated with these proceedings at all. As a Director and Chief Executive of the Company Mr Venables is entitled to be privy to discussion affecting every aspect of the Company's business.

'Mr Sugar, still less Mr Sandy, who is supposed to report to Mr

Venables, is not entitled to arrogate to himself functions which are properly those of Mr Venables.

Please take instructions and revert, making full disclosure for the basis of the enquiry, so that Mr Venables may give the matter his attention on the basis that will enable him sufficiently to deal with reasons for Mr Sugar's questions.

It occurs to us that our respective Clients should sensibly agree to the appointment of a forensic accountant (auditor) to investigate the financial affairs of the Company and that Mr sandy should step aside so that any investigation that needs to be undertaken will not cause him embarrassment, as Mr Sugar's close confidant. If the proposal is agreeable, we propose that Mr Lemar of Cooper and Lybrand be appointed to undertake the investigation.

We also propose that the terms of reference be to investigate player transactions and financial arrangements between the Company and other members of the Board, and connected persons.''

(What a way to run a football club! Heaven help us if this had taken place during the Season!)

Mr Mann: ''Mr Venables is quite happy to answer any questions, but he was not happy to be put under pressure of that kind at the very time when he had this litigation. If necessary, he will undertake that information after these proceedings.

''So far as the other two matters are concerned they are the subject of audit and the information must be information to which Mr sandy as Financial Director is already privy. It is simply indicative of the way that Mr Venables has been harassed in one way or another ever since the reported termination the service agreement, and the order that was made. We hope that the campaign in the press was not by way of Mr Sugar's direction.

''The leaking of material in Mr Sugar's affidavit to the press which Mr Venables has not been in a position to answer.

(Sub judice?)...

''Coming back to the order of the 14th May, it is relevant to whether the interregnum is working, or not. Or if not, who is the cause of it not working!

''On the 17th May there was a meeting of the Board, the purpose of which was to have been the termination of the consultancy service contract with Mr Ashby, Mr Venables' personal assistant. Secondly, the meeting was to consider the position of Mr Crystal. That meeting was called very late: On Friday the 14th immediately after the order was made.

"Mr Isaacs (partner at Mr Venables' Solicitors) has sworn evidence in these proceedings putting that matter before the Court on the basis that it was an example of conduct getting pretty close to contempt, intending to make Mr Venables' position untenable, immediately after that order was made."

We quote from Mr Isaacs' affidavit:

"Events which I shall describe, put in hand by Mr Sugar, immediately after the order was made, were calculated both to create uncertainty and, whether intentionally or not, to undermine the efficiency of the order.

"The Judge's order was designed to place Mr Venables in a position that he had been, so that the business of the Company could be carried on exactly as before. I shall explain, Mr Venables has informed me, and I believe that on or about 11 pm on the 14th May 1993 he received notice of a Board meeting to take place on Monday 17th May 1993 at 2pm for the purpose of ratifying a decision to terminate the service of Mr Ashby, by way of his Company, Gearbury Ltd."...

(Here we have an assistant to Terry, acting as General Manager, confirmed by the way he signed some letters, performing a service contract which was given to one of his companies. In normal circumstances, the advantages of this procedure means that the man's 'wages' are invoiced with appropriate VAT added and paid in full by way of invoice, without PAYE or NHI deduction. these deductions are then determined by what he draws out of Gearbury as salary.... Consequently, he becomes a contractor to, and not an employee of, Tottenham Hotspur Plc. That is why he is described as a 'consultant')....

"It is also the purpose of this meeting to convene a Extraordinary General Meeting to remove Mr Jonathan Crystal from the Board."

"This was done because Mr Sugar was not pleased with Mr Crystal's line in supporting Mr Venables.

"There is a memorandum from Mr Sugar to Mr Crystal. I quote:"

'In due course you will receive the minutes of the above mentioned Board meeting of the 17th May..... In broad terms the Board ratified my decision to terminate the use of Mr Eddie Ashby's consultancy firm. As there is a shareholder holding more than 10% of the Company shares, and therefor am able to ask the Board to call an EGM for the purposes of removing you from the Board. Before I make that decision, I thought it would be right to consult with the Board. I accordingly asked their views on the suitability of you being a Board member of this Company.

'Mr Berry and Mr Sandy gave their views on your performance in the past, and Mr Alexiou gave his view based only on your behaviour at the Board meeting of the 14th May.'

(The Board meeting at which they sacked Terry!)

'Unanimously, those Board members felt that you certainly do not act in an independent manner and that your decisions seem to be blinded by your loyalty to Mr Venables. Four Directors felt that your removal would be most appropriate. I believe that Mr Venables refrained from commenting. It would be appropriate for there to be an EGM for the purposes of removing you, but this would incur a lot of costs by way of printing and postage, if you do not agree to resign.'

Mr Isaacs' affidavit:

"While therefore Mr Venables accepts the direction of the Board, the fact remains that the termination Mr Ashby's contract has, and I believe must have, been calculated to cause Mr Venables and staff at Tottenham maximum inconvenience and corresponding confusion.

"Mr Venables would, of course, has he been consulted, rather than have the termination of Mr Ashby's services presented to him as a fait accompli, have been prepared, as he informed him, I believe, to consider the appointment of a replacement for Mr Ashby until his own position had been resolved.

"However, no proposal was put to Mr Venables.... Mr Venables has now such a proposal."

Mr Mann then pointed out in clarification that Terry had agreed to Mr Ireland standing in that position temporarily.

Mr Isaac continued:

"The position of Mr Crystal is just a pertinent. As again seems to be acknowledged, Mr Venables has come to rely very heavily on Mr Crystal for advice as to the propriety of certain decisions affecting Tottenham, but now Mr Sugar is proposing Mr Crystal is to cease to be a Director. I infer that this, too, was calculated to cause Mr Venables inconvenience, as well as to isolate him in the deliberations at Tottenham both at staff level and in the Boardroom.

"We understand, although we also stand to be corrected, that the proposal to remove Mr Crystal at an EGM has 'now been suspended....' "

(I suspect that Mr Crystal offered his resignation, since we know that did actually resign on the 4th November 1993.)

"The position is that Mr Sugar does not regard Mr Crystal as an independent Non-executive Director and pays little, if any, regard to him. Indeed as you know already, he has even threatened him in the manner of giving evidence."

(Details of this matter are given in the following chapter, the hearing of the 15th June.)

"We submit strongly that the evidence shows, both by t he events of the 17th May and the calling of a Board meeting at a very inconvenient time, and the request for information, that a systematic attempt to make the interregnum unworkable has been made.

"Mr Venables, on the other hand, does everything that he can to make it work, and provided parties deal sensibly with each other, then there is absolutely no reason why he should not do so.

"Of course, the longer the interregnum, the more difficult the position may become, but that is an inconvenience for all parties, because as I have already submitted, the possibility of a replacement for Mr Venables being appointed would seem to be a remote hope, rather than an actual possibility."

Mr Isaacs then dealt with two footballing matters concerning the Gary Lineker and Teddy Sheringham transfers.

"I will deal with them very quickly, but it is Mr Sugar's integrity with which I deal.

"If you would look in the affidavit headed, 'The sale of Mr

Lineker'. This is an affidavit sworn by Mr Sugar that found its way to the press before we received it.''

Quoting from Sugar's affidavit:

'Another example of Mr Venables' so-called misunderstanding was when I realised that Tottenham was only receiving £850,000 for Mr Lineker as opposed to the £4 million that Mr Venables had spoken of in our second meeting.

'I questioned Mr Venables about this and reminded him he told me that Tottenham would receive £4 million for Mr Lineker. Mr Venables laughed and told me that the deal was worth £4 million to Mr Lineker but that nobody could possibly have believed that Tottenham could have received over one million pounds for Mr Lineker. I, myself, as I have explained above, had not previously been involved in the football business and, therefore, had no experience as to what individual players might or might not be worth, and relied entirely on Mr Venables.

'Now having been involved with football for two years, I know that such an old player would be worth only approximately one million pounds, but it must be remembered that I was taking Mr Venables totally on trust as the expert in football in what was only the second meeting I had with him to discuss this matter.

'Indeed, Mr Venables said that we were receiving over £1 million for Mr Lineker, but this was not strictly a accurate. In fact, we were receiving £850,000 from Grampus 8 which was the Japanese company to whom Mr Lineker was being transferred and the balance was being made up by Mr Lineker waiving a cash payment that Tottenham would have to pay him in the future. As a result of this, my faith in Mr Venables' business acumen was declining further, as another result of this I insisted that Mr Venables keep me informed in the future in relation to all major transactions.

'Mr Venables agreed to do so. At a meeting with Grampus 8's agent, Mr Venables and Mr Lineker's agent, I asked If I could have directed access to the people in Japan, because I had a great deal of experience negotiating with the Japanese from my position of Chairman and Managing Director of Amstrad Plc.

'The Grampus 8 agent told me that he would deal with the matter. I believed the reluctance of the Grampus 8 agent to allow me to negotiate directly with Japan was at the full value of what

Grampus 8 was actually paying for Mr Lineker, but not being disclosed. Reluctantly I agreed.'

"For the record we look at Terry's version of this:

"The allegations which Mr Sugar makes in connection with the sale of Gary Lineker are ludicrous to anyone who knows anything about football. the circumstances of the sale of Gary Lineker were these. John Homes, Mr Lineker's agent,came to me with information that Mr Lineker wanted to go and play for a club in Japan, that under the terms of the deal negotiated with the Japanese club, the club would get £850,000 immediately, and on top of that, Mr Lineker would waive the £150,000 still due to him as part of his signing fee on August 1991.

"The deal was very attractive because it had been struck in August 1991 and Tottenham would be able to retain services of Gary Lineker for another year and still receive £850,000 at a time when we very much needed it. As at August 1991, in any event, Gary Lineker only had two years of his contract to run, and I had already been concerned about whether he would have sufficient motivation to finish it. There was no question of Gary Lineker being worth £4 million at that time. He was originally purchased for £1.2 million from Barcelona aged 28 and he was obviously worth considerably less aged 31. the effect of that transaction was that Tottenham were getting their money back for him. The alternative would have been to let him serve out his contract and get nothing at the end. it is absolutely incredible that Mr Sugar should state that his faith in my business acumen has declined as a result of this purchase."

An affidavit from Mr Homes' independent company adviser and Director of Park Associates:

'I am employed as personal adviser to Gary Lineker and have been so for more than ten years. I was party to all the negotiations regarding the transfer to Grampus 8 from Tottenham. In and during the early part of 1991 I was approached by two organisations who informed me that they represented a Japanese football corporation which was interested in Gary Lineker.

'I receive many similar approaches and my policy is always to listen to any propositions put forward. I did my normal investigations and ascertained that the organisations who had approached me were representing Toyota and in fact were backing a Japanese football club, Grampus 8.

'Mr Lineker and I then met with the representative of Grampus 8 in order to progress matters further. After the meeting we were satisfied. Thereafter, I informed Mr Venables, who was then the Manager of the club, of the approaches which had been made to me. I informed Mr Venables these were still in the preliminary stages and would get back to him. Unbeknownst to Mr Venables, Mr Lineker or myself it was ascertained that Tottenham Hotspur had, through Mr Dennis Roach (another agent) put in action negotiations concerning Mr Lineker's transfer to an Italian club.

'I never mentioned the figure relating to the transfer of Mr Lineker to Grampus 8. I have read Mr Sugar's affidavit. I just cannot understand how Mr Sugar can mention a figure of £4 million. All I can say is that it must have been Mr Sugar's personal feeling as to the worth of Mr Lineker, but certainly this figure was never mentioned.

'I refer to the last part of Mr Sugar's affidavit when he talks about the meeting that took place between Mr Flood, Grampus 8's agent, myself, Mr Lineker and Mr Venables. Mr Sugar does not mention that Mr Lineker was also present at this meeting. I recall that Mr Sugar wished to deal direct with the Japanese and it was his view and not that of Mr Venables that Grampus 8 would pay a considerable amount more that on the table. I would further point out that Mr Flood was extremely experienced in negotiating with the Japanese, HAVING NEGOTIATED MRS THATCHER'S TOURS OF JAPAN PREVIOUSLY.

'I can confirm that there was no other reason for Mr Flood dealing direct with the Japanese, despite what Mr Sugar seemed to indicate. Mr Sugar does not seem to appreciate that Mr Lineker's acceptance of the deal is critical. Furthermore Mr Lineker wished to continue his playing with Tottenham only to the end of his contract which was at that point two years hence. Had he done so tottenham would not have received any transfer fee whatsoever.

'The suggestion by Mr Sugar that the full amount Grampus 8 is actually paying for Mr Lineker is not being disclosed, is ludicrous both to me and my client.'

''Now we look at the Sheringham transfer according to Sugar's affidavit:

'Following this, Mr Venables was made aware that a striker at Nottingham Forest, Mr Sheringham, was unhappy living in the Midlands and wished to return to the South of england and bought a flat in Woodford, London. As a consequence of this Mr Venables embarked on negotiations with Mr Brian Clough, then the Manager of Nottingham Forest.'

(In the interview with Graham Smith, he stated that his services and those of Frank McLintock were required because of the difficulty of the two Managers negotiating directly.)

'Shortly after this spoke to Mr Venables on the subject and he told me THAT MR CLOUGH LIKES A "BUNG". He explained that Mr Clough wished to receive a payment personally for selling Mr Sheringham. I told Mr Venables that it was absolutely out of the question. I HAD NEVER HEARD ANYTHING LIKE THIS BEFORE AND IT WAS CERTAINLY NOT THE WAY THAT TOTTENHAM OR I WOULD CONDUCT BUSINESS. I believed Mr Venables mentioned this to me one and told me what usually happened in these cases was PEOPLE WOULD MEET MR CLOUGH IN A MOTORWAY CAFE AND MR CLOUGH WOULD BE HANDED A BAGFUL OF MONEY. At this I told Mr Venables I did not wish to discuss the matter again and that he should not even mention it to me again.'

Terry Venables' response to this very serious allegation was as follows:

'Mr Sugar's allegations concerning the purchase of Mr Sheringham are unfounded. I find much of what I said inaccurate to the point of being bizarre. The purchase of Mr Sheringham had nothing to do with wanting to live in London. I approached Nottingham Forest solely because he is such a good player, I wanted him for the Club. I worked very hard to try to get him before the start of the Season, August 1992.

'I put out feelers through our Club's scanner, Ted Buxton, to Ron Fenton, Brian Clough' Assistant. He suggested a minimum of £2 million. About halfway through pre-season training Mr Sheringham came to London and made contact with me through

Graham Smith. I met Mr Sheringham at the Royal Garden Hotel. Mr Sheringham said Nottingham Forest was willing to let him go and he would be interested in joining the club.'

(Graham Smith told us Sheringham would have walked on water to play for Tottenham.)

'He then returned to Nottingham. There followed periods of uncertainty during which Nottingham Forest appeared to have changed their minds. We were unable to conduct further negotiations. I tried to speak to Brian Clough but he would never take my calls.

(It is extraordinary that a football manager of such fame and high profile should refuse to talk to another!)

'I knew that during this period Graham Smith and Frank McLintock were trying to push the deal, because Mr Sheringham had decided he definitely wanted to move. It was not until quite into the Season that the club went ahead with the purchase of Mr Sheringham. By then Graham Smith had reverted to me to say that Brian Clough was not going to sell for less that £2.1 million.

'The reason why the price was pushed up by £100,000 was that Nottingham Forest wanted to get their money back on Mr sheringham and had overlooked in initial negotiations an engagement fee of £100,000 which had been paid for him.'

(Terry does not say, nor has Frank McLintock indicated to whom this engagement fee was paid. Does he mean that Sheringham received £100,000 when he signed from Millwall, or was that a fee paid to McLintock or First Wave Sport Management?)

Terry continues:

'I had no direct contact with Brian Clough, since all my negotiations at that time were conducted with Mr Fred Reacher, the Chairman of Nottingham Forest Football Club.'

'Neither Mr Smith, nor Mr McLintock were involved in the negotiation of the transfer fee. Eventually the fee was finalised between myself and Mr Reacher of £2.1 million, I kept the Board informed of what was happening throughout, mainly through Mr Sugar. The allegation that I told Mr Sugar that Brian Clough "liked a bung" is untrue. I never used that expression, I have never used those words or words to that effect to Mr Sugar. As to what I am alleged to have said to Mr Sugar about Mr Clough meeting people in motorway cafes to collect his bags of money, that really is a lot of nonsense. I certainly never said any of that to Mr Sugar, and he is either making it up or he is repeating something he heard from some other source; That is all I have to say about that.'

(At this point in the proceedings, when this affidavit was being read, the Vice-Chancellor intervened to ask about the £50,000 that was paid over in banknotes.)

Mr Mann: "That is the reference to that, I will deal with that later. Those are the matters concerning Mr Lineker and Mr Sheringham, which those individuals are concerned about and for which reason I have mentioned them.

"Our primary point on the interregnum is that it works. The only reason it may not work is if unnecessary obstacles are put in the way in bad faith. So, as to balance of convenience, we would say, it being accepted that somebody of Mr Venables' calibre has to be in employment in the interim until the petition is hear, Mr Venables is the very man who ought to be there doing it, doing the job."

There followed legal arguments and submissions by Mr Mann which were similar to those advanced at the first hearing on the 14th May. He told how one share in Tottenham Football Club, held by Mr Gray was transferred to Mr Sandy on the 14th May giving the PLC total control of the Football Club. He further stated how Eddie Ashby had done an excellent job, and that there were no criticisms of his work. He also alleged that Colin Sandy did not have 'significant qualifications'.. although he is however, qualified as a taxation accountant, ATII, a qualification of great value in all the various dealings of the modern day football club.. He told of the attempts by Terry's solicitors in April 1991 to buy out Scholar and Bobroff and how they all came to nothing until Sugar arrived. He reminded the Court of Sugar's statement on the day of agreement, June 21st 1991... 'At last Spurs have a more secure future. Terry Venables has a remarkable reputation and commands the affection and respect of the Team, the Club's supporters and its employees.'

How Terry said on the same day..

'It has been a long road but in the end I believe that we have come up with the right combination. The chance to stay with

Spurs and play a real role in its future is all I could ever have wanted. Let me say the support of the fans and the loyalty of players have kept me going through these difficult months.'

At that point the Judge adjourned.

Later in the day Mr Mann sought to introduce an affidavit from a Mr Staunton, a Spurs supporter since 1966, shareholder and Club member. Mr Heslop suggested that there was no time for this piece of evidence to be introduced, but Terry's counsel insisted and in the end was allowed to introduce the affidavit, which read:

'On the 25th June 1991 Mr Sugar and Mr Venables put forward a mandatory cash offer for which they offered to pay 75p per share. Through the media and in the offer document they presented their ownership of Tottenham Plc as a partnership, and at that time I noted they would each hold an equal part of the share capital.

'At the start of the offer document, there is a page entitled 'A letter from Mr Sugar and Mr Venables'.. From that letter it was clear to me that they were effectively in partnership, and they did not want shareholders to accept the offer which they were forced to make under the City code'. I doubt if I would have sold, but the partnership between them dispelled any thoughts that I might have to do so. The shares were attractively priced, given that they were at that time suspended.'....

There was also an affidavit from Bernie Kingsley, Coordinator TISA:

'I started supporting in the mid-1960's and regularly attended matches. Since the 70's I have attended both home and away matches. Like many supporters I bought shares in the original flotation (1983). I subscribed for 200, but only received only 100 in the "scale down".

'In 1990 when news of the Company's financial difficulties and the possible involvement of Robert Maxwell became public, I attended a public meeting and as a result became a founder member and a coordinator of TISA.

'Having supported Terry Venables in his attempts to purchase a major share in TH Plc., during the first half of 1991, I did not sell my shares as specifically requested by Mr Sugar and Mr

Venables, because I had confidence in the new management, particulary in their stated aim to combine their expertise. There were numerous references to their working together and I noted that Mr Sugar and Edennote intended in due course to enter into an agreement, regulating disposal of shares, which SEEMED TO ENSURE THE LONG-TERM STABILITY THE COMPANY HAD PREVIOUSLY BEEN LACKING.

'When the Company sought an injection of capital through its 4-for-7 rights issue at £1.25 per share, I took up my full entitlement. The terms of this offer document again reiterated the progress was making under its new management; Mr Sugar stating that "We now have in place the necessary financial, commercial and football expertise to operate the group effectively.'....

(Note the intention of Mr Sugar and Edennote to reach agreement regulating acquisition and disposal of their shares as above, was again re-stated.)

'With the lifting of the suspension of the PLC shares, TISA received a number of requests regarding how our members could buy shares and we sought to find a method that would minimise the transaction costs. I intended to participate in this myself. Shortly afterwards, in February 1992, the Company enquired more generally in the match programme as to whether other supporters wished to become shareholders. It received around 500 replies. TISA was then approached by Colin Sandy with a view to help the Company's scheme as well as our own. At one stage we proposed that instead of buying shares on the open market, the Company should sell some of the ISSUED SHARE CAPITAL thereby allowing supporters to put additional funds directly into the Board. (Meaning shares that were issued by Tottenham for sale but which hadn't yet been taken up).'

Mr Mann: ''The problem was that Mr Venables preferred a different route from that of having a Rights Issue.''

(Presumably because he could not envisage taking up all that was being offered to him, without having to borrow more, whereas he knew that Sugar could readily afford to take up his shares which would give him an advantage.

Conversely, Terry preferred to mortgage the ground to raise funds, but as Roger so clearly stated to me, that was not possible because of the state of the ground and the enormous amount of money that would be needed to bring it up to scratch, and of course, the resultant astronomical interest and capital payments.

Although that can be seen by all to be Terry's concern, in fact Sugar's route has been successful in as much as the ground has improved consistently since 1992 and will shortly be all-seater with good overhead covering all around, and catering and toilet facilities showing a massive improvement.)

Mr Mann then referred to the 'agreement' that was allegedly confirmed at a meeting at the Grosvenor House Hotel. He admitted that there was some conjecture as to all of that, stating however, at the same time, that there definitely <u>was</u> an agreement.

Then he tells of a particular meeting at Scribes, where many take place, between Venables, Sugar and Crystal. Venables fully discussed the inequality that would result if the Rights Issue went ahead. He states again that Mr Sugar assured Mr Crystal and Mr Venables that "Even if he (Sugar) picks up all the shares they have a shareholders' agreement, and it would not affect the status-quo so far as the original agreement was concerned."

The Rights Issue was agreed on the 28th November 1991 at a Board meeting, but it was agreed to postpone the issue until July 1992, allowing Ashby time to seek the other route to raise the finance. At a meeting at Brentwood between Ashby and Sugar, Ashby alleges that Sugar stated: "I will agree to place all the excess shares on the market, but I do not think that it would be very successful because of the price at which they would have to be offered (£1.25).. but I will agree to a standstill agreement which will prevent me out-voting Mr Venables."

(All this, of course, may have been agreed by Alan Sugar before Sandy carried out an investigation into Ashby's background and then began examining certain invoices and transactions. It seems to me that Sugar was willing and open about retaining the status- quo, until the doubts, and according to him, the evidence of 'questionable dealings' began to raise its nasty head. Even the supporters were almost totally behind Terry until certain news became public. It would be fair to say that during my many interviews with supporters, concern about Terry's dealings have divided their loyalty.)

Mr Mann nevertheless tried to persuade the Judge that the only reason Terry had agreed to the Rights Issue was because of the undertakings Sugar had given Ashby and Crystal at the two meetings. He introduced a letter that Venables wrote to Sugar, after the meeting at the Grosvenor House Hotel on the Thursday 21st November 1991:

'Dear Alan,

I confirm the context of our agreement this morning concerning the refinancing of Tottenham. We adopt a strategy as follows:

A) Gascoigne monies received from Lazio.

B) You provide a commercial mortgage/loan of £4 million against the Stadium.

C) We secure bank overdraft facilities of £2 million.

D) If by 31st July 1992 you are unable to realise your mortgage/loan plus the 'Scholar' loan I will fully support the 'Rights Issue' by Tottenham at your discretion.'

(You will note that there is no mention of an agreement to secure Terry's base of equality!)

Mr Mann suggested that this agreement was drawn up to give Venables time to raise the finance. He said that the agreement between Ashby and Sugar was recorded by a solicitor, a Mr Salber, acting for Venables, as a result of a 'phone call from Ashby to him...

"At 9-40 am, on the 22nd November 1991, I made a manuscript i.e. telephone attendance note of the said conversation, summarising Ashby's instructions. I sent a copy to Martin Isaacs, marked urgent:

'Eddie Ashby called 9.40 am this morning who said he would be at the 'Grand Hotel' at midday. The following was raised.

1) It is most likely that the Gascoigne money will be available.

2) Alan Sugar has agreed to underwrite a rights issue at £1.25p per share which will have the effect of raising his shareholding to 47% and dilute Terry's to 23%.

However Alan Sugar has agreed to do the following:

Either a) place his additional 24% in the market at £1.25, (difficult to place), or b) enter into a standstill shareholder agreement so that he is restricted from voting his additional 24%, so as to oust Terry. Please could we urgently look into this and telephone the YAOKE KUMI BANKERS to discuss how this can be done.'

Mr Mann: "A draft agreement was produced to Mr Sugar by Kanter Jules and Grangewood (Terry's solicitors) dated 26th November 1991. It was not signed by Mr Sugar because he gave Mr Crystal his personal assurance."..

(You will remember that Alan said that he could not sign any agreement until the issue had taken place!)

The agreement stated:

'1) 'Following the Rights Issue... (Note <u>FOLLOWING!</u>)... Alan Sugar will hold more shares in Tottenham than Edennote. Such difference being referred to as 'The surplus shares', Sugar's surplus. None of the parties will buy or sell without the written agreement of the other.

2) Alan Sugar will use his best endeavours to procure that the 'Sugar surplus' will be disposed of by placing, (on the Stock Market), or by some other method to be agreed by Sugar and Venables within five years. Such disposal will not be to an associate.

3) For so long as the "Sugar surplus", but in any event not exceeding five years, from the date hereof, Alan Sugar will irrevocably and unconditionally agree with Terry Venables that he will exercise all voting rights and powers attached to half the Sugar shares and derivative shareholding as Terry Venables may from time to time direct.'

"That is to give support to the telephone attendance note sent by Mr Salber to Mr Isaacs, the agreement prepared by Kanter Jules and Grangewood."

The Judge then enquired as to whether Terry was in the same position at the time of that agreement as he was now. Mr Mann immediately picked up the implication that Mr Sugar could have used, anyway, a casting vote as Chairman for overruling Terry on the Board, effectively saying that the inequality in shareholding made no difference.

The Vice-Chancellor: "What you have told me so far is that what was agreed originally was that Mr Sugar was to be Chairman, and understandably was going to have control of finances and Mr Venables was to be a Director, and understandably to have control of the football side. The agreement that you refer to has no bearing on that matter, and the original agreement is not broken by an issue of new shares."

Mr Mann: "What I have said is that they would maintain a balanced Board."

The Vice-Chancellor: "Is that a term of the original agreement:"

Mr Mann: "Yes, I am at fault for having stated that."

The Vice-Chancellor: "what do you say, even as by implication, was agreed?"

Mr Mann: "What we say is they would simply not be in a position either of them, because of there being a balanced Board."

The Vice-Chancellor: "What do you mean by a 'balanced Board'?"

Mr Mann: "their votes would control the composition, 50/50 of the Board of the Company."

The Vice-Chancellor: "But they did NOT!.. They did NOT! There is Mr Sandy, Mr Crystal and Mr Berry!"

Mr Mann: "I accept that buy so far as they were concerned, there would be a balanced Board and they would not be able to out-vote the other. That is the implication!"

The Vice-Chancellor: "I do not follow. they would not be in position to out-vote the other?.... they were two of five Directors, so at Board meetings I do not see what that means."

(Mr Mann then tried to impress the Judge that the arrangement meant that they were not able to out-vote each other. That was what he meant by a 'balanced Board', each having 50/50 say. But of course the salient point is that on a shareholders' vote, it was Berry that had the power. For he controlled 8% and added to Sugar's now 46% that would give them jointly absolute control. The point now is whether Alan had the right to add his 46% to that of Berry's or to any of the small shareholders. On reading the purported agreement drawn up after the Grosvenor House and Brentwood meetings prepared by Terry's own solicitors, there seems to be nothing to prevent that, unless of course had signed that agreement. With this becoming the real issue the way for Mr Heslop became clear.

It was perhaps at this point in the proceedings that Mr Mann might have felt that matters were not going entirely his way. He sought to argue that neither Sugar nor Venables could out-vote each other. Should Terry have sought an adjournment at that time to discuss this issue, because it seems to me that the road the Judge was going down was fraught with danger?)

Mr Mann: "You have seen a proposed agreement regulating those additional shares. It may be that the constitution of the Board would seem to be inconsistent with the plain expression 'balanced Board'. That is a Board which must answer to 50%. So far as they were concerned a balanced Board, and we say that it is implicit, that they would not out-vote each other so at least to be at odds with their arrangement. That they would not be altered.. OF COURSE IF THERE WERE OTHER DIRECTORS AND THOSE DIRECTORS WERE FULLY INDEPENDENT THEY WOULD BE EXERCISING THEIR VOTES IN ACCORDANCE WITH THEIR DUTIES AS DIRECTORS. It is as the result of the agreement of the 26th November that Mr Venables was happy about the Rights Issue."

The Rights Issue letter states that Alan Sugar will take up his entire share issue at 1.658821 million at a cost of £2,073,526, while Edennote will take only 640,000 of its entitlement, at a cost of £800,000. There is also mention of the fact that revenue can re re-lied upon from the sale of Gascoigne, Lineker and surprisingly at that time, Gordon Durie; (who in fact was sold in November 1993. (£1.2 million to Rangers F. C., Scotland).

Mr Mann, after summarising much of what we have already included, later blamed Sandy for a lot of the troubles at the Club. He admitted that Ashby had been found to be an undischarged bankrupt but pointed out that berry had been criticised by the DTI report for his part in 'Blue Arrow'.

According to Venables... "Mr Sandy was always questioning and interfering with heads of departments under my control... It had been apparent that Mr Sandy resented Mr Ashby and was keen to secure his departure. Mr Ashby has not sought to inter-fere with Mr Sandy.... I am sure that the clash between Ashby and Sandy would not have arisen if Mr Sugar had acted to restrain his employee.'

Mann makes mention of how Sugar usurped power of the commercial enterprises from Ashby and how Sandy sacked two members of that department and appointed two of his own choice. Additionally, Alan wanted a corporate lawyer as Company Secretary instead of relying on the Non-Executive Director, Jonathan Crystal.

He mentioned Alan Sugar's dissatisfaction:

"It is accepted that the hype surrounding the new 'kit' produced good INITIAL returns, but there has been a dramatic down-turn. There is no stock control and there is no-one capable of dealing with the major issues confronting this department."..

Then he introduced an affidavit from a Mr Pay who was in charge of commercial activities at that time. 'The opening of a new shop in the East-End resulted in a lot of stock being taken. (Does he mean being taken over to the East-End, physically, as against being stolen?).' 'Mr Sugar expressed a great deal of disappointment that the data-base was not up and running at this point. He had hoped that a great deal of progress had been made in that area so that we could exploit non-football-related merchandising opportunities. Progress was now being made with Mr Sandy.

'Mr Rollo, the overall Commercial Manager, does have his uses but he does have to be driven.' (Rollo is still there at December 1993, seen most recently at the Spurs-Liverpool game 18th December, presenting a gift to Holsten Pils., who have sponsored Spurs for the last ten years)

'Amstrad people have on various occasions done good deals for Tottenham. Mr Sugar also stated that he was unhappy with the unfair criticism that surrounded the King-For-The-Day and other match-day promotions. It was agreed that the football industry would become larger and more complicated in the future and with that in mind it was suggested that Mr Venables should concentrate in that area.'

Mr Mann: "Mr Sugar wanted to take more control of what is happening in the Club."

"Mr Venables was critical of the recent action taken by Mr Sandy to dispense with the accountant in the merchandising division and to immediately replace him with another body, without any reference whatsoever to Mr Ashby or Mr Venables. Mr Sandy explained removal was merely a temporary replacement.

"Mr Berry expressed concern at the tone of the meeting. In his view football is the most important item and rest is just peripheral. Mr Venables has too much to do as Chief Executive and team coach, but as probably the best coach in the world, he must control the football team.

"Mr Sugar agreed this should be the one job that Venables should be responsible for, but that he should be responsible for the financial issues that support the football operation.

"There followed a discussion on those specific areas and it can be seen that Mr Sugar wants to take over more areas of the overall operation."

(No-one in their affidavits suggests that Alan Sugar wanted to interfere with the football side of things. Clearly he was aghast at the lack of control at Tottenham compared to the smoothly computerised operation at Amstrad and desired to bring Tottenham up to that standard. If it is alleged that Terry was submitting non-appropriate invoices and handling things on an ad hoc day-to-day personal basis, this clearly would not satisfy the efficient and provenly successful Chairman.)

Mr Mann then pointed out how Alan wanted to take control and that Mr Pay and a Mrs Calvino were sacked by Sandy on 22nd November. Although they would be dismissed for 'gross misconduct' they would receive 4 weeks pay. Later Sandy offered better terms and Mr Ashby was asked to approach them. Solicitors are now being instructed in that issue. (More litigation?)..

Mr Venables accepted the position of Mr Sugar taking over the commercial activities and hoped that that would end the difficulties arising in their relationship, but on the 21st January 1993, Mr Sugar wrote to Venables, that letter reproduced to open this chapter.

Mr Mann: "That lengthy correspondence represents the point it seems when the breakdown occurred. The trouble is that there was no attempt at resolution by actually sitting down. Mr Sugar and Mr Sandy together, we say, embarked on a course of conduct which was in itself wrongful, in bad faith and unfairly prejudicial to Mr Venables and all shareholders. Mr Sugar, in order to achieve his objective of arrogating control for himself, has acted in bad faith and in breach of his duties owed the Company as a

Director thereof and as being guilty of misconduct towards the Petitioner and has demonstrated his own unfitness to be Director of the Company.''

To conclude the days matters in summary, we reproduce some of the relevant statements made by some of the people involved.

Mr Venables: 'Mr Sandy was always questioning and interfering with heads of departments under my control. for example Mr Rollo and Mr Barnes. It has been apparent that Mr Sandy resented Mr Ashby and was keen to secure his departure. Mr Ashby resented Mr Sandy's attempt to interfere on his management field of activity. Mr Ashby has not sought to interfere with Mr Sandy. It is not true to say as Mr Sugar does that Mr Ashby insisted that the Club's accounts be my personal responsibility I am sure that the clash between Ashby and Sandy would not have arisen if Mr Sugar had acted to restrain his employee. I felt it untrue to treat Mr Ashby differently than Mr Berry, particularly as he was not a Director of the Company.'

(This refers to Crystal producing a DTI report on Berry which Terry suggests is equal to Ashby's own questionable background in business.)

Mr Pay: 'Mr Sandy mentions that I had not realised that I was expected to report to him on stock control matters relating to our merchandising. Certainly this did arise during discussion. It became clear to me that Mr Sandy regarded himself as my boss, whereas I had been taken on with a view to reporting to Mr Ashby.'

(Who took him on? Is he a partner with Ashby in some of his companies? If Sugar thought this, then he would certainly have Sandy taking a close view, especially with Ashby's reported dealings in up to 43 other companies, most of whom were bankrupt or nearly so!)

Pay continues: 'As far as I was concerned the person to whom I was supposed to report within the context of my duties was in a most fundamental position and of great importance and could not understand why he did not see this in the same light.''

Mr Crystal: 'At some time unknown and undisclosed to the Company's Board of Directors and prior to the 6th May 1993, Mr Sandy BEGAN AWARDING HIMSELF £1,000 PER MONTH

304

PERSONAL EXPENSES........ CHARGED TO THE COMPANY!

'The services of Mr Sandy were provided to the Company by Amsprop Ltd, another in the Amstrad Group. No formal agreement exists in relation to that. Mr Sandy has been renumerated £4000 per month and at the Board meeting on the 6th May he disclosed that he also considered himself entitled to claim £1,000 per month expenses. At no time prior to that Board meeting had Mr Sandy ever made such a suggestion!

'In the early part of 1992 a Mr Simmons was introduced by Mr Sugar and Mr Sandy to advise of the new installation of the new computer system. Mr Simmons was an employee of Amstrad Plc. He was permitted to charge his personal expenses to the Company without prior authorisation.

'Between October 1992 and February 1993 Mr Sugar and Mr Sandy proceeded on the basis that the entire computer system would be linked to the computer main-frame at the Brentwood premises, entirely without prior authorisation. Mr Venables was NOT MADE AWARE UNTIL THE NEAR-COMPLETION IN FEBRUARY 1993, by which time, given the equipment that had already been installed, there was no other practical alternative.

'The original plan was that the entire computer equipment and operational staff would be under the control of Mr Venables. It was now under the control of Mr Sandy. The information systems manager was now Richard Simmons, who worked at Brentwood and is employed by Amstrad. He reported directly to Mr Sandy.'

Venables states:

'Like many of my generation, I have never been trained to used and never envisaged that I should be writing information on a system. However, as Chief executive, with such wide responsibilities I clearly needed to have it under my control with access to the management system in my office. For that reason Mr Simmons did not come up with any idea of linking it to Amstrad at Brentwood.'

(The new system shows an integrated system and is not externally linked to departments at Tottenham.)

'Although Mr Ashby was very much involved in the early stages, my efforts to placate Mr Sugar led to me taking him off the project, which also led to my own total exclusion. I regret that decision because Mr Sandy did not produce information requested.'

Mr Pay: ''There was a new warehousing system which caused a lot of unrest. The way management accounts were prepared were to discount (reduce) profits by the value of unpaid cheques at the end of each account period (monthly) that had a direct effect on what Mr Sugar said at a Board meeting in October that the Merchandising department was not making money. I believe that the department was making money but the management accounts produced by Mr Sandy, for what ever reason, simply were not accurate. They were deliberately drawn up so as not to show the true situation.'

(In accounting, expenses which have been incurred during an accounting period are charged to that period's profits, regardless of whether they have actually been paid or not.)

Mr Heslop finally stood to mention that there were 32 alleged particulars of the Respondent's bad faith, and that his position was impossible, for although the Judge had suggested that these be handed to him at the close of the first day's proceedings, 4.15 pm, he had little time to examine them or check on their accuracy, and was against there submission. They formed part of the revised petition which was discussed at the beginning of the day's revealing events.

The Judge asked what his problem was. What he had heard was evidence in support of the petition. Heslop answered:

''I cannot stop my friend making whatever submissions he likes about the evidence, I accept that, but what I am anxious to do is to prevent amendments being allowed to the petition without the Respondents having a fair opportunity to consider whether the amendments are properly formulated and whether there is evidence to substantiate each and every one of them.''

The Vice-Chancellor: ''These are allegations. That is all. In the ordinary way you would not find that it is necessary for him to give evidence of the sort that you would accept.''

Mr Mann came back and referred to the agreement between Tottenham and Amshold that effectively awarded Mr Sugar a £50,000 per annum emolument. Then he refers to an agreement where Tottenham did not receive any money from a broadcast that he purports Alan Sugar agreed to..

"My Lord, we say the allegations are all supported by evidence."

The Vice-Chancellor: "Yes".

Mr Mann: "If Mr Heslop is satisfied."

The Vice-Chancellor: "I don't suppose he is for one minute!. What you have been doing is reading bits of evidence put in by your clients. You have slightly changed direction. The emphasis from the beginning was that this is in effect a partnership case, but as amended the petition becomes something rather different, and that is something rather different.

"I think that the best thing is for me to call a halt for today and perhaps overnight you and Mr Heslop can get together and see if you can agree as to what is going to be the method of proceeding which is likely to result in the least time being taken up in the Court."

DAY 1 ENDS.....

(Was the writing on the wall for Terry Venables?)....

THE HEARING OF FRIDAY 11th JUNE.

Mr Mann opened by informing Sir Donald that he had listed the additional evidence and that he had handed a file of those to Mr Heslop. The Judge replied that he was looking at saving time as 'someone has to pay the costs.'

Mr Heslop stood to advise the Court that he thought that Mr Mann should take his own course, but that he was handed the file at 8.45pm, the previous evening, and he hadn't had time to digest it. What he proposed was to take the Judge to the important and relevant issues on both sides.

Much of the morning's repartee had been a repeat of evidence submitted the previous day and on the 14th May, but did contain some very interesting fact.

Our summary includes most of what everyone had to say by way of affidavit, the letters, the statements, the evidence.

One item that was not mentioned yesterday was Terry's criticism of the running of the commercial departments:

'Mr Pay became Sales Manager of the merchandising department after the departure of Mr Freedman, and it is true to say I was unhappy with the way that the division was running. Considering the turnover, the profit margins should have been greater.'

The gist of a letter to Venables from Pay suggests again that he tried to implement stock control and stock accounting and looked for back-up from Sandy's department, but never received same, he alleges. He says that he found the assistance to be inadequate, but that it was he that got the blame for Sandy's inadequacies, and he was accordingly, sacked.

Mr Mann: "Mr Pay had been discharged from the service of the Company. Mr Sandy was running the merchandising from December 1992, and there was nobody other than Mr Sandy to run it. Mr Sugar proposed that he received remuneration and the Board's approval on the basis that it be to run the merchandising department."

(I think that he is referring to the £50,000 that Sugar awarded to one of his companies in respect of his personal service, not, as may be read, an additional salary for Sandy. Sugar was now in overall charge of merchandising).

Mann continued: "In due course another gentleman was introduced and employed by Sugar, called Mr Gilbert. He was effectively doing the same job, and that cost the Company £40,000."..

Mr Gilbert stated: "Mr Sugar introduced to the Company, a Mr Harvey, on the 28th January, a personal friend of his, to supervise the merchandising department."

Jonathan Crystal confirmed... "At that meeting Harvey stated that he would not want to be paid for his services to the Company. The Board accepted his generous offer. On the 3rd June 1993 I attended a Board meeting. I was handed copies of the accounts for the merchandising. I noted that Mr Harvey had been awarded £40,000 expenses!"

Crystal and Venables provided further information about another Board meeting on 6th May, some eight days before Terry was finally dismissed. Crystal told of the independent report that Terry had prepared to survey the computer system that had been introduced on £25,000's worth of obsolete Amstrad equipment.

"What it tells me is that there is serious concern relating to the system which has been installed along with the host system at Amstrad. Mr Sugar dismissed the report out-of-hand."

Venables confirmed that the report was critical of the computer system. The particular criticism was that information had to be obtained from the finance department and could not be assessed by the Chief Executive.

Mr Mann: "That for the Chief Executive with overall responsibility for all the operations of the PLC was to Mr Venables, very unsatisfactory."

(Well, Tel had said that he knew nothing about computers anyway!)

Crystal also referred to the abortive Board meeting, held at Highbury, the night they played Tottenham in the final Premier League game of last season.

He said that the one share held by Gray was transferred to Sandy without a formal arrangement approved by the Board and that the meeting was not called correctly, and of course he later received a letter from Berry confirming that. He mentioned every occasion that he believed Alan Sugar behaved in an ad hoc manner, not relying on the conditions laid down by the Company Articles, and indeed by Company Law.

Later, after considerable restatements of things that had either been recorded in this hearing or the previous one, Terry's counsel read out statements in support of his client:

From Bill Nicholson.. 'Whilst I am not aware of the details of any dispute such as there may be at Board level, I cannot think how the interests of the Club and shareholders can best be served by permitting such a good football man as Mr Venables surely is to leave."

From Gary Mabbutt, after stating what a good coach Terry is and after saying how the players were happy with him etc.:

'I am not aware of the details of the dispute such as they may be between Mr Venables and Mr Sugar. I do not wish to appear to be taking sides....'

From Neil Ruddock, who had joined Tottenham in 1986, and who was later kicked out by Terry, and who was then re-signed from Southampton, and who has now departed to Liverpool..

'When I heard the news I was absolutely floored. extremely upset. The team would be wrecked by Mr Venables' departure. I would probably wish to leave the Club, if Terry were to leave and so would some of my fellow team members.'

Ruddock made a statement which had already been published in the Daily Mirror on Friday 14th May:

'It would be an absolute tragedy if Terry Venables left the Club. He has worked extremely hard with the players to get the best out of them. There is a real art to understanding the needs and character of each player and without any disrespect to Doug Livermore and Ray Clemence, all our achievements are due to his input and efforts.'

Mr Mann went on to read a handwritten letter from Ruddock headed TRANSFER REQUEST 4TH JUNE...

"Dear Mr Venables,

"Owing to the uncertainty of the future of Tottenham Hotspur F.C., I feel that it is in my best interest to be placed on the transfer list. The reason for this is when I first joined Tottenham I was informed by yourself that you would renegotiate my contract at the end of my first season. Approximately three months ago we had a meeting regarding a new contract. I was assured by yourself that in principle we had reached an agreement, that I was ready to sign at the end of the Season. Unfortunately since then there has been a problem regarding your future and I have now been informed that the deal that we agreed in principle will not take place until after the litigation. Then there is still no guarantee that our agreement in principle will be honoured. As much as I appreciate your situation as explained at our meeting, I need to resolve my financial problems I encountered by moving to Tottenham.

"Finally, I would like to make it clear to yourself that you have the full support of myself and my family, and I wish you every success in the coming weeks."

Mr Mann said that the letter was a direct effect of the removal from office of Terry Venables.

(Ruddock was after a £150,000 loyalty bonus — as Terry described it. He had been at Tottenham for only one season, having been kicked out once before by Terry, yet he wanted a new contract. As Jimmy Greaves wrote in the Sun on Saturday the 18th December: "Why do footballers deserve new contracts immediately they have signed one. If footballers sign a contract for three years or so, then they should stick to the terms, until the third year and then renegotiate. They already have freedom of contract. Other members of the public can't sign new contracts so quickly. Why footballers?"...

Ruddock has been branded as disloyal by many Spurs supporters. If he loved Terry so much why not wait until the result of the hearing? I suspect that it might have been considered politically favourable for him to ask for a transfer while all this was happening, perhaps, in order that Mr Mann could read the letter out in Court. As everyone knows, Ruddock moved to Liverpool for an enormous fee, and all credit to Ossie for letting him go while making a good profit for Tottenham.)

The Vice-Chancellor: "What would the proposal be? The Board approve new contracts or that Mr Venables approves....

Mr Mann: "No, the Board do it on Mr Venables putting them up for approval."

The Vice-Chancellor: "Let us be clear what that means. Is the Board going to simply rubber-stamp Mr Venables' decision or is the Board in its unhappily divided state going to be asked to make a decision?"

Mr Mann: "No. The position will be that Mr Venables will make proposals to the Board and Board, in the best interests of the Club, will decide what it is right to do in connection with any particular proposal."

The Vice-Chancellor: "That is the five present members of the Board?"

Mr Mann: "That is the six members of the Board."

The Vice-Chancellor asked who were the six? Mann told him there was Mr Alexiou, Mr Crystal, Mr Venables, Mr Sugar, Mr Sandy and Mr Berry. The Judge asked whether that was the same now as before the litigation of the 14th. Mr Mann told him that Terry had autonomous authority up to £50,000. The Judge asked whether the same applied to out-going players. Mr Mann, after consulting Terry, said that Terry was responsible for 'transfers out', and the Board just rubber-stamped the deals.

Mr Mann resumed after the luncheon adjournment by reading some details provided by Vinny Samways:

311

'I joined Tottenham when I was twelve years old, at a time when Keith Burkenshaw was Manager. I signed straight from school at sixteen when I became an apprentice, then one year later became a professional. I first worked under Terry when he came from Barcelona.'....

Vinny went on to reiterate what Ruddock said and praised Terry in similar fashion, as did Gary Mabbutt, and closed with the words: 'If Terry were to leave, it would be a great shame. It would not be in the interests of the team or the players. Many youngsters have been tried out in the first team and they would be worried about keeping their position in the first team. Terry has a very good rapport. In my career, I can say to date that out of all the managers I have worked for, all of whom have been extremely good, Terry has been the best.'

Mr Mann also produced a number of faxes and letters from supporters, and one from Eric Hall who forecast the possibility of transfer requests from Justin Edinburgh, Steve Sedgeley, David Howells, Vinny Samways and others.

(All in support of Terry Venables, none knowing of the forthcoming television programmes that would report on shady dealings, dodgy invoices and suspicious payments that was all taking place out of their domain. How do they feel now?)

More legal argument followed before a long submission reiterating what we already know, but highlighting the alleged faults of Alan Sugar: altering Board minutes; presenting a contract for personal gain signed and agreed but without the Board's authority; buying computer equipment without the Board's authority; purporting to hold and rely on an irregular Board meeting; irregular and unlawful conduct; charging expenses without authority, unfair prejudice and finally bad faith.

Mr Mann suggested that it would be a waste of time hearing Sugar's evidence, because it would be another version of the same facts.

Before admitting that he could not take matters much further, he pleaded that the interregnum, the period of Terry's temporary reinstatement, was working satisfactorily.

The Judge accused him of going over the same ground.

Again there are many legal arguments that I consider would

bore the reader and again we summarise the Barrister's submissions, detailing the relevant statements.

In response the brilliant Mr Heslop adopted what can only be described as the simple and most effective argument. All the submissions and all the evidence and all the 'slagging-off' in the world could not overturn the simple fact that Terry Venables was dismissed by a majority of the Board. Any agreements that he may or may not have had with Alan Sugar were not binding on all the members of the Board of Directors, and that the Court could not overrule the decisions of a legitimately elected Board of a public limited company.

Alan Sugar's alleged bad faith and behaviour were issues which could be aired at a trial later and which should play no part in these intermediary proceedings. Should Terry continue, then the full value of the evidence could be reiterated and used against the Board and Alan Sugar, specifically.

Effectively, nothing else needs to be said. The fact that the ensuing arguments in the legal papers took usage of more than twenty two printed pages only serves to support how meticulous and articulate Barristers are. They also repeat themselves frequently!

In order that Mr Heslop should not think that we make preference towards Mr Mann, we detail below his argument, summarised, but with the very clever and assured words that he uses.

. "I do not accept," Mr Heslop said, "that there are serious issues to be tried on the issue of whether Edennote should be entitled to relief in the petition. On analysis of the evidence, I will be submitting that your Lordship does not have to take a view on disputed facts.

If your Lordship would look at what is said about an agreement between Mr Venables and Mr Sugar, it was proposed that shares would be purchased as to 50% for Mr Venables and 50% for Mr Sugar. That would have no bearing on what has happened. Mr Venables is removed from office. They agreed to be Chairman and Chief Executive and that has been achieved. The only question is as to whether there will be a further term of the agreement, or whether he had legitimate expectation arising from the dealings, that not only would he be there, but he would be there forever, or as long as he chose to be."

The Vice-Chancellor: "What is said is that there was a joint venture. Mr Venables and Mr Sugar agreed their respective positions and the shares that they would each purchase. That is what they arranged and that is what is said."

Mr Heslop: "It may be said, but the question is why should the Board of a public limited company be saddled with what at best is a private or side agreement between Mr Sugar and Mr Venables, for what is suggested as a potentially indefinite period?

"The point is that whatever side agreement, and I do not accept that there was one, may have been reached between the parties, it was a decision not of Mr Sugar, but of the Board of the Company, that Mr Venables should be removed, and the Courts will not enforce an agreement entered into between entrepreneurs that will have the affect of fettering the discretion of the Board of a company. The further point is that Mr Venables was not removed by Mr Sugar because he packed the Board with more Directors that Mr Venables. Mr Venables has been dismissed by a majority of the Board. Mr Berry and Alexiou, who it has not been suggested are nominees of Mr Sugar, stand by that decision. What has happened to the word 'balanced' mentioned by Mr Mann is that this word has been converted to mean that neither side shall appoint more Directors than the other. That has not happened. Can I just say that the articles of the Company entrust the management of the Company's affairs to the Board of Directors That is almost the inevitable position. Shareholders are simply not entitled to be consulted, or decide for themselves whether a Chief Executive ought or ought not to be dismissed. the third point I make is that Mr Venables was appointed to his position by the Board on behalf of the Company and not by Alan Sugar. The decision of the 14th May is one taken by the majority of the Board.

"In my submission there is no credible evidence of bad faith, and also true under clause 459 under which this petition is brought, that the Court will not intervene in a management decision, whether it be to dismiss a Chief Executive, or terminate a contract with suppliers, or whatever. The Court cannot substitute its commercial judgement for that of the Board. Hence, my Lord, the Court will be wary of intervening.

"The next point is that Mr Venables has been removed as an employee, albeit the most senior employee, but it is important that he has not been removed as a Director. The distinction is important, because it leads on to my next point. That is that the removal of Mr Venables involved the exercise of no votes by Mr Sugar, or any other shareholder, in contrast to the position that would arise if he had been dismissed by a vote of shareholders. That means that in the alleged agreement, which provides for neither party using its votes to oust the other, that simply has not happened. The further point is that the shareholders have no right to change the decision of the Board. They cannot in any other company change what they don't approve of, that the Board has decided upon. That means that shareholders in general cannot complain. Mr Venables has no right in the absence of exceptional circumstances to ask the Court to reverse the decision. His remedy is to sue for breach of contract.

"My submission is that your Lordship allows the dismissal to take effect and no interlocutory relief should be granted. As I said, in ordinary circumstances a Chief Executive who feels that he has been aggrieved, sues the Company for breach of contract and takes a Queen's Bench action. That is the end of it. Much of the evidence which is before your Lordship goes to an issue which is not before the Court. It is a serious issue to be tried in a trial. The agreement between the two parties has been foisted on the Board and they cannot be expected to honour that. It cannot be shown that the Board, the Company or its members had any knowledge of such an arrangement. The question to the Board is 'Have you agreed that Mr Venables, regardless of his competence as Chief Executive and not as Manager of the football side, can have a job for life?"

The Vice-Chancellor: "Is this the point you make? You say that there cannot be legitimate expectancy here, even if there was a binding agreement, because the other members of the Company did not know about it, and that is your point."

Mr Heslop: "Yes, absolutely! The agreement states that 'This agreement sets forth an entire agreement of each of the parties." That is the point. Of each of them and not of anyone else!"

Mr Heslop referred to many of the affidavits that were presented by Mr Mann and some letters which we have already seen, but effectively, and indeed, most effectively, he had nullified the Courts' authority on the matter.

They adjourned until after the week-end.

THE HEARING OF MONDAY 14th JUNE.

For hours Mr Heslop ran through the evidence alleging its inconsequence to the issue. There was, however, late in the day, a long speech that summed up much of Terry's and the players' statements and the state of Tottenham in as much as the way it was being run while the injunction stood to effect. Perhaps, to conclude these four long days of legal arguments, we should endure what he said...

Mr Heslop: "Mr Venables is a Director. We heard today an undertaking that nothing would be done to remove him from this Directorship. We are happy for that and thankful for it, but it would be surprising if the other shareholders thought for a moment that depriving a 23 per cent shareholder of a Directorship in the Company would be a wise course. Mr Venables as a Director is entitled to attend all Board meetings and to be provided with information for that purpose sufficient to enable him to exercise his fiduciary duties as a Director, and he will have to involve himself in that exercise in consideration of the very such matters which he would be dealing with as Chief Executive, though as a supervisory exercise and not in participation and reporting to the Board.

"As his role of management and Chief Executive is principally at the training ground, away from the Board, and negotiating player contracts and the like, it is very unlikely that at the Board meeting itself or before the change represented by his departure, if that is to be, would be very different. Who is going to do the work he is doing now? A manager has to be employed. It is not suggested seriously with all respect to them, Mr Livermore and Mr Clemence would to the contractual work which has to be done. It would have to be done by a new manager, and Mr Venables in the Board room applying his talents properly will have to decide whether or not the decisions are proper and sensible ones. That really is the most invidious position for both him and a new manager, if one could be found to take on the job.

"Mr Venables' regard to contracts in any event is pretty limited now. He undertakes as far as contracts are concerned to present them to the Board in the usual way. He might even go beyond that. Then if he is to be regarded as solely in the position of a Director, he reviews his own decisions or the decisions that he might have been involved in, in the same way. To interpose a new manager in circumstances where calibre cannot be guaranteed, in order to preserve in favour of the Respondents a status quo, would be wrong. It is not just a case of negotiating contracts which have expired or run out.

"Contracts which have to be entered into or renewed are very important. I can mention four: Mr Ruddock if he stays, Messrs. Walker, Howells and Sedgeley. Their contracts need to be lengthened and the reason is as the season proceeds, their transfer value. There is no argument from Mr Sugar about the reasons for that, and the reason for that is nobody on the Board at the moment has the faintest idea how a manager's job is performed. The implications are that, if a new manager is got in, he may or may not be of the best calibre, and Mr Venables for the protection of the shareholders interests will have to participate to the same extent and with the same degree of assiduity and with the benefit of as much information to protect the shareholders' interests as he did before.

"What it comes down to is that it is regrettable that the petition has got to be got on as quickly as possible because there is no satisfactory interregnum other that that which pertains today. I could say a lot more. If I do so, I will reiterate what I have already said in my opening submissions and I do not want to do that.

"One short comment about the effect of an injunction and the unsuitability of a specific performance order in the case of service contracts, the order that exists today is not one specifically enforcing the service contract. It is one which a shareholder is entitled to, enforcing an understanding. The incident of it is that Mr Venables has maintained his position under his service agreement. It is not the direct result. Where a party is entitled to a prohibitory injunction, then the reverse of the coin is that the party is entitled to a mandatory order. That means Mr Venables, in order to protect Edennote's position, must remain as Chief Executive in the interregnum."

One item offered in evidence, not yet mentioned, is worth noting.

Mr Heslop makes reference to the circumstances involving the payment of £58,750 made to First Wave. You will recall that Graham Smith and McLintock both said that Frank received a call from 'someone at Tottenham' to come and collect his money and when he arrived he was handed a bag of cash. According to a Sugar affidavit, McLintock demanded the money at the time that Sheringham was about to sign, saying that he wanted the cash before he would allow Sheringham to sign any contract.

The Vice-Chancellor: "There is an allegation that Mr Sandy and Mr Sugar acted in bad faith for the purpose contrary to the interest of the Company. As far as Mr Sandy is concerned, was that the only reference in the petition to him acting in bad faith?"

Mr Mann then intervened and pointed out that there was also the matter of the agreement with Amshold, £50,000 per annum which was arranged by Mr Sandy.

The Vice-Chancellor: "In the actual evidence what follows are criticisms of Mr Sugar."

Mr Mann then pointed out that throughout 1992 Mr Sandy was Sugar's nominee.

The Vice-Chancellor: "That is an allegation that Mr Sugar has sought to interject. Now I am going to rise for a few moments and I will give my judgement at 3.30 pm."

THE VICE-CHANCELLOR, SIR DONALD NICHOLLS. THE WISDOM OF SOLOMON?

Tottenham Hotspur is one of the country's leading football clubs. Tottenham Hotspur Football and Athletic Company Ltd is wholly owned by Tottenham Hotspur Plc. About 70% of the shares are held by two parties, Amshold holding about 48% and Edennote 23%.

The controllers of those shares, effectively Mr Venables and Mr Sugar have unfortunately fallen out. The question before me today is what should be done about running the affairs of Tottenham, until the proceedings started by Edennote can be tried.

To anyone who is even the most passing acquaintance to English football, Terry Venables needs no introduction. He has been described as an institution in the football world. Equally, alan Sugar needs no introduction; he is a household name as a successful entrepeneur.

Tottenham in 1990 were facing financial difficulties having built a new stand at the ground costing more than £9 million.

In 1991 Mr Sugar and Mr Venables purchased between them almost 48% of the shares in Tottenham and were described as the 'dream ticket'.

Unfortunately the arrangement has not worked as hoped and intended. Clearly both Mr Venables and Mr Sugar are forceful, stone-willed, determined men. On occasions they can be touchy.

The voluminous evidence, extending in all to over 2,500 pages, is not untypical of the evidence frequently produced on unfair prejudice petitions. Misunderstandings were followed by disagreements, bickering and rows. Board meetings became increasingly confrontational. By May '93 acrimony had reached the stage when, in practice, it had become impossible for these two talented men to work together any longer as Chairman and Chief Executive.

So on the 14th of May Mr Sugar acted. The Tottenham Board, by a majority, summarily determined Mr Venables' service contract and in consequence he ceased to be Chief Executive. The vote was Mr Sugar and Mr Sandy in Favour, and Mr Crystal against. By reason of his personal interest, Mr Venables was disqualified from voting. Mr Berry abstained. However, Mr Berry made it clear that had it been necessary, he would also have voted in favour of the resolution to dismiss. The Director since appointed, Mr Alexiou, has said that he also supports the dismissal of Mr Venables.

Edennote immediately launched these proceedings under S459 of the Companies Act.

edennote seeks an Order that Amshold must sell its share to Edennote and an Order restraining Tottenham from acting on the resolution of the 14th of May and from extending Mr Venables' service contract.

319

What should be done until the trial? There are many areas of dispute. Clearly the proceedings cannot be tried for some weeks at best. The trial itself would be expected to last for at least a month. So I have to decide whether justice and commonsense, marching hand in hand, require me to give directions about the running of Tottenham over the next few months.

The service and management contracts have now been terminated by Tottenham. That has happened. If that was in breach of the terms of those contract, Edennote and Mr Venables have grosvenor for damages. Neither of those two have brought a claim for an Order compelling Tottenham to carry on with those contracts, as distinct from a claim for damages or wrongful dismissal.

For long, the law has recognised that in most cases contracts for personal service cannot sensibly be made the subject of Court Orders in respect of specific performance. IF PARTIES CAN NO LONGER WORK TOGETHER, NO ORDER OF THE COURT CAN CHANGE THE POSITION.

The second point to note is that success by Mr Venables in the present proceedings, and if Mr Venables can find the very substantial amount required to buy out Mr Sugar, he may yet find himself once more at Tottenham's Chief Executive. I note that Mr Sugar has offered to buy out Mr Venables.

Thirdly, it follows that there will be some continuing uncertainty about Tottenham's future, and the role of Mr Venables at the Club, so long as the present proceedings remain on foot. Mr Sugar has offered an undertaking not to take any steps to remove him from the Board pending the trial. Board meetings will therefore be very difficult; feelings are running high, and the enforced cooling-off period has done nothing to lower the temperature. Mr Venables and Mr Sugar remain at daggers drawn.

Against this background I have to balance two matters in particular. On the one hand, there is the advantage to the Club of Mr Venables remaining to deal at least with important football matters. In addition, Mr Venables is very popular with the supporters and players. I have seen 700 letters expressing support. On the other hand, his return makes the smooth running of other aspects of the Club extremely difficult for everyone.

Given the neutral hostility and mutual lack of trust, employees and Directors are placed in an impossible position. This inevitable leads to a paralysis if continued for any time and which cannot be in the best interests of the Club.

The Court will do what is just inequitable in all the circumstances.

At the time of the original mandatory cash offer in July 1991, and later at the time of the Rights Issue in December, nothing about any side agreement relating to the respective appointments of Mr Venables and Mr Sugar was disclosed to shareholders. There was nothing to suggest that the Board of Directors did not have the normal right to hire and fire.

'THIS BEING SO, I DO NOT THINK IT WOULD BE RIGHT OR SENSIBLE FOR ME TO MAKE AN ORDER OVERRIDING THE MAJORITY DECISION OF THE BOARD AND RESTORING MR VENABLES TO AL OR SOME OF HIS FUNCTIONS AS CHIEF EXECUTIVE UNTIL THE TRIAL. WHETHER MR VENABLES' DISMISSAL WAS IN THE BEST INTERESTS OF TOTTENHAM IS NOT A MATTER FOR THE COURT TO DECIDE. THAT IS A MATTER FOR THE TOTTENHAM BOARD TO WHOM THIS DECISION IS ENTRUSTED UNDER THE COMPANY'S CONSTITUTION.

I shall therefore not make an Order as asked. I shall rise now for a few moments and sit again to hear any applications there may be regarding costs or other ancillary matters."

After the break, Mr Heslop's assistant Mr David Mabb submitted to the Judge that the Sugar side should be awarded costs against the Venables side for the hearings of the 14th May, 25th May and the present application.

Mr Mann for the Venables side argued that the proceedings were brought by a clear breach of contract, which has yet to be heard that the Judge should make a different cost than normal, even though the opposition had effectively won. He asked that the Court recognises the unlawfulness of what brought the proceedings about. He asked that the cost Order should be held pending the possibility of a success in making Mr Sugar sell his shares.

The Vice-Chancellor: "I THINK THE RIGHT ORDER I

SHOULD MAKE IS THAT THE PETITIONER SHOULD PAY THE RESPONDENT'S COSTS OF THE APPLICATION, IN-CLUDING THAT WHICH CAME BEFORE THE COURT OF THE TWO PREVIOUS OCCASIONS.''

This hit Terry where it really hurt. No job, no income, and the costs as well!...

There was still an application to jail Alan Sugar in contempt of Court proceedings. A date was set for the following day.

THE APPLICATION TO JAIL ALAN SUGAR — 15th JUNE

WHAT IS AN EASTENDER?

Terry Venables was recorded as having stated that Alan Sugar was not 'An Eastender'. By this I am certain that he meant the statement to reflect his idea of an Eastender as opposed to where the man actually was conceived or brought up.

Having known Mr Sugar during my formative years and later during my teens I can assure you that Alan Sugar is indeed a product of that erstwhile geographic region that takes in such places as Bethnal Green, Shoreditch, Hackney, and Mile End, plus a few districts who like to include themselves within the boundaries. Being an Eastender implies loyalty, usually from one fellow human being to another; there is a code — an ethos. Not grassing on 'your mate' is paramount to the thinking. Shout and rave at an adversary, yes; but never grass him up. If you know that he is, for example having a bit on the side, you don't tell his missus, no matter what harm he has done you.

But Alan Sugar no longer seems to respect that basic human emotion that is supposedly inherent in his breeding: that which surely must be in his blood. Anything goes!

To be frank, I remember the boy as a bit of a wimp who definitely did not accompany the crowd of lads each and every second Saturday to White Hart Lane, from rail stations such as Bethnal Green, Stratford, Hackney Downs, Rectory Road and Stamford Hill: Alan was not among the giggling lads that went to the game eager for victory and the joy that a good result would bring which would be carried on during Saturday evening pursuits.

Alan Sugar would seem to have grown out of that idealistic state and settled for hard nosed, aggressive ambition, regardless of the cost to him and to others.

Particularly the others!

During the course of any business, and I defy Alan to argue this point, a certain amount of ducking and diving is endemic to survival. When he started Amstrad on several thousand pounds of borrowed money, I am sure that he had to use every ounce of guile to help the Company along. In football, the same ducking and diving is essential to survival and success. He is not so naive as to pretend that his sensibilities were affected when he told the world that Terry said 'Sign the cheque leave it to me, these things are done in football.' Alan feigned shock and revulsion at such a suggestion.

Having stated the above, I would not wish it to be felt that I condone graft or under-the-counter payments or 'bungs'. But it isn't an ideal world. It's a jungle out there!

If Mr Sugar was so affronted, why did he authorise the cheques in the first instance? Then, there was his condemnation of Eddie Ashby. Now, I will not defend this man's past, or his continuance of company liquidations or his personal bankruptcy. Alan knew that Terry had appointed the man as his back-stop, whatever he may have called himself on paper, and indeed it was Alan Sugar as Chairman of the Club who appointed Eddie to investigate the possibilities of raising money by mortgaging the ground. It was Colin Sandy who later took out a personal check on Ashby, and who created the seed of doubt with Sugar, as a result of his findings.

The high profile of assaulted sensibilities that Alan Sugar demonstrated was impressive to the readers of certain newspaper articles, and viewers of a television production on Channel 4, Dispatches.

That integrity was not demonstrated when on the 1st of June 1993 he found himself in the company of a witness in the hearings, whom he threatened if the man disclosed certain previous confidentialities.

Subsequently, on the 15th of June 1993 he found himself apologising to the Court for his behaviour, while facing a charge of Contempt of Court: Effectively, a committal to prison proceedings brought about in the first instance by Terry's Company Edennote Plc, later withdrawn, but viewed seriously by the Vice-Chancellor Sir Donald Nicholls.

Details of that hearing appear below. The trial was held on the 15th of June 1993 in the High Courts of Justice, Chancery Division before the Vice-Chancellor Sir Donald Nicholls. Again Mr Martin Mann QC and Mr Michael Gadd, instructed by Terry's Solicitors Messrs. Kanter Jules Grangewood appeared on behalf of Edennote, while Alan Sugar in his own right (Amstrad were not, of course, cited), was represented by Lord Irvine of Lairge QC and Miss Siobhan Ward, instructed by Messrs. Herbert Smith, Solicitors.

Incredibly, the result of the case was determined in favour of Alan Sugar as a result of the hooligans that daubed paint on his car, and damaged it, and who graffiti'd his house as well as those that caused pandemonium in the forum of the Court. I am certain that had they known that their actions would be taken into consideration when the Vice-Chancellor made his decision, and that their actions would be paramount to that decision, they would have not behaved so abominably.

HERE IS THE LEARNED JUDGE'S DECISION

Case No. 004296 of 1993.

THE VICE-CHANCELLOR.

I HAVE BEFORE ME AN APPLICATION FOR <u>THE COMMITAL TO PRISON OF MR ALAN SUGAR</u> FOR A CONTEMPT OF COURT COMMITTED ON THE 1st. OF JUNE 1993 IN THE COURSE OF A DISCUSSION HE HAD WITH A POTENTIAL WITNESS. THE APPLICANT NO LONGER WISHES TO PROCEED WITH THE APPLICATION.

IN THAT REGARD MR SUGAR IS A FORTUNATE MAN.

I HAVE CONSIDERED WHETHER, SINCE THE COURT NOW KNOWS OF THIS INTERFERENCE WITH THE ADMINISTRATION OF JUSTICE, I OUGHT STILL TO PROCEED. THE COURT ITSELF HAS AN INTEREST IN SEEING THAT INTERFERENCES WITH THE ADMINISTRATION OF JUSTICE DO NOT TAKE PLACE AND, IF THEY DO, THAT THEY ARE DEALT WITH APPROPRIATELY.

THE POSITION IS THAT MR SUGAR HAS SET OUT IN HIS AFFIDAVIT EVIDENCE A DETAILED ACCOUNT OF WHAT HAPPENED AND OF WHY, MISTAKENLY, HE ACTED AS HE DID. HE HAS ACCEPTED THAT HIS CONDUCT AMOUNTED TO A CONTEMPT, AND HE HAS EXPRESSED UNRESERVED REGRET FOR WHAT OCCURRED. IN THESE CIRCUMSTANCES I HAVE NOT FELT IT NECESSARY TO CALL ON MR SUGAR'S COUNCIL TO ADDRESS ME AT LENGTH ON THE EXTENUATING CIRCUMSTANCES PUT FORWARD BY MR SUGAR IN HIS AFFIDAVIT. BUT I SHOULD SAY THIS. IN CONSIDERING THIS MATTER, I HAVE VERY MUCH IN MIND THAT OVER THE LAST FEW DAYS AND WEEKS SOME OF THE BEHAVIOUR OF SOME OF THE SUPPORTERS OF TOTTENHAM HOTSPUR TOWARDS MR SUGAR HAS BEEN DISGRACEFUL. THEIR BEHAVIOUR IN COURT WHILE THE COURT WAS SITTING WAS EXEMPLARY. ELSEWHERE THIS HAS NOT BEEN SO. EVEN WITHIN THE PRECINCTS OF THE COURT MR SUGAR HAS BEEN SUBJECTED TO PHYSICAL INTIMIDATION AND ABUSE AND THREATS. THIS BEHAVIOUR WAS ITSELF A CONTEMPT OF COURT. PARTIES, HOWEVER UNPOPULAR THEIR CAUSE MAY BE WITH SOME, MUST NOT BE DETERRED FROM COMING TO THE COURT BY THE THREAT OR THE FEAR OF SUCH BEHAVIOUR. IT GOES WITHOUT SAYING THAT MR VENABLES WAS IN NO WAY RESPONSIBLE FOR THIS. BUT IN MY VIEW MR SUGAR HAS BEEN SUFFICIENTLY SCARRED BY THIS VILIFICATION AND ABUSE AND THREATENING BEHAVIOUR FOR IT TO BE INAPPROPRIATE FOR ME TO TAKE ANY FURTHER ACTION OVER MR SUGAR'S OWN ADMITTED CONTEMPT. I SHALL THEREFORE MAKE AN ORDER ONLY IN THE TERMS OF THE DRAFT PUT BEFORE ME.

The Witness that was accosted verbally by Alan Sugar was Mr Jonathan Crystal QC, Barrister, who was also a Non-Executive Director of Tottenham Hotspur Plc, responsible, as he saw his position, for the vetting and approval of legal documents submitted to Tottenham. Except of course, when Alan Sugar decided to ignore this position and go full steam ahead to arrange and authorise contracts that he appeared to preclude from the learned Mr Crystal's observations.

It is alleged that at a meeting with Sugar, the Chairman threatened Mr Crystal with ruination if the man issued a fuller and more comprehensive affidavit indicting Mr Sugar for greater breaches of Company Law than those which had already been committed, and for his authoritarian and dictatorial attitude, contrary to democratic proceedings that Mr Crystal demanded.

UNEASY LIES THE HEAD THAT WEARS THE CROWN!

THE FINAL SOLUTION
29th July 1993

(Although it was the Sugar team that were applying to have Venables place into court sufficient monies to cover their assumed costs, should he lose his fight, it was still Edennote who were described as 'The Petitioners' as they had been throughout all the hearings to date.)

Appearing for Edennote was Mr Alan Steinfeld QC and Mr Michael Gadd, and Miss Harrington, still as ever instructed by Kanter, Jules, Grangewood, Solicitors.

Appearing for Tottenham Hotspur Plc, Amshold Ltd, and Alan Sugar was Mr Philip Heslop QC and Mr David Mabb, instructed as ever by Messrs. Herbert Smith, Solicitors.

Summary of events. Hearing of the 29th July

Mr Heslop: "My Lord, I appear on behalf of three respondents, Tottenham Hotspur Plc, Mr Sugar and Amshold Ltd. This is an application for security of costs pursuant to s276 of the Companies Act. There is a late development, that being that just before your Lordship came in I was told and then handed an affidavit which appears to have been sworn by Mr Venables. I have had no chance to consider it, but it is rather startling because, amongst other things, it contains what are said to be draft accounts of the Petitioner for the year 31st March 1993."

Mr Justice Harman: "Any further evidence would need special leave."

Mr Heslop: "Yes…. What I was going to to do was this; I had proposed not to trouble your Lordship by taking up time reading the evidence in the order in which it appears. What I was proposing to do was to make submissions to your Lordship on the footing really of just the main points involved, drawing your Lordship's attention, to the material exhibits and extracts from the affidavits in support.

"Not having had a chance to consider this latest evidence, we might hear from my learned friend now or at a convenient moment to make his application, but can I say that given the history of this matter I would oppose the introduction of any further evidence.

"Your Lordship will see that on the 24th of June the Registrar gave directions for evidence on this application and then he adjourned the hearing over until the 19th July.

"My evidence was sworn on the 2nd of July and no evidence in opposition had been served by the deadline on the 15th of July, and application was made to the Registrar to extend the time for him (Terry) to serve his evidence. His reasons were that the papers had been sent to Counsel, but they had not had time to deal with them. This was opposed by Mr Gold of Herbert Smith acting for Mr Sugar and the Registrar declined to grant any extension that would adjourn the application.

"Now, the story of the 19th was supported by an affidavit the details do not matter for a moment, save that in paragraph 2 he sets out his reasons for seeking an extension. There was missing, the 1992 and 1993 audited accounts (of Edennote Plc). Mr Venables goes on to make much of the difficulties with Landhurst Leasing...."

(Readers will note the mention of the Landhurst Leasing agreement brought into question by the Dispatches programme on Channel 4, when Terry was purported to have borrowed a million pounds against one hundred thousand pounds worth of assets that he didn't own in the first place!)

"...which he thinks will be of significance to his application."

(To introduce new evidence, i.e. the set of draft accounts for 1993.)

"What happened then is that my learned friend, Mr Mabb told your Lordship about other difficulties which I think that your Lordship was not impressed by, in the SEVENTH affidavit of Mr Venables which was served on the 23rd of July."

Mr Justice Harman agreed.... "Absolutely...."

Mr Heslop: "Summarising it..." (the affidavit) "...it deals with various matters thought to be relevant including exhibiting what were said to be the audited accounts which are dated the 23rd July and it goes on to say that there has been no resolution of the dispute with Landhurst Leasing and that the 1993 accounts were not at that time, ready.

"In the light of all that, it is an intolerable position for the applicant, given the extensions of time that have been made and the orders that have so far been made, to have to deal with an application prepared on the basis of evidence filed so late, and then to be faced with any additional evidence, particularly of such significance as it is, of the 1993 accounts.

"It is a matter for your Lordship and my learned friend to satisfy you, as to whether he should be allowed to introduce this now or at some convenient later date."

Mr Steinfeld: "If I make that application, my Lord, may I first of all say that we of do apologise profusely for the late...." (Interrupted by the Judge.)

Mr Justice Harman: "Mr Steinfeld, I observed last week that if papers were lodged before 6 pm. last night I would endeavour to read them all before sitting today, on the grounds that we are on the very end of 'Term', there is very little time and I am under huge pressure, or the court is under huge pressure of work. I spent a few hours reading it last night. I am ready to hear this matter now. It is grossly unfair to the Court as a public matter to load evidence at ten-thirty or even ten o'clock when I sit extra early to accommodate you."

Mr Steinfeld: "That is putting it rather high if I might say so. Your Lordship has not seen the Affidavit; it is a short affidavit. It is only in fact...."

(Judge interrupts again. Seems that Steinfeld has lost this one even before it gets going!)

Mr Justice Harman "But the accounts cannot be short!"

Mr Steinfeld: "The accounts are short, they are just figures bringing the '92 accounts up to date, and if I might respectfully say so, that while we apologise profusely to your Lordship and to the court, you are dealing with an application for security for costs where your Lordship has to exercise, at the end of the day possibly a very delicate discretion, and it is fundamental in the interests of justice that discretion ought to be exercised with the most up-to-date evidence that is available."

Mr Justice Harman: "What is fundamental to the interests of justice, is that both sides are given a proper chance to appreciate the matter and that, the Court chance also."

Mr Steinfeld: "Could I just tell your Lordship, without actually reading the affidavit, what the affidavit deals with? First of all it...." (Interrupted again.)

Mr Justice Harman: "Mr Steinfeld.... The date for evidence was the 15th of July. You were out of time. You made an extension on that day. That extension was down to Friday the 23rd July, so, you are already in 'mercy'. You received assistance and the substantial evidence was filed on Friday the 23rd July.

Mr Steinfield: "My Lord, I take the point.... The affidavit of Mr Venables which you have seen, stated that preparation of the '93 accounts had been delayed, mainly because of the negotiations with Landhurst Leasing, which were expected to come to fruition and in the result, he said in his affidavit in paragraph 7, that those accounts are...'in the course of preparation...' Venables describes in that affidavit what he had been told they were going to...." (Interrupted again!)

Mr Justice Harman: "It looks very much as if the preparation of these accounts has been arranged to arrive at 10 a.m. on the morning of this Hearing."

Mr Steinfeld: "Well.... With respect there is no evidence to suggest that."

Mr Justice Harman: "No, but it is a strong inference from your conduct."

Mr Steinfeld: "Well.... No, things have happened as your Lordship can see, coincidentally in the negotiation with Landhurst Leasing which broke down on the 22nd of July, one day before the expiry of the time to swear in the affidavit. That meant that the 1993 accounts had, so to speak, had to be put back on ice and re-prepared. The evidence shows that they were being prepared on the basis that there was going to be some form of settlement. The accounts have now been prepared. Your Lordship say the 29th July. That is within six days, which is not a great deal of time for the accountant to get round to re-prepare the accounts. That is the first thing that has been dealt with. We have also put into the accounts a letter from the accountants verifying the results, the basis upon which they have been prepared and which provides the up-to-date position."

Mr Justice Harman: "Which your clients ought to have prepared weeks, if not months ago."

Mr Steinfeld: "Well, if that had been possible…. We are not late in terms of the statutory obligations."

(He means the ten months after year end Directors are allowed to produce accounts of limited companies to Companies House.)

Mr Justice Harman: "No, but on the face of this application which you have known about for — 2 months?"

Mr Steinfeld: "Yes…. Well, the second point dealt with in the affidavit is really by way of a rejoinder to the point that Mr Gold…" (Herbert-Smith, Sugar's Solicitors) "…made in his reply."

Mr Justice Harman: "You are not entitled to rejoinder evidence…" (Rejoinder evidence is third part opinion.) "…and you know that!"

Mr Steinfeld: "I am not entitled to it, but I am telling your Lordship what the point is. In Mr Venables' affidavit he refers to the fact that those loans that are shown as being loans due after one year are in fact loans made to the Company (Edennote) by himself, or companies which he…." (Interrupted again.)

Mr Justice Harman: "What DO the accounts say?"

Mr Steinfeld: "They simply say…." (Interrupted again.)

Mr Justice Harman: "They DO NOT say, 'loans by Directors' — They should say that…! The accounts, you are now saying, are wrong?"

Mr Steinfeld: "No, with respect, I do not say that — That may be a matter of issue here — I believe that is right. Certainly the auditors of Mr Venables' Company take the view that what has to be shown in relation to the notes regarding transactions with the Directors is loans made to Directors…. Not loans made BY the Directors — Loans which have to be permissible. Be that as it may we do have evidence now of the break-down of the figures and it is a very important matter because Mr Venables in his latest affidavit and I, on his behalf, before your Lordship, would be offering an undertaking to subordinate that loan to the potential claims of respondents."

(What he is saying is that Terry loaned money from Edennote, and he is prepared to 'charge' those loan notes on behalf of the Company, to Sugar, as a sort of security against the legal costs that Venables/Edennote may get stuck with if he loses his proposed legal actions.... Later you will discover that Edennote had no money, only the shares in Tottenham, anyway, and so the 'loan note' offer is potentially useless! Particularly as Terry owned Edennote virtually outright, and the Company was effectively established only to control the interests that they have in Tottenham Shares. Edennote is a Holding Company, has a share capital of 50,000, and has issued the whole 50,000 shares to Terence F Venables and Edward Ashby. In the official papers of the Company, Terry is shown as owning all the shares, while Ashby, a 'L Gillick' and a 'I Yawetz' are shown as Directors, but without any actual shareholding. It is interesting to note that I Gillick was appointed on the 12th March 1991, but resigned 2 months later on the 17th May.

At the end of the trading year, 31st March, 1992, Terry and or others on the Board had loaned Edennote £53,000, but they had borrowed from the Company, some £112,00.... Effectively he, or others with him owed Edennote £59,000. By the way, Terry had only paid in cash some one quarter of the £50,000 shares he bought in the Company!)

Mr Justice Harman: "And why was that not thought of until this eleventh hour and fifty ninth minute?!"

Mr Steinfeld: "Well, can I just say.... Yes, the reason is that at the time it was thought that the negotiations with Landhurst Leasing would clarify the position in relation to the assets of Edennote. We are offering it and it is a matter of importance."

Mr Justice Harman: "It is a matter that has been raised and an issue for weeks, and only as the clock is about to strike midnight does this offer come up!"

Mr Steinfeld: "Well, there is the general principle as you will know, that a court ought to decide matters on the basis of the evidence which is before it. Of course...." (Interrupted again.)

Mr Justice Harman: "Evidence which is properly before the court, Mr Steinfeld, in the proper rotation and in accordance with orders which have been made."

Mr Steinfeld: "Of course, that is why I am asking your Lordship for leave to introduce this evidence."

Mr Justice Harman: "Special leave?"

Mr Steinfeld: "Yes. But that does not prevent introduction, even during the trial...." (Interrupted again.)

Mr Justice Harman: Mr Heslop has had no opportunity — I understand that it was only handed to him outside the court. How can he make any sensible submissions to me, opening his case without having any chance to read the affidavit, because of your WILFUL AND DELIBERATE LATENESS?"

Mr Steinfeld: "Well, we do not accept that the lateness is wilful and deliberate.... So far as the 1993 accounts are concerned, with respect, that cannot...." (Interrupted again.)

Mr Justice Harman: "There is lateness in producing evidence."

Mr Steinfeld: "That cannot be stigmatised as being wilful and deliberate lateness when one is simply putting in something that has occurred. That is to say the reasons why they were not prepared previously...." (Interrupted again)

Mr Justice Harman: "I hear what you say, Mr Steinfeld!"

Mr Steinfeld: "In our submission the evidence ought to be allowed in. It is not lengthy. I could understand if Mr Heslop was being faced with a very lengthy affidavit. He is only being faced with an additional 2 pages. The information is essential when presenting the facts of Mr Venables' loans to and from the Company. So our submission to your Lordship is that, with apologies for the lateness of that evidence...." (Interrupted again.)

Mr Justice Harman: "Apologies...? How much apology have you offered me...?

Mr Steinfeld: " I commenced my submissions with an apology!"

Mr Justice Harman: "A perfunctory word...!"

Mr Steinfeld: "Well, we are sorry and I have said that."

Mr Justice Harman: "An order made on the 19th July giving you extension to the 23rd and in flat defiance of that, you come in on the morning of the 29th after I have pre-read the whole case, and the whole thing is ready.... 'Oh, no...! Disrupt it.... Start again, Mr Justice Harman'...."

Mr Steinfeld: "Well, we are NOT starting again...! I mean, really.... With respect to your Lordship, and I hope that you do not take this unkindly.... (Interrupted again!)

Mr Justice Harman: "I do not take it very kindly that I should have spent quite a lot of hours, quite late last night, reading this not insubstantial bundle, and I am told that the whole approach which I formulated to the evidence has got to be re-thought because of this new evidence."

Mr Steinfeld: "Of course I cannot comment upon that approach your Lordship may have formulated. It does not in fact add a great deal more. What Mr Venables said in his affidavit as to what the 1993 accounts will show is in fact simply corroborated by what they will show. It will be a matter of your Lordship to weigh that up, but it does not actually ADD anything."

Mr Justice Harman: "If it does not ADD anything.... Why do you want it?"

Mr Steinfeld: "I am not saying that it does not ADD anything in terms. It should not add anything in terms of any formulation that your Lordship has already put into your mind, in regards to your approach to the evidence. But of course I cannot tell what views your Lordship may have formed. So far as the...." (Interrupted again.)

Mr Justice Harman: "Preliminary views...."

Mr Steinfeld: "Preliminary views.... So far as the offer to subordinate the loan is concerned and your Lordship may criticise that as being late.... Nevertheless the offer, once made, is something that clearly has to be taken into account even if made late. It is a decisive matter in the exercise of your Lordship in his discretion and the fact that it is made late is obviously something that can reflect itself in how your Lordship deals with the costs of this application generally. But it is an offer made. It has to be in our submission considered when made and of course in order to give 'meat' to the offer made, to find out exactly what it amounts to, one has to see the evidence.... The very short evidence.... As to what the Company owes to Mr Venables and see therefore what affect on the...." (Interrupted again.)

Mr Justice Harman: "Can you formulate to me now the undertaking that you are offering to the Court?"

Mr Steinfeld: "Well, the undertaking by Mr Venables...." (Interrupted again.)

Mr Justice Harman: "How much?"

Mr Steinfeld.... (Procrastinating and referring to files)...: "Exact sum...er.... I can tell your Lordship is...sorry..., if I can give you the figure...." (Interrupted again.)

Mr Justice Harman: "You said it was very easy. It seems to be taking a very long time."

Mr Steinfeld: "I can tell your Lordship it is in the letter...it is £1,134,351."

Mr Justice Harman: "And what are you offering of that sum?"

Mr Steinfeld: "We will offer that this debt...." (Interrupted again.)

Mr Justice Harman: "That is due to Mr Venables from the Company (Edennote Plc)...?"

Mr Steinfeld: "Yes it is. That is what the evidence now shows."

Mr Justice Harman: "And what does Mr Venables undertake in relation to that sum?"

Mr Steinfeld: "Mr Venables agrees that that sum will be subordinated to ANY CLAIMS OF THE RESPONDENTS."

(At this stage we would mention that Edennote according to the 1993 annual accounts registered at Companies House had a bank loan for the shares purchased of £2 million, an overdraft of £2,000 and creditors of £292,000. The share value which was vested in the Company amounted to over three and a half million without any form of discounting, therefore Terry was effectively worth the difference. A) Could they sell such an amount assuming by this time Sugar had withdrawn his original offer to buy, B) could Terry even get the price that they were valued at and C) if he sold those shares would he have any further claim to return to the position of Chief Executive, and buy Sugar out.

He was pledging everything that he had to convince the Court that if he ultimately lost, he would be able to pay both his and Sugar's legal costs. Should he lose, he would have only the equity in the shares. Clearly Edennote had no funds....)

Mr Justice Harman: "All creditors of this Company?"

Mr Steinfeld: "All the creditors, indeed, yes!"

Mr Justice Harman: "Is subordinated to ALL the creditors as

at this day?"

Mr Steinfeld: "As at today, yes."

Mr Justice Harman: "And including the Respondents claims in respect of costs to be incurred?"

Mr Steinfeld: "Incurred...and to be incurred, yes."

Mr Justice Harman: "Thank you.... At least I have it clear now."

Mr Steinfeld: "Your Lordship has it clear and indeed if necessary we could even go further if that was being suggested, and agree that rather than subordination that they could have an express charge over the debt, which might in fact improve their position but subordination is probably the simplest...." (Interrupted again.)

Mr Justice Harman: "I would not think that that WAS VERY SATISFACTORY."

Now, Sugar's Barrister, Mr Heslop stands....

Mr Heslop: "My Lord, there are a number of problems about what my learned friend is saying which I will deal with in due course. This occurs to me my Lord, that since your Lordship has been offered this undertaking, and it is unsatisfactory, that it has been drafted in this way, frankly...," (Interrupting Heslop now.)

Mr Justice Harman: "That is why I wanted it on the tape now."

(These are the tapes from which these transcripts have been summarised and to which we refer in our leader that thank Messrs. Harry Counsell and Co for their help.)

Mr Heslop: "I'm obliged, but since your Lordship has been told that, and accordingly, it is something which may or not not weigh in how you look at the matter, what I would submit rather than give my learned friend what would not be a good ground for any possible appeal, but nevertheless a ground by arguing that your Lordship has not taken into account evidence.... Might it be convenient that my learned friend takes us through the additional evidence...? Would that help?"

Mr Justice Harman: "That is most helpful, Mr Heslop.... Mr Steinfeld, I will propose to give you special leave to file this affidavit, sworn when...?"

Mr Steinfeld: "This morning, I believe."

Mr Justice Harman: "Upon terms that no costs of this affidavit shall be any part of your costs of this hearing. That is a requirement of the leave that I shall give you."

(First blood Terry Venables. He has got his late evidence through, attempting to prove that he is worth sufficient for the ultimate legal bill. The wise Mr Heslop notes that if he had resisted and the Judge agreed to his objection, this might have given Terry some excuse to appeal against the decision if it went against him, at some later stage.)

Mr Justice Harman: "Is it 'punched' so that I can add it to my batch of documents, if not why not? How can one do business if one has got no documents properly prepared?"

Mr Steinfeld: "We have got copies for your Lordship. The 'punching' has not been attended to, but it will be."

Mr Justice Harman: "I WANT PUNCHED COPIES PLEASE!"

(Steinfeld then punches the 2 paged affidavit and has it delivered to the Judge. Then he reads it to the Court.)

Mr Steinfeld: "This is the affidavit by Mr Venables: In Paragraph one he identifies himself and refers to the purpose of the affidavit. In 2, he produces a copy of a letter written by Edennote's Auditors (Crouch Chapman), the terms of which are self explanatory. I will just go onto paragraph 3 before we come to the exhibits. He produces the draft accounts for the year ending 31st March with a copy of a letter sent by his solicitors. Perhaps we can look at those."

Mr Justice Harman: "Would it not help to finish this?"

Mr Steinfeld: (Quoting from Terry's statement) "As Director of the Petitioner (Edennote Plc) I am able to say that the only events of any significance relating to the financial position which have occurred since the 31st March 1992, are as follows.

1) The termination of the Management Agreement.

2) The loan made by Mr Yazman (£250,000) to Edennote Plc has been renegotiated to the extent that all interest accrued thereon has been waived. The only amount outstanding to Mr Yazman relates to the principal sum."

Mr Justice Harman: "Is there a letter from Mr Yazman confirming this?"

Mr Steinfeld: "No, there is not. I refer to the auditors letter. 'I

339

confirm that the amount owed to me by the Petitioner as at the 31st March 1992 was'...." (Reading a statement by Yazman.)...(Interrupted again.)

Mr Justice Harman: "1992?"

Mr Steinfeld: "Yes, 1992...."

Mr Justice Harman: "So that is not up to date?"

Mr Steinfeld: "Yes, but the letter does confirm the exact amount. You will see in a moment from the draft accounts the current indebtedness of Edennote Plc to Terry Venables is not less than one million. In fact, when you look at the letter, you will see the exact figure set out there. The figure which I gave to your Lordship was taken from the exhibit. If it is considered necessary to do so, in order to resist the Respondents' application, I am willing to undertake to the Court be subordinated to any claim against Edennote or Terry Venables.

"For some reason the investments which were previously put down as a fixed asset have now been showed as a current asset...."

(What Steinfeld is saying is that Edennote's holding in Tottenham Hotspur Plc, is now being shown as a 'TRADING' item, and not one that is 'FIXED'. Therefore, in doing this, Terry is suggesting that he intends to sell the shares, by moving this item into another category in the balance sheet of Edennote.)

Steinfeld contin.... "I am unable to...."

Mr Justice Harman: "That means that it is held for trading purposes and not as an investment!"

Mr Steinfeld: "That might be a possible explanation for it."

Mr Justice Harman: "Is that not THE ONLY possible explanation?"

Mr Steinfeld: "One would have thought that would be the...." (Interrupted again.)

Mr Justice Harman: "Can you suggest to me another reason?"

Mr Steinfeld: "I cannot, and do not think that it is necessary for present purposes to do so. You will see that the current assets which include the investment which we know as the BOOK VALUE (COST) of the shares in Tottenham Hotspur Plc is...." (Interrupted again.)

Mr Justice Harman: "That carries a cost NOT AT MARKET VALUE. I thought that they had to do this?"

Mr Steinfeld: "I think market value is considered LOWER than cost."

(Tottenham shares had dropped after Terry's dismissal!)

Mr Justice Harman: "I thought one had to put them in at market value."

(Now Terry's stated equity in those shares that he had declared at 1.13 million has been challenged....)

Mr Steinfeld: "Well, current assets would be.... I think the normal accounting practice is to put them in at the lower of the valuations."

Mr Justice Harman: "Exactly.... That is what I suggested to you."

Mr Steinfeld: "Yes, if the market value is considered to be less than they cost, then that ought to be substituted."

Mr Justice Harman: "I think that on your stockbrokers valuation, you might be able to place one million of these shares at 71p."

Mr Steinfeld: "I think that the stockbroker is being very conservative with that view."

Mr Justice Harman: "If he is right, the market value is substantially less."

(Let's summarise this asset.... Edennote at the 31st March held 3,542,938 shares (22 per cent) in Tottenham which cost Terry £3,264,000. Assuming that two million were charged to the Bank who loaned him the money to buy most of them, he would have 1,542,938 shares unencumbered.

Except that he had borrowed £250,000 from Yazman secured by the shares, which leaves, 1,292,938 shares.

Now we know that he had to mortgage 450,000 to his Solicitors, although this was not brought out in Court, presumably because that mortgage was not effected until a month after this hearing.

Therefore, effectively, assuming he was able to overcome the 'actual' charge made to the 'Bank' on those shares, which you will read about later in this chapter, his purported unencumbered quantity represented a net subordinated asset of only 842,938 shares to call his own. At the market value these represented £598,486 at 71p each.

This is of course nothing like the value Steinfeld offers to subordinate to the Respondents.

Of course, this still may be enough to pay Sugar's legal bills if Terry lost, and there is the question still remaining, that if Tottenham contributed all or part of Sugar's legal expense then why, as a major shareholder in Tottenham Hotspur Plc, should Terry not receive a contribution, too, from that same source?)

Mr Heslop: (Standing now, having heard and noted the unsympathetic encounter between Steinfield and the Judge, obviously annoyed at the late attempt to introduce new evidence)....
"My Lord, I will deal with those submissions at the appropriate time, what I was going to do first of all was to just take you through the chronology of events.

"31st March, draft accounts for Edennote Plc, which are exhibited in the first affidavit. Total assets worth some £3,482,000.... Total liabilities, some £3,869,000, which shows a net deficit of £427,000, with a loss shown for the period of £439,000...Mr Gold (Sugar's Solicitor), if your Lordship takes the volume of affidavits on this application, in the 2nd affidavit, refers to these draft accounts and he makes a point that why they had been exhibited in the first place was unclear.

"Mr Pottesman (A Director of Edennote between May 1991 and April 1992) has stated that the financing SHOWN IN THE DRAFT ACCOUNTS HAS BEEN CHANGED SINCE THEY WERE PREPARED FOR THE 31st MARCH 1992.

"The effect of this statement is such that the Respondents are unable to ascertain the financial status of the Petitioner...."

(Pottesman leaves Edennote and then provides evidence for use by Sugar?...)

Heslop contin.... "He goes on to make the point that the draft accounts indicate that Edennote's only assets are its 3.5 million shares in Tottenham and valued at 94p — the mid-market quotation on those accounts, while the market price was £1.04p. He said that it was a matter of conjecture whether a buyer could be found for such a large block, and the Petitioner's only income appears to be dividends on these shares, and what was his income under the management agreement with Tottenham...."

(Who is it that might wish to spend about three and a half

342

million pounds buying a minority interest in Tottenham, with no guarantee of a board seat, and with Alan Sugar as Chairman...?)

Heslop contin.... "He goes on to deal with another item in Mr Venables' first affidavit, which deals with what can only be described as a tangled background to the financing and security interests in relation to the shares. He refers to an extract in that affidavit to a letter of the 26th June, written by Pan Financial Insurance to Edennote setting out the basis upon which that Company guaranteed repayment by Edennote of two million pounds borrowed from Norfina for the purpose of buying the shares. IT WAS ORIGINALLY REPRESENTED IN THE EVIDENCE THAT IF TERRY VENABLES LOST HIS JOB AS CHIEF EXECUTIVE THERE WAS A DEFAULT CLAUSE UNDER THE FINANCING ARRANGEMENT...."

(In other words, if Terry loses his job, which he did on the 14th May, the £2 million would then become repayable!)

(We are advised by a spokesman at Norfina that Terry refinanced his loan to the Bank of Liechtenstein in November 1992, and therefore the possible foreclosure did not arise! At least NOT because he had been fired from his job.

Terry had experienced difficulties in repaying the loan with Norfina, but borrowed sufficient from the Bank of Liechtenstein, to bring the account up to date with them before then re-financing.

Norfina, in fact, demanded this before allowing a re-finance operation....

In his conversation with me in August 1993, Venables had specifically stated that he had managed to keep the interest payments up-to-date, but not according to Norfina!, who were getting ready to foreclose, anyway.)

Heslop contin.... "Then Mr Gold refers to another affirmation of Mr Pottesman on the 20th May in which he says that the letter on the 26th March was no longer relevant to the Petitioner's current financial position. Mr Gold says that he believes this demonstrates the uncertainty that surrounds their finances. So just by way of background one starts with the initial evidence which is then immediately contradicted by Mr Venables' own Solicitor...."

(Melvin Jeffrey Pottesman was Terry's solicitor, and works, according to the 1993 lists of solicitors, as a partner in Kanter, Jules, Grangewood.)

Heslop contin…. "Then going on with this chronology, on the 31st March 1992, audited accounts which are included in Mr Venables' affidavits, are summarised here as showing total assets of £3,482,000 with liabilities of £3,869,000, with a net deficit of £387,000, and the accounts showing a loss of £399,000. On the 14th May, the order of Mrs Justice Arden made ex-parte, on very short notice granting 'relief' had the effect that Mr Venables was to remain in office. Then a petition was presented on the 17th May. The Respondents gave, on the 20th May, two clear days later, their intention to apply on the 25th May for the discharge of the injunction granted by Mrs Justice Arden.

"Mr Sandy is the Finance Director of Tottenham Hotspur Plc, and refers in his first affidavit to the discrepancy between the number of shares SAID TO BE unencumbered and the number of shares appearing in the Company search. The Petitioner has not filed any accounts for the period with the Registrar of Companies. Despite the fact that under the Companies Act, the accounts for the year ending 31st March 1992, a draft which has been exhibited, should have been filed by the 31st January 1993…."

(Previous mention of the statutory ten months allowed to file accounts have been made, but originally Venables' Barrister suggested that they were NOT out of time!)

Heslop contin…. "The draft accounts give me cause for concern as to the ability of the Petitioner to make good his undertaking. Edennote's only asset appearing to be the shareholding in Tottenham. I have reason to believe that it would be difficult to find a buyer at the current market price for this large block of shares. Venables has no income as the management contract has been terminated. Although Edennote is a 22 per cent holder of shares in Tottenham, it is NOT entitled to a like amount of the profits; merely to dividends which are paid.

"Sandy, in his affidavit, then mentions the interest that Mr Venables has in a number of companies. Now this is important, my Lord, because of the undertaking for subordination to you is a

344

matter of concern because there is discrepancy. NOW on the original evidence he states that £1.4 million due to Mr Venables or companies controlled by him, and the evidence now before us which says that it is broken down into a million, unqualified, due to Mr Venables personally...."

(Heslop gets interrupted.)

Mr Justice Harman: "The undertaking offered is £1.134 million."

Mr Heslop: "Quite.... It is now said contrary to the evidence sworn on Friday 23rd July that the money is owed to Mr Venables personally...."

(Interruption again.)

Mr Justice Harman: "I realize that."

Mr Heslop: "The reason for the concern is that from the inquiries that have been made, Mr Venables' financial affairs, so far as his other companies are concerned, give cause for concern. He exhibits a schedule listing companies of which he is aware, indicating searches made at the Companies House on 17th May: 'In respect of the only two of the companies which are filed, showing that Transatlantic was wound up by the court on a creditor's petition on the 3rd of February and that Terry Venables Ltd had net assets of only some £39,000 at the 30th of June. In addition Scribes West Ltd, which I believe is the Scribes Club, has received notice from the Registrar of Companies dated the 20th April, 1993, indicating that it will be struck off the Register unless it shows cause within three months that it should not be.'

"That, as you will recall, has been overtaken by events because the evidence of Mr Gold shows, in reliance of a report made to him by Messrs. Ragg & Co in Birmingham, that there is an outstanding winding-up petition against Scribes West Ltd due to be heard on the 16th August.

"The immediate point of all this is that if Mr Venables' affidavit of the 23rd of July is correct and the debt, whether it is 1 million or 1.43 or whatever, is due to companies, as opposed to Mr Venables personally, one needs to know which companies — we have not been told — because if they are debts due to...."

(Interrupted again.)

Mr Justice Harman: "It was put to me expressly on the

footing that it was personally due to Mr Venables and that he had personally given an undertaking. He plainly cannot give undertakings on behalf of the companies and if it is due to the companies he is misleading the court."

Mr Heslop: "I am obliged. Obviously, any such undertaking would run into problems of preference and goodness knows what, if any of the companies concerned were interested in the debt. And the other consideration as to why one has to approach such an undertaking with considerable caution is, given the evidence not only of the other companies referred to but the current evidence about the petition out against Scribes West and the fact that one knows that a petition against Venables has only recently been settled, one has then to take into account the question of whether or not there are any personal guarantees given in relation to any of the corporate indebtedness because, if there are — one has not been told — then again the question of whether or not an undertaking to subordinate a claim would be valid in the event of a call on the guarantees leading to an insolvency or bankruptcy of Mr Venables is a matter again which raises problems. So, for those reasons certainly I am going to encourage your Lordship to take little account of the offer to subordinate and, in any event, that does not solve the problem even on the latest balance sheet.

"Going back to my chronology — the affidavit of Mr Sandy, of course, was concerned with the cross undertaking of damages. At that point there has been no order for costs made. On Monday the 24th of May — Mr Gold says, 'In Mr Sandy's affidavit sworn on the 21st of May, Mr Sandy refers to the financial position of Mr Venables. On behalf of all the Respondents, I put in issue the matter of the Petitioner's financial standing to support the cross-undertaking in damages given to the court.'

"So, the question of the Petitioner's financial standing was in issue, and that is material, not least to the weight your Lordship would give to evidence being put in this morning.

"Then, on Thursday the 25th of May, the Respondents (Sugar, Tottenham and Amshold), applied to the Vice-Chancellor to discharge the injunction (The 'Relief' granted to Terry on the afternoon he was dismissed). The Petitioner sought an adjournment to swear evidence in reply, not having done that, and there were various difficulties owing to religious festivals (Jewish Holidays adhered to by Venables' Solicitors) which made it impracticable, they said, to deal with the matter as quickly as the Petitioner (and Sugar, no doubt!) would have wanted, and then there was that Vacation, so the Vice-Chancellor adjourned the matter, the injunction staying in place meanwhile.

"The effective hearing of the application began on the 10th of June and that was before the Vice-Chancellor. It went over till the 14th June. Now, on that day my learned friend, Mr Mann, obtained leave to put before the court a further affidavit. It arose in this way. The Vice-Chancellor asked my learned friend, Mr Mann, during the course of his opening, he said 'Well, where is the evidence that your client is in a position to buy the Petitioner's shares in the event that he succeeds? Do not I need some evidence before the court' "

Mr Justice Harman: "That is Rule 9."

Mr Heslop: "That is absolutely right, which was a point we raised."

Mr Justice Harman: "It is mandatory, as far as I understand the rules."

Mr Heslop: "Yes, it is a mandatory requirement. Even dealing with Mr Sugar's shares there was a problem and the Vice-Chancellor wanted evidence. Mr Mann said it was not necessary at that stage. I made submissions on why it was necessary. Mr Mann then showed me in front of the court a letter which he was hoping would be satisfactory: I said it was not and on the Monday morning, an affidavit surfaced — and I want to take you to it: An affidavit of Mr Chapman."

Mr Justice Harman: "I have it and I have read this."

Mr Heslop: "I am obliged. Now, what you need to see here is that he apparently confirmed as you have seen from the latest evidence (he also apparently acts for the Petitioner personally) — he says that he is dealing with and he says: 'I can state from my own knowledge as the partner concerned with the corporate finance affairs of Mr Venables' Companies that, subject to contract and Stock Exchange approval and other statutory or corporate approval, the Petitioner is in a position with others to purchase all the shares of Amshold and Mr Sugar, its or his nominees, at the price which Mr Sugar has offered the Petitioner for his shares.'

"I do not accept that evidence in this form can possibly be what I would call credible evidence for the court to proceed on; it is so wishy washy."

Mr Justice Harman: "It is mere assertion."

Mr Heslop: "Well, it is and you know that hidden in the words 'subject to contract and Stock Exchange approval and statutory or corporate approval' there contains a welter of difficulty for anybody seeking to mount a bid — but the starting point is: who is providing the money? What I will be showing you is that, notwithstanding the deficiencies on this affidavit, this is a clear representation that the petitioning company would be good for acquiring the Respondents' shares. And what one sees in Mr Venables' affidavit when it comes to the 23rd of July is a resiling, in my submission, from that clear assertion, and one also sees from Mr Gold's further evidence, which I will go to in a moment, that Mr Venables very recently has apparently been seeking to solicit the help from at least one entrepreneur in support of his funding, which is consistent with, in my submission, the assertion of Mr Chapman that the funding is there. In any event, I will show you that in a moment.

"If I can go to Monday the 14th of June, the same day, the judgment of the Vice-Chancellor."

Mr Justice Harman: "One is plainly entitled to report the decision of the Vice-Chancellor, and counsel before the Vice-Chancellor can tell the Court what went on, but the exact words I do not think I can take until the learned Vice-Chancellor has approved them."

Mr Heslop: "Well, I would respectfully submit that it depends on the words and their context. One can see that sometimes there may have been misreporting, but one would have thought, given that this has been exhibited to Mr Gold's affidavit for some time, that if the...." (Interrupted again.)

Mr Justice Harman: "I am merely being cautious. I think that unapproved transcripts have to be treated with a considerable degree of caution."

Mr Heslop: "Even allowing for that, even if one accepts that as a proposition, the upshot of what the Vice-Chancellor said was that the Petitioner faced real difficulties in success on this petition, and so underwhelmed was the Vice-Chancellor by the strength of the Petitioner's case that that was a decisive factor in not granting the interlocutory relief sought. I am not going to read it because that would take too much time. Can I just direct your...." (Interrupted again.)

Mr Justice Harman: "I have read it through."

Mr Heslop: "Can I direct you to just a few points? The Vice-Chancellor says: 'The voluminous evidence extended in all to over two and a half thousand pages, being not untypical.' The point being that the Court had before it effectively the case and it was not a question of simply having just a little bit of evidence and time available. There was a lot of material that the Vice-Chancellor had before him. Then one can go to the balancing exercise, where he balanced the advantages to the Club of Mr Venables not being there. He says: 'If matters had rested there I might have been attracted by a course not urged by either side, which <u>would involve Mr Venables continuing to deal with football matters but not otherwise.</u> However, there was a further fact which has weighed with me. It concerns the prospects of success of these proceedings, in deciding whether and how to exercise the wide powers under the section, the Court would have regard not only to the company's constitution but also to equitable considerations arising from expectations created by dealings between its members. The Court would do what was just and equitable in all the circumstances. But there is a major difficulty facing Mr Venables.' And then he goes on to deal with what these major difficulties are, because the.... (Interrupted again.)

Mr Justice Harman: "I saw that and the whole inconsistency between the alleged oral arrangement (The one where Sugar was supposed to have promised Terry that his additional shareholding would provide no material advantage to Sugar, as they 'had an arrangement'), if it was made, it was wrongly suppressed for the public documents, where it would plainly have been material and proper."

Mr Heslop: "Absolutely. I took the Vice-Chancellor in some detail through mandatory cash offer documents and the rights issue document, which carried the usual responsibility, and there are express representations that all the arrangements and agreements were contained in the documents and these led to the legitimate expectation said to arise which, coming to its logical conclusion, would mean that he would be able to stay forever, as far as one can understand it, were not mentioned, and I took his Lordship to the two authorities on the point, as you may recall. One is Blue Arrow and the others is Ring Tyre and both of which, I am afraid it was me, argued unsuccessfully that, notwithstanding the representations made in a public company's documentation, there can be room for a residual expectation, and those submissions on both occasions were rejected by Mr Justice Vinelott and Mr Justice Peter Gibson. Where a man puts his name to a public document he simply cannot be allowed to argue, in my submission...." (Interrupted again.)

Mr Justice Harman: "It is the whole public process."

Mr Heslop: "Well, it has unthinkable consequences. He concludes: 'Even so, with the background of formal documents and published information, Venables' case that he or his company, Edennote, had been unfairly prejudiced as shareholders by the recent actions of Mr Sugar, is fraught with difficulty' and then he concludes that it is a matter for the Board, therefore, as to how to deal with Mr Venables. Certainly the thrust of it is very clear and it indicates the Vice-Chancellor did not think that the case even really passed the appropriate hurdle of being a sufficiently strong case. That when I come on to address your Lordship to the material factors to take into account on security for costs of applications, it is important: it is important for the Court to assess the strength of the Petitioner's case, or, in this case, the lack of it.

"Going back to my transcript: The Vice-Chancellor ordered that the costs not only of that hearing but of the two previous outings, that is the ex-parte application before Mr Justice Arden, May 14th, and my application on the 25th of May to discharge the injunction, should be paid, albeit not immediately, by the Petitioner. He gave directions on the following day which will have effect of an expedited trial. At the moment the trial I am told is to float to the 1st of November. The Petitioners I think have given an estimate of four weeks. My junior has given an estimate

350

(and I agree with it) of five weeks, and that is on the basis that we have not yet had discovery, we have expressly reserved the right to amend that, as it is our duty. But the implications of that plainly are that the costs of the trial itself are bound to be substantial, and you will recall that my application is being made for security up to the close of discovery and that I have expressly reserved my right to seek further security for the period up to trial, because at that point the Court will have a much better picture of how long the trial is going to last. There is no point at this stage guessing.

"Then, the 18th of June, a letter from the Respondents' solicitors to the Petitioner on a bill of costs and reply on the 21st — not accepting that there is any entitlement."

(Terry denying that he was responsible for Sugar's costs!)

Mr Justice Harman: "I have read that."

Mr Heslop: "I am obliged. The point is made that this is going to be done in tranches, if the Court grants security on this application...." (Interrupted again.)

(If the Judge accepts that Terry can proceed further but will have to pay money or securities to the Court then Terry wants to pay them off!)

Mr Justice Harman: "Mr Heslop, one point: On the letter it says that the order is not for taxation and payment forthwith. The form of that order was that they do pay costs and I thought that that carried an inevitable implication that they were to be taxed and paid forthwith?"

(Taxed: A term used by Courts and Solicitors to mean that costs submitted by solicitors will be 'taxed' i.e., assessed by an independent cost draughtsman before being approved by the Court.)

Mr Heslop: "It has not been taken by the Respondents — The point I think that one does have to make is that when in that paragraph — which is important and I am obliged — where it says, 'We do not believe that your client has a right to apply for security in respect of such costs' — whether or not they are payable forthwith, it is a misconception to think that you can only apply for costs to be incurred as opposed to costs which have been incurred and have been awarded in favour of the Respondents, even if not to be paid until due course. I do not know whether my

351

learned friend is going to argue that, but I need not for the moment take any more time on that point. Anyway, the upshot of the correspondence is that the request seeking to avoid this application was declined. Going back to my skeleton, on the 22nd of June the application for security for costs was launched. On Thursday, on the application of the Respondents, on the 24th of June, the Registrar gave direction and then the rest of this you know because I have taken your Lordship to it.

"My learned friend a moment ago emphasized that: 'The company 'will' be able to pay the costs.' There is a little bit more to it than that. The section provides that, 'Where in England and Wales the limited company is plaintiff in an action or other legal proceedings the court having jurisdiction in the matter <u>may</u>' — so it is self-evidently discretionary — 'if it appears by credible evidence that there is reason to believe that the company will be unable to pay the defendant's costs if successful in his defence, require sufficient security to be given for those costs and may stay all proceedings until the security is given.' So, one cannot just look at the words 'will be able to pay'; one has to look at it in the broader phrase: 'credible testimony that there is reason to believe.' Self-evidently, until costs have to in fact be paid you never actually know. What the Court has to do, is form a view based on the evidence before it when the application is made as to whether or not there is reason to believe that the company will be unable to pay the costs, and that is the appropriate test that I would invite you to bear in mind."

Mr Justice Harman: "It is 'reason to believe' not 'is convinced' or 'is satisfied' or anything like that. It is the lower test."

Mr Heslop: "Certainly. It is not a particularly onerous test to trigger effectively the Court's jurisdiction. The question then is whether or not as an exercise of discretion on the particular facts of the case security ought to be given. And I will be submitting that on any view of this evidence, including the latest evidence put in, that certainly there is credible testimony before you that there is reason to believe that the Company will be unable to pay the Defendants' costs. Just to get the point out of the way, I think there can be no dispute about that and I was not going to deal with that further unless my learned friend sought to raise it.

"If I can then turn to the evidence, there is one preliminary point to make which is important. If you could go to Mr Gold's second affidavit, he says, 'On this basis it is a matter of concern to the Respondents that there is no up to date independently audited financial information on the Petitioner. The draft accounts show a company that is in serious financial trouble. On this basis I believe that the Petitioner will be unable to pay the Respondents' costs which have already incurred and the costs which will be incurred should this matter proceed to trial.' And he goes on to say, 'It appears from the matter that I have referred to herein that the Petitioner is insolvent.'

"Now, just pausing there plainly as matter of logic if the Company (Edennote), is insolvent it will not be able to pay the costs, but is not essential on an application to show that a company is insolvent; what one is really looking for is to see whether it has got the wherewithal when the time comes to pay the costs. Given Mr Gold's conclusion, one would have expected in the evidence in opposition to see Mr Venables saying 'Mr Gold is wrong. For the following reasons this company is not insolvent and, furthermore, it will be able to pay the Respondents' costs in the event that they are successful in the future' and so on. The first and perhaps the vital point is that you will not find such assertion in the evidence of Mr Venables or any other evidence filed on his behalf. If I have missed something my learned friend, Mr Steinfeld will tell you, but the fact of the matter is that the thrust of Mr Venables' evidence is to seek to make points on the particular accounts in order to ameliorate (Improve, make better), what otherwise is their rather unfortunate effect, but nowhere does he go on oath — and I invite you to draw the conclusion that he cannot — to assert that he is able to pay these costs.

Having made that general point, could I then turn to the '92 accounts. Your Lordship is not in fact given an adequate explanation for the delay. Mr Pottesman, you will recall from the affidavit seeking an adjournment on the last occasion, talked about the difficulties with Landhurst but, in any event, when you look at them they show a loss and an excess of liabilities over assets. What I wanted to do was just to draw your attention to a number of facets of this. Page 1, under results and dividends, the group profit amounts to £290,000. That is, in my submission, purely an accountant's statement, because that is consolidating the results of the Company, Tottenham Hotspur Plc, into this Company, and you know that, whether or not one can properly consolidate, is apart from anything else a matter not only of having an appropriate shareholding...." (Interrupted again.)

Mr Justice Harman: "Active involvement...."

Mr Heslop: "Significant management influence, I believe is the relevant requirement."

Mr Justice Harman: "Anyhow, it is purely accountancy."

Mr Heslop: "Exactly. It is not accepted that it is appropriate to consolidate, at least now and whatever it was in '92. But the important point in terms of cash or one's ability to settle debts — it is simply neither here or there. What one must look for is the balance sheet and, indeed, the cash flow position and the overall financial position of the company concerned. On page 1, you will see Mr Venables and Mr Yazman are the two current Directors so far as one can tell. I think the other three gentlemen are all partners or associated with Mr Venables' solicitors. It refers to the acquisition of the shares, movement in fixed assets. It is difficult to square the treatment here of the shares of these fixed assets with the way in which it is now sought to suggest that they are — namely, some sort of trading stock."

Mr Justice Harman: "Reclassify them as a trading stock."

Mr Heslop: "Yes. Then it refers to post-balance sheet events. Now, given this is the 23rd of July, '93, when these accounts were prepared, it is a bit startling to refer to the entry into a management agreement with the Club but not to refer to the events of the 14th of May which involved the termination of that contract and subsequent matters, but there we are. You can see that the two year bank loan is to be replaced by a two year term loan repayable on the 31st of October, and I take that to be a reference to the Bank Liechtenstein loan secured (By Terry's holding in Tottenham Plc). Then there is a note as to how the accountants find it possible to consolidate, which I am not concerned about, although it might be thought to be a little odd.

"Anyway, on these figures the consolidated balance sheet is irrelevant, in my submission. The balance sheet shows a deficit of assets and liabilities of £387,000 — and one will come on in a moment to deal with the current figures. The basis of accounting is that the Directors have indicated their continued financial support of the company for the foreseeable future. That is not unimportant any more now than it was then because, of course, that then depends on Mr Venables' personal financial status, and the evidence indicates that certainly a number of his other corporate ventures were in dire trouble and who knows what implications would follow for him personally in the event that Scribes West, for example, were to go into insolvent liquidation. There is a point said by Mr Venables, that it is impossible to deal with goodwill and write it off in an appropriate way. It is a short point but Mr Gold in his second affidavit, disagrees with that, on the basis of advice from Touche Ross. He says that it is certainly possible and he gives a figure, as you may recall, of £200,000, which it would be thought appropriate to write off. It is not accepted that there is any difficulty. The effect of not writing off is favourable in terms of trying to present the position of the company.''

(Not 'writing off' the goodwill means that the assets of the Company are overstated. Goodwill is usually written off after it is paid for, sometimes over a period of time.)

''Then there is the loss of £398,000 which you do not get out of the consolidated figures. Then over the page, the market value was approximately £3.3. million at the 31st of March and that is based on a 94p valuation. The important point about that is that for the purposes of these accounts and considering the company's position, and indeed the '93 accounts which have also surfaced — my learned friend has accepted that if market price is lower than cost, that is the figure to work on, and that immediately leads to the valuation. There are just a few points to make about the valuation. The assumptions made by them, on the basis of which they can then value a million shares (albeit with this hefty discount) themselves merit some attention because they are assumptions which do not prevail in the current circumstances. It says in that letter: 'There is little doubt that in the current circumstances where the dispute is ongoing it would be extremely difficult to identify any potential purchasers of the shares. Indeed, the market side (The size of a block of shares that could reasonably be disposed of on the Stock Exchange) at the moment is a mere thousand shares, indicating that the price is merely a basis for discussion. It follows that only when the dispute is resolved one way or another could we envisage such a block (Terry's assumed one million unencumbered), being placed. At that point in time, assuming there was then certainty as to both the shareholding, the ownership and the management direction of the company, and on the assumption that some indication would be given as to the current financial performance of the company, it should be possible to identify potential purchasers, although you will appreciate that football clubs are rather a special type of investment. They are not a natural investment for major institutions but, with that qualification, given a certain amount of notice, a matter of weeks, buyers could be found for such a block of shares.' One has to take that rather into account because it basically means, certainly at the moment, those assumptions are not met and, accordingly, even the discounted valuation must be regarded with considerable scepticism. I think what...." (Interrupted again.)

Mr Justice Harman: "I think what they say is, 'Today we couldn't sell it.' "

Mr Heslop: "That is what they are saying. There is no price today, that is the problem, that is what they are really saying. No price or a negligible one. And that only when the matter is entirely resolved, on the assumptions contained here, do they think given time that they might be able to find a buyer. It is my submission that the discount down to 71.25p, far from being a conservative valuation, as my learned friend has suggested — I think can be regarded with a good deal of scepticism, for this reason: that to buy a 22 per cent block of shares in this company.... (Interrupted again.)

Mr Justice Harman: "This is a million."

Mr Heslop: "Yes, a million, but to buy a million shares in a company which represents the percentage it does without certainly.... (Interrupted again.)

Mr Justice Harman: "It is about 8 per cent, is it not?"

Mr Heslop: "I think it is, yes, without a seat on the Board it is

the sort of investment which is unlikely to appeal to investors —
not only major institutions, self-evidently, but pretty unlikely to
appeal to any entrepreneur who might be interested in investing
in a football club.''

(He fails to add 'particularly as Alan Sugar is the Chairman
and main shareholder', which in some people's eyes might also
prevent them from being interested in buying one million shares,
or just 8 per cent of Tottenham.)

"So, the fact of the matter is that, far from being a conservative
valuation, I would submit that this is really a generous valuation.
But even if you did not accept that, even on these figures it has a
significant impact immediately on the financial position of the
company.

"The only other points to make on the '92 accounts — this is
the Bank Liechtenstein, as I understand it: bank overdraft/trade
creditors £249,000. Those are not identified but certainly on
these accounts would be difficult to see where his loan fitted in.
All one is told at that stage is that Mr Venables under amounts
falling due over one year, other loans: £1.473 million. The
evidence that has been given to the Court — if your Lordship
goes to Mr Venables' affidavit, Mr Venables says, 'As at the 31st of
March, '92, £1.473 million was liable to the Petitioner
(Edennote), with a liability to myself and companies which I
control, incurred by reason of my and those companies have
loaned to the Petitioner a substantial part of the money needed
to acquire shares in Tottenham. The position was the same at the
31st of March, '93 and continues to be the same today.'

"So, on the 23rd of July it is being asserted that the £1.473 is
a loan from Mr Venables and companies which he controls. If
you could go to the latest affidavit, 'Under creditors falling due
after more than one year, analyzed as follows: from '92 figures
being audited. Furthermore, it is our belief that Mr Venables'
loan will exceed a million pounds in the final '93 accounts,
although we can give no guarantee of this' and they then break
it down and one can see there that, in contrast to what was said
on the 23rd of July, the 1.473 figure given in the 31st of March
accounts does not involve apparently loans to Mr Venables and
the companies controlled by him; it appears to involve a loan at

the balance sheet date of £1.223 million odd to Mr Venables personally and a separate loan of £250,000 to Mr Yazman. Given that it is said at the 31st of March, 1992 that Mr Yazman was owed a quarter of a million, one has to go back to the '92 accounts and say, 'Well, if he is....'' (Interrupted again.)

Mr Justice Harman: "How do you reconcile this with other statements?"

Mr Heslop: "You cannot...! That is my point. And worse, if there can be anything worse, it is difficult to reconcile that in terms of what is said under other notes. The fact of the matter is that one or other of the explanations has to be wrong, and you are faced with SWORN EVIDENCE from Mr Venables that the entire debt (£1.473 mill) is owed to him or companies controlled by him, and then the assertion contains in Chapman's letter which says 'In our belief Mr Venables' loan, one cannot help noticing....' " (Interrupted again.)

Mr Justice Harman: "What this shows is that of that £1.473 million, not a ha'penny is due to any company controlled by Mr Venables, contrary to his oath. Certainly a quarter of a million of that amount is due to Mr Yazman."

Mr Heslop: "Yes...."

Mr Justice Harman: "It makes his oath a little difficult."

Mr Heslop: "Well, I think it points him in an impossible position. One sees from his latest affidavit when it now says: 'I confirm that the amount owed to me by Edennote at the 31st March 1993, was £1.233 million, odd, as stated by Chapman's. The current indebtedness of Edennote is therefore less than a million pounds. He fiddles around with detail. He does not deal with the obvious point, and that is that what he is now saying is inconsistent with earlier sworn evidence. That leaves a matter of considerable concern.

"What is not shown is Mr Venables' personal wealth. He shows loans to and from Edennote and indebtedness to other companies that he controls, some of whom we know to have winding-up orders against them or at least applications to wind up. He in all cases is both Director and shareholder. Examining the accounts Mr Venables is owed £50,000 net, and this appears to be in the figure of £175,000 shown as outstanding debtors. We do not even have audited 1993 accounts. We have not been given sufficient information to be able to rely on these figures.

Mr Justice Harman: "Since the 1992 accounts show these as the only assets, the recoverability MUST be important."

Mr Heslop: "My submission is that the recoverability is in doubt, given that we don't know the companies controlled by him, and from whence these assets derive. We are not satisfied that he has not chosen to identify these companies which are said to be the debtors and to their standing. He has not advised us to whether there are personal implications for him in these companies, particularly those that are insolvent or are about to go into liquidation.

"May we examine the Bank Liechtenstein loan? Edennote obtained 3.5 million shares and that 1.5 million of those are unencumbered. A company search shows that only 381,000 shares are unencumbered. Chubb Insurance Company accepted the liability against collateral of the shares for Bank Liechtenstein from Norfina, who originally advanced the loan, and their financial document states: 'All monies and the discharge of their obligations and liabilities now or hereafter due owed or incurred by Chubb under the insurance policy as made between Chubb and Edennote and the counter indemnity executed in favour of Bank Liechtenstein, Edennote as beneficial owner has charged to Chubb by way of first fixed charge, 2 million shares in Tottenham Hotspur Plc... ALL THE COMPANY'S RIGHTS TITLES AND INTEREST TO AND IN ALL STOCKS SHARES, BONDS, NOTES WARRANTS AND SECURITIES OF ANY KIND WHATEVER, WHETHER MARKETABLE OR OTHERWISE, THE PURCHASE OF OR SUBSCRIPTIONS FOR WHICH BY OR WHOLLY HAS BEEN FINANCED BY EDENNOTE OR WHICH HAVE BEEN DELIVERED TO OR TO THE ORDER OF CHUBB, INCLUDING WITHOUT LIMITATION ANY SECURITIES HELD BY OR ON BEHALF OF NOMINEES...."

Mr Heslop is still speaking.

(There you have it.... Even though Chubb were directly placing a charge over only two million of the shares, they were effectively requiring an authority over ALL the assets of Edennote.... Terry therefore, had NO unencumbered assets, including the

1.233 million shares that he offered to subordinate, and which he claimed were not encumbered.)

Mr Heslop then reads out further clauses which include Chubb's rights over dividends received from the shares, and all income received, interest and other income whether paid or payable. Even Terry's income into Edennote was charged...!

He then suggests that Architect, Mr Yazman's interest in Edennote is mysterious. He loans Edennote £250,000 in exchange for a like amount of shares, without interest being charged on the loan. He is described as a director of Edennote Plc.

Then he turns to the dealings with Landhurst Leasing, who claim that they are not owed money by Edennote, because their loan was owed by someone or some company other than the Petitioner.... (NOTE: The Channel 4 Dispatches programme.) Later he speaks of the administrators of Landmark (in liquidation) not having a liability to Edennote. He states that if Edennote did owe Landhurst money, that would have a serious effect on their balance sheet. Their liabilities would be greater. He also states that 'no income stream' has entered Terry's financial picture. Then he refers to the dividend of £106,000 that Terry received from his sharcholding in Tottenham and the likelihood of receiving a similar amount this year. Mr Heslop points out that the dividend is subordinated to Chubb under the agreement (noted above).... He further mentions that £200,000 in interest to Bank Liechtenstein has accrued up to the end of the 1992 March 31st accounts and by July 1993 stands at £227,000.

"The Petitioner is also facing legal costs of 'at least £300,000 accrued to date'. In addition there is a liability now to Bank Liechtenstein of £2.6 millions, and that does not include current interest...."

(It could be reasonably assumed that Terry had to borrow more than he originally loaned from Norfina to settle their debt which was in arrears. Often there are 'penalties' of not only accrued interest but for settlement of the debt before a certain period.)

Heslop then suggests that Terry has personally guaranteed the Landhurst Loan, which Channel 4 described as 1 million pounds, and that Terry's financial position had worsened because of having no income since the end of the financial year for his companies, 31st March, and his final dismissal from Tottenham on the 14th June 1993.

"As we regard the Petitioner's evidence as being weak rather than a sham, we submit that you have the discretion to seek security from the Petitioner in order to secure the eventual costs of the Respondents."

Finally Heslop refers to an offer made by Venables of £450,000 to Sugar for the costs, which result from the offer made to Terry by Sugar for the termination of his contract way back in May. That had lapsed, and was made by Sugar in order to prevent the litigation which has resulted. In other words, no guarantee of compensation for the loss of two and a half years unfulfilled contract was now on the table.

Had Terry taken that, everything that has since happened including some of the cruellest accusations and allegations against him and others, could have been avoided.

After Heslop refers to Terry's ultimate intention of buying out Sugar if he wins and at that time having the means to do so, rather than at the present.

Mr Justice Harman: "One of the best encapsulations of this matter is contained in another case. On the one hand one must not use the section to stifle litigation, that would be oppressive, but on the other hand it is oppressive to a defendant to be sued by a insolvent company."

Heslop then says that Terry had threatened an action against Sugar for wrongful dismissal but that they were unaware of any proceedings, despite the newspaper headlines, and that such an action would be strongly contested. He asks the Court for security of £335,000 being his costs to date and some that he will actually incur in the future, and with leave to increase that amount should further costs be incurred. The 'tax Draughtsman' had indicated that he would agree a figure of £265,000. The Judge has his discretion.

Then Barrister Steinfeld rose to speak for Mr Venables and Edennote Plc.

Mr Steinfeld: "There are altogether three matters which you have to determine.

"The first is whether your Lordship has the jurisdiction to

make the order sought.

"Secondly having been satisfied on that, whether in all the circumstances, security ought to be ordered.

"Lastly, what the quantum of the security should be.

"Can I deal with the question of solvency? You have to decide that by reason of credible testimony that there is reason to believe that the Company will be UNABLE to pay the defendant's costs. It is clearly upon us to satisfy the Court in that regard. My submission on that can be put very briefly. That on the latest evidence, the indication is that Mr Venables agreeing to subordinate his loan, bearing in mind that he lost his petition against dismissal, he is now free to sell his shares. So, by the time of a proposed full trial (October/November 1993), there is no reason to suggest that he will be unable to pay the costs.

"We recognise that there is an apparent discrepancy in Mr Venables evidence. Looking at the point, we now see that the discrepancy and that being the figure of £1,473,000 is in fact give or take the figure referred to in the draft accounts, under 'Other Loans'...."

Mr Justice Harman: " I have found it easier to use your exhibit which you produced this morning, the letter from Chapman's on the 29th July, because it has got all the figures very neatly set out."

Mr Steinfeld: "What I wanted to show you was where the amount figures in the 1992 accounts. The notes to the accounts are what I wanted to show your Lordship. You will see under 'Creditors' amounts falling due over one year, 'other loans' and that is where the figure comes from."

Mr Justice Harman: "THAT DOES TELL ONE A TERRIFIC LOT...OTHER LOANS!"

Mr Steinfeld: " Your Lordship sees 'other loans' in which Mr Venables is both director and shareholder of the companies, and that amount is £53,000."

Mr Justice Harman: "Borrowings are £53,000, Loans are described as £112,000."

Mr Steinfeld: "All that I can tell you is this.... That when Mr Venables swore his affidavit he had wrongly assumed that the £1.473 million was a reference to the loans that he had made

PERSONALLY combined with the loans that his Companies had made."

Mr Justice Harman: "Grossly careless."

Mr Steinfeld: "It is careless. What Venables had not appreciated was that that figure was composed of his personal lendings which at 31st March stood at just over £1.2 million, and that Mr Yazman's loan of £250,000 were dealt with."

(Very simply: Terry and his other companies had lent Edennote £1.473 millions, including Yazman's quarter of a million. Take his loan out and you are left with £1.2 millions approx.)

Mr Justice Harman: "All you are telling me is that his evidence is not worth the paper that it is written on!"

Mr Steinfeld: "I am saying that he made a mistake...." (Interrupted again.)

Mr Justice Harman: "It is totally inaccurate on every possible foot."

Mr Steinfeld: "I have given you an explanation for that discrepancy."

Mr Justice Harman: "It does not give me great confidence in Mr Venables' financial abilities."

Mr Steinfeld: "If I may say so, I am not here to extol his financial abilities."

Mr Justice Harman: "I have got to rely on that because of his assertions in his affidavits."

Mr Steinfeld: "Well, HE HAS NEVER ASSERTED HIMSELF TO BE A PERSON WITH GREAT FINANCIAL ABILITIES!"

(Coming from Terry's own Counsel, that really says it all! Perhaps there is little wonder in Sugar wishing to grab the reins for himself under the expert operational control of Colin Sandy, Tottenham's Financial Director....)

Steinfeld contin.... "He has great abilities but they do not lie in his FINANCIAL ABILITIES and these sort of errors can occur when evidence is being prepared, perhaps in something of a hurry. I apologise."

Mr Justice Harman: "A hurry...? You've had an extension from the 23rd July!"

Mr Steinfeld: "Well, it is still not a great deal of time. Be that as it may, an error was made. Your Lordship may well say that he cannot give much credence to...." (Interrupted again.)

Mr Justice Harman: "You are telling me that I should not place much credence on Mr Venables' evidence, are you not?"

Mr Steinfeld: "NO I AM NOT...! What I am saying is that it was unreliable in so far as it referred to the £1.473 millions as being a liability which included the liabilities of the companies. It plainly did not. To that extent it is unreliable, yes, the figure is RIGHT (in total).... Mr Venables is owed well in excess of a million pounds. Then his agreement to subordinate that figure to the claims of all creditors, including the Respondents, transforms the balance sheet."

Mr Justice Harman: "If I have got to draw a hypothetical balance sheet as at, say, Christmas Eve, when you have just got Judgment, I would have to change the valuation of the Tottenham Hotspur shares. I have got to alter it by reducing the liabilities by £1.134 million, being the subordinated amount of Mr Venables' loans. I have then got to increase the liabilities by the costs on your own side to the end of a proposed four week trial and I have got to increase it by the liabilities for costs to the Respondents at the end of the trial. You tell me that having re-drawn that balance sheet, I shall find out that there is a surplus...?"

Mr Steinfeld: "Well, one obviously would have to go carefully into the figures. There is a further factor that you have not mentioned. You will have to assess the worth of the value of Tottenham shares at that time."

Mr Justice Harman: "I have to take the best evidence of that from the stockbrokers. I may have my own views. I have also got to add in, on the liabilities side, the interest accruing on the Bank loan of £2 million, which will not have been offset by income."

Mr Steinfeld: "Then you have to assess the likelihood of dividends."

(This is all conjecture. The assumptions in the first instance were that Terry eventually won the trial, in which case surely Sugar would be responsible for the costs. Then the Judge assumes that Terry will hold on to his shares until then and does not pay any interest in the meantime, obviously because Terry has declared no form of income. Should Terry sell before October/November, then he would forfeit the right to buy out Sugar....)

Then Steinfeld turns to the expected dividend perpetrated by the undisclosed profits of Tottenham at that time. The Judge suggests that it is not for public disclosure and he would have to clear the court…. Steinfeld suggests that he works on a certain figure, indicated in the board minutes, deducts what Sugar and the Board want to retain in reserve, and then calculates what Terry as a 21.8 per cent shareholder would receive. Steinfeld agrees that the amount may not leave him with any surplus but goes a long way towards the costs and refutes the claim that Edennote will be unable to pay the costs.

AT THE TIME THE YEAR END FIGURES FOR TOTTENHAM HOTSPUR Plc GROUP WERE NOT KNOWN. AT THE TIME OF WRITING WE ARE ABLE TO DETAIL THE ITEMS RELEVANT TO THIS CASE:

OPERATING PROFIT, YEAR ENDING 31st MAY 1993	£3,158,000
ADD INTEREST RECEIVED OR RECEIVABLE DURING THE YEAR	£203,000
TAXATION: PAYABLE	£305,000
PROFIT AVAILABLE FOR RETENTION AND DISTRIBUTION	£3,056,000
DIVIDENDS	£801,000
PROFIT RETAINED IN RESERVE	£2,255,000

THE DIVIDEND FOR THE YEAR AMOUNTED TO £801,000

TERRY DID NOT SELL HIS SHARES UNTIL AFTER THE FINANCIAL YEAR END. THEREFORE HE RECEIVED IN TOTAL, GROSS, £174,618… BY WAY OF HIS OWNERSHIP OF 3,542,938 SHARES, EQUAL TO 21.8 PER CENT.

TAKE OFF TAX AT, SAY, 30 PER CENT AND HE WOULD HAVE RECEIVED, NET, £122,233.

Not enough for his own costs and not enough to pay Sugar's as well, should Terry lose this case!

Mr Steinfeld: "The fortunes of Tottenham at Christmas Eve are not known, and therefore we cannot evaluate the shares at that time. They could go up and they could go down. Your Lordship knows the Government health warning on stocks and shares.

"May I draw your attention to the letter of offer sent by Mr Sugar to Mr Venables of the 6th May. It is stated as being Private and Confidential, and is subject to contract without prejudice. You will recall that the Petitioner was criticised for not mentioning that letter in the ex-parte hearing of the 14th May. Basically, Mr Sugar makes an offer of just under £3 million, the purchase price paid by Mr Venables.

'I will enter into contract and pay for all your shares, subject to getting Stock Exchange clearance.'

"The fact still remains that Mr Sugar made this offer on the 6th May. Mr Sugar by all accounts is not a person who can be described as 'OTHER THAN A REALISTIC BUSINESSMAN', and he was making this offer and it does provide an indication which your Lordship is entitled to take into account."

Mr Justice Harman: "A special person.... Yes, because he wanted to get rid of all this row and not to have all this hassle. It does make him special at this time."

Mr Steinfeld: "I can see that point, but he was nevertheless prepared to offer that as a...." (Interrupted again.)

Mr Justice Harman: "Mr Steinfeld, I entirely see that he made the offer and it seems to me that it would be mad not to think that on the 6th May Mr Sugar was keen to avoid all the row and all the costs and the public nonsense that goes on in these cases and to get rid of it. For that reason he would make that offer, and it seems to me entirely understandable and natural and would have a value to him; but once the row started the value has gone."

Mr Steinfeld: "Could I just make one further point and that is with regard to why the auditors have felt it right to treat the shares as no longer being a fixed asset but as a current asset.... First of all, these are draft accounts and they have not yet been accepted, although they are being shown, hot, as it were, off the auditors' press. They have not been accepted by Mr Venables as being necessarily the form of accounts that will be presented to Companies House. Your Lordship should not infer that that indicates any less of an adherence by Mr Venables to his stated policy of wishing to retain those shares, and, indeed, TO BUY OUT MR SUGAR'S SHARES IF THE COURT GIVES HIM THAT ORDER."

Mr Justice Harman: "The trouble being Mr Steinfeld, that you pressed me to let this evidence in on the grounds that it showed an improvement in current assets...." (Interrupted.)

Mr Steinfeld: "I DID NOT! I asked your Lordship to let the evidence in to show what — I used the word 'current' in a different sense, meaning the current state of...." (Interrupted again.)

Mr Justice Harman: "NO...! You referred to the current assets and the change from a £2 million deficiency to a million credit. That can only be achieved if the shares are held as a trading stock for disposal."

Mr Steinfeld: "That is right, but that really is not a matter of any materiality: Your Lordship is not concerned with the treatment of assets in the balance sheet. Your Lordship is only concerned with the overall financial position. I was saying to your Lordship that he should not draw any inferences in regard to Mr Venables' intention in relation to those shares."

Mr Justice Harman: "I am not concerned with his intentions. I expect auditors to present accounts on the instructions of the Directors of the Company."

Steinfeld then explained that the movement of the assets was made only because it was not yet determined as to whether Terry would be able to purchase Sugar's shares and that on June the 14th he had lost his fight to be reinstated.

Steinfeld then pointed out that in a ruling by the Master of the Rolls, the important word when deciding on security of costs is the word 'may', indicating that Mr Justice Harman was not obliged to do so. Mr Justice Harman then suggested that he preferred that ruling or the balance that was decided by another judge, Mr Justice Megarry.

Steinfeld suggested that whilst, of course it is unfair for any defendant to face proceedings where if he wins he may have difficulty in recovering his costs from the other side, that nevertheless is a feature of litigation. Mr Justice Harman replies, there is no jurisdiction to protect defendants pursued by wholly impecunious individuals against fairly hopeless actions.

Mr Justice Harman refers then to Lord Denning, who said, 'Whether the company has a reasonably good prospect of success'.

Steinfeld says, "My Lord that in this particular case you do not have adequate material to come to a view one way or the other.

We say that Mr Sugar has suborned (induce, especially in cases of bribery to commit perjury or other crime)...the interests of the Company to his own personal interests or to the interests of his major public company of which he is the Chief Executive.

"My Lord, could I just perhaps in the five minutes before the adjournment make one further point in relation to discretion. It is one actually amerged in the Board minute. Never, in our submission, could a case like this be more regarded than a straightforward dispute between shareholders. If you would turn to that minute, and in particular the line 'Mr Sugar pointed out that the costs would be much greater': and those costs have been entirely financed by the Company (Tottenham Plc) and will continue to be so financed. If I may refer to a judgment that you yourself made in 1991. You referred to whether or not costs that had been incurred constituted a misapplication of company funds. The declaration was that every payment made out of funds of the company, being a payment of the costs or expenses with a view to financing any defence or opposition to the petition presented by the plaintiff, involved a breach by the defendants in the action who were both Directors in the company and Respondents to the petition. This under the articles of association of the company and in breach of their fiduciary (given in trust), duty as Directors."

Steinfeld then states that in his view that expressed the law as it exists and that Alan Sugar is showing a wrongful application of the Company's funds.

"In the present circumstances, the Company (Tottenham) financed the first application on the 14th May. That must be a wrongful application of funds. This application is not made in that sense with clean hands. All the costs, not just that part which pertains to the Company, have been heaped onto the Company and now security is sought for those costs, and the Court ought to say: 'We will have none of that!' Of course if the application is dismissed, Mr Sugar may well come back to the Court and offer to pay his part."

Mr Steinfeld promised that he would only be taking up 20 minutes or so of the Court's further time before Mr Heslop stood up, and the Court adjourned for a break.

After the break Mr Steinfeld quoted several similar cases but made the specific point that demanding security might hinder the case of the Petitioner, and in particular, that this petitioner was being hindered directly by the fact that it was Sugar and the companies being 'defended' by him that was causing such hindrance....

"If the Plaintiff had to provide security for the costs it might have to abandon the action altogether because of its impecuniosity and then the Judge had to take all the relevant facts into consideration. Mr Venables is a small company making a claim where the full backing of the Company itself (Tottenham) is providing funds to finance the defence."

Referring to another case, that of Parkinsons, the Counsellor stressed that in that case the Judge was not able to direct a security of more than £1,500. He further stressed that Mr Sugar, utilising Tottenham's funds, must not be allowed to use that financial strength to put unfair pressure on Venables.

"We say that Petitioner, Edennote Plc, has at all times been known by the Respondents to be a company with its sole assets until May of this year, two assets only: One, its shares in Tottenham, and, two, its management agreement with the Club. The management agreement which provided the sole income for the Company to live on was cut off, and we say improperly and oppressively. That leaves the shares, which either must be traded or be 'charged'. At the moment sale of the shares is virtually impossible: Any sale by Mr Venables of these shares will undermine his ultimate claims and objectives. Now is a very bad time given the state of the Company to try to sell those shares."

Mr Steinfeld then described how there was an undisputed partnership between Venables and Sugar and tried to direct the Judge into believing that had the two protagonists not bought their shares through their respective companies, the case would be between two men only. The Judge suggested that the advantages of purchasing shares through the companies were accepted but that there are also disadvantages which Venables must accept.

"I think on the ground that if you make a bed you have to lie

369

on it...."

Mr Steinfeld then suggested, coming to the end of his submissions, that Edennote has a substantial claim against Tottenham and that the Judge should bear that in mind, outside of the offer to subordinate Edennote's shareholding. He refers to the letter sent to Terry by Sugar offering him the sum of £450,000 in full and final settlement of his cancelled contract. The letter was sent on the 6th May, but we know that Heslop had previously suggested that the offer was in order to prevent the proceedings which had taken place in May and June, and effectively was then withdrawn. Steinfeld ignores this point.

Sugar's letter goes on to say: "No doubt you will wish to consult with your advisers on this matter. I would point out to you that part of this offer of purchasing your shares is NOT AN ENTITLEMENT TO SOMEONE WHO IS ASKED TO LEAVE HIS EMPLOYMENT, and it is this part of my offer which I would point out to you is the most valuable in the settlement."

(We have stated throughout this book that even without the advantage of retrospective knowledge, surely Terry MUST have considered acceptance a better path than the one which has resulted in almost his total demise in credibility and employability. Had he accepted that offer to purchase his shares, held by Edennote, and the cash against the loss of contract with his Company, he would still have had the opportunity to mount a claim for losses, damages, on the basis of his personal employment contract. Sugar's offer only being in respect of the contract with Edennote.)

Mr Steinfeld then takes the Judge to 'quantum' the amount of costs that would need to be secured if the Judge deems that necessity. A bill of £340,000 had been submitted by Herbert Smith, Sugar's Solicitors. Steinfeld points out that the 'Taxation Cost Master' suggests that he would have difficulty in justifying the amount of time charged and recognises also, that there are some duplications on the bill. He refers to a comment that Counsel is much in demand and are charging above the standard rate at these times.... The Judge confirms....

"To use a vernacular expression...a party is entitled to have a Rolls-Royce, but cannot expect the other side to pay the costs of a Rolls-Royce. I hope that Mr Heslop will not be the slightest bit insulted if I say that that is the present case."

Mr Steinfeld submits that the amount of costs should be limited to £265,000....

Mr Steinfeld apologises for over-running the 20 minutes he asked for and gives way to Rolls-Royce, Mr Heslop, the Barrister who represents Mr Sugar, Tottenham Hotspur Plc and Amshold Ltd.

Mr Heslop: "My Lord, there are just a few points.... The costs of litigation.... There are two answers: One of principle and one of fact. Because of the way that it has been put I would rather turn to the facts first.... No bill has yet been submitted to any of the Respondents by Herbert Smith. Mr Sugar has accepted that he will take advice from Herbert Smith as to the 'apportionment' of any bill sent as between the respondents. Advice that has been given is that costs of the Petition representing a dispute between shareholders are in principle, costs that must be borne by the individual shareholders, and Mr Sugar and not by Tottenham Hotspur Plc. In contrast, the Company may well have a legitimate interest in having an injunction which was made against it and had an impact on it. It may well be that a proportion of the costs of the injunction can properly be attributed to the Company."

Mr Steinfeld asks whether any money has been paid to Herbert Smith, 'on account', even though no bill has yet been submitted.... Mr Heslop confirmed that no monies had as yet been paid by Tottenham or anyone else.... The Judge expressed his relief of that as he had been worried by the insinuations of Steinfeld that all the costs were being met by Tottenham.

Mr Heslop then pointed to a number of other cases similar to the one being heard, and where it was considered that it was not necessarily improper for the Company to pick up the costs. He referred to Blue Arrow which involved Mr Berry, who is currently on the Tottenham Board. "Accordingly," he says, "there is simply nothing in the point that my learned friend has made."

Mr Heslop, after further references to points of law in previous cases:

"The real problem, leaving aside the subordination, is that if you look at the '92 accounts, and the '93 draft accounts for

371

Edennote Plc, the shares which have been offered as security do NOT in fact secure the loans made to the Company. One does not like to emphasise that too much, but it has got to be said that at the end of the day, a crisis would be caused were the security holders... (He means Chubb and Bank Liechtenstein) "...to take a view on that."

(If you recall those two companies have tied up all the income, dividends and virtually every asset 'owned' by Edennote in the agreement even though they have taken a direct charge on only £2 million.)

"That is a matter that is outside the Petitioner to influence. It is a matter for Chubb or the Bank and even if they took a different view, THEN ALL THE SUBORDINATION IN THE WORLD COULD NOT HELP...! Inevitably, extra shares would have to be sold or some other funds would have to be injected. Much of the misfortune has been brought on Edennote by other events and the income cut-off. In fact that would only generate an extra £12,500 per month, which is relatively modest in relation to the overall woes that the Company appears to be facing. My learned friend again used in support of his submission that the actions of the Respondents (Sugar) could have contributed to the difficulties of the Petitioner (Venables), and then he said it would be unfair since there were only the shares and income from the management agreement, now terminated, if shares had to be sold. The point about that is one does wonder first of all how the Petitioner's existing costs have been or will be funded."

(Does he know...? Is he guessing...? We know that in August, a little after this final hearing, how Terry paid his solicitors!)

"One assumes that if my learned friend is right, it will not come out of the sale of shares, and the fact of the matter is that there is nothing in this application which requires shares to be sold. It is a matter for Mr Venables to decide how he can fund any order for security, but if in contrast to that it leads to a sale of shares, which is the fall-back relief, the order that his shares are bought out, there is no reason why in appropriate circumstances, the Court cannot take into account all of this matter under its general jurisdiction.... None of these points in my submission, the evidence shows that there is good reason to believe that

Edennote will not be able to pay the bill, and why an order should not be made. There is no argument regarding the fact of whether Mr Venables owned his shares personally. The fact is a company is a creature purely of statute....

My Lord, those are my submissions in reply. It is my overall submission, that this a case more than made out. The discretion of the Court should be exercised in favour of the Respondents and the amount should be sufficient to protect the Respondents from what otherwise may be the consequences, that it will not get the costs incurred...."

BRIEFLY, THE JUDGMENT:

The Mr Justice Harman: "Substantial evidence was sworn by Mr Venables. The Respondents replied to that evidence. The evidence contained substantial criticism of and doubts about the financial status of Edennote Plc and Mr Terry Venables with reference to the lack of any audited accounts for 1992 and the draft accounts for 1993 until very recently.... Where a limited company is the plaintiff in an action or other legal proceedings, the court may in the absence of credible testimony, that there is reason to believe that the Company is unable to pay the Defence's costs, require sufficient security to be given for those costs. Thus the Court has to have before it credible testimony which gives reason to believe that the company will be able to pay its costs.

"On the 14th June the Vice-Chancellor refused to continue the injunction and ordered, unusually, the Petitioner to PAY THE RESPONDENTS' COSTS of the applications before him. He also gave instructions for a full trial to commence on the 1st November next.

"I have to conclude that at the end of all the proceedings, probably in December, that the Company will then be unable to pay the costs of the Respondents. It is quite clear that this Company at present is far from adequately capitalised. The balance sheet as at 31st March 1992, shows fixed assets being investments at £3,264,000, and sundry debtors at £218,000. On the other side, creditors due within one year £2,396,000. A net surplus of £1,086,000. And then there are further creditors falling due after one year of £1,473,000, which leaves a deficit of £387,000. By the 31st March 1993, there was a very slight improvement, the deficiency being shown as £345,000.

"The statute requires me to look at the inevitable very large costs after the end of the whole trial. I have no idea what the total costs will be, but I cannot believe that they will be less than £450,000. The Respondents' costs will be something in excess of £600,000. The liabilities of Edennote at that time could be well over £1 million.

"ONE CAN SEE THAT ON THESE FIGURES THIS COMPANY CANNOT BE SAID TO BE IN A POSITION WHERE I HAVE REASON TO BELIEVE THAT IT WILL BE ABLE TO PAY ITS DEBTS.

"THEREFORE IN MY JUDGMENT, THERE IS JURISDICTION TO AWARD SECURITY FOR COSTS AGAINST EDENNOTE PLC.

"There is no difficulty in my considering this application for security on behalf of all 3 Respondents (Tottenham, Amshold and Sugar.)."

(So Tottenham CAN pay towards Sugar's costs!)

"It is notorious that 'Rolls-Royce' quality litigation is very desirable for the client getting it, but it is not proper to be visited on the other side. The bill submitted is £340,000, and the draughtsman's estimate is £265,000. I therefore will come somewhere in the middle at £300,000. I am minded to give the Petitioner 21 days to satisfy."

So that was it! Poor old Tel! Where on earth was he going to find £300,000 within three weeks on top of the £450,000 he already owed his own solicitors?

Effectively these proceedings ended, probably for all time, certainly for as long as Alan Sugar is in control of Tottenham, Terry's adventure and participation in the football that he professes so profoundly to love.

Had it never occurred to him, or had he not been advised, that he would have been better off to take the money that was on offer from Sugar and run? Had he agreed to sell Sugar the shares held on his behalf by Edennote, he might well have been able at the same time to have negotiated a deal in respect of his personal employment contract.

The only result of all the expensive litigation has been the washing of much dirty linen in public. Criticisms have been made about all the parties but it is probably Terry's credibility that has suffered the most, since matters connected with his dismissal from Tottenham have left a bad taste in the mouth of people who had previously regarded him as a hero.

Nevertheless he is still highly regarded for his abilities, especially as a football coach, and my best wishes go out him and his family, on a personal level.

Only time will tell whether the major changes at Tottenham will bring further success to the club, and I wish Alan Sugar every success in his attempts to make Tottenham great again.

The best result of this horror story will be success for Terry Venables, Alan Sugar, Osvaldo Ardiles, Tottenham Hotspur and football in general, which surely, needs urgently to clean up its image.

LETTER TO TERRY VENABLES

Dear Terry,

Assuming that you have bothered to read the previous pages you will know how bloody upset I am feeling at the discoveries I have made about your business dealings; because Terry, since 1989 I have held a regard for you above and beyond that of the average supporter. It was you who gave me inspiration to live, and now, I, like so many, have become disillusioned.

After the op. I felt fortified with a strength not previously felt. I had lost any fears that I might have had, so after reading this, don't bother with thoughts of litigation, for what I am saying is the nearest to the truth. It is time for someone somewhere to re-mind you what you have done. If you sue I shall defend and you will have to assure my legal representatives of your ability to pay my costs should you lose, and if you win I have nothing of any value, so you can place me among the Eddie Ashbys of this World in as much as you can make me bankrupt.

I don't know how it all started, the business dealings and cor-ruption that you continually deny. Can you honestly hope that the public will believe that in transferring Teddy Sheringham you did not even talk to Clough? Can we accept that he stood by and let Fred Reacher do all the trading? Then, to sell him at roughly the same fee that they paid Millwall for him? He was, as he is at Spurs, their top goal-scorer, and Graham Smith wishes us to be-lieve that Forest wanted to off- load him. That, when they were near the bottom of the League with that appalling start they had which ultimately saw them relegated and Clough retiring.

Then there is the McLintock business. He says someone at Tottenham rang him and he went along and was handed a bag of notes. You say he demanded cash and Alan says that Teddy wouldn't have been allowed to sign if Frank wasn't handed 50k before his signature was placed on the contract. Appeal all that you wish, but it stinks, doesn't it? Then there is Graham Smith really confirming that the whole thing was as Alan had suggested it, except that Smith had to have his cut first.

The Bailys are the tip of the iceberg. There are so many companies that you, alongside Eddie Ashby, have been involved in that have caused misery and despair to unassuming creditors that you ought to stop and consider just what you two have done. What has Ashby got on you that you sacrificed your career and credibility and your position at Tottenham for?

Any mug could have seen that Sugar was not going to stand for that relationship, and your loyalty was to Tottenham, the Company and the supporters, not to a man with a questionable business past. It was not you who saved Tottenham, but Alan Sugar. He even lent you the money, initially to buy your bloody shares! I know that in your eyes he was a goon when the insiders of football surveyed his antics, but do you honestly think that a man like that was going to remain ignorant of what goes on in football for very long? What about the business with Mr Pay? Suddenly a man accused of being in some sort of partnership gets the job in the commercial department at Spurs and there are stock shortages and low profit returns?

You can't possibly expect the world to accept continual protestations of innocence and Sugar to be wrong on all counts.

Then there was the interest on the loans that you took. The finance company indicated to me that they were getting ready to foreclose. You were never earning enough to pay that back, you had to get the money from somewhere, didn't you?

How about Santin? That really is something else! A restaurateur negotiating with lawyers and bankers and top club officials, and his services valued at two hundred thousand pounds. My word, I could have got you the finest Italian/English speaking lawyer for about one tenth of that. Then the guy invoices Tottenham from a non-existent Swiss company, and gets paid in cash. Couldn't you appreciate that Alan Sugar upheld your position with the deal, even though he was highly suspicious, by allowing the invoice to be paid. Didn't that man deserve any respect from you? He was your Chairman! The Chairman of Tottenham Hotspur, a Club that means a great deal to me and to thousands of others.

If Tottenham are relegated because of the intricate 'loan' deals you made with the likes of Paul Stewart etc, it will be down to you. Alan has pleaded for an armistice and I hope that the FA see that the rotten elements have been removed and he will run a straight Club and Company. That's how much good you have done us since your return from Spain.

Having said all the above, I have to admit to being worried about today's reports in the Sun declaring that you will be our next Manager of England. Half of me wants that to happen, the other half, the one of disillusionment, disappointment and annoyance says no, you are only fit as far as football goes, and the other matters go too deep to be pushed to one side.

Although I was a sincere Terry Venables supporter, I am a Tottenham supporter first and foremost.

El Tel, you have let me down. You have let Tottenham down. You have let the supporters down. Worst of all you have let yourself down!

Guy.

"THERE ARE NO WHOLE TRUTHS, ONLY HALF TRUTHS....

THE END.